FAMILY STRENGTHS

FAMILY STRENGTHS

POSITIVE MODELS
FOR FAMILY LIFE

EDITED BY
Dr. Nick Stinnett
Dr. Barbara Chesser
Dr. John DeFrain
Dr. Patricia Knaub

University of Nebraska Press
Lincoln and London

Copyright © 1980 by the University of Nebraska Press
All rights reserved
Library of Congress Catalog Card Number 80-50917
ISBN 0-8032-4125-9 (cloth)
ISBN 0-8032-9122-1 (paper)

In the interest of timeliness and economy, this work was printed from camera-ready copy prepared by the editors.

Manufactured in the United States of America

TABLE OF CONTENTS

v

SECTION   PAGE

SECTION

Contents

SECTION

PAGE

ACKNOWLEDGMENTS

Sincere thanks are expressed to each of the authors who has contributed to this book and also to each of the participants at the Second National Symposium on Building Family Strengths for their contributions. Special appreciation is expressed to Dr. Hazel Anthony, Dean, College of Home Economics, University of Nebraska-Lincoln, to Dr. Roy Young, Chancellor, University of Nebraska-Lincoln, and to the University Foundation, for their support and encouragement of the National Symposium on Building Family Strengths.

Much gratitude is expressed to Mrs. Ward Sybouts for her superior typing and editing. She kept typing even when a new granddaughter was born. Invaluable editorial contributions and encouragement throughout the preparation of this book were provided by Nancy Stinnett. Special thanks are extended to Diane Franzen, Marion Kaple, Charlotte Jackson, and Virginia Woodward for contributions and help with the National Symposium on Building Family Strengths.

Appreciation is also expressed to Jacque Taylor, Nancy O'Donnell, and George Hart for their assistance in the manuscript preparation.

INTRODUCTION

Enriching family life is a quest to which the National Symposium on Building Family Strengths is dedicated. To fulfill this dream depends upon knowing what are the qualities of strong families; it also depends upon developing a positive model of family life which can be used in our educational, research, and counseling efforts. How can family strengths be developed? Some of the most prominent and knowledgeable family life and human development professionals in the nation have shared their expertise in addressing this question at the National Symposium on Building Family Strengths during the last two years.

The Second National Symposium on Building Family Strengths, in similar manner to the first Symposium, attracted approximately 600 registrants from 34 states and two foreign countries. The National Symposium on Building Family Strengths has generated much interest in developing a positive family life model. During the last two years, building family strengths has been an increasingly frequent theme of educational programs and research. The National White House Conference on Families identified family strengths as one of its themes.

The present book, *Family Strengths: Positive Models for Family Life,* is the second book to emerge from the continuing series of National Symposia on Building Family Strengths. The readings in this book are authored by family life educators, practitioners, and researchers from 20 states and Canada, representing 21 universities and colleges, as well as a number of other institutions and agencies from all regions of the nation.

The readings in the book are represented in the following sections:

    I.   Perspectives on the Family
   II.   Marriage Relationships
  III.   Parent-Child Relationships
  IV.   Parent-Adolescent Relationships
   V.   The Middle and Later Years
  VI.   Building Strengths in Families with Special Needs
 VII.   The Role of Education in Building Family Strengths

One asset of this book is that the readings represent diverse approaches to building family strengths. Among the authors are outstanding counselors and other practitioners, researchers, and both university and public school educators.

The content of the book includes descriptions of existing
programs as well as proposed model programs, proposed family social policies, descriptions of various forms of family
life education, sharing of research information, and discussions of methods and techniques for building family
strengths.

While diverse approaches characterize the book, the readings are bound together by similar themes, including (1) the
constructive use of conflict; (2) the development of support
systems in building family strengths; (3) the importance of
applying existing social science knowledge in developing
policies and programs concerning families; (4) the importance
of self-esteem in developing fulfilling interpersonal relationships; (5) the role of philosophies and techniques of
family life education in enriching family life; (6) the importance of nurturing the family unit throughout the life
cycle; (7) a preventive approach to family difficulties; and
(8) an emphasis on further enriching successful marriage and
family relationships, as well as a remedial approach to
those in trouble.

The concept of family strengths and the belief that family
relationships can be enhanced are the major themes which
characterize this book.

As described in the previous book, *Building Family Strengths:
Blueprints for Action,* the concept of family strengths is
defined as those relationship patterns, interpersonal skills
and competencies, and social and psychological characteristics which create a sense of positive family identity, promote satisfying and fulfilling interaction among family members, encourage the development of the potential of the family group and individual family members, and contribute to
the family's ability to deal effectively with stress and
crises.

Family strengths can be developed. The future of the
family can be bright, and the positive potential for the
family is great. This book, *Family Strengths: Positive
Models for Family Life,* is dedicated to that potential.

Nick Stinnett, Chairman
Department of Human Development
  and the Family
College of Home Economics
University of Nebraska-Lincoln

I. PERSPECTIVES ON THE FAMILY

The articles in this section provide a general look at families and family interaction. They deal with the idea of building family strengths in the context of the entire family. Articles in other sections focus more specifically on one aspect of family life, such as marriage or on particular family types such as families with a handicapped member.

Dr. Ned Gaylin provides an appropriate beginning by making a case for the family as the most permanent of all our social institutions. He views the family as essential to mankind, and urges the adoption of attitudes and social policies that enable families to thrive.

Dr. Douglas Gunn defines the idea of creating an identity for a family. Such an identity helps a family recognize the unity and purpose of its life. Photographing family events, perpetuating rituals, and telling the family story are ways of creating family identity.

Dr. Anne M. Juhasz presents human interaction, individual identity, and the development of intimacy as three interwoven aspects of family cohesion. Early parent-child contact is vital to the development of identity. Positive identity and positive interaction allow the establishment of intimacy.

Family therapy is presented by Dr. Augustus Napier as an approach to improving family life by treating troubled individuals as members of troubled families. He suggests providing help in a nonclinical setting to all families at critical times in the family life cycle.

Dr. Edward Zigler and Dr. Kirby Heller conclude this section by reviewing social conditions that attest to the need to give more attention to the social policies that affect children and families. Existing programs which are contrary to social science knowledge are cited, as well as examples and suggestions of policy and programs consistent with social science knowledge.

Dr. Ned L. Gaylin
Department of Family
and Community Development
University of Maryland

IS THE FAMILY IN DANGER?

Late twentieth century America has rediscovered the family. Pick up any newspaper or periodical, either popular or scholarly, and one can find some "expert" opinion of the family-- generally in negative terms: "The family is weakened and in need of strengthening; it is imperiled, obsolete, or dying," we are told.

I tend to be a bit overwhelmed by the family's place as America's new cause célébre. I am not sure whether the discovery is a blessing or a curse, but I tend to be a bit conservative and wary of zealousness in American fads. I become a bit edgy over the rash of figures, often hastily generated, to bolster claims of social scientists, politicians, or journalists.

Figures abound to heighten the drama of the plight of the American family: Two out of every five marriages end in divorce; illegitimate births have nearly tripled since 1960; 15 percent of American children live in single-parent homes (double that of 25 years ago), etc. Do these not attest to what has been termed the "calamitous decline of the American family?" Perhaps--in any case it does not sound good.

But the other half of the story is, that of the 40 percent of divorced individuals, over three-fourths remarry. Furthermore, the two-thirds of our population who marry for life stay married longer due to the increased life span. Despite what recently appeared to be a declining marriage rate (but which actually proved to be a delayed marriage trend), America is still the most marrying country in the world (Glick & Norton, 1977).

A few years ago, famed American behavioral scientist, Ann Landers, asked her readers whether or not, if they had it all to do over again, they would have children. An overwhelming majority--70 percent of all those who responded--

5

adamantly declared they would not. The lament caught national attention as proof of Americans' antifamilialism. But some months before that, in a representative probability sample of over 2,500 families assessed by Yankelovitch and associates (1975), 83 percent reported they were doing well personally, and 93 percent of the sample ranked the family as their number one priority. Yet, not too many people have heard of that study.

I do not mean to sound either cavalier or unconcerned about some of the apparent social trends and their impact on the family. Indeed, I have often enlisted similar figures to call attention to changes in the social climate. However, I have grown wary of apocalyptic scare tactics, specifically when they lead to crisis intervention approaches to broad social issues, and particularly as they apply to an institution so basic to human society as the family.

The helical movement of social history has recorded such crises before, and over more protracted periods than two or three short decades, which when placed against the longevity of the family as an institution, represents a mere freckle in time. Rather, what I would like to suggest is that while the family seems to be changing somewhat, the implications of that change--for me at least--are not totally clear. Furthermore, I am not quite so ready to side with many of my colleagues who perceive the family as a somewhat outmoded, dysfunctional social unit, nor am I so ready to rush in with preconceived notions as to how we should repair the old model.

When a social institution, particularly one so central to human existence and survival as the family, does not appear to be synchronized with the prevailing social climate, at least two possibilities exist: either the institution is inadequate (our usual assumption), or, on the other hand, the institution may be fundamentally sound, but the social milieu in which it operates may be in flux and/or awry. Because the prevailing ethos of an entire culture is difficult to evaluate, let alone modify, we rarely choose the latter alternative as tenable. Rather, we look for scapegoats.

Our latest rediscovery of the family, I submit, is but a symptom of our most recent burgeoning social concerns and anxieties. The family is fundamental to society (though there are those who would contest that premise). It serves as the paradigm for all of our social relationships. It is the introducer of the individual to society and vice versa. It is the mediator between man and mankind. Indeed, it is so primary an institution as to be basic to our very humanness. Therefore, when the course of our lives goes smoothly, we tend to take the family for granted. Only during periods of stress (either personal or social), upheaval, or rapid social

changes, does the functioning of an institution so focal to
our uniqueness as beings come under scrutiny. Because of its
central position in both our individual personal development,
as well as its role in our cultural and social articulation,
the family often takes on the additional burden of being scape-
goat to our fears.

ANALYZING THE FAMILY

From the personal point of view, we are each a kind of expert
on the family. Virtually all of us have had some kind of
family experience, and each of us carries with us memory
traces of what family was to us. The memory effect creates
difficulties because memory is selective. Over time, we tend
to maximize and romanticize the positive, as the more painful and onerous experiences submerge, or become poignant punc-
tuation marks in the totality of our recollections. This
effect is further enhanced by our growing older, which changes
our relationships to our parents, siblings, and children.
Actions of our parents, which as children we considered intolerable, grow more understandable as we ourselves become
parents and rear children of our own. Our contemporary mythology tends to heighten the effect by romanticizing and ideal-
izing love, marriage, and family relations. The Waltons and
Sada Thompson's portrayal of "mother" in the television series,
"Family," are examples of this.

Moving to the other extreme, historians and social scientists attempt to delineate the course of the family through
time, but rarely is there consensus with regard to the eti-
ology of the various adaptive forms the family has taken, or
for that matter, why. We have studied the family across cultures and with structural and functional analyses, but by
and large, the mystery of the tenacity of the institution
remains. Throughout man's history, the family has accommodated through economic, political, religious, and technological cataclysm, modifying itself and adapting, but continually surviving as an identifiable and indispensible social
unit. Thus, neither the microscopy of our individual recollections, nor the telescopic objectivity of twentieth century
behavioral science, has unraveled the secret of the family.

What is becoming eminently clear, however, is that the
analysis and understanding of the family cannot be taken
lightly and/or left to crisis-oriented bandaid solutions.
Thus, while I agree in principle with many recent observers
of and advocates for the family, I contest the continual use
of pejorative rhetoric in describing the present state of
the family. Continual allusion to the family as being in
need of strengthening is not only confusing, but deflective

from a course of positive social action which could enhance
the quality of our lives.

I would suggest that rather than view the family as de-
caying and in need of repair to fit a fluctuating social
milieu, we look to the possibility of reevaluating our social
policies in a manner which will better accommodate familial,
and therefore, human priorities. Traditionally, in examining
the course of cultural growth, development, and decline, we
have noted that civilizations in a state of decay have had
weakened family structures. From these observations, the
conclusion often drawn is that the deterioration of the family is a cause of a culture's demise. I contend that a careful study of civilizations, such as ancient Babylon, Greece,
Rome, or more recently Nazi Germany, would verify that the
seeds of decay, that is, the breakdown of human concerns,
of ethical judicial systems--all that we consider noble exercises of the human spirit--were prelude to and causes of, rather
than caused by the decay of the family structures of those
cultures. Furthermore, in each of those cultures, the family
was the last tenacious bastion of human integrity to give
way. Just as the family is the root of our orientation, so
too is it the last blossom.

THE ETHOS OF MODERN AMERICA

I suspect that history will look upon the first two hundred
years of American history as the flowering of the age of the
individual. Our Declaration of Independence articulated the
rights of each human being to "life, liberty, and the pursuit of happiness," and did so at a moment in time when the
vast resources of its newly formed nation were readily utilized by the tremendous growth in science and technology.

It is at this point that the institution of the family
becomes focal. While many modern observers of the scene see
our rapidly expanded technology as the major factor contributing to our present dilemma, technology is but one of at
least three intimately related tropisms which affect our
orientation and values. These are: technocentrism (our
faith that science can solve all our problems); presocentrism
(our preoccupation with only the immediate); and egocentrism
(our self-centeredness). Technology in and of itself is
perhaps the most benign of these forces, yet taken out of
context, it looms as primary (Gaylin, 1975).

If the vast American frontier and the industrial revolution set the stage for the developing ethos of twentieth
century America, it was the birth of the behavioral sciences
in the late nineteenth century which cast the characters.
Perhaps no one individual had so great an impact on this

aspect of the drama as did Sigmund Freud. His theory gave
additional emphasis to the psychological rights of the individual set against a repressive cultural backdrop. America,
even more than Europe, was fertile soil for the conceptualization of mankind, and embraced it. Thus, the curtain rose:
the plot of the drama, an unintentional opposition of man
against society and vice versa, which has culminated in the
creation of our individualistic, present-focused, techno-
logically-oriented value framework.

It should be noted that Freud's message was not one of
antifamilialism. On the contrary, his entire logic with regard to the nature of civilization is based upon the central
role of the parent-child relationship. Nonetheless, his focus
was the individual, and his theory found wide acceptance in
this country, because it complemented our developing cultural ethos of individualism. It gave credence and support
to the American Dream that each man or woman is in control
of his or her own destiny, the captain of his or her soul.

Thus, repression and guilt have become dirty words in
late twentieth century America. Individual psychotherapists,
marriage and family counselors, and educators have become so
concerned with the liberation of psychic functioning from
"irrational" cultural constraints that the question of morality has become virtually taboo. The equating of morality
(a general interpersonal ethical code) with sexual moralism
(rules defining sexual conduct) has reinforced the avoidance
of this area of concern within the helping professions. In
like fashion, terms such as "duty" and "obligation"--good,
strong words, previously used to define role relationships
within the family--have been studiously avoided. They seem
inhibitory to individual achievement and success. They appear antithetical to the American spirit of the rights of
life, liberty, and the pursuit of happiness and the unwritten
spirit of competition. The irony of all this is that without repression and guilt, and duty and obligation, there can
be no society.

I have been discussing the concept of guilt with local
parent groups, and have discovered that guilt can be dangerous to discuss in public. I have been verbally stoned by
some, upon suggesting that a guiltless society is no society
at all, and that our children need to be taught how to develop and appreciate their sense of guilt. For three generations, modern American parents have lived with modern
psychological thought; such heresy appears counter to all
that psychotherapeutic agents have been advocating for the
past half century.

When the dust settles and discussion continues, invariably it is decided that I have been using the wrong word.
I am told that I am using "guilt," when I really mean

"conscience." Perhaps I should distinguish between rational
and irrational guilt, or better still, I, in good social
science tradition, should develop a new term. I point out
that the common dictionary definition of guilt is perfectly
adequate to my meaning, i.e., "a feeling or feelings of
culpability," and that as such it is vital for the monitoring of our own behavior. When I further point out that a
concept of guilt is basic to a concept of conscience, and
that both are crucial to our understanding of social responsibility, of morals, and of ethics, I am implicitly accused
of behaving and talking more like a theologian than a psychologist.

Discussions of such issues are tolerable in our society
in a religious or romantic context, not in a scientific one.
However, because they are inherent in our broader humanitarian ideals, we cannot totally denigrate or abrogate the basic
ethical underpinnings of our society. Rather, we see them
as somewhat anachronistic, unpragmatic, and simplistic for
our sophisticated twentieth century American life styles.
We suspend them, encapsulate them, or set them aside for
special times or occasions. That is, "ethics are ethics,
but business is business."

FAMILY IS ESSENTIAL AND ENDURING

At the risk of belaboring what may seem obvious, allow me
to turn momentarily to the Decalogue, the Ten Commandments,
to which my research on the family has led me. Here is the
code which perhaps best embodies the moral foundation of our
society. I have found it an amazingly elegant and pragmatic
document. I am quite surprised at the lack of knowledge which
many have regarding its basic tenets, let alone its inuendo
and interpretation. By some 3,000 years, it predates our
rediscovery of the family as focal to civilization.

In an informal research endeavor, I have begun asking
students at the beginning of the semester if they know the
Ten Commandments and their ordering. They all seem a bit
surprised at being asked. It may shock you to learn that after
some thought, most of our brightest students can give about
six out of the ten (generally the last--and that is important
to note). Nearly none, however, can order them.

In the first place, there are two distinct orders naturally divided by the two tablets. The first five are pre-
scriptive--the "thou shalts"--and are generally taken to deal
with man's duties and obligations to God (or if you prefer,
the "Cosmos"). The second tablet deals with the prohibitives--
the "thou shalt nots," and concerns man's relationship to
man.

My concern here is primarily with the Fifth Commandment. When I ask students which commandment follows the fourth, it is rare to hear the correct response immediately. Generally, the first impulsive response from a member of the group is "Thou shalt not kill." Only after some thought is the Fifth Commandment, that which is the foundation of the family, given--"Honor Thy Father and Thy Mother." Most are quite surprised with the recognition that the establishment of the family and the highlighting of the sanctity of the filial bond precede admonishment concerning the sanctity of life. This commandment establishes a reverence for those from whom we issue, which seems somewhat ironic in light of relatively recent recognition of the disenfranchisement of the aged-- our collective parents--in modern American society.

Whether one considers the Decalogue divinely given, divinely inspired, or as an evolutionary refinement and crystallization of man's concern with his relationship to the physical and interpersonal environment, the role of the family in that conceptualization is impressive. Whether one be theist, atheist, or agnostic, it is difficult to discard a code of ethics which has withstood at least 3,000 years of social evolution in favor of 100 years of technological revolution. Despite our technological expertise, there is little to indicate that man's basic nature has changed so substantially in over 30 centuries (let alone in one) as to justify the scrapping of our noblest efforts in the arts or in ethics in lieu of those of science. Even the most rabid iconoclastic futurist would be, I think, at least a bit discomfited at the prospects of such a trade-off. Man's hand cannot operate without his heart, for to do so would make him other than human. The family is, has always been, and is likely to remain, the home for the heart. Indeed, it may take different forms and serve different needs at varying points in time; but its identifying characteristics of at <u>least</u> <u>two</u> <u>biologically-bound</u> (or <u>simulated</u> <u>as</u> <u>through</u> <u>marriage</u> <u>or</u> <u>adoption</u>) <u>individuals</u> <u>in</u> <u>an</u> <u>age</u> <u>articulating</u> <u>environment</u> would appear to be as close to a permanent social structure as mankind has as yet fallen heir to, and certainly more satisfying than any we have yet designed.

There are those who will be quick to point out that these are times the likes of which we have never had before. At no time in the history of the world has mankind ever been so flooded with information and so exposed to so many differing cultural patterns via the ease of travel and the omnipresence of television. The very technology which has created our affluence and our expansion has given us a capacity for destructiveness beyond the dreams of just 100 years ago.

This is the message of many of our social commentators: of Toffler (1970), who has chronicled our future shock, of

Henry (1963), who has shown us cultural relativism to the
point of atomism, and of Mead (1970), who sees us as "immigrants in time," inadequately prepared for a future totally
different from our experience. It is in this context that
we are told the family is incompetent to deal with the world
of tomorrow.

PROTEUS--MAN OR FAMILY?

A noted personality theorist, Robert Lifton (1969), has even
suggested that modern man is psychologically evolving into
a new breed of individual to accommodate to our culturally
relativistic, presocentric, stimulus-bombarded time; a breed
of man who is in constant flux, shifting identity, uncom-
mitted, continually experimenting with himself, as well as
the world around him. Lifton calls this being of the future,
"Protean Man," after Proteus, the old man of the sea in Greek
mythology, who had the ability to change his shape to all
forms of being and matter, and had at his disposal knowledge
of past, present, and future.
     Lifton (1969), however, notes a flaw in our modern Pro-
teuses. He sees them as

     . . . experiencing a break in the sense of con-
     nection which men have long felt with the vital
     and nourishing symbols of their cultural tradi-
     tion--symbols revolving around family, idea
     systems, religions, and the life cycle in general.
     Today we perceive these traditional symbols as
     irrelevant, burdensome, or inactivating, and
     yet we cannot avoid carrying them within us or
     having our self-processes profoundly affected by
     them.

     Lifton (1969) never quite resolves the apparent paradox,
because it is my belief that despite the clarity and cogency
of his observations of the modern scene, he has misread the
metaphors within the myth of Proteus. For unlike presocentric man, Proteus related to past, present, and future. Despite the various forms he took, he had integrity through
time. His father was Neptune and his mother the sea--the
source of all life on this planet. Indeed, his very name
has been used by modern science to signify that which is the
source of all life--"protein." Man, on the other hand, is
barely aware of his past, knows not his future, and has difficulty in understanding the present. He is neither god nor
demigod (as was Proteus), but the seeker of God. Man is the
wanderer, the questioner.

But what then of Proteus? I submit that the image of Proteus befits the concept of the family. It is the family which knows past, present, and future. Through parents and grandparents, through uncountable generations, the family relates us to our heritage, back to the first man, and beyond that to our Protozoan past in a continuous and unbroken chain. So too does the family engage us with our present, through siblings and through familial analogues by which we order our societies. Our language is replete with continual reference to familial bonds. Finally, the family speaks to our future through our children and their children's children. It is the only representative of immorality presently available to us.

In different times and in various cultures, the Protean family may indeed take different forms: at one time a large, extended multigenerational clan, at another place the rudimentary, two person, single-parent and child, but nonetheless it remains a family. It is the whole which defines us as parts, and wherein take place the rites of passage that we as human beings have grown to accept as central to our existence: our beginning, our coming of age, our joining, our generating, and our parting.

Societies may attempt to constrain and mold the institutions to some idealized pattern of Utopian ends, but when these constraints strike at the heart of familial priorities, they invariably fail. Thus, the communal structures of Russia, Israel, and Czechoslovakia, for example, are beginning to show signs of devitalization as more and more parents in these countries seem to want a greater share in the rearing of their children. So too, are large companies in the United States meeting resistance in their heretofore wanton moving of executives, as families protest the sense of anchorlessness such moves create.

This is not to suggest that there is some ultimate family form towards which we must planfully direct ourselves. Indeed, that which makes the family so pivotal to us as a human species is its very Protean adaptive quality. It is this very same quality which makes it so difficult to legislate policy for facilitating the family's task of mediating between the individual and the culture. Thus, talk of the decline or demise of the family is as diagnostically naïve, as talk of strengthening it is prescriptively misleading.

ENABLING FAMLIES

What is therefore needed is not so much a plan for strengthening families, as an attitude for enabling them. Some may think this is a semantic argument. Strengthening implies

a knowledge of endpoint or ideal. I make no such pretenses.
We have tried that route. With all good intentions and far
too little knowledge, we have intervened with cultures and
subcultures, imposing social standards which at a given moment seemed appropriate to a select number of policy makers.
Public housing, head start, or more infamously, prohibition,
are examples of such. These were noble but naïve
efforts aimed at improving our lot. Because they presupposed
one idealized model applied to a broad spectrum of problems,
their effectiveness was less than spectacular.

On the other hand, enabling, or as the theme of this book
purports--building family strengths, suggests a multiplicity
of facilitative means for preventing problems. It implies
lifting impediments rather than structuring solutions. It
is freeing rather than constraining. Such is the kind of
public policy needed for dealing with the Protean family looking towards the world of the future.

While enabling does does imply a panacea, neither does it
imply a stance of laissez faire. On the contrary, we have
tried that, too, and with little success. We were shamefully
one of the last industrial nations to develop and adopt a
system of social security, and then only out of the crisis
and desperation of a cataclysmic economic depression. Since
that upheaval, we have done pitifully little to enhance our
social welfare system, which is widely recognized as hope-
lessly inadequate and badly in need of restructuring. For
example, how can a nation as wealthy as ours, dedicated to
its humanitarian principles, tolerate the irony of an infant
mortality rate which ranks us seventeenth among all nations
in the world, while our per capita medical expenses rank us
first?

This is but one obvious example of the paradox with regard to our policies affecting the family. Our transportation systems tend to accommodate to cars, not to people,
which in turn affects the way our communities are structured.
How can we train children in the practical skills of being
wise consumers, when our communities are laid out in such
a way that our young cannot make individual purchases until
they are old enough to drive? There are more insidious dan-
gers to this phenomenon. Shopkeepers see our young as potential hoodlums, because they have no exposure to our children during their formative years, and vice versa. We have
depersonalized the many transactions which, but a few years
ago, were meaningful exchanges and learning experiences for
both young and old alike. We cannot continue such practices
without questioning their repercussions.

On the most mundane scale, I have found that our school
systems and community agencies--those institutions most directly concerned with our young--adopt policies and make

decisions which have, albeit small but cumulatively enormous, an erosive impact upon our familial activities. Teachers, in attempting to meet increased demands upon them to produce higher group test scores, assign increasing amounts of busy work, with little regard to what their colleagues are simultaneously assigning, and what, if any, free time will be left for the family. School bus schedules are established so that a family with children in more than one school cannot possibly breakfast together. Lunchtime, we long ago relinquished, so that the dinner hour is often the only time remaining for repast. And, because of extracurricular activities, we often must forego even that brief period of potential familial replenishment.

We have begun to recognize that many of our twentieth century-created institutions cannot fulfill the needs nearly so easily nor economically as the community and the family once did with relative effectiveness. Thus, we now speak of deinstitutionalizing our sick, our aged, our retarded, and our handicapped. But through the process of training towards depersonalization and disaffiliation, there is no place in our families or communities to house them.

Our young cannot be taught respect for the aged, compassion for the infirm, nor grief for the departing when they have not even minimal contact with such individuals, either in our homes or near them. We have segregated, sterilized, and deodorized our interpersonal environment to the extent that we face only mirror images of ourselves in our day-to-day dealings. We have decanted our children (to use Aldous Huxley's imagery) into a perhaps brave, but not very caring new world.

Now it is time to take stock. It is time to realize that rights and privileges are corollaries of duty and obligation, and that both conceptualizations are axiomatic to life, liberty, and the pursuit of happiness. It is time to understand that teaching and learning are reciprocal enterprises. As the old teach the young, so too, through examining and evaluating their own behavior, do the old learn, and thereby does our society advance. It is not so easy to shave the sharp corners of our consciences with an inquisitive child in tow. This is the message of family--the very heart of society which pumps in circular fashion, the life blood of our culture.

Yet, we who pride ourself as being the most advanced culture the world has ever seen, remain one of the last major nations of the world without an articulated national policy for the family. Our intent, however, screams quietly for the world to hear. Our lack of action regarding the family, along with our denigration of it, is indeed our policy. We are at a juncture now. Once more we have rediscovered the family. What we do with that discovery may well decide our future. It may well decide whether we will survive as a distinct and viable society, or whether, like those of ancient Greece and Rome, it shall be read about as a valiant social venture which inherently sowed the seeds of its own destruction.

REFERENCES

Gaylin, N. L. On the quality of life and death. *The Family Coordinator*, 1975, *24*, 247-255.

Glick, P. C., & Norton, A. J. Marrying, divorcing, and living together in the U.S. today. *Population Bulletin*, 1977, *32*, 5.

Henry, J. *Culture against man*. New York: Random House, Inc., 1963.

Lifton, R. J. Protean man. *Yale Alumni Review*, January, 1969.

Mead, M. *Culture and commitment*. Garden City, New York: Doubleday & Company, 1970.

Toffler, A. *Future shock*. New York: Random House, 1970.

Yankelovitch, D. *The American family report*. Minneapolis: General Mills, Inc., 1975.

Family Identity Creation: A Family Strength-Building Role Activity

Dr. C. Douglas Gunn
Department of Home Economics
and Family Ecology
University of Akron

Settling in a chair and accepting the baby from
Matilda, his mammy spoke almost conversation-
ally. "George, yo' chilluns been wantin' to ax
you sump'n--" She turned. "Ain't you, Virgil?"
Chicken George saw the oldest boy hanging
back. What had they primed him to say?
"Pappy," he said finally in his piping voice,
"you gwine tell us 'bout our great-gran'daddy?"
Matilda's eyes reached out to him.
"You's a good man, George," said Kizzy softly.
"Don't never let nobody tell you no different!
An' don't never git to feelin' we don't love you.
I b'lieves maybe you gits mixed up 'bout who you
is, an' sometime who we is. We's yo' blood,
jes' like dese chilluns' great-gran'pappy."
"It's right in de Scriptures--" said Matilda.
Seeing George's apprehensive glance, she added,
"Everything in de Bible ain't sump'n hard. De
Scriptures have plenty 'bout love."
Overwhelmed with emotion, Chicken George moved
his chair near the hearth. The three boys squatted
down before him, their eyes glistened with anticipation, and Kizzy handed him the baby. Composing
himself, he cleared his throat and began to tell
his four sons their gran'mammy's story of their
great-gran'pappy.
"Pappy, I knows de story, too!" Virgil broke
in. Making a face at his younger brothers, he
went ahead and told it himself--including even
the African words.
"He done heared it three times from you, and
gran'mammy don't cross de do'sill widout tellin'
it again!" said Matilda with a laugh. George
thought: How long had it been since he last heard
his wife laughing?

17

> Trying to recapture the center of attention,
> Virgil jumped up and down. "Gran'mammy say de
> African make us know who we is!"
> "He do dat!" said Gran'mammy Kizzy, beaming.
> For the first time in a long time, Chicken
> George felt that his cabin was his home again.
>
> --Alex Haley, *Roots*, p. 555

The purpose of this paper is to offer a role interpretation of certain family activities involving the telling of a family's story and the creation of a family identity. It will be claimed that we may profitably identify as role enactment certain activities within the family which deal with the creation, nourishment, and transmission of the family's concept of its identity. It will be urged that this role--which I term the family identity creation role--take its place with others in the lists of role behavior studied and researched by students of the family. It will be argued that this role behavior within the family lies at the very heart of what it means to have family strengths as distinct from strengths accruing to individuals who happen to be living in families. This paper is not a definitive treatise on the family identity creation role, but an attempt to bring the existence and importance of that role to the attention of workers in the field of family health and development.

FAMILY STORY: THE CENTER OF FAMILY IDENTITY CREATION

First, let me point clearly to the kind of activity I have in mind when I write of family identity creation role enactment. The quotation from Alex Haley's *Roots* with which we began gives us a perfect example. The elder member of the family--in this instance, Chicken George--sits down to tell the story of his family to the younger members assembled. It doesn't really matter that they've heard it before; the purpose and effects of the story-telling role enactment are clear in the paragraphs quoted. The telling of the family story ties the hearers and tellers together in a unit; it transforms a cabin into a home. Telling the family story creates family identity. Those hearing the story for the first time learn their true identity--as when Chicken George tells the little boy Uriah (Haley, 1976, p. 656), or when the author himself hears the story from the griot or African storyteller (Haley, 1976, p. 718). Those who already know the story and have heard it before experience a reaffirmation of their sense of family identity through hearing it again.

Thus, the role enactment to which I am referring is basically that of "telling the family story." But there may be much more to telling the family story than just sitting down and verbalizing a narrative. Alex Haley had to spend a tremendous amount of effort and time to recover his family's story so it could be told. Telling the story may necessitate finding out what the story is, preserving the story, and transmitting it from generation to generation through writings or documents. Hence the role activity connected with transmitting the family story and thereby building family identity can include not only the work of the oral narrator but that of the archivist, the documentary researcher, the antiquarian, the photographer, the conservationist, and the writer. It may also involve the skills of the genealogist, the historian--and the mythmaker.

Family story may be told or supported by pictures, photographs, maps, drawings, rituals, pageants, or the display of treasured artifacts, but the narrative feature still remains central. This is because a family's story is basically the narrated tale of a family over time. It differs from family history in that it includes more than the chronicle of events, personages, and facts pertaining to the family. Story includes also the myths, values, meanings, and interpretations which turn the chronology of history into a total fabric of narrative which stands as a source of identity in the present. Michael Novak's excellent definition of personal story can be translated into that of family story:

A "story" ties a person's actions together in a sequence. It units past and future. It supplies patterns, themes, motifs by which a person recognizes (or someone else recognizes) the unity of his or her life. (1971, p. 60)

The key word here is unity. Story--whether of a person or of a family--supplies patterns, themes, motifs by which the unity of personal or family life may be recognized. In *Roots*, Kunta Kinte's progeny see in his life and in the story-heritage he left a set of patterns, themes, and motifs which gives them a sense of belonging, a sense of family unity and identity. ". . . de African make us know who we is!" This is accomplished not merely through knowledge of chronology or genealogy, though such knowledge may be a part of the story. It is the story itself as told and retold within the family context that elicits this sense of unity. And a great deal of the magic of this family story, one must admit, lies in the role behavior of the succession of narrators into whose hands the tradition is passed and entrusted.

THE CONCEPT OF FAMILY IDENTITY

Before we discuss further a family identity creation role,
we need to look closer at the concept of family identity
itself. Family identity is analogous to the concept of personal identity important in a number of studies in psychology
and sociology. We will examine the use of the concept of
personal identity in several works and comment on its ana-
logical applications to a parallel concept of family identity.

Perhaps Erik Erickson's formulation of personal development is the place to begin. For Erikson (1968), identity
formation is an essential task of adolescence. The task is
one begun in infancy, however, and one in which the interaction between the individual and his or her community is essential. In the process of achieving a sense of personal
identity, the youth becomes recognized by the community as
distinct from other youth and as an individual in his or her
own right (Erikson, 1968). The development of a style, of
a distinctive way of doing things, of the sense of who one
is and might become is integral to this concept. There are
two poles to this sense of identity: a feeling of well-being
with oneself and a feeling of acceptance in community (Erikson, 1974).

An an analogue to this concept of personal identity, our
concept of family identity will have these two polar aspects.
On the one hand, the family's identity looks back to its
history and foward to its future--and to its mythology composed of "patterns, themes, motifs by which [it] recognizes
the unity of [its] life" (Novak, 1971, p. 60). On the other
hand, the family's identity is involved with the larger community in which it lives--the formulation of the family story
which embodies a family's identity must set it into the context of the wider community in a way which will be acceptable
to the family members themselves. In other words, a sense of
family identity creates a symbolic image of "the family" in
the minds of family members. That symbolic entity may have
its codes of honor, its ways of doing things, its canons of
right and wrong. But perhaps most importantly, the symbolic
entity created by a sense of family identity gives a context
to family life from which meaning can be derived and personal
satisfaction obtained from the family experience.

> Identity is a coherent sense of self. It depends
> upon the awareness that one's endeavors and one's
> life make sense, that they are meaningful in the
> context in which life is lived. (Wheelis, 1958,
> p. 19)

Here, Wheelis uses the word "identity" in its ordinary
lay meaning. He sees our society as one in which a person's
sense of having an identity has largely been lost--hence
the many quests for identity he documents in our society--
and the creation of the problem of finding one's true identity itself. We may ask about an analogous situation of the
family. If the individual needs a coherent sense of self,
cannot we say that the family likewise needs a coherent sense
of its own place in the scheme of things? If families are
to exhibit strengths, if they are to be capable of pulling
together and collectively overcoming difficulties, it would
seem that they, too, need an awareness that their cooperate
lives and endeavors make sense, and that family life is
meaningful in the context in which the family lives.

Other social commentators have noted attempts of individuals to search for identities. Fashions, cults, crusades,
and various other collective movements offer to many the hope
that some kind of identity can be found (Klapp, 1969). Others
are so rejecting of identities they derive from the everyday
routines at home, school, or work that they seek alternative
identities in hobbies, inner experiences, travel, and the
like (Cohen and Taylor, 1978). The point here is that a
number of studies document the fact our usual role behavior
is often unpalatable for our identity formation. In other
words, many of us don't want to be defined (or identified)
as merely the role performers we look like to the wider
society. We believe there is more to us than shows. House-
wives want to see themselves as more than performers of the
homemaking and child care roles; workers at various jobs reject the notion they are merely the perfomers of role activities they despise.

In the quotation from *Roots* above, we notice the same
dissonance between a family's visible roles in the larger
society and its felt sense of identity. The kidnapped African
Kunta Kinte insisted to the end of his days that no matter
how much massa and the dominant white society wished to turn
him into Toby (a slave), he was in reality Kunta Kinte--a
free African man with a home, village, friends, and family
of his own. As his family developed over time, this heritage
from their African ancestor was kept and remembered; the
struggle of this family became one of sustaining a sense of
family identity quite counter to surface reality. The family refused to allow its sense of identity to become defined
by the roles imposed upon the family members. Various techniques were evolved to keep alive this collective vision of
who they were--religion, hard work, conscious distancing,
subterfuge, and just plain fantasy. But primary was the
repetition of the family story--a reiteration and oral re-
minder of who the family was, providing an occasion for the

family to renew again an appropriation of the patterns,
themes, and motifs which gave unity to their lives.

Role expectations imposed by society today can hardly
be as oppressive for most of our families as they were for
the transplanted African-American families of ante-bellum
times. But family roles in society are still rarely palat-
able enough that all families wish to conceive of their identities as synonymous with their collective role activities.
Just as the larger society could indentify a family as a
family of slaves in earlier days, so today it can attempt to
imprint an identity upon a family against which the family
must struggle. A family's identity as viewed by the larger
society tends to be composed of the collective role functioning of its members. Thus, a family becomes known or
identified by its social activity, its work roles, its community service, and so on. Some families may be happy enough
with the family image thus created. But others--and perhaps an increasing number of others--may feel there is more
to their family's identity than comes through to society's
view via role behavior. As our society becomes increasingly
bureaucratized, depersonalized, computerized, and to the extent that each social unit becomes interpreted in economic
or productive terms, this feeling is likely to increase. It
is my surmise that many families today find themselves in
about the same position as Haley's family; the sense of identity transmitted by the expectations of the larger culture
is an impoverished and deadening one. This possibility may
go far to help explain the popularity of the novel and television production of *Roots*--among whites as well as among
blacks in our country.

Family identity, then, may be interpreted as a necessary
developmental task for any family. Some of the content of
the family's identity may come from its collective role activity as perceived and reflected by the larger society. Increasingly, families may find such identities insufficient
for building a feeling of family self-worth, purpose, and
self-esteem. This feeling that a family's role activity is
not enough to provide a satisfactory sense of family identity is parallel to feelings widely reported in our society
that individuals find it necessary to quest for identity far
afield from their work-a-day role activities.

FAMILY IDENTITY CREATION AS ROLE ACTIVITY

I will now ask whether activity leading to the creation of
a family identity should be interpreted as a role enactment.
Is it useful to conceive of the activities leading to the
creation of family identity as role behavior?

The most suggestive work on role behavior in the contemporary American family is that of Nye et al. (1976) as
reported in *Role Structure and Analysis of the Family*. Nye
and associates distinguish eight roles within the family:
the child socialization, child care, provider, housekeeper,
sexual, therapeutic, and recreational roles. Should we add
to these roles a ninth--a family identity creation role?

Family identity creation activity fits well into this
conceptualization of role behavior outlined by Nye et al.
(1976). The behavior we are considering is not sex-linked,
and does not define a position, although its association with
a particular position or status within the family may be
normative. (The telling of the family story is most often
initiated by elder members of the family, and in any case
the nature of the activity implies that of necessity the
role-taker must be authoritatively informed about the tradition to be transmitted.) Activity associated with a rehearsal
of the family story may be shared by two or more members of
a family. (In our example from *Roots* quoted above, we note
that the storytelling function seems to have been normative
for grandmother Kizzy; however, in the episode quoted above
the role activity is taken by Chicken George himself and
shared with his oldest son Virgil.) Story-telling activities
appear to be similar to other family role activity in that
there is a complementarity involved; there must be listeners
if one is to tell the story, just as there must be viewers of
family photographs as well as those who take them. As with
other previously identified family roles, such concepts as
role strain, role competence, and role identification apply
(Nye et al., 1976).

Activity designed to create family identity has a long
history. However, the recognition of this activity as role
activity yielding a sense of family identity has been lost
in many families. A conceptualization of any family behavior
as role activity has the advantage of raising to consciousness the activity itself for purposes of study and rational
decision making. Interpretation of family activity in terms
of role behavior spotlights such activity for scholars and
researchers to consider as well. For these reasons, it
seems salutary to recast activities leading to a creation of
family identity into role terminology.

Much activity which can serve to build family identity
seems to be performed in contemporary families with little
sense of direction or purpose. For example, photographic
activity capturing the important moments in the growth of
children is sporadic and haphazard in most families, with
a minimum of planning and sense of purpose involved. Events
are often recorded on film, but dates, names, and places are
eventually lost to memory. Often enough, the family will

merely feel impelled to "take some pictures of the kids" to
send to grandparents because "it's been a long time since
we've sent them anything." To identify a family identity
creation role as bona fide role activity within the family
is to encourage a more conscious, orderly, and purposive approach to that type of activity.

FAMILY IDENTITY CREATION RELATED TO OTHER FAMILY ROLE ACTIVITY

Following a principle of parsimony, Nye and his associates
(1976) wished to identify as few roles as possible as long as
each role conceived did not subsume unduly diverse behaviors.
The type of activity with which we are concerned--the telling of the family story for purposes of family identity crea-
tion--would seem to have little to do with child care, provider, housekeeping, sexual, therapeutic, or recreational
roles. The activity does, however, seem linked with behaviors
typical of the child socialization and kinship roles. We
will look at each of these in turn and ask if our hypothesized family identity creation role can be subsumed under
one or more of these previously identified family roles.
    Viktor Gecas, in his discussion of the child socializ-
tion role, summarizes it as follows:

> Socialization, in our usage, is limited to the
> social and psychological development of the child.
> It refers to those processes and activities with-
> in the family which contribute to developing the
> child into a competent, social, and moral per-
> son. Specifically it involves such activities as
> teaching children what is right and wrong, devel-
> oping in them a sense of responsibility, develop-
> ing competence in eating and dressing properly,
> in doing school work, and generally in inter-
> acting with others. The particular manner or
> style of parent-child interaction, such as the
> amount and kind of discipline, support, and com-
> munication characteristic of the relationship,
> is also an aspect of the socialization process
> which may be consequential to the products of
> the process. (Nye, 1976, pp. 33-34)

Clearly, the telling of the family story has much to
do with child socialization under this definition. It would
seem that the telling of the family story is a "particular
manner or style of parent-child interaction", and that the
results of successful transmission of that story would touch

on areas of right and wrong, responsibility, and interaction with others.

However, there would seem to be <u>more</u> to the telling of the family story for purposes of building family identity than mere socialization of children. Much family storytelling activity takes place among older family members--often without youngsters present. We may further note that the African storytellers who informed Haley of his own family's origins transmitted their lore not only to their society's children but to older members as well (Haley, 1976; Blockson, 1977). In mediaeval times, the storytellers and court poets of Northern Europe extolled the adventures of patron families not only for the benefit of the young but for the enjoyment and edification of adults (Vigfusson & Powell, 1883). In our contemporary society, activities such as genealogical or heraldic research are performed by and for the mature quite as much as for the socialization of the young (Wagner, 1972; Doane, 1960). Within the modern family, it is the elderly as much as the young who benefit from the reminiscences, the scrapbooks, the photographs, the mementos, the recounted adventures of the family. While socialization of children is a part of family identity creation, it is only a part: the role is more complex, and is directed toward welding the family into a unit more than simply bringing the children to a level of knowledge or compliance with adult standards. The family identity creation role impinges directly upon all members of the family and is enacted for the benefit of all.

The telling of the family story would also seem to have much in common with the kinship role identified and discussed by Howard M. Bahr (Nye et al., 1976). Bahr lists characteristics of ideal kindred relations norms relating to: (1) participation in rituals and ceremonies; (2) promotion of the welfare of family members; (3) making personal resources available to family members; (4) trust in the kindred; and (5) maximizing communication. As the kinship role is developed, it becomes clear that the central focus of the role in modern society is on communications between the nuclear family and relatives not living within the same household, such as aunts, uncles, grandparents, etc. It must be admitted that the telling of the family story and a subsequent development of a sense of family identity will have a positive effect in promoting such communications. Again, there seems a difference in direction. Family storytelling is an internal activity with strong implications for the kinship role. The building of a sense of family identity is conceptually distinct from (and perhaps a prerequisite for) the building of strong ties from the nuclear family to more distant kin. We can see this difference in families which have

few or no known living relatives to whom a kinship role can
be directed. Kinship role activity depends upon the existence of living relatives to whom communications and relations may be directed; the family story and its building of
family identity can go on independent of this factor. This
is because family story conceptually unites not only presently living units of the family but unites the family's past
with the present and points to its future. Schematized on
a time-chart, the kinship role works laterally to link living
kin to the nuclear family; the family identity creation role
includes this but further reaches into the past and antici-
pates future generations to supply ". . . patterns, themes
and motifs by which a [family] recognizes . . . the unity
of [its] life" (Novak, 1971, p. 60).

Our situation seems to be this: the creation of family
identity through transmission of the family story has the
hallmarks of role behavior and decided affinities with the
child socialization and kinship roles outlined by Nye et al.
(1976). However, family identity creation activity goes beyond these roles in its impact and intent; family identity
creation activity as here developed focuses on the entire
family rather than on the children or the family's living
relatives. While child-socializing activity and kin-
communications may be part of this proposed role, they are
neither its exclusive nor its primary intent. The aim of
family identity creation activity is to build the family into a unit which conceives of itself as a living entity with
an integral past and an anticipated future--an entity of
which each member is an important part.

FAMILY IDENTITY CREATION ACTIVITY AND ITS
SUPPORT TO BUILD FAMILY STRENGTHS

The need for a sense of family identity in past and present
times can be demonstrated. We have interpreted this activity as role activity in contemporary society. We shall now
turn to a consideration of family identity creation as enacted in contemporary family life and consider implications
of such activity for those who would help build family
strengths.

We may conveniently identify four distinct concerns
around which family identity creation activity is oriented
in contemporary family life.

1. Concern with telling the family story. This is the
kind of narrative activity to which we have often referred
in the quoted excerpt from *Roots*. In many families today,
the stories of previous generations, of "father when he was
young," of "mother when she was a little girl," are passed

on by the older members of the family. Unfortunately, we live in a busy age when these stories may fall on deaf ears; a generation may be uninterested in such stories and fail to transmit them. It is well known that many older family members may have such stories to tell but that they often have only other older people to tell them to.

This suggests first of all a program to make families conscious of their heritage and of the need for conserving and preserving oral traditions. Many of the stories and anecdotes may be reduced to writing, or at least recorded on tape while older family members are still available to impart them. Efforts expended in this task can, in themselves, provide occasions for strengthening a sense of family identity, and bring family members closer together. At least one popular publication incorporates such activities in a program to strengthen family ties (Nutt, 1976).

Further, the existence and importance of family story may be lifted to consciousness. It has been suggested that an interpretation of such storytelling activity as role activity within the family is a step in this direction. Telling stories is an art, and like any art can be improved with practice and conscious effort. There are immediate rewards to those who acquire this art and are able to communicate a sense of family identity and a sense of history to younger members of the family. Practice in reading aloud and in declamation used to be a part of everyone's education; perhaps this skill ought to be revived and encouraged by those who would build family strengths.

More traditional genealogical and family historical research work may be necessary if the family story is to become known, let alone transmitted to younger generations. The tracing of family ties and history has many facets, from library work to face-to-face meetings among relations. All such activities united in a common goal to piece together the family story may provide excellent activities to bring a family together physically as well as conceptually.

2. <u>Concern</u> with <u>photographing</u> the events of the family. Since the invention of photography in 1839, the family has had access to a powerful technique for preserving family traditions, events, and memories. Most families in America attempt to record the benchmark occasions on film—whether they be formal family portraits, snapshots of a new baby, pictures of the youth before departing for college, wedding pictures, or whatever. Most families retain such photographs taken at key times in the past; perhaps few are able to preserve them intact over several generations, and fewer yet to pass them on with the necessary explanatory information or accompanying story.

Conservation of pictures from the past is a growing concern for museums and art collectors, and should be of concern to those who would encourage families to transmit their family stories. Preservation and conservation of photographs are techniques which can be learned--and in this case, are techniques which are potentially family strengthening. Boxes of old photographs need to be resurrected from the attic and shown to older members of the family to learn what occasions in the life of the family they capture. Who were these people? How are they related to us? What did they do? The answers received need to be carefully written down and the photographs themselves documented and preserved. There are better and worse ways of doing this--gluing photos in an album is not the best way of preserving them for future generations. The dissemination of better methods appropriate to families-- not necessarily to museums--for the conservation of family photographs has begun (Davies, 1977) but needs encouragement and efforts on the part of students of the family.

Primary concern, however, needs to be given to linking photography to the family story. Photographs when separated from the family story become mere collectibles and relics of the past. They lose their life and their ability to remind us of something special and important. Hence, the need for documentation of the photographs is even greater than the need for their conservation or preservation; the images can be duplicated or copied, but once separated from their place within the family story they become meaningless.

3. Concern with preserving and perpetuating traditions, rituals, and distinctive ways of doing things. Each family comes into existence with ways of doing things inherited from the families of origin of both parents. Each family must pick and choose what features will be kept, which passed over. Perhaps the suggestion of a more conscious approach to this process will lead families to the creation of new-old life styles built on combined heritages as a step in building family strengths. Even, for example, if a family is composed of members of two religious faiths and one faith is chosen for the newly constituted family, there may well be ways of honoring the existence and importance of that other, not-chosen religious heritage. Conscious efforts at keeping certain identifying rituals and traditions from the past can be an exercise in building family strengths. Of course, these efforts can also mire the family down in endless functions and meaningless repetitions if they become separated from the family story or if they merely become a burden upon one or a few members of the family. For the student of the family, however, it is suggested that a return to a once popular topic--that of ritual in family living (Bossard & Boll, 1950)--

might be salutary in developing methods whereby families might consciously strengthen their identities.

4. <u>Concern</u> <u>with</u> <u>mementos</u> <u>of</u> <u>the</u> <u>past</u>. We live in an age which is interested in nostalgia and in relics from the past. Many families retain physical mementos belonging to their ancestors--grandfather's watch, great-grandmother's wedding dress, pieces of furniture, or antiques once owned by members of one's family. Often these relics are accompanied by stories such as, "This is the chair in which your grandmother rocked your mother to sleep when she was a baby." Again, the danger is that the story will become detached from the relic and the artifact will merely become an antique alongside other pieces of bric-a-brac.

The task is again one of documentation and the reduction of oral tradition to written form. Efforts also need to be made to document the transfer of such memorabilia from one generation to another so that all sisters and brothers may know who has great-grandfather's watch. Photography may likewise come to the rescue; if every child cannot have great-grandfather's watch, perhaps each may have a photograph of it to show to his or her children. Conscious efforts to record at least some of the physical surroundings of the past-- and of the present which will one day be someone's past--can be made. Future generations will be grateful to those who took the time and possessed the foresight to encourage in this manner the development of a family identity.

* * * * *

So Dad has joined the others up there. I feel
that they <u>do</u> watch and guide, and I also feel
that they join me in the hope that this story of
our people can help alleviate the legacies of
the fact that preponderantly the histories have
been written by the winners.

This is the last paragraph of Haley's book *Roots*, with which we began. Perhaps it points to the most important reason for looking to this area of family identity in the building of family strengths. Most families--whether white, black, or of whatever race or clan--will perhaps feel they are not among the "winners" of society. Few of us will count presidents or kings among our ancestors; few will feel their family has enacted a pivotal role in world history. However, if society does not allow us to see ourselves as winners, we still nevertheless must refuse to see ourselves as losers. As *Roots* and its popularity and aftermath indicate, the power of family story to pull together a family

and give it identity, dignity, and strength is as strong today
as ever. The key to such family identity lies in transform-
ing the bric-a-brac of the past--the genealogies, the boxes of
photographs, the mementos, the rituals, the anecdotes--into
a family story which has the power to unite the present generation with its past, and which reveals patterns, themes,
and motifs by which a family can recognize the unity of its
life. The recognition of a family identity creating role
within the family--a role which can be appropriated and shared
by any number of individuals within that family--can go a
long way toward the strengthening of family life in this day
and age.

REFERENCES

Blockson, C. L., & Fry, R. *Black genealogy*. Englewood Cliffs,
    New Jersey: Prentice-Hall, 1977.

Bossard, J. H. S., & Boll, E. S. *Ritual in family living*.
    Philadelphia: University of Pennsylvania Press, 1950.

Cohen, S., & Taylor, L. *Escape attempts*. Harmondsworth:
    Penguin Books, 1978.

Davies, L. *Shoots: A guide to your family's photographic
    heritage*. Danbury, New Hampshire: Addison House, 1977.

Doane, G. H. *Searching for your ancestors*. (3rd. ed.).
    Minneapolis: University of Minnesota Press, 1960.

Erikson, E. H. *Dimensions of a new identity*. New York: W.
    W. Norton, 1974.

Erikson, E. H. *Identity youth and crisis*. New York: W. W.
    Norton, 1968.

Haley, A. *Roots*. New York: Dell Publishing Company, 1976.

Klapp, O. E. *Collective search for identity*. New York: Holt,
    Rinehart & Winston, 1969.

Novak, M. *Ascent of the mountain, flight of the dove*. New
    York: Harper & Row, 1971.

Nutt, G. *Family time*. DesPlaines, Illinois: Million Dollar
    Round Table, 1976.

Nye, F. I., et al. *Role structure and analysis of the family*. Beverly Hills/London: Sage Publications, 1976.

Vigfusson, G., & Powell, F. Y. *Corpus poeticum boreale*. New York: Russell & Russell, 1883.

Wagner, A. R. *English genealogy*. (2nd ed.) New York: Oxford University Press, 1972.

Wheelis, A. *The quest for identity*. New York: W. W. Norton, 1958.

Interaction, Identity, and Intimacy: The Glue That Cements the Family

Dr. Anne McCreary Juhasz
School of Education
Loyola University of Chicago

INTRODUCTION

Currently among sociologists and psychologists there is heated debate about "What is a family?" At one end of the continuum is the traditional, committed for a lifetime, monogamous structure. At the other extreme is the single person residing alone, considered a family. Between lie various combinations of informal, formal, structured, and reconstituted groups.

A majority of problems facing these groups revolve around either legal or relationship aspects, and the focus, in many instances, is sex-related and includes many dimensions, such as development, learning, attitudes, behavior, freedom, adjustment, use, and abuse. Divorce, desertion, separation, remarriage, unwed pregnancy, child abuse, incest, spouse abuse, bisexual and homosexual households, cohabitation, working mothers, day care for children, dual career families are representative of the issues facing modern families.

It is within the family framework that patterns for effective living and loving can best be instituted, practiced, and perfected. Intimacy, identity, and interaction together form the glue which cements relationships within the family and allow children, as they enter the adult world to form families, which are held together with that same glue, and are strong enough to withstand the pressures of a changing society.

In terms of optimal developmental progress and sound mental health, it is almost impossible to visualize consolidation of identity, growth in intimacy, and human interaction as separate processes. Through interaction, we achieve a sense of identity, experience intimacy, and learn to understand and come to terms with our own sexuality and with that of others.

INTERACTION

The key, the beginning point, is interaction, a process that
can be either verbal or nonverbal, physical or nonphysical;
it is one which continues from the moment of birth throughout the total life span. Interaction is a fundamental prerequisite for knowing oneself. The feedback which accompanies and follows interaction allows the individual to form
ideas of who and what he or she is in relation to others and
in various situations. This sense of identity is an important factor in the capacity to develop intimacy, which in turn
leads to interaction and further searching for understanding
and insight into oneself. Thus, the circular reaction continues throughout the dynamic, active life of the individual.
     Also, if sexuality is to be considered, as it should be
within the context of human development and experience, understanding will be facilitated as we gain insight into some
of the important interactions, some of the crises in identity
formation, and some of the problems in establishing intimacy.
Whether one favors the psychoanalytic, the social learning,
or the cognitive theory of sexual development, the beginning
point will be birth and early infancy, and many problems which
occur later in life will have their roots in this period.
Thus, the Eriksonian epigenetic chart of developmental crises
offers an appropriate point of departure. His framework is
also especially relevant here because of his inclusion and
ordering of the identity and intimacy crises.
     Briefly, Erikson (1963, 1965) feels that during the first
year of life, the infant must develop a sense of trust. Trust
develops when the mother or caretaker consistently meets the
infant's need for comfort and attention. From one to three
years, the major task is that of developing independence
and self control, a feeling of what is me and not me, and
a feeling of pride rather than shame in relation to me. From
three to six years, the task of sex-role identification and
feelings of initiative, rather than guilt, are foremost. Six
to eleven years is the time when competence in academic skills
and social relationships is important, and puberty is the
time for trying on adult roles, consolidating identity, and
building heterosexual relationships. This leaves for young
adulthood the task of establishing intimacy and the ability
to love in a mature fashion.

Parent and Child Interaction

Most research on early relating and its later consequences
has dealt with animals or with some unique rather than normal population. However, there are applications and implications for normal human development. Perhaps the most

extensive research has emanated from the Primate Laboratory
at the University of Wisconsin at Madison, where Harlow and
his colleagues (Suomi & Harlow, 1972), working with monkeys,
have observed the importance of "contact comfort." They
found that baby monkeys, raised with surrogate mothers, would
in times of crisis or tension prefer the mother who provided
warmth and softness, rather than the one who provided nourishment. Even more important, in terms of understanding sexual
behavior, were the findings with regard to babies raised with
surrogate mothers, who merely provided warmth or food, but
never censure, cuddling, or interaction. When they became
adults, those monkeys had tremendous difficulty learning appropriate heterosexual behavior. It was almost impossible
to breed them, and those who did have offspring were very
poor mothers who neglected their infants, and, in fact, treated
them as they had been treated by their surrogate mothers.

   In addition, monkeys raised in isolation from peer members developed typical schizophrenic reactions, such as roll-
ing up in a fetal ball, rocking, and head banging. Only when
therapy included interaction with much younger playmates did
they begin to learn appropriate play and social roles. It
was also interesting to note that whatever the type of mother,
for monkeys, the affectional response was long-lasting. They
spent hours looking through the glass window of the Butler
Box at the mother.

   While research findings based on animal behavior cannot
be generalized to humans, nevertheless strikingly similar
findings have been reported. Infants, deprived of contact
with humans and emotional feedback did not fare well. Recent medical research has tied lack of tactile contact to
dermatological problems in infants (Harlow et al., 1969). Infants have actually died of no other cause than wasting away,
grieving, and refusing to eat. In fact, treatment for such
cases is a surrogate mother to provide emotional and contact
comfort. The persistence of the affectional response has
been noted in cases of child abuse, where the child chooses
to keep returning to the battering parent, and when old
enough to talk, lies about injuries to protect the parent.
Also, the modeling of parental behavior is evidenced in the
fact that many battering parents were themselves the victims
of parental abuse.

   A Canadian documentary film, *Warrendale*, shows the treatment of severely emotionally disturbed youngsters and young
adults. Treatment was based on the idea that without the
basic foundation provided by the establishment of a sense
of trust in infancy, the individual cannot move forward to
the next stages of heterosexual or even homosexual relationships. In order to develop the sense of trust in these
severely disturbed people, a one-to-one relationship is

established with a guiding adult who takes the patient back
to infancy, and holds, rocks, cuddles, and feeds warm milk
from a bottle, in an attempt to fill in this missing stage
of development of trust.

Some extremely fascinating and important research is
being carried on by Dr. M. Klaus at Case Western Reserve
Medical School. Klaus (1975) has been involved with a series
of projects on the importance of early parenting, especially
interactions and intimacy. Similar to the work of Harlow
and colleagues, initial impetus to the Klaus studies came
from animal research. Klaus has investigated the first moments after birth, and the effect on the infant of immediate
contact with the mother.

Experiments with baby lambs showed that the first 15
minutes are crucial in terms of mother-infant attachment.
When infants were taken away for the first 15 minutes, 40
percent of the mothers destroyed the baby. If the infant
were left with the mother for the first five minutes, the
mother mothered all the babies. If the mother and infant
were together for the first 15 minutes, she mothered only
her own baby. Consequences for infant rats and chimps were
not so startling; if the baby were not given to the mother
for 24 hours, the rat would care for it but not so well.
Under similar circumstances, the mother chimp would mother,
but also to a lesser extent.

With human mothers, it has been found that after 10 minutes with the wrong baby, it is hard to change; mothers somehow feel that the first baby must be the right one. Human
mothers, who were given their nude baby at once and allowed
extended contact daily and alone with the infant, demonstrated
quite different behavior than mothers in a control group.
They did not want to leave their babies during the first
week, they picked up and soothed the crying baby, fondled
the infant more, had more face-to-face contact, and during
the one-month visit to the doctor's office kept a hand on
the infant. It is reported that one-third of battered babies, and one-third of the babies who fail to thrive or have
maturational disorders, were separated from their mothers at
the time of delivery.

Cross-cultural research in Brazil and Guatemala reveals
that more mothers, who were given their babies immediately,
chose to breast-feed the infants than did those who did not
have contact. In Sweden, study of the father-infant attachment is under way, based upon the same practice of giving
the nude infant to the father immediately after birth.

Other interesting findings on interaction and attachment involve the importance of eye contact, and lining up
the mother's and infant's faces. The one-day old infant will

actually imitate, by sticking his or her tongue out, and moving in rhythm to the mother's voice. Findings on early attachment have implications for adoption, multiple births, and for grieving mothers. According to Klaus (1975), two basic rules governing parental-infant attachment are: (1) "attachment to one"--the mother to a single infant; thus, the problem with multiple births; and (2) "one cannot detach and attach at the same time." He states that a woman grieving the loss of a loved one at the time of the birth cannot mother at that time.

This type of research serves to highlight the importance of parenting, and these researchers are following up longitudinally on subjects in their studies. It will be interesting to observe these children at adolescence, and to note their patterns of interaction, problems of identity formation, and their capacity for intimacy. At this point, Klaus (1975) recommends that the mother be allowed to be alone with her naked newborn infant for the first 45 minutes of life.

Interacting as a Sexual Being

So far, I have been discussing early interaction between parent and child, and its importance in laying the foundation for healthy later relationships. This provides the groundwork; I would now like to concentrate on some of the problems of the adolescent and the young adult. These are problems for which there are few answers and little research to guide us at this time, and have to do with interacting as a sexual being.

Interacting in terms of anatomy, physiology, and techniques for insemination, procreation, contraception, and abortion are not included in the discussion, mainly because these are not the difficult areas to understand. Audiovisual materials and self-help manuals and clinics facilitate easy, objective presentations of information on these topics. There is really nothing new when it comes to sexual behavior. People have always been interested in it, participated in it, and left behind both primitive and sophisticated records of how and when. A well-trained, skilled technician can produce erection, ejaculation, and orgasm. So when we think of understanding sexuality, this simplistic, mechanistic approach is not what we mean. However, it seems somewhat ironical that these are the aspects which have received the most attention and which arouse the most controversy. Perhaps the reason for this is that, in our attempts to understand and to explain and educate, we have isolated the factual and the objective, taken it out of the affective context, which is the only place where it is meaningful,

and in this way have stripped away the most positive connotations of sexual interaction.

Just what, then, does interacting as a sexual being mean
and what does it involve? Are all interactions sexual in
nature? Do we interact primarily as males in a masculine
way, or as females in a feminine way? Do men react and interact differently with men and with women, and is the same
true for women? Do males and females interpret interactions
and responses to them differently? When do human interactions
become sexual interactions? Is sexual arousal or attraction
in the interaction the distinguishing factor, and is this
what we are uptight about? Do our ideas about what is proper
sexually inhibit our capacity to interact? What role does
the liberation of women play? Has spontaneity been elimin-
ated and, in our materialistic society, do we, as Libby
(Libby & Carlson, 1973) suggests, utilize an exchange theory
in interrelationships, where actual interaction in a situation is present or future oriented, and costs, rewards and
profits are weighed and evaluated, which results in ranking
inteactions and decisions on a continuum from consensual to
accommodative, depending upon the stakes and the price to
be paid?

IDENTITY

Partial answers to some of the questions about interrelating
will be provided as we proceed to examine the importance of
identity, and the manner in which one establishes the dimensions of his or her sexual self.

Sexual Indentity

With few exceptions, an infant's sex (male or female) is
firmly established at time of birth. Almost the first thing
the attending physician says is either, "It's a boy," or
"It's a girl." Biological, constitutional, hereditary, con-
genital, and maturational components are spelled out, except
in the case of hermaphrodites.

It is the next stage, that of sex-role identification,
which is a major task, and one of prime importance to the
individual. Experts agree that by three years at the latest,
the child has a firm idea of whether he or she is masculine
or feminine, and that after six years, it is practically impossible to change this orientation. However, there are at
least three theories about the manner in which this takes
place. According to the psychoanalytic or Freudian theory,
the earliest identification for an infant is with the mother.
Thus, the male child desires the mother, fears paternal

retaliation, and so identifies with the father as a means of escaping. The girl, in this situation, shifts her love object to the father, but learns the complementary sex role.

The second major theory of psychosexual identification is the social learning theory, which hypothesizes that the child identifies with the major rewarder, and models behavior after that which is rewarded. In this context, it is interesting to note that girls usually receive and learn from positive rewards, such as "That's a good girl!" while boys primarily learn from negative sanctions such as, "Boys don't cry!"

The third theory is a cognitive-developmental theory set forth by Kohlberg (1974), in which the child who is identified as a boy selects, organizes, and structures his perceptions from his social world to fit the label, "I am a boy. Boys do this. Therefore I do this." Each of these theories has been discussed and argued, and Freudian terminology is part of the layman's language--oedipus complex, penis envy, etc. However, even Freudians have varying interpretations of the identity problem. Social learning theory has spawned a mountain of research on the effects of father absence, working mothers, merging sex roles, female teachers, and varied infant caretakers on male sex-role identification. There are as many answers as there are questions, and research results mainly reflect the characteristics of the specific sample populations from which the data were collected.

In terms of sexual identity, then, infants are born either male or female, and by three years of age have identified with either masculine or feminine sex roles, usually that which is fitting their gender at birth. However, transsexuals are an example of individuals who biologically are one sex, but identify with the opposite. Again, there has been much research into the factors which influence this opposite sex-role identification. The persons who identify with their appropriate sex role usually prefer it, adopt it, and learn to perform it more or less adequately, according to the prescription set forth by society. The final stage in establishing sexual identity is that of developing or selecting sex object preference--preference for either homosexual or heterosexual contacts and experiences.

There is an increasing body of literature in this area on the characteristics and behaviors of homosexuals. With the publication of the Wolfenden Report in Britain, and more liberalized views, increased acceptance of homosexuality as a normal variation of sexual behavior has taken place. Actually, between homosexuals and heterosexuals, there appear to be more similarities than differences. Some persons believe the one factor which bothers heterosexuals the most, when it comes right down to it, is that, for the male

homosexual, a vagina is not essential for sexual intercourse;
for the female homosexual, a penis is unnecessary. Otherwise,
heterosexuals do everything that homosexuals do. Homosexuals,
however, do encounter many more legal and social problems.

Problems

Now that the components and concepts involved have been presented, I would like to consider some of the problems which
face the individual in establishing sexual identity.

Incidentally, in focusing on sexual identity, I do not
mean to imply that this is the overwhelming aspect of the
self-concept, or that self-esteem rests entirely on one's
idea of one's masculinity or femininity. Actually, I know
of no research which investigates the old chicken/egg dilemma, that is, "Am I a good person because I am a good woman?"
or, "Am I a good woman because I am a good person?" This
question may become even more cloudy with the merging of sex
roles and the accompanying overlap in the dimensions of each.
It may become more difficult for children to identify as
either a male or a female, and to determine which are masculine and which are feminine attributes. Children may wonder,
"Which am I?" as well as, "Who am I?"

This dilemma is even more inclusive; Elkind (1973) sees
parental value structures as the matrix of identity formation for the child. The same vagueness exists here, and
as a result, the adolescent in search of personal identity
has nothing to rebel against. When the opportunity for reality testing against parental models is unavailable, the adolescent is forced to turn to peers and to public figures.
The doubling of the number of broken homes in the last decade, and the causal relationship between juvenile delinquency
and family disruption, are evidence of the dilemma. In addition, society's pressures on children do not fit with developmental pressures. Society presses for academic achievement
and intellectual pursuit just when the children's biggest
problem and consuming worry is how to relate.

Also, we expect identity closure and solution to the
crisis at an early age. Offer, Marcus, and Offer (1970),
in a longitudinal study of normal adolescent males, found
they were very insecure and unsure about who they were and
where they were going, especially in terms of sexual relationships. At age 19, many still had not completed the identity solution. For girls, there are also problems. One
study of adolescent teenage girls seeking abortion indicated
that their identity was insecure and not yet firmly established. Their ability to love and to be loved was just
emerging, along with new and little-understood feelings of
femininity. The loneliness of the girls pervaded the study.

They had failed to form any close relationships, and were attempting to prove their femininity and maturity by getting pregnant, since that is what mature women do.

Investigations of the incidence of adolescent non-virginity reveal an interesting trend. A reversal has occurred. While the number of non-virgin females is increasing, the number of virgin males is rising. In addition, numbers of college-age males complaining of impotence is on the upswing. Emphasis on having the female achieve orgasm has placed heavy pressures and anxieties about possible performance-failure upon young people.

Very often sexual problems are a cover-up, either conscious or unconscious, for some other identity problem. Many of the uses and abuses of sex are tied to an inadequate self-concept. Very often, people use sexual activity as a way, and a poor one, to manage other personal problems.

Nor is the problem of identity solved once and for all at adolescence. While the work of Masters and Johnson has added to our knowledge of the physiological sexual response, this knowledge, disseminated to the public, has promoted anxiety and apprehension about sexual ability, potency, and techniques. In this respect, exposure to the mass media, enlightenment, and education have backfired. In addition, the greater acceptance of contraception, with the resulting freedom from fear of pregnancy; increased freedom to have premarital and nonmarital sexual intercourse; growing independence of women; acceptance of the idea that personal preference (not chronological age) is what determines the sex-activity span of the individual; and encouragement to seek openness, self-enhancement, and equality have forced adults to make an effort to find a new identity. So the occurrence of a second, or middle-aged, identity crisis is increasingly common.

No longer can we speak of identity as something static which can be attained, especially sexual identity. Rather, for the majority of people, it will be a constantly developing and changing aspect of personality and behavior, to be enjoyed and developed throughout the life span; it will be through interacting with others that identity will be defined.

INTIMACY

Of the concepts with which we are dealing, perhaps the third one, intimacy, has the highest emotional loading in terms of sexual connotations. Indeed, one of the dictionary definitions of this term is, "illicit sexual intercourse." You will recall that the work of Harlow and his colleagues and Klaus demonstrated the need for contact comfort, the need for intimacy unrelated to sexual intercourse, from the moment of birth.

Definitions of the word intimate tend to come closer to what a majority of young people today mean and are looking for when they speak of intimacy, that is, "a close association, a close friend, pertaining to one's deepest nature, essential or innermost." This is what comes through in the research findings on premarital intercourse and cohabitation. A majority of young people are neither promiscuous nor sexually permissive. They approve of sexual intercourse if both partners feel affection or love for each other. Interviews with students who set up living arrangements together reveal that sex and sexual intercourse are not the main motivating factors. Some cohabiting students have never had intercourse. Rather, the desire for close companionship, someone to interact with and to share with, a need to get to know members of the opposite sex, and to know how one relates to them are important. Also, of prime importance are loyalty and emotional security. Students who have premarital intercourse say that this enhances their relationship with their partners. Those who refrain say that this has the same effect.

Overlap and Interpretation

Whatever the dimensions and definitions of intimacy, it is here that identity and interrelating overlap and merge. Certainly, the rate of sexual intercourse has increased. Today, almost 80 percent of males and 60 percent of females (compared with 50 percent and 25 percent respectively in Kinsey's studies) will have had coitus by the time they leave college. Some young people see this as a means of discovering their identities, or resolving crisis. Erikson (1965) places the intimacy versus isolation crisis after the solution of the identity crisis, and it would seem that identity diffusion or confusion would result from too early sexual encounters. If success and positive reactions do not accompany this attempt at intimacy, premature identity closure or loss of sex-role identity could occur. Adolescent experimentation with sexual intimacy experiences could lead to early closure and commitment, or to promiscuity. It has been found that early initiation into dating results in more dating partners, and more frequent dating. Often such youngsters marry in adolescence to escape conflict at home, and the two partners have similar problems which draw them together. This can precipitate a triple crisis--adolescence, early marriage, and parenthood. Perhaps the increasing divorce rate is tied to too early movement toward intimacy, before resolving the identity crisis--the outcome of which is fidelity.

The result might be that the person in love married, but was unable to be faithful because of insecure identity.

Returning to the concept of contact comfort as an aspect of intimacy, and to isolation as the result of failure to achieve intimacy, a simple experiment performed by the late Sydney Jourard (1964), the originator of touch-taboo research, is relevant. The experiment demonstrates the way in which our background and culture can cut us off from establishing intimacy and from resolving this crisis. Jourard sat in coffee houses in various cities in the world, and made a note of how often someone touched another person in a period of an hour. The results were as follows:

San Juan	180
Paris	110
Gainsville	2
London	0

A reporter did the same experiment in Toronto, Canada, in a suburban shopping center coffee shop and in a west end cafe frequented by Italians. The count per hour in the first case was three; in the second, sixty-three.

Speaking of causes of withdrawal and alienation, Jourard (1964) says:

> The day begins with a rush through breakfast, the hurry to go to work, and the mechanized, meaning-less, fragmentary quality of the work itself.
> . . . Anybody would shriek in protest if he al-lowed himself to feel the violence to which he is subjecting himself. This depersonalization and mechanization result is some novel substitutes for human contact--like the electric vibrators which barbers use, and the "Magic Fingers" gadget that you find in many hotel beds, a coin-operated gizmo that rocks a person into relaxation without human intervention. It seems that the machine has taken over another function of man--the loving and soothing caress.

Jourard would have been appalled to read of a Japanese invention, a simulated-womb-type water bed with a carefully regulated mother-heart beat, for continuation of the fetal atmosphere. This can be used with premature infants, or with difficult babies. Even the heart-beat machine alone has an immediate soothing effect, which has psychologists worrying about overuse and its effect on the activity level and cognitive development of children.

It is noteworthy that a characteristic complaint which marriage counselors, gynecologists, urologists, and family doctors have heard repeatedly in their offices, often to the tune of tears, is:

He never touches me unless he wants to go to bed.
If he would just put his arm around me once, sort
of affectionately and friendly-like, or rub me
without lust, I'd fall down in a dead faint.

Throughout the discussion of interaction, identity formation, and intimacy, the sexual component has been interwoven, since sex is not something we do, it is something we are. We can never be far removed from our sexuality--as a means of communication and interaction, as an expression of intimacy, and as declaration of our identity.

CONCLUSIONS: THE PROBLEMS

What, then, are some of the major problems in developing intimacy, identity, and interaction in the family setting? Is understanding our sexuality, being proud of it, and accepting it as a basic and valuable part of us and others a necessary prerequisite to family strength? Can we view sexuality as a combination of our manner of interacting, presenting and thinking about ourselves, and sharing our warmth and closeness with others? Are interaction, identity, and intimacy important dimensions which compose the glue which cements a family? And if so, are we prepared to work toward their enhancement in the family setting?

At present, some of the roots of our problem, and barriers to its solution, lie in society itself. William Coffin, Chaplain at Yale University, has stated:

A society that places people in the category of
things and values the ability to purchase above
the ability to relate, is a society where young
people will grow up confused as to behavior and
values. (Rhymes, 1964, p. 34)

This seems to be borne out by both observation and research, which indicate that we utilize sex as something to be used for gain, for exploitive reasons, to sell things, as a bribe, as a weapon of anger or revenge, as a status symbol, as a reward, to demonstrate masculinity or femininity, and to prove independence from parents. This, by the way, is not a new trend. Over 20 years ago, Kardiner (1954) wrote:

In a competitive, success-oriented society, where
failure is automatically accompanied by loss of
self-esteem and increase in anxiety, hostility and
egocentricity, one can expect that sex activity
will be torn out of the context of social usefulness and will be carried on without concern for
the welfare of the person with whom it is achieved."

Kardiner (1954) feels that it is unrealistic to expect
sex morality to follow a course which differs from the morality prevailing in the society at large, and that sexual activity will thus become reckless and destructive.

Kohlberg (1974), in tracing the development of moral
reasoning, points out that there is nothing in the act of
sex per se that is either right or wrong. He has found culturally determined universal moral stages, but is not sure
that this is true for sexual dilemmas which are much tougher
than other types, because nothing has been morally specified
in the sexual situation. Erikson (1965) has questioned
whether early freedom in the direct use of sexuality would
make humans freer as persons. He says that we do not have
to act out every alternative concretely in order to learn.
Premarital sexual experience is not necessary for sexual
fulfillment, either for men or women. This we can learn
quickly and can learn together. If attitudes toward sex are
positive, primary pleasures are not distorted by lack of
experience. Erikson feels that chastity gives the relaxed
security and the time to be sexually creative, and that humans do not seek release and rest the easiest way. Man seeks
tension, challenge, even barriers and limitations at times,
simply for the joy of overcoming them.

Lieberman (1973) has said, "Young people, if they know
where they are going, can take sexuality also in their stride,"
while Luckey (1973) warns that we must stop quibbling about
the insignificant things like, "What is a family," and,
"Are we grown up enough to see explicit sex films?"

I have now completed the circle. I began by emphasizing
the importance of the earliest infant-parent contact. I return to conclude that in the long run, it is the quality of
the parenting which has the most influence on how well individuals deal with problems of sexual behavior and sexuality. Will parents help children to build positive self-
concepts, to find out who they are and where they want to
go? Will parents allow children to develop their capacity
to think, to consider available alternatives, to evaluate
the probable outcomes, to make decisions on this basis, and
to accept the responsibility for their actions? Will the
children of tomorrow be taught to feel enough and to care
enough about not only themselves, but also those with whom

they interact, identify, and are intimate? Menninger (1971) sees our task as broader than just understanding sexuality. He sees it as meeting the needs of struggling, concerned youth in search of gratifying solutions to the problem of being human.

No doubt the answer to helping young people to better understand their sexuality is a difficult task for a generation of adults who are struggling to understand their own. The process is not easy but the desired product--stronger families--merits the effort.

We need to recognize the problems and to be willing to establish as viable goals (1) the acceptance of the interrelationship between identity, interaction, and intimacy, (2) the understanding of sexuality, and (3) the need for special parenting skills. With this as a basis, hopefully we can produce the glue to cement stronger families.

REFERENCES

Erikson, E. *Childhood and society* (2nd Ed.). New York: W. W. Norton and Company, Inc., 1963.

Erikson, E. *Insight and responsibility*. New York: W. W. Norton and Company, Inc., 1965.

Elkind, D. Culture, change, and their effects on children. *Social Casework*, 1973, *54*, 360-366.

Harlow, H. F., Schlitz, K. A., & Harlow, M. K. The effects of social isolation on the learning performance of rhesus monkeys. In C. R. Carpenter (Ed.), *Proceedings of the Second International Congress of Primatology* (Vol. 1). New York: Karger, 1969.

Jourard, S. *The transparent self*. New York: D. Van Nostrand, 1964.

Kardiner, A. *Sex and morality*. New York: Bobbs-Merrill, 1954.

Klaus, M. *Infant-parent reciprocal interaction*. Paper presented at the Conference on Identity, Intimacy, and Interaction, Department of Home Economics and Family Ecology, University of Akron, and the Ohio Council on Family Relations, October, 1975.

Kohlberg, L. A cognitive developmental analysis of children's sex role concepts and attitudes. In E. Maccoby (Ed.), *The development of sex differences.* Palo Alto: Stanford University Press, 1966.

Kohlberg, L. Moral stages and sex education. In M. S. Calderone (Ed.), *Sexuality and human values.* New York: Association Press, 1974.

Libby, R., & Carlson, J. A theoretical framework for premarital decisions in the dyad. *Archives of Sexual Behavior,* 1973, *2,* 165-173.

Lieberman, J. E., & Peck, E. *Sex and birth control: A guide for the young.* Scranton: Thomas Y. Crowell, 1973.

Luckey, E. B. Parenting: Challenge and commitment. *The Family Coordinator,* 1973, *22,* 163-166.

Menninger, R. W. Decisions in sexuality: An act of impulse, conscience, or society. In D. L. Brummon & A. L. Barclay (Eds.), *Sexuality: A search for perspective.* New York: D. Van Nostrand, 1971.

Offer, D., Marcus, D., & Offer, J. L. A longitudinal study of normal adolescent boys. *American Journal of Psychiatry,* 1970, *126,* 917-924.

Rhymes, D. *No new morality.* London: Constable, 1964.

Selye, H. *Stress without distress.* Philadelphia: Lippincott, 1975.

Suomi, S. J., & Harlow, H. F. Social rehabilitation of isolate reared monkeys. *Developmental Psychology,* 1972, *6,* 487-496.

Primary Prevention: A Family
Therapist's Perspective

Dr. Augustus Napier
Institute for Marital and
Family Counseling
Atlanta, Georgia

FAMILY THERAPY

Family therapy is an exciting field. It is a uniquely
American invention in that it works. With a family that is
family motivated and not too terribly stressed, and with a
therapist with some experience, family therapy is a dramatic
improvement over other types of therapies we have had in
the past. It is really exciting to see us tackle problems
like alcoholism, drug abuse, child abuse, juvenile delinquency, and serious marital problems with the family as the
contact. I think one of the reasons that family therapy is
working is that we have taken a different attack--a radically
different attack from what the Freudian tradition was. Freud
was aware that families were disturbed--the families of his
patients. He was aware of the contacts of disturbance in
the system. What he chose to do was to try to emancipate
the patient from the family--to work with patients who had a
good chance of doing that. In fact, he liked to work with
patients who had a private income, and who did not depend
on their families.

I think that has been the history of individual therapies,
and that fits with another American ideal--strengthening the
independence and the autonomy of the individual, helping them
leave their families, separate from them, and to "become individuals." It is a valid thing to do. But when it is done,
it has put the patient/client in contact with the system because of the enormous loyalty that the individual has to the
system and its problems, because of the person's awareness
of his or her part in that system, and because of an unwill-
ingness to upset the system in order to pursue his or her own
growth. So individual therapy I think, in the main, has
failed because it did not take into account the needs of the
family from which the individual patient came. Those needs,

49

as we now know, are real. Disturbed individuals come out
of disturbed families. Those families need help along with
the person who represents that family when contacting an
agency or practitioner.

Family therapy has been for a number of years a sort of
treatment to use when everything else fails. Fortunately, it
is becoming something else. It is becoming a regular part
of the mental health system. It is a radically different
approach in that it redefines the patient or client as a
social, biological group. But many of us who work regularly
with families in clinical centers are aware that we are there
under pretty tragic circumstances. The point where we see
the family is pretty late in the family's history, in the
family's choice of alternatives, and in their evolution over
time in a certain direction. A lot of times as I sit down
with the family, I find myself feeling angry, and saying,
"Why weren't you here ten years ago? Why did this particular,
negative event in the family happen? Why wasn't there somebody there at a point where this family's history diverged
very powerfully in the direction that has now brought them
to a pretty severe crisis with a lot of damage?"

A FAMILY VISITED

I want to take some common problems that I see in the clinic
and describe them to you, tell you a little bit about what we
are doing to alleviate some of those problems, and then fanta-
size about what might have been different in those families'
histories if somebody had been in contact with the family at
certain periods of time and had done something different.

I want to start off with a family which haunts me; whose
history and story haunt me. I find this true of a lot of
families I am working with; I carry around their dilemmas
with me, work on them when I am on the plane, or think about
what I should have said last session that I did not. The
picture I have now is of a very small family. I will call
the wife Sandra and her son Danny. Sandra is in her late
twenties. She is a sort of stocky woman, attractive, soft,
sort of sad; she is there with her son who is the age of my
son. Her son's name is my son's name so I can identify with
him sometimes. Sandra is crying in the session, and she
spends most of the session crying. This is a new development
for her. When she came into therapy, she was concerned about
her son; she had been abusing him periodically, getting furious, and beating him. We had been working together for about
three or four months. Sandra has stopped abusing her son.
That particular problem has ceased. As she cries, she wonders

if she is losing her mind. She thinks she may be going crazy.
She feels peculiar to be crying about something which happened ten years ago, to be grieving about a person who has been
out of her life supposedly for that time. Her present period
of grief, which has been intense, was set off by the shooting
death of a casual friend in a robbery at a convenience store,
and that in combination with the kind of therapeutic work we
have been doing precipitated her into an acute sort of grief.
What she is talking about as she is crying is her former husband and Danny's father, and she speaks of him warmly and
tenderly. She visited the places where they had courted as
adolescents, and that added fuel to her grief. What she is
really asking is why did he kill himself, what did she have
to do with it, and how could it have happened otherwise?
Among her other thoughts are that an important part of her
life is missing, and how she did indeed love him. She is simply going through the process of grieving that everybody needs
to do sometimes, but which she had put off for a long time.

At the time her husband, Dan, killed himself, she had
filed for divorce, and for understandable reasons. He had
been involved with drugs, was having an affair, was spending
much of his time hallucinating, and was gone massive amounts
of time. She felt both assaulted and abandoned by what he
was doing. In the context of what had happened in her fam-
ily--she had been abused by her father and not supported by
her mother--it is pretty understandable that her husband's
action had a significant kind of symbolic meaning for her,
and that she was, in fact, running from her own history. As
she and I talk about what happened to Dan, she mentions that
he was adopted at age five. She suspects that her husband's
adopted father was also his biological father. He spent the
first five years of his life with his biological mother, who
had four other children. His mother experienced much rejection by her family, as well as by others, for having an il-
legitimate child, and finally, I think, gave up and placed
this boy up for adoption. He was eventually, after a period
of about six months, adopted by what we suspect was his biological father. Of course the fact of this psychological
issue did not make things easier for his adopted mother, and
set him up for a second rejection.

What was going on with him during the time just before
he committed suicide was a lot of usage of LSD, in which he
would go to a cemetery and sit at the foot of a statute of
Jesus and talk to the statute. He was obviously psychotic,
and he was obviously pushing my patient to reject him. He
had a powerful sense that he was going to be rejected, and he
provided lots of excuses for it. And it came. It was sort
of a final confirmation for him that life was indeed rejecting, and so he shot himself.

This couple, and certainly he is there as we struggle with the grief, represents the most serious problems which we see in the clinical setting, and they are the kind of problems which can be most harmful to kids. These problems represent an overwhelming intrusion into a child's life--in this case Sandy's sense of being overwhelmed by her father's anger, unsupported by her mother. The other side, her husband's experience in life, was one of a series of rejections. Rejection is the most untouched, undeveloped area of injury to children. I think that we as a culture are dumb about the security needs of kids; we essentially do not see them. As I think back to Dan's death, which we are now struggling with, I wonder if there were not somebody during the process of his being adopted who did not know that the adoptive father was his biological father, and did not know or could not have known what a massive rejection a five-year-old would experience at being put up for adoption.

REJECTION

Most of the severe dilemmas which we see in a clinical setting have to do with experiences of loss or rejection in the family. These come from a variety of incidences. We frequently see families where the parents are always gone, and there simply was not enough time or energy. The kids grew up feeling like nobody really cuddled them. We see individuals whose families sort of unintentionally set up a rejection experience. For example, one that I remember clearly was when my wife was leading a play group for a number of kids-- these were three-year-olds--and they were sitting on the floor playing. One of the kids was sort of listless, looked confused, and really did not join in with the other kids. I said to my wife, "What's wrong?" She replied, "Don't you remember? That's the child whose parent a year and a half ago went for three weeks on a skiing trip in Europe and left her with a babysitter." That is a fairly minor thing I suppose. It happens often in families, but it is the kind of dynamic I think we are not sensitive to--that kids are extraordinarily vulnerable to rejection.

I am going to talk more about some of the various forms this takes in other situations. A common situation in families is one where a child grows up in a family which looks relatively intact and relatively nurturant, but where one particular child, because of the dynamics of the family, experiences repeated chronic distancing by the parents. I saw one family that looked great. Their only problem was that their middle child was suicidal. The family looked like the all-American ideal. The problem was that there was a kind of chilliness in this marriage. There was a kind of cool, rejecting quality, and both parents had two kids on their team. The middle child of five was on nobody's team and nobody really noticed that this kid had fallen in the cracks of the teaming of the parents. Essentially, this child inherited the negative "vibes," as it were, from both parents--vibes that had to do with feelings towards each other. It produced an acute crisis for a period of years. But the violence was very quiet, very subtle, and it had to do with repeated patterns of interaction--over and over in that family. These patterns are difficult for us to be aware of and difficult for families to see.

The questions of how we can help families who are dealing with the more profound issues of rejection and intrusion in their families are very difficult questions, and I think they have to do with how we can be involved with the primary care-givers for that family's system during the early parts of its life cycle. For example, the abusive family is one which is isolated, that does what it does within its own walls, with a lot of insulation in those walls from the surrounding so-ciety. A few key individuals may have a chance to know what is happening within that family. They tend to be the doctor, perhaps the minister, and perhaps the teacher. To reach these early childhood assaults, it is going to take a very alert, informed kind of awareness of what happens in families, if we are going to help these kids before they become symptomatic.

THE ADOLESCENT IN CRISIS

Another common crisis that we see in the clinical setting is the adolescent in crisis. Let me talk about Tom. Tom is 16, which seems to be a magic age for adolescent crises. He has been involved in minor drug use; he has experimented with some harder drugs, but he is not a drug addict. He has terrible grades, he stays out late in defiance of both his parents, and he seems to be able to talk to nobody. He does not have a close group of friends, and he really is alienated from most of the family.

When the family comes for therapy, Tom will not talk to me. His family has trouble getting him there, and he looks like the one troubled person in a concerned family. He looks rebellious, angry, unpleasant--a difficult character. As I begin to work with the family, I start with the father, be-cause he is usually on the outside of this thing and may give me a view of the family that other people cannot. As I start to learn about the family, I find that they have a cycle

which they go through, and it takes me a good while to discover what this cycle is. The cycle starts when Tom does
something which irritates mother. One of the things which
he does that disturbs mother is that he promises to do some-
thing--take out the garbage, do his homework, or whatever--
and he then disappoints her. What I later discover this
means is that father does the same thing in a more subtle way
to mother. He has been promising her for years that he would
make some changes in his work schedule. He has been promising
her for years that he would take more interest in the kids.
He has let her down a lot of times. She is furious about it.
She is afraid to bring it up with him. When Tom does the
same thing, he catches it from mother.

Another thing I learned later is that mother felt a similar kind of letdown from her father, and when Tom does something that disappoints her, it not only sets off her anger
at her husband, but her anger at her father; what Tom catches
is a "double dose" of mother's anger. Tom reacts belliger-
ently. He senses the extra voltage in this. He senses that
it is not fair, that what he has done is out of proportion
to the reaction he is getting from mother. He says a lot of
abusive stuff to her; he really assaults her verbally, and
she begins to cry and essentially says, "I give up, I can't
deal with this. This is too much for me." At that point,
she calls in Tom's father. Tom's father has overheard this
fight, and he has gotten more and more furious as he has heard
the way the boy is talking to the mother. Of course he is mad
at himself for the fact that he lets her down too, but he
does not know that; he does not admit it. He comes in and he
really lets Tom have it. He really bludgeons him into sub-
mission. He tells him in no uncertain terms that he is not
to talk to his mother this way.

Tom feels scared by his father's anger and is overwhelmed
by it. Mother sees what Tom's father is doing. She gets upset that he is being so brutal. She says to him, "You're
being too heavy-handed with Tom. Back off, you're being too
harsh." Her husband turns to her and says, "Well, what the
hell do you expect me to do? You called me in here to help
you, and now you tell me I'm being too strict. What right
have you to tell me how to behave with my son anyway?" They
get into a small fight which lasts about two minutes at the
most. During this fight, mother does what she rarely does,
which is to stand up to father. She does it in the name of
her son, who has riled her. Meanwhile, Tom's sister, who
is 13, and who really has a close relationship with mother
(Tom is very jealous of this close relationship) is on the
sidelines. She is completely left out, feels scared about
all the anger, disconnected from mother, and afraid about
the parents' fighting.

Tom gets upset about what is going on with his parents. He feels like he is to blame. He then decides to run out of the house. He leaves the house, and his parents do not know where he is going. They are upset about what has been going on with him. They are suddenly distracted from their fight, and focus on Tom as he leaves to go they know not where. When Tom comes back, you can bet he is going to have something to tell them. It is going to be upsetting to them-- something that he did or almost did. They are going to have to struggle to get it out of him.

What nobody notices is that everybody in the family is part of this crisis. Underlying Tom's intrusion into the outside world is (1) a lot of tension between the parents, (2) the fact that mother cannot stand up to father, (3) the fact that father is disconnected from the family and is not involved enough with the kids, (4) that Tom is jealous of the younger sister and wants to provide some way of wedging himself in between mother and sister, and (5) that Tom is aware of father's distancing and wants to provide father with an excuse to get involved.

Tom is also aware of the fact that his parents have pretty serious marital problems. Thus, when he gets his parents to fight, which is part of the secret agenda in this whole thing, he then cooperates further by leaving the family as a way of helping the family regulate the intensity of the fight. That is, he gets his parents to talk to each other, and then he leaves to regulate the intensity of that fight. This is the kind of complicated, intricate cycle of events which families get into with disturbed adolescents. Tom is not simply a victim of his parents' forces; he gets a lot of power by the fact that they are divided. But underneath his symptoms there is a lot of concern about the family as a unit and a lot of unconscious awareness of the family's dilemmas, and that the family as a unit has worked out this complicated cycle as a way of dealing with some of its problems.

The price which Tom is paying for helping his family is essentially failure in school, a sense of not being able to trust parents and adults, and a sense that life is pretty hopeless; he inherits and takes on the burden of the family's low morale. I am pretty optimistic about Tom's chances. I think we know enough to help a kid in his situation out of that particular dilemma. The cycle which Tom is going through can get worse. The family can organize all of its negative feelings about itself and its members around Tom, and the whole family can agree that the way for the family to survive is for Tom to be extruded from that family. We do see kids in whom this cycle has gone so far that the family's solution to this problem is essentially to extrude one of its members.

Most of the time, if we get there in time, if we manage some of the intricacies which are required in treating these families, Tom's dilemma and the family's dilemma are imminently treatable. It involves treating more than the marriage. It involves treating the system because Tom is a powerful part of that system, just as his 13-year-old sister is. We need change of that whole circle, and most of the time we also need change in the family of origin. We find that as we work with these families, many times we need access to mother's family and father's family. That is certainly true in the case of Sandra and her son. We will bring in Sandra's parents to work on the abuse which occurred in her childhood. We will bring in her in-laws to work on the death of her husband, their son. In Tom's case, because some of mother's problems of feeling let down by men involve so significantly her own father, we will bring in that family too. What I am acutely aware of is that Tom's family should have been treated ten years before this.

Most of the problems in adolescence are identifiable in elementary school by an alert referral source. There are millions of families out there with latent crises--marital struggles which are disguised in the interactions with the kids, where essentially the marriage remains stable because of the sacrifices of the kids in keeping that marriage stable. An adolescent like Tom has learned that his mother is one down in relationships with father, and in his own way Tom is trying to help his mother get one up in that system.

Kids are acutely sensitive to the dilemmas of their parents, but the stress of trying to help with those dilemmas is too much for most kids. They usually show signs of that stress very early if we are alert to pick them up. Kids' behaviors are something that teachers are most aware of, and I think that the best chance for finding these families early comes from teachers who live with kids' stresses day-by-day, and who become sort of substitute parents. The kids act out the same problems with the teachers that they do with parents. So, in a sense what we need to do is to find families where kids know about the hidden marital crisis, and essentially precipitate that crisis into a marital crisis. We need to find these families before the child, as therapist, has gone too far in his or her career. That is a difficult thing to do. I am going to talk a bit later about some of the problems in intruding upon the life space of families in order to reach their situations.

MARITAL CRISES

Another extraordinarily common situation today in family therapist work is the marital crisis itself. Lots of families are coming for help pretty late in the history of the marital issues. Always the marriage is in some ways polarized, and the polarization takes several basic forms. One way in which the couple is polarized is around the question of whether this is a meaningful relationship, a meaningful union.

I am seeing a family (husband, wife, and three children) now where last session the father finally decided he was going to get a divorce. He has been hedging about it for a number of times and he finally said it definitely, "This is it, I'm going to file for divorce." What happens to the family is like a death. The family is grieving. Everybody in the family is crying. The family is mourning essentially the death of the marriage. It happens right in sight. It is like a relationship dies within an hour or two in front of your eyes. As the husband talks about what is behind the death of his commitment to the marriage, which his wife does not feel, I ask him how they got married and what got them together in the first place. He said, "Well, I was young, I was insecure, and I needed support. She was a good German woman, and I'm from a German family." He chose to marry her out of a kind of security need. She would take good care of him. She had an entirely different feeling. She said, "He's a very handsome guy," and added she just melted whenever he came near. She obviously had a whole different experience than he had. Nobody helped that guy, that couple, look at whether their relationship had a real sense of emotional commitment. I suspect there are a lot of relationships which get started because in our culture we tend to choose a mate at the same time we are leaving home; that is, as these two psychological climates come together, we are facing the world outside the family at the same time we are expected by society to find a life partner. A lot of marriages occur because of the security needs of the people involved. We are essentially finding a family substitute so that the world does not feel so lonely.

We really do not help couples take a look at what they are going into, and I am not sure as I think about it how we can do it. Increasingly, ministers are making a real effort to talk to couples before marriage. Most of the time, they see couples during the kind of crazy period where essentially the unreason of the situation is enforced. There is a great amount of sexuality in the relationship. There is a lot of insecurity and panic, and the invitations are often sent out.

It is really not a very good time to take a look at whether or not this is a good thing to do now. As I think about what could be involved in helping couples take a look at their commitment to getting married, I feel sort of "ify" about it because it is a sacred decision. I would not want to treat it lightly. I would not pretend to give couples advice about what to do with something that vital. But I think we could do a much better job of helping couples step back and at least say, "Is this the right time?" if not to question whether or not this is the right person.

FAMILY SCRIPTS

I think there is another way that we could help couples as they get married, and I think that involves helping them take a look at the family scripts they each come in with. Let me give you an example. I saw a couple recently, and the man is a successful person, a professional who said he has been spending years keeping his pencils lined up. He is a methodical, compulsive person who has worked hard at being organized and doing the right thing. He is currently afraid he is going crazy because he is not keeping his pencils lined up anymore. When I say going crazy, I mean he has extraordinarily intense fits of anger which result in his beating holes into wallboards at home, and really frightening both his regular therapist and his wife. What sets him off is his wife's cool, analytical distance, and it is exactly what he grew up with. His parents took good care of him. They did everything right, just the way he has tried to do everything right, but they did it coolly. They did it all at a distance. He grew up with a kind of shell of adequacy. He did things right too, but underneath there was a kind of panicky desperation, "If I don't do things right, I'm going to be what? Starved to death, killed, rejected?" He experienced a kind of terror about the coolness that existed in that family. What has happened is that finally he has bumped into that same coolness with his wife. He is now a very scared, very frightened one and a half-year-old kid who really needs a nurturing parent, and his wife cannot do it.

The wife's life space is organized in a very different way. She grew up in a close family where her parents were always there. They were supervising a lot of her thoughts and actions, and while they were supportive and she felt generally good about them, the problem for her was that she was never allowed to be separate. She never really got permission to move out and leave them and be herself. She wants the experience of being separate, single, alone, and in charge of herself. What that does to her husband, of course, is to replicate for him the sense of rejection. This makes him make lots of demands, which makes her pull back, which makes him make more demands, which makes her pull back, and they go round and round.

A lot of marriage crises are organized around these contrasting scripts and differently organized behavior patterns. For example, the person who wants intimacy, support, closeness, togetherness, and fears rejection is organized in a way to pursue other people, to look for help and support. They often marry somebody who is organized to seek space, to seek independence, territory, freedom, and economy. What this does is that each person is protected from finding the thing that they think they want. They set up a situation where their marriage replicates the dilemma in their family of origin, but also where they are protected from knowing about the other fear which they have. The person who is so eager for closeness underneath is also afraid of it. The person who is so eager for freedom underneath is also afraid of it. So they marry somebody who provides them with a replica of the service aspects of the family of origin, and they then do the dance to free themselves from that pattern; however, underneath there is another agenda where both of them really have fears about both intimacy and rejection. They share these dilemmas, but they act out the dilemmas by taking separate parts in the dance.

It is really not a difficult thing to sit down with a couple before they are married and to look at the family scripts; to look at the rules in the families of origin. For example, if one family had rules against anger because it was prohibited, and the other family had traumatic episodes with anger, you can know this couple is going to have trouble with anger. They are going to have trouble processing conflict. If the wife has this kind of experience of never having been free, and the husband has a kind of deep hunger for intimacy, and they take a look at those needs as they come into marriage, they can get some idea what they are going to face when those two family systems, those two scripts, those two agendas collide in the marriage; and collide they will.

We could also help the couple learn what they cannot do for each other. Many couples get into trouble as they move into marriage by promising to be the therapist, to be the parent, to be the substitute, the fill-in for what they did not get as kids. "I'll try to be your therapist if you'll try to be mine." If couples can be warned not to do that, not to expect that kind of help from a marriage, then what they are spared from developing is maybe the kind of intense, symbolic relationship which develops as a marriage crisis unfolds; that is, the marriage becomes the kind of staging ground for the issues coming out of early childhood. These become symbolically reenacted in the marriage. One of the reasons that the symbolism becomes so powerful is that each has tried to be the parent to the other one, and has inherited with that all the associations of the parent. If we can help couples early learn not to be therapists to each other, we might save them some of the pain of disentangling from this complicated symbolism.

DIVORCE

One has the feeling with a couple who is divorcing that a process is going on which is so primitive, so powerful, so charged with emotional electricity that the best one can do is try to guide the electricity so it does not become destructive. Intervention earlier in the marriage life cycle would, I think, short-circuit some of the development of that intensity.

The divorce crisis is often the process of psychological birth. It is the first time both people really experience being individuals, and the experience is against a background of defining self against other; that is, "I am me because I am not you." If couples could go into marriage with an expectation that there is not any escape from aloneness, then I think they would have a much better chance of not having to be reborn out of the kind of symbiotic development which many couples have.

We have a number of crises today which have to do with post-divorce. I think probably a lot of the increase in teenage pregnancy, the increase in suicide rates in adolescence, and a lot of the problems we are seeing in kids have to do with the emotional fallout that comes post-divorce.

I saw a family last week in which the girl is 17, and her parents had been divorced for three or four years. Her father had remarried, and for the past couple of years the daughter has been in a pitched battle with the father, and the battle has gotten more intense as he did remarry. As the family comes into therapy the father and new wife, who have marital problems themselves, have united around throwing this girl out. She is really out on the street. She has been taken in by a youth service agency. What has happened is that she has essentially represented her mother in a fight with her father. Her mother is now in another state. She has taken mother's revenge against father, and in the process sacrificed herself massively. She is working to keep her parents married; she is working to keep father in touch with mother, and mother in touch with father. In some ways, she is working to keep father from remarrying and starting a new life.

Many of these kids would not have to go to extremes if work with the family of the divorcing couple--the entire family--were routine. That is, every divorce should ideally go through a process of therapy whereby the kids are disentangled from the battle of the parents and warned to stay out of it, and where the parents are given permission to work on getting divorced over a period of time. I am not sure a divorce ever really occurs if there have been kids. I think that we kind of legalize bigamy. Couples might as well face this--the new wife is going to live with the old wife because of the kids. A very complicated process of working through divorce is helping these systems accommodate each other. The members of the systems accommodate each other, helping the child accommodate feelings of disloyalty if they make attachments to the new parent, helping the parents deal with leftover anger at each other, and helping this entire network in a sense become a kind of extended family because of the needs of the kids.

PREVENTION AND INTERVENTION

As I think about prevention in the family, I have a sense of the immense number of families in crises right now, and of the needs just to treat those families. I guess that is where I have put my energies. I have a sense that if we as a society could make some changes, we could do some things very differently with the family which might make this kind of treatment unnecessary, or at least a very different experience. What I think we need as a culture is a lowered pain threshold for certain kinds of experiences. I think we have a kind of straight back, stiff upper-lip quality about certain kinds of life experiences.

For example, I think most families do not have a way of validating the need for help when certain kinds of things happen, such as the birth of a child, the death of a parent. I just overheard someone talking recently about a woman who is losing in the same year her sister, who is in a foreign country, and her mother, both from cancer. That family needs some kind of help and intervention. It should be routine, but it is not. I think we have a sense of putting off getting help with certain problems because we do not understand the validity of the need for help in certain areas. I think we need to de-clinicalize, as it were, what the psychologists might call health-seeking behavior. We have in this country a lot of effort to seek help, but most of it is disguised.

SOME PSYCHOLOGICAL ISSUES

Most help-seeking for psychological issues is disguised under
looking for a pain medication for imaginary pains from a
physician--that kind of disguised attempt to get help. I
think the only way the kind of input most families need as
they move through their crises can be available is for it
not to be seem as treatment, but as part of the normal flow
of the human fabric of society. I think we need a lot more
awareness of psychological issues.

As I sit with families, I feel myself as really kind of
stupid about the complexity which I am facing. I feel like
it is bewilderingly complex. I think that it is a real complexity; that is, I think what happens in families is, in
fact, terribly complicated. As a society, we have not addressed some of the most fundamental areas. For example,
we have not really looked hard at the basic dependency needs
of kids; we have not been realistic about those. It is nice
to be able to say that a three-months maternity leave is
all right, but that is not really all right for kids and
mothers. It is really pretty stupid to think of that as
enough, to not make it easier for mothers to continue to care
for their kids at work or wherever. I think we do not know
nearly enough about what happens when there is an interrup-
tion in the normal security needs of kids--when mother is
hospitalized, when father is away for two years because of a
job transfer to a foreign country, or when there is a death
of not the parent but the grandparent. For example, there
is a study which shows that schizophrenia in a child is fairly
strongly correlated with the death of that child's grandparent within two years of the birth of the child. The grandparent now, not the parent. What I suspect is happening is
that the parent is strained from both sides--the pressure to
fulfill the child's needs, and the loss of support from the
grandparent.

I do not think we really understand what happens to kids
when they are adopted and they are put in foster placement.
I think there is a lot of obscuring of the real psychological
violence which occurs in kids when these profound intimacy
attachments are interrupted early. That is the area I think
we need to look at harder.

I think there is a host of other areas where we need more
awareness. For example, we need to know more about symbolic
behavior in kids. I did a consultation recently with a family where a 16 year-old is acting up sexually and it is pretty
self-destructive stuff. She is adopted; she lost her father
two years ago, and her real nurturant parent was her father.
They were really close. But her relationship with her father

was sexualized because of his needs. For her, the needs were nurturant. His meeting some of those needs provided a sort of sexualized tinge. When her father died, what happened is that she went looking for a substitute through sexual acting-out with men. She was really looking for nurturance, and she was also reenacting her fantasies of what happened with her biological mother, because she had discovered she was an il-legitimate child, and she was redoing some of that kind of fantasy of what her real mother was like and what happened to her. It was very clear she was planning to get pregnant. When the question was raised about how she was handling her birth control, she indicated she was not using any. The workers said something about, "Have you thought how hard it is to get an abortion and how expensive it is?" She said, "Oh, I'd never do that." So clearly, she was planning to get pregnant, planning to have the child, and keep it this time. She would do the same thing her mother did, but with a different twist. It is tuning in to that kind of symbolic level, where kids act out their feelings, that we need in order to be able to reach the real dilemma behind the be-havior.

SYSTEMS OF HUMAN INTERACTION

We also need much more awareness of systems and how they op-erate. We tend to think in a very linear way; that is, I often find myself when I am sitting with a family thinking, "Father is doing this to son and that's the problem." I think top to bottom--force acting upon an object. I do not think in terms of the very complex circular patterns of in-teraction where all of the forces in a family are interacting at the same time to produce a sequence of events which is repetitive, and where the totality of forces in that system is determining the outcome. It is very difficult to think in something other than a straight line, such as a person acting upon another person, or a persecutor acting upon a victim. I think we have a lot of work to do in addressing ourselves to the network in which human distress exists. Sometimes, one of the problems in thinking about the full system is the kind of complexity it leads us into if we are going to treat that system.

A family which I consulted with recently consisted of mother, three kids, mother's boyfriend, mother's mother, mother's ex-husband, and his parents. All were living in a four-block radius, and former husband and wife were living next door to each other. That is the kind of complexity we address if we are really going to extend ourselves to clusters

of people interacting powerfully with each other, and shaping
each other's destinies. We need permission to invade privacy. We have a myth in this country that you leave people
alone, and that you mind your own business. The metaphor
for this, which our culture brings up occasionally, is that
the person gets shot in the streets and nobody comes. That
is more than a metaphor, because there are people around us
whose business we are trying not to mind is a pretty tragic
business. Somehow we as a culture need permission to invade
each other's privacy, and to ask about what's going on over
there, and to somehow be available. That is a really difficult issue. What therapy is basically, I think, is permission to speak your mind, say what is, and talk about what
is real. Therapy would go out of business, I believe, if we
as a culture could do that. The closest I come to it, probably, is saying to somebody, "You look like you are having a
rough time. I think you ought to see a therapist." That is
probably as close as I come to it. Because of my work, I
tend to back away from doing anything more. That kind of
"breaking the rules," about what can be talked about and what
cannot, is one of the basic things our society has to address.

STRATEGIC INTERVENTION POINTS

We need to find points in the normal life cycle where there
is a chance of making a difference. Those points tend to be
when there is normal high stress in any family system. Programs offering assistance to young parents, I think, are extremely vital. A problem I see in the ones we have now is
they often do not include father. Father is tremendously
important in families, often primarily because of his absence.
I think his absence starts at birth for the kids. It is a
point where he most vitally needs to be in.

There is a crisis in every family around the issue of
whether the child is going to "take" in school; in other
words, cope with school. The school is a miniature for our
society as a whole, and we ought to look hard at every kid
who does not adapt to it. It is a model for everything which
follows. Any child who is having trouble adapting to that
system needs help, and we ought to make changes in the system
too. We should help each family with the crisis they have as
they ask themselves, "Is our child going to be able to make
it in this system?"

We have adolescence as a normal crisis because adolescents
are normally psychotic I think. Our country is struggling
with some basic questions around adolescence. They center
around simplistic questions like, "At what age should an

adolescent be when when he/she drinks?" But underneath this
what we are asking as a society is, "What does it take to be
an adult?" "What does it take to be judged independent, competent, and free to go out in that world?" We need to look
at the various stages when adolescents acquire that kind of
maturity, and to help families create some kind of ritual
of coming of age, which would include meeting certain criteria for being "independent." We need to help families adjust to the fact of their kids' independence and leaving,
because by the time an adolescent has been in a system for
eighteen to twenty years, they are very much a part of that
system. The system grieves their loss and needs to adjust
to it, and I suspect that when we really look at what it takes
to leave home, we would be very surprised to find it takes
some people fifty years to do it. It is a very difficult
job, if it ever happens, and hopefully it never completely
happens. We can come back and be closer than we ever were
sometimes.

The ritual of marriage is an important point, and at
times of extraordinary stress in the family, such as divorce,
separation, deaths, serious illness, or job loss, we need to
be there to help families. We need to create a social context where the family is a more humane place to live. To do
that, I think we need change in almost every institution in our
society. I am not optimistic that it will happen. We live
in a culture which is exciting, stimulating and creative, but
it is also anxious, disorganized, and full of a lot of hostility, and we tend to put off until tomorrow changing and growing, if we can. I suppose I am part of the whole thing of
being in the emergency room trying to stop the flow of blood,
when maybe I ought to be out trying to teach people not to
play with knives and guns.

I am delighted that so many people involved in the National
Symposium on Building Family Strengths are interested in the
positive and preventive approach--that gives me hope.

Strengthening the Family by
Strengthening Social Policy in
Behalf of Children and Families

Dr. Edward Zigler
Sterling Professor of Psychology
and
Dr. Kirby A. Heller
Bush Center in Child Development
and Social Policy
Yale University

INTRODUCTION

The myth that we are a child-oriented society continues to
exist in this country. Yet the condition of our nation's
children is poor and getting worse. This statement is sub-
stantiated by a host of disturbing social indicators documented in several sources, such as the Carnegie Council report, *All Our Children* (Keniston, 1977), and the report of
the Advisory Committee on Child Development of the National
Academy of Sciences (1976). Problems faced by parents and
children in four areas--health, child abuse, child care,
and out-of-home child placements--will be described to highlight the invalidity of the myth.

SOCIAL INDICATORS

Infant Mortality

Although the United States is considered the world's most
technologically advanced nation, fifteen countries have lower
rates of infant mortality (Advisory Committee on Child Development, 1976). Even more shocking is the disparity in
infant mortality rates between whites and minority groups, as
well as between regions of the country. This country's ranking among nations drops to 31 when only non-whites, whose rate
of infant mortality is twice as high as that of whites, are
included. Similarly, there were 14.9 deaths per 1,000 births
in the Pacific states in 1973, as compared to 21.6 deaths
per 1,000 births in the southeastern section of the United
States. This high mortality rate is due to a host of factors
unrelated to our medical knowledge: poverty, poor sanita-
tion, malnutrition of the mother, and lack of proper medical
care. Statistics on teenage pregnancies are enlightening.

Complications during pregnancy and delivery, as well as the
risk of having infants in poor health, are greatest for women below the age of twenty. Experts had believed that this
was partially due to the physical immaturity of the young
mothers. However, a recent study in Copenhagen found that
teenage mothers given proper care had the least complications
in childbirth (*New York Times*, 1979). This study illustrates
that the high risk status of pregnant teenagers is due to
societal rather than biological conditions.

Health

Statistics on the health care of children are also grim. Priorities in federal spending are clearly not directed to children. In 1970, only one out of seventeen federal dollars for
health care was spent on children (Keniston, 1977). One-third
of the nation's 60 million children received inadequate health
care, with little access to primary care, immunizations, and
early treatment of disease (Advisory Committee on Child Development, 1976). Despite the ability to eliminate infect-
ious diseases through immunizations, epidemics continue to
occur. For example, epidemics of measles in 1969, 1971, and
1974 were the result of nearly half of the children between
the ages of one and four failing to get the proper inocula-
tions (Knowles, 1977). Once again, poor children are the
least likely to receive the necessary preventive care and
have little access to health services until they enter school,
at the age of six.

Childhood accidents continue to be the greatest single
cause of death for children between the ages of one and fourteen (Furrow, Gruendel, & Zigler, 1979). Among western countries, the United States has the second highest rate of childhood deaths due to accidents, and is ranked first in deaths
caused by firearms and poisonings. Motor vehicle accidents
are the leading type of accidental death for children of all
ages, yet there are few preventive efforts to protect children. Both children and parents need to be educated about
traffic risks, and the use of infants' and children's auto-
mobile seats and restraints should be encouraged.

Foster Care

More than 500,000 children are not living with their families,
but instead are in some type of out-of-home care (Edelman,
1979). The foster care system, presumably representing only
temporary care until decisions about permanent placement can
be made, subsidizes children indefinitely. Statistics on
the number of children in foster care are difficult to collect. This is itself an indication of the poor state of

monitoring of children in the system. It has been estimated
that more than 250,000 children are in foster homes. In contrast, only 169,000 children were adopted in 1971 (Advisory
Committee on Child Development, 1976). Children are moved
from home to home, and attempts are often not made to re-
unite the children with their families. In a survey conducted by the Children's Defense Fund (1978), 52 percent of
the children had been out of their homes for more than two
years, and 18 percent of the children removed from their
homes had been moved more than three times. The report by
the Children's Defense Fund documents serious neglect by the
state and federal governments of children for whom they are
responsible, as well as unnecessary separations of children
from their parents, with little opportunity for reconstitu-
tion of the family. Despite the evidence that patterns of
parental visiting best predict whether children will return
home (Fanshel & Shinn, 1978), agencies have no specific policies concerning parental visits. For example, efforts are
not made to place children with willing relatives, parents
are sometimes not told where their child has been placed,
children are placed far from their communities, or even out
of state, and parents are either not allowed to visit the
children in their foster homes, or are not given transportation subsidies. Children in the public welfare system are in
a state of limbo; there is reluctance to either return the
children back to their families, or to terminate parental
rights so that the children may be adopted. Not surprisingly,
minority and handicapped children are overrepresented in the
population of children without permanent homes.

Institutional Care

Between 250,000 and 300,000 children are placed in public and
private residential centers and institutions (Advisory Committee on Child Development, 1976). While many children need
specialized services, public officials acknowledge that children are often inappropriately placed in institutions (Children's Defense Fund, 1978). The type of institution, rather
than the characteristics of the child, can determine the label
the child receives (e.g., mentally retarded, emotionally disturbed). Occasionally, an expose of an especially horrifying
institution will catch the public's attention for a short
time, but few long-term changes are made. For example, in
1965, Blatt and Kaplan visited five state institutions for
the mentally retarded, and described these field trips in
their photo-essay, *Christmas in Purgatory* (1966). Ten years
later, Blatt returned to find no substantial changes; still
evident was the poor care, the lack of activities, education,
and recreation. Even a new small state institution costing

$65,000 a year per resident contained no exceptional facilities or services (Blatt, in press).

Child Abuse

Equally shocking are the statistics concerning child abuse and neglect. Although for a variety of reasons it is difficult to estimate the number of cases of child abuse per year (e.g., cases not reported, bias in the types of children who get reported, problems in the definitions of abuse and neglect), estimates range from a conservative 500,000 (Light, 1973) to four million adults who were aware of at least one incident of abuse (Gil, 1970). An estimate commonly quoted is that of the National Center on Child Abuse and Neglect--1,000,000 cases reported per year.

Perhaps even more frightening is the amount of physical violence found in the American home. Gelles (1979) reported that 63 percent of respondents in a survey described having at least one violent episode with a child between the ages of three and seventeen in one year. Extrapolating from the data based on his survey, he found that between three and four million children have at some time been kicked, bitten, or punched by parents; between 1.4 and 2.3 million children have been beaten up; and between 900,000 and 1.8 million children have had a parent use a gun or knife on them. In one year (1975), between 1.4 and 1.9 million children were vulnerable to physical injury from parental violence. Clearly, the less than $20 million provided by the Child Abuse and Treatment Act can barely begin to address the problem.

Instances of legalized child abuse occur in America's public institutions, e.g., schools, correctional settings, and homes for the mentally retarded or otherwise handicapped. Documentation of institutional abuse is found in the research by Blatt and his colleagues described above (Blatt, in press; Blatt & Kaplan, 1966), and Wooden's *Weeping in the Playtime of Others* (1976). The Supreme Court's decision on corporal punishment is an indication of the nation's attitude towards children. Ruling on a case in which two junior high school students received severe beatings, the Court upheld the use of corporal punishment in the schools (*Ingraham vs. Wright*). The message clearly conveyed to parents is that corporal punishment is an appropriate method of discipline. Violence toward children is sanctioned when it is labeled corporal punishment, and abhorred when it is labeled child abuse. Newberger and Bourne (1979) discuss the court case of *Landeros vs. Flood*, in which a physician could be sued for malpractice by not reporting bruises which were legally inflicted by a teacher.

Child Care

The last area to be described concerns the need for child care.
This issue does not elicit the emotional reaction associated
with child or institutional abuse. There is no widespread
public outcry for day care. Child advocacy, labor, and women's rights groups have failed to form a single effective
lobby capable of overcoming the public fears and myths about
day care. Yet the need for alternative child care arrangements exists. In 1977, 6.4 million children under six had
working mothers, and 22.4 million children between the ages
of 6 and 17 had working mothers. Data from HEW in 1976 indicate that only 1.6 million licensed child care openings
exist in centers and family day care homes. While some of
the needs for child care are being met by informal arrangements (e.g., care in one's home by a relative), unmet needs
also lead to lengthy waiting lists, unaffordable private care,
and less than optimal arrangements. In addition, more than
two million children between the ages of seven and thirteen
come home at the end of the school day to an empty house
(*Congressional Record*, 1979). In a study of 11 and 12-year-
olds in Oakland, Rubin and Medrich (1979) found that 47 percent of the children had to babysit for younger siblings after
school. Children who are themselves in need of supervision
are instead solely responsible for providing it.

Not much is known about the modal kind of care children
are receiving, since research tends to focus on high quality
day care centers, the least common type of substitute care.
An exception to this pattern of research was the study by the
National Council of Jewish Women (Keyserling, 1972), in which
11 percent of all licensed non-profit centers were rated as
poor in quality, 51 percent were rated as fair, 28 percent
were rated as good, and only 9 percent were rated as superior.
Proprietary centers fared worse: 50 percent were considered
poor, 35 percent were fair, 14 percent were good, and 1 percent was superior. Finally, the percentages for family day
care were: 14 percent were rated as poor, 48 percent were
fair, 31 percent were good, and 7 percent were superior. These
figures probably overestimate the quality of child care, since
most care is provided in unlicensed homes which are not ac-
countable to public authority. Yet unlicensed settings are
not the only culprits in this situation. Even among licensed
centers, standards and monitoring are often lax. Staff/child
ratios, which are part of the Federal Interagency Day Care
Requirements (FIDCR) for children from six weeks to six years,
have been suspended since 1975. After four years of study
and consideration, the proposed new standards do not promote
the optimal development of children in child day care. In
fact, the suggested standards are less stringent than many

state licensing requirements. One suggested option for a
staff/child ratio is one adult for <u>five</u> infants. These recommendations do not differentiate three-month-old infants from
two and one-half-year-old toddlers, but include all infants
younger than two and one-half years. These proposed standards
are truly regressive. The debate concerning day care can no
longer focus on whether it is or is not good for children;
rather, ways to improve and expand the current system need to
be explored.

SOCIAL TRENDS

The needs of children, outlined above, should be considered
against the backdrop of two recent social trends. The first
is the increased labor participation of women. Dramatic
changes in the number of working mothers have occurred in
the last two decades, especially mothers of children under
six. For example, in 1950, 22 percent of all mothers were
working. In addition, 14 percent of mothers having children
under six were employed. In 1960, the comparable figures
were: 30 percent of all mothers were working, as well as
20 percent of mothers having children under six. In 1978,
53 percent of all mothers, 44 percent of mothers having children under six, and 60 percent having children between the
ages of six and seventeen were employed (Rivlin, 1978). The
percentages are higher for mothers in single-parent households: in 1978, 56 percent of mothers with children under
six and 71 percent of mothers with children over six were
employed (Rivlin, 1978). Clearly, the mythical American family with two parents, one working and one taking care of the
children, does not describe the majority of American families
today. Services provided to children and families will have
to take into account these changes in the status of families.
   The second important social trend is the increasing cut-
back in spending. In recent years, both inflation and unemployment have been high, producing hardships for many families.
A survey by Yankelovich, Skelly, and White in 1974-1975 found
that Americans had less faith in the economy than they previously had, and no longer were optimistic about future pros-
perity. In addition, tax revolts, such as the one leading to
Proposition 13, have led to cutbacks in spending on social
services by state and federal governments. Thus, it is unlikely that new programs designed to fulfill the needs of
children and families will be funded.
   The lack of funding is not the only problem in the delivery of necessary social services. Many public services
which are currently provided have an anti-family bias, and
are not cost-effective. One such system is out-of-home care.

The average monthly payment for foster care is $254; the average monthly payment for institutions is $575. Preventive services to families at risk, as well as adoption subsidies to insure a permanent home for children, could be considerably cheaper than both of these (Edelman, 1979). The Children's Defense Fund report (1978) on out-of-home care described the removal of three preschool children from their home and their placement in foster care, because their mother could not afford to pay $250 to fix the broken furnance. Blatt (in press) presented statistics from two studies in New York comparing types of care for mentally retarded individuals. Cost per year per resident in small group homes was $6,700. The best residential care provided for the mentally retarded which Blatt observed was a community-based service by foster parents costing $8,500 per year. In institutions, costs were $35,000 per individual per year. Providing quality care for people with special needs is not necessarily the most expensive alternative.

What are the solutions to this array of problems? More specifically, how can the knowledge we have gained about the nature of the developmental process be applied to implement solutions to these problems, and begin to meet the needs of children? In some cases, an adequate knowledge base does not exist. For example, the dynamics producing child abuse are not well enough understood to predict which abused children will grow up to themselves abuse their own children, and which of them will not. In most cases, however, social science research which can be useful in the formation and implementation of policy concerning children and families does exist. Is this information utilized by this nation's policy makers? The answer to this question is complex. Too often, solutions to children's problems seem to be based on social fads and questionable assumptions about development. An effective utilization of social science knowledge, and a meaningful collaboration between social scientists and governmental decision makers do not seem to be the norm.

In recent years, interest in studying the utilization of social science knowledge in policy making has grown. The questions which we have raised related to the apparent lack of use of research in child development apply to most areas of social science and public policy. While an extensive review of this work is beyond the scope of this paper, a brief digression exploring some of the issues in the utilization of social science research is useful. In the next section, problems, myths, and unrealistic expectations in the application of research to policy making will be described. More realistic approaches to the utilization of knowledge about human development to constructive social policy will be offered.

PROBLEMS IN THE UTILIZATION OF SOCIAL SCIENCE KNOWLEDGE

One problem commonly cited as causing a failure in the utilization of social science knowledge is the conflict in values between social scientists and policy makers (Mayntz, 1977; Weiss, 1977, 1978; Weiss & Bucuvalas, 1977). Social science is presumably value-free, while policy decisions are made in a value-laden context. This dichotomy is misleading, however. Research in the social sciences is not value-free, and even the most basic research takes on the values of the investigators. These are evident in the questions which are asked, the methodologies used, the presentation of results, and the interpretation of the data. Research in child abuse demonstrates the influence of the values of the investigators on the way problems are studied. Three approaches to understanding child abuse will be briefly compared. (See Parke and Collmer, 1975, for a detailed analysis of each approach.)

In the psychiatric analysis of child abuse, investigators assume the causes of abuse are within the parent, who is ill or abnormal. The research, therefore, focuses on identifying those traits or characteristics common to abusive parents. The solution to abuse advocated by those working within this model is typically individual or group psychotherapy. The second approach, the sociological model, views child abuse as a response to stress and frustration in one's everyday life, as well as the social values of one's culture. Conditions such as the cultural attitude toward violence, housing conditions, job-related stress, unemployment, poverty, family size, and social isolation, rather than inherent factors in the individual, contribute to child abuse. Control of abuse in this framework results from changes in societal values and conditions (e.g., the elimination of poverty). Researchers working within the social-situational model of child abuse study the patterns of interaction between abusing parents and their children, and the conditions under which abuse occurs. Factors such as use of discipline, the child's role in abuse, and interferences in mother-child attachment are viewed as important contributors to child abuse. Because the cause is not the individual but the context in which abuse occurs, intervention efforts emphasize the modification of maladaptive behaviors by both partners in the interaction. From this brief description of three approaches to child abuse, the close relation between the values of the scientist, the hypotheses proposed, and the outcomes of research can be seen.

Another example of the value-laden nature of psychological research is the tendency to blame the individual for his or her problems, rather than look for causal factors within the situation (Caplan & Nelson, 1973). Although two of the models of child abuse discussed above did identify the causes of the problem in the environment, these analyses were not typical of psychological approaches. The nature of the discipline leads to the study of intrapsychic causes of phenomena. Solutions, therefore, would not be externally based, but should result from change within the target group. Thus, researchers studying the underachievement of minority children label the children and their families as "problem groups," rather than identify the school and the educational system as the root of the problem.

A second conflict between social science research and policy making which is frequently cited is that research is often viewed as basic, not applied, and irrelevant to social problems. This position is clearly not accurate. Within the last decade, the amount of funding for applied research has increased dramatically. In 1977, the federal government spent nearly $2 billion on the production and application of social knowledge, a majority of which went to research (Study Project on Social Research and Development, 1978). In addition, evaluation requirements are written into many new social programs. Clearly, the federal government is looking toward social scientists for answers to their questions.

Perhaps the major problem in the utilization of social science research is that social scientists are perceived as not providing clear answers to appropriate policy questions, while policy makers are not asking questions in ways which would lead to valid and reliable research. Each group, therefore, does not supply the information necessary for effective collaboration.

Expectations concerning the types of questions which social science research can answer need to be revised. Those who expect single studies to have an impact on policy are likely to be disappointed, for the effects of such studies are usually small or nonexistent (Cohen & Garet, 1975; Cohen & Weiss, 1977; Rich & Caplan, 1976; Weiss, 1977, 1978). Furthermore, answers that single-study research can provide are more likely to come from an in-house research staff of a federal agency (Caplan & Rich, 1977).

If single studies do not have an impact on policy, what is the effect of accumulated research in any one area? Typically, the result of the proliferation of research on a topic is not to more adequately or definitively answer a policy question, but to introduce additional complications (Cohen & Garet, 1975; Cohen & Weiss, 1977). This seemingly negative consequence does, however, have advantageous effects. Although research many not provide a consensus from which to draw undisputed solutions, it can lead to a clarification of differences and perspectives, as well as improved research methodologies. Evaluations of Head Start exemplify

how research can be both contradictory and complex, while
leading to a more sophisticated and useful understanding of
the effects of early intervention. After the early and primarily negative findings of the Westinghouse evaluation of
Head Start in 1969, questions about proper assumptions, subject selection biases, analyses, and program goals arose.
Improved statistical techniques (e.g., the Campbell-Evans
debate concerning regression artifacts), a range of methodologies (e.g., Shipman et al. case study approach), an interest in outcome variables other than school achievement
(e.g., changes in community institutions, utilization of
special education classrooms), and a focus on process within individual programs all contributed to a complex and murky
picture of how early intervention programs affect children.
Yet this is not a regrettable situation. When the question
is complicated, it deserves more than a simple "yes/no"
answer (see Datta, 1976, 1979, for an analysis of the effects of evaluations on Head Start).

Based on the above discussion, it is obvious that to
understand how social research is used in social policy,
one must clarify the meaning of the term "use." Weiss (1978)
has discussed at length many possible uses of research in
policy making, and a summary of some of these interpretations will be described below.

USES OF RESEARCH IN SOCIAL POLICY

Ideally, research can be used for problem solving. This is
the most common understanding of the relation between research and policy, yet the link least likely to occur. This
approach assumes that a concrete and well-defined problem
needs to be solved, and that empirical evidence can be used
to help generate a solution or choose among several alternatives. The more subtle assumption is that there is consensus among decision makers on the goals for the policy in
question, a condition rarely met. Caplan (Caplan, 1975;
Caplan & Rich, 1977; Rich & Caplan, 1976) interviewed 204
policy makers in the executive branch of the federal government who were asked: "On the basis of your experience in
the federal government, can you think of instances where a
new program, a major program alternative, a new social or
administrative policy, legislative proposal, or a technical
innovation could be traced to the social sciences?" Although
82 percent of the respondents replied yes to this question,
their examples were not empirical studies, nor did the information they cited guide specific policies. Rather, their
use of social knowledge was a subtle process, relying on
ideas and principles derived from the social sciences.

Research can create its own use. Weiss (1977, 1978) refers to this model of social science utilization as the "knowledge driven model." Borrowed from the physical sciences, it
assumes that due to the compelling nature of basic research,
applications are bound to follow. This is unlikely to occur
in the social sciences.

Research can be used as political ammunition. Even after
policy makers have reached decisions and are unlikely to be
influenced by research, they may use social science knowledge
to bolster their argument. This is neither an unethical nor
unimportant use of research, as long as the information is
not distorted and is accessible to all sides.

Related to the above use is research which advances self-
interest. For example, policy makers can delay taking an
action, arguing that the needed evidence is not available.
This was the case in the four-year moratorium on staffing
regulations in the federal day care standards, pending the
results from the ABT National Day Care Study and the "Appropriateness Report" from HEW to Congress. Social scientists
also serve their own interests by having an influence on
policy, gaining governmental funds, and advocating their own,
usually liberal, views.

The last use of social science research to be discussed
is the most amorphous, but perhaps the most important: "research as conceptualization" (Weiss, 1977). This definition
of use encompasses sensitizing policy makers to new issues,
turning research problems into policy issues, clarifying alternatives, and supplying a common language. Although this
is a "softer" use of research than is commonly desired, it
can have far-reaching implications. Generalizations from
the accumulation of research in an area can, over time, change
the climate of ideas and become a part of the social consciousness. The negative aspect of this type of use of research in policy is that myths and social fads become part
of the knowledge which is accessible and utilized by the
public. Unfortunately, these myths often remain unquestioned,
and become the basis for new policy and further research.

This use of social science research can be clearly seen
in the formation of Project Head Start. Social and political
forces, in combination with the prevailing social science
theories, converged in the mid-1960's to form this important
social program (see Zigler & Anderson, 1979, for a more detailed description). The revival of scientific interest in
the role of the environment in human development, and the
design of educational intervention efforts for children of
the disadvantaged, in combination with the Civil Rights era
and the War on Poverty, all influenced the development of
Head Start. A novel alliance between child development experts and social policy makers was created.

Thus, the use of broad principles based on social science
knowledge can and does affect social policy. In the remainder
of this paper, several principles of development, based on
decades of work in child development, will be outlined. Examples of policies which are contrary to these principles,
as well as examples and suggestions for ones which are consistent with our knowledge, will be offered.

PRINCIPLES OF DEVELOPMENT

The first principle is that a child's development is continuous, and that the child benefits from a sense of continuity, both between the stages of his or her life, and
between the spheres of his or her life. For the past twenty
years, workers in the field of child development have sought
some magic time in a child's life in which to optimize development. Some have claimed that this magic period is the
nine months *in utero*; others have emphasized the first three
years of life; others have said that the true critical period
is the first three years of elementary school.

According to the principle of continuous development,
each of these periods is a magic period. Intervention programs for children should be designed in such a way that
children's needs at these specific stages are met. Of course,
it is advantageous to begin meeting children's needs as early
in life as possible. However, it is never too late to intervene effectively to optimize the development of children.

The principle of continuity also implies that children
will benefit from consistency in the environment. On a
most obvious level, the lives of children removed from their
homes need to be stabilized. Earlier in this paper, the
number of children in out-of-home placements and the number
of times children in foster care changed homes were described.
Revisions of child welfare laws are needed. The current
child welfare bill in Congress targeting funds for adoption
subsidies, as well as preventive and support services, is
a first step. Children who must be removed from their families should be placed in the least restrictive setting, pre-
ferably with relatives, and close to their families. Reviews of children in the welfare system should be made periodically, and if children are not to be returned to their
families, termination of parental rights should be hastened.
Above all else, a permanent, secure, and supportive home for
children should be found.

Consistency in the environment does not apply only to
children in foster care or institutions, but to those who
spend some time away from home each day. Children who attend day care programs, from the most informal to the most

structured, need consistency. The status of child care providers needs to be upgraded to avoid rapid staff turnover. Family day care workers are responsible for about half of the children in child care who are under six. They suffer from isolation, underpay, and inadequate training. An expansion of the Child Development Associate program could begin to address the problem of staff training. Caregivers are certified through competency examinations, so that child-care workers with experience, but without academic degrees, can qualify for a CDA degree. Innovative programs, such as family day care networks, toy lending libraries, and affiliations between family care providers and more stable centers, can also aid in solving some of the problems in the family day care system.

Parents should be encouraged to participate in the child's out-of-home setting. Although many working families may not be able to find the time to actively work in the child's day care setting or classroom, they should remain in close contact with the child's other providers. In order to provide a child with a sense of continuity, genuine partnerships must be established between professionals and the families who they serve. A model for such a partnership exists in the Head Start program, in which parent involvement is critical. Programs such as the Brookline BEEP project are demonstrating the value of parental involvement in elementary schools as well.

Related to the first principle of continuity is the second principle of child development: the most important influence on the development of the child is the family. Children need a one-to-one relationship with a caring adult. The growing recognition of this principle has led to the development of programs designed to improve parenting skills. Thus, in Home Start, professionals work not with children, but with parents. Such programs help parents develop realistic expectations for their children's behavior, and gain confidence in their child-rearing abilities.

Recently, child development education has been expanded to reach people before they become parents. George Hecht, the founder of *Parents Magazine*, has observed that young people are almost completely unprepared to assume the responsibilities of child rearing. The Education for Parenthood program was developed to introduce students to the topic of child development. More importantly, students are given the opportunity to gain firsthand experience with children in supervised settings.

The need for primary prevention has been emphasized throughout this paper. With some outside aid, parents can often handle the stresses and frustrations that all too frequently result in the breakup of the family. Home visitors

or parent aides can help the abusive or potentially abusive parent deal with some of the problems he or she faces,
by being a role model, a teacher, and a good listener (Adnopoz,
1979). Crisis day care centers and parents' groups have also
been developed to help control child abuse. Ideally, not only
families at known risk, but all American families would have
access to needed services.

The most important support that could be offered to families would be for one parent to have the option of raising
a child at home, without having to sacrifice necessary income. This may involve income-maintenance policies, family
allowances, maternity or paternity benefits, or flexible working hours (Kamerman & Kahn, 1979). Many European countries
have successfully implemented these policies.

The third principle is that children as a group are heter-
ogeneous, and show a great variability on every characteristic which can be measured. This variation relates only
minimally to social class and ethnic factors. Children with
diverse abilities have diverse needs, and rather than expect
children to match the characteristics of any single program,
programs should be developed that can be tailored to fit the
needs of each child and his or her family. The ideal intervention program would not consist of one uniform national
program, but centers in every community with a variety of programs to meet the range of needs represented by children and
families. The model for this policy of the future already
exists in the Child and Family Resource Program. This
community-wide delivery system links a variety of programs
and services to children and families, in areas such as early
childhood education, parent involvement, health, and nutrition.

Parents need options in child care which match their life
styles and philosophies. The present system tracks children
so that poor children attend one type of center, while more
affluent children go elsewhere. Government funds for day
care should subsidize whatever options the parents choose:
babysitting in the home by relatives or non-relatives, family day care, or center care. The criteria which parents use
to choose child care are complex. While several surveys have
shown that cost, location, and convenience of hours are critical to the decision-making process (Unco, Inc., 1975), an
intensive research project based on a case study approach
indicates that this is too simplistic. Lein (1979) found
that parents sought a caregiver who was reliable, warm, and
protected their children from physical danger. She also
found that parents varied in how important they considered
certain features of day care, such as an emphasis on cognitive development, supervision, exposure to different values,
and the discipline and control provided. Options in child

care which mesh with parents' needs and desires can augment, rather than undermine, family life.

Certain groups of children and families have special needs, and deserve priority in receiving support. Three groups of children should be considered first in expanding and designing new programs: children from families with low income and/or a single, working parent, handicapped children, and bilingual children.

Attempts to meet the variable needs of children do not imply that programs should try to change children to fit into one uniform mold. Pluralism and diversity are healthy, and cultural variation must be respected. Our emphasis on options reflects this belief. Caution by professionals is always required, to avoid the tendency to believe that as "experts," no one, including parents, can make better decisions for children.

The fourth principle is that full human development involves more than the formal cognitive system. Development of character, personality, and values is equally as important as the acquisition of intellectual skills. This "whole child" principle leads to the rejection of the view that higher IQ scores and school grades are the ultimate goals of educational intervention efforts.

For this reason, the "back to basics" movement represents a threat to educators committed to the whole child view. Skills in reading and mathematics are important, but social competence should be the ultimate goal of education and intervention. At least three factors must be considered in a definition of social competence: physical and mental health, formal cognitive development, and optimal emotional and motivational development. Unfortunately, measures of social, emotional, and motivational development are difficult to construct and validate. Yet, many adequate measures of such variables (e.g., effectance motivation, expectancy of success, self-image, learned helplessness, and creativity) do exist (Zigler & Trickett, 1978), and child development researchers can contribute by refining these measures, as well as developing new indicators of social competence.

The fifth principle concerns the relation between children and their social and nonsocial environment. In the past, the direction of causality was perceived to be unidirectional--from environment to child, and from parent to child. A more accurate description would include the reciprocal effects of both the child on the environment and the environment on the child. Of course, if the environment falls below a mininmum level of quality, the damage to the child can be drastic. But recent views of child development have emphasized the nonpassive nature of the child (Bell, 1968; Piaget, 1952). Based on this principle, programs

designed to alter only one partner in an interaction are not
adequate. The focus of change should be on the interaction,
and all participants' perceptions of this interaction. Revising a course curriculum is not enough, if the child expects to fail and the teacher expects the child to fail.
Therapy for abusing parents is not enough, if the child's
contribution to the abuse and the eliciting conditions are
not taken into consideration.

Social policy based on the notion that hereditary factors are all-important, or environmental factors are all-
important is doomed to failure. Expectations based on the
complete malleability of the child (e.g., expecting compen-
satory education to erase differences in achievement levels
across all children), or lack of hope in the possibilities
for change (e.g., expecting that schooling will not have an
effect on future success) ignore the complexities of the individual in a changing enviroment.

The final principle to be discussed is the broadest; it
concerns all the institutions which influence the development
of the child. The child's development is not determined only
by the parents' child-rearing techniques. Children encounter
many environments and social institutions in their development, and are affected by all of them. The family is, of
course, critical, but so are the schools, the community, and
the media. America's children are affected by social forces,
such as the state of the economy, the length of the industrial work day, the geographical mobility of industrial employees, the availability of day care, the ever-changing regulations concerning the availability of food stamps, and a
thousand other decisions made at the federal, state, and local
levels of government.

Advances in research are not enough to improve the lives
of children. While we believe that the principles which have
been outlined should be the base upon which effective social
policy is formed, we also believe that helping our nation's
children should not wait for all the necessary or relevant
knowledge to be produced. As we have discussed, social science
research is often underutilized, misinterpreted, and above
all, takes an exceedingly long time to influence the social
consciousness of the public. We must, therefore, take a broad
view of our responsibilities to children and their families.
When the media manipulates and exploits the child consumer,
we must speak out. When government policy, by commission or
omission, threatens our children's well-being, we must speak
out. If we are concerned about the lives of America's children, we must become nothing less than social activists on
their behalf.

REFERENCES

Adnopoz, J. *Parent aides: Effective supports for families.* Unpublished manuscript, Yale University, 1979.

Advisory Committee on Child Development. *Toward a national policy for children and families.* Washington, D.C.: National Academy of Sciences, 1976.

Bell, R. Q. A reinterpretation of the direction of effects in studies of socialization. *Psychological Review,* 1968, *75,* 81-95.

Blatt, B. The pariah industry. A diary from purgatory and other places. In G. Gerbner, C. J. Ross, & E. Zigler (Eds.), *Child abuse reconsidered.* New York: Oxford University Press, in press.

Blatt, B., & Kaplan, F. *Christmas in purgatory.* Boston: Allyn & Bacon, 1966.

Caplan, N. S. The use of social science information by federal executives. In G. Lyons (Ed.), *Social research and public policies.* Hanover, New Hampshire: Dartmouth College, 1975.

Caplan, N., & Nelson, S. On being useful: The nature and consequences of psychological research on social problems. *American Psychologist,* 1973, *28,* 199-211.

Caplan, N., & Rich, R. F. *Open and closed knowledge inquiry systems: The process and consequences of bureaucratization of information policy at the national level.* Unpublished manuscript, University of Michigan, 1977.

Children's Defense Fund. *Children without homes.* Washington, D.C.: Author, 1978.

Cohen, D. K., & Garet, M. S. Reforming education policy with applied social research. *Harvard Educational Review,* 1975, *45,* 17-43.

Cohen, D. K., & Weiss, J. A. Social science and social policy. Schools and race. In C. H. Weiss (Ed.), *Using social research in public policy making.* Lexington, Massachusetts: Lexington Books, 1977.

Congressional Record, January 15, 1979, S76-77.

Datta, L. The impact of the Westinghouse/Ohio evaluation of the development of Project Head Start: An examination of the immediate and longer term effects and how they came about. In C. C. Abt (Ed.), *The evaluation of social programs*. Beverly Hills, California: Sage, 1976.

Datta, L. What has the impact of Head Start been? Some findings from national evaluations of Head Start. In E. Zigler & J. Valentine (Eds.), *Project Head Start: A legacy of the war on poverty*. New York: Macmillan Free Press, 1979.

Edelman, M. W. Children instead of ships. *New York Times*, May 14, 1979, A19.

Fanshel, D., & Shinn, E. B. *Children in foster care: A longitudinal investigation*. New York: Columbia University Press, 1978.

Furrow, D., Gruendel, J., & Zigler, E. *Protecting America's children from accidental injury and death. An overview of the problem and an agenda for action*. Unpublished manuscript, Yale University, 1979.

Gelles, R. J. Violence toward children in the United States. In R. Bourne & E. H. Newberger (Eds.), *Critical perspectives on child abuse*. Lexington, Massachusetts: Lexington Books, 1979.

Gil, D. *Violence against children: Physical child abuse in the United States*. Cambridge, Massachusetts: Harvard University Press, 1970.

Kamerman, S. B., & Kahn, A. The day-care debate: A wider view. *Public Interest*, 1979, *54*, 76-93.

Keniston, K. *All our children*. New York: Harcourt, Brace, Jovanovich, 1977.

Keyserling, M. D. *Windows on day care*. New York: National Council of Jewish Women, 1972.

Knowles, J. H. (Ed.). *Doing better and feeling worse. Health in the United States*. New York: W. W. Norton, 1977.

Lein, L. Parental evaluation of child care alternatives. *Urban and Social Review*, 1979, *12*, 11-16.

Light, R. Abused and neglected children in America: A study of alternative policies. *Harvard Educational Review*, 1973, *43*, 556-598.

Mayntz, R. Sociology, value freedom, and the problems of political counseling. In C. H. Weiss (Ed.), *Using social research in public policy making*. Lexington, Massachusetts: Lexington Books, 1977.

New findings on teen pregnancy. *New York Times*, April 29, 1979, E7.

Newberger, E. H., & Bourne, R. The medicalization and legalization of child abuse. In R. Bource & E. H. Newberger (Eds.), *Critical perspectives on child abuse*. Lexington, Massachusetts: Lexington Books, 1979.

Parke, R., & Collmer, C. Child abuse: Interdisciplinary review. In E. M. Hetherington (Ed.), *Review of child development research* (Vol. 5). Chicago: University of Chicago Press, 1975.

Piaget, J. *The origins of intelligence in children*. New York: International Universities Press, 1952.

Rich, R. F., & Caplan, N. *Instrumental and conceptual uses of social science knowledge in policy-making at the national level: Means/ends matching versus understanding*. Unpublished manuscript, University of Michigan, 1976.

Rivlin, A. *Childcare and preschool: Options for federal support*. Washington, D.C.: Government Printing Office, 1978.

Rubin, V., & Medrich, E. A. Child care, recreation and the fiscal crisis. *Urban and Social Change Review*, 1979, *12*, 22-28.

Study Project on Social Research and Development. *The federal investment in knowledge of social problems* (Vol. 1). Washington, D.C.: National Academy of Sciences, 1978.

Unco, Inc. *National child care consumer study: 1975*. Washington, D.C.: U.S. Government Printing Office, 1975.

Weiss, C. H. Introduction. In C. H. Weiss (Ed.), *Using social research in public policy making*. Lexington, Massachusetts: Lexington Books, 1977.

Weiss, C. H.   Improving the linkage between social research
and public policy.   In Study Project on Social Research
and Development (Eds.), *Knowledge and policy: The uncertain connection.*   Washington, D.C.:   National Academy
of Sciences, 1978.

Weiss, C. H., & Bucuvalas, M. J.   The challenge of social
research to decision making.   In C. H. Weiss (Ed.),
Using social research in public policy making.   Lexington, Massachusetts: Lexington Books, 1977.

Wooden, K.   *Weeping in the playtime of others.*   New York:
McGraw-Hill, 1976.

Yankelovich, Skelly, White, Inc.   *The General Mills American
family report 1974-1975.*   Minneapolis: General Mills,
1975.

Zigler, E., & Anderson, K.   An idea whose time had come:
The intellectual and political climate for Head Start.
In E. Zigler & J. Valentine (Eds.), *Project Head Start:
A legacy of the war on poverty.*   New York: Macmillan
Free Press, 1979.

Zigler, E., & Trickett, P. K.   IQ, social competence and
evaluation of early childhood intervention programs.
American Psychologist, 1978, *33,* 789-798.

II. MARRIAGE RELATIONSHIPS

The marriage relationship is the central relationship in most families. Since marriage is the foundation upon which family strengths are developed, it is important that this relationship be fulfilling. The second section of this book focuses upon understanding and enriching the marriage relationship.

The article by Dr. David Mace and Vera Mace establishes the theme that marriage is the foundation stone upon which family strengths are developed. They discuss the occurrence of marital conflict and effective, constructive ways of dealing with it. Their article also delineates the essential qualities for developing a successful marriage.

The article by Dr. Jack Buerkle, Donald Eckard, Rhonda Jacobs, and Jay Bolick explores the influence of individualism on the families of today. Their article also emphasizes the importance of good communication patterns, empathy, and constructive ways of dealing with conflict. Implications for counselors are discussed.

Dr. Michael MacLean's article discusses a model for improving communication patterns among retired couples. The model involves a sequence of interactions, beginning with the discussion of past family events of a non-threatening nature and moving to progressively more personal and meaningful matters. Some critical aspects of retirement are also considered, such as lowered income and decreasing physical abilities.

Dr. David Mace
    and
Vera Mace
Founders of Association of
    Couples for Marriage Enrichment
Winston-Salem, North Carolina

MARRIAGE: THE FOUNDATION STONE

We want to begin by emphasizing the title of our topic, "Enriching Marriages, The Foundation Stone of Family Strength."
That is what we believe about marriage. The marriage relationship is central to any attempt to strengthen families.
Yet, there is an unfortunate tendency among many family life
professionals to avoid the topic or even the word, marriage.
Too often when the term marriage is referred to, it is done
in a negative context. I've encountered this again and again
and it gives me some concern. So I want to plead with you
as family professionals to try to defeat this avoidance of
the topic marriage--this avoidance of the word marriage.
    There was a time when sex was a word we did not use. We
did not talk about it. That's gone. There was a time when
death was something we did not talk about, but that is going
now. It distresses me deeply to find that professionals in
the family field are evasive about marriage. I hope by saying that I may cause you to reflect on the central importance
of the marriage relationship to any functioning family.

WHAT IS HAPPENING TO MARRIAGE
IN OUR COUNTRY TODAY?

Marriage is changing very profoundly. We can view marriage
on a spectrum which includes three different kinds of mar-
riages--the old traditional marriage, the marriage of today
in transition, and the marriage of the future.
    The traditional marriage was the conflict-excluding mar-
riage. The husband up there in a commanding position, the
wife down below in a responding, submissive position. All
marriages and families were like that in the ancient world

for the simple reason that all human cultures were hierarch-
ically structured on the basis of authority and obedience.
This was the only way that they could be held together--by
the use of power by a leader, a king, and so forth, and sub-
mission to that power by others. Relationships in the old
world were almost all vertical--up and down.

The family in its simplest form is simply a factory which
manufactures people. That is what a family is. Because human life is limited and people get old like we are doing, and
die as we shall do, you have to keep feeding in replacements.
So the family is the factory which feeds in replacements. The
job of the family is to manufacture people, and to make them
the kind of people who can contribute positively to the culture to which they belong. In those old days, the kind of
people who were needed in a hierarchical culture were people
who knew what their place was and how to keep it. So the
old family was right for the old world.

But then when democracy came and some people over here
made the astounding statement, "all people are created equal,"
which was a complete denial of everything society had been
based on before, something happened. A little later, when
it was realized that an inescapable implication was "all men
and women are created equal," we were really in a new world.
So what we are doing today is creating a new world in which
relationships are not vertical but horizontal. Consequently,
we have to create new families to produce people who can
live in a world where relationships are horizontal.

What is happening today is that marriage and the family
are struggling through that colossal transition in their
roles. What we did was to take that fellow down from his
high eminence. We took him down and then we put her up be-
side him, and we said they belonged side by side and that
was beautiful and everybody expected wonderful marriages, but
it did not happen. It did not happen for a very simple reason.
When you change a one-vote system into a two-vote system you
are headed for trouble--plenty of trouble. And that is what
we did. We thought they would always vote the same way and
everything would be sweet and beautiful but they did not and
it is not. So what we have done is to open the marriage
relationship wide to conflict--a division of opinions, differences, disagreements--and what has happened today is that
millions of marriages in America have become conflict-avoiding
marriages. Because the couple could not tolerate the pain
of their incessant disagreements and conflicts, they put a
wedge of insulation between them. They shut each other out
at all levels.

What we find in marriages today is that couples have decreased the number of areas in which they communicate in-
depth and in which they cooperate in-depth, until their

relationship becomes shallow. They do not want it to be
shallow, and they are disappointed and they feel it has failed. As a result, you too often have another couple on the
divorce list. The marriage of today is the conflict-avoiding
marriage. Where do we go to from there?

There are some people who want us to go back to the old
hierarchical system. I do not think we are going to do that
because we are living in a democratic world, and I believe
democracy is going to survive. So, the only way we can go
is to go forward to the conflict-resolving marriage, accepting the fact that marriage, as a close interpersonal relationship, has got to experience conflict. That is part of
its nature. By dealing with and using that conflict creatively, we can produce really effective, close interpersonal relationships.

FUTURE PROSPECTS OF AMERICAN MARRIAGES

Let us take a look at where American marriages are in the
process of transition. Of course when you talk about marriage and divorce statistics, it is rather confusing because nothing stands still, so they should be taken in ap-
proximation. All American marriages today, in terms of
their future prospects, can be placed in four classifica-
tions. The first classification is the highly successful
marriages. About ten percent of them are going to be highly
successful marriages--not more than ten percent. They are
not going to need any help at all. The remaining ninety percent of American marriages need help if they are to reach
their full potential. In the most fragile group, forty percent of these marriages are going to fail and end in divorce.
Then in the in-between group, we still have fifty percent
of American marriages and what are they? We've divided them
roughly into two groups--one group being in danger of dissolution and the other group, which is growth oriented. This
classification is an estimate, but within these intact marriages which do not end in divorce, there are many very bad
marriages. We did not realize that in the past. We assumed
that all couples who stayed together had beautiful relationships, and even our early studies of juvenile delinquency
were built on that assumption, which was quite inaccurate.

The truth is, now that we know about battered wives and
battered children and battered husbands and many other dis-
tressing things that go on in marriages that do not break
up, we know that many of these marriages are in poor shape
even though they hold together. We have estimated half of
the marriages to be in that category. They range from marriages

which are very bad indeed to marriages which are pretty bad
but have some good features. Then we have the group of marriages which could be called, on the whole, good marriages,
and they range from the almost highly successful to the almost not very good. There are fifty percent of our marriages
which are not going to break down, but on the other hand they
are not going to be all that they could be because they will
not get the help they need.

Of all the couples who divorce, over seventy percent will
remarry a second time, and then the second time they will go
through the same process--more than forty percent of them
will fail again. Some of them will be good; some second marriages are very good indeed. Those are the prospects for
American marriage.

WHAT HAPPENS AFTER THE WEDDING?

The wedding is the beginning of a marriage. As I shall be
saying to you later, we are greatly mistaken when we say
that a wedding is a marriage; it is not. A wedding and a
marriage are not the same thing, although we use the words
interchangeably. Following the wedding, marriages begin to
take shape. It is our opinion that the first year of marriage is pretty critical for most marriages. The pattern
of interaction between the couple emerges and takes shape
in that first year, and sometimes it is a good pattern, in
which case the marriage will keep on growing, and sometimes
it is a bad pattern, in which case the marriage will probably go on deteriorating. There may be a very few marriages
which stay just as they are all the time, but that is probably only an intellectual concept. These are what we call
the plateau marriages--the marriages that just do not go
anywhere, but just get stuck in ruts and remain there.

A number of marriages begin to deteriorate very soon
and some deteriorate very slowly. Many marriages, according to the studies over a lifetime, get worse over time,
and that need not happen but it does. Many of these marriages deteriorate quite quickly down to the point of separation or divorce. Some of these marriages deteriorate
only very slowly and only a little. But these are the marriages which progressively deteriorate, forty percent of
them ending in divorce. The others stay in some kind of
state of incomplete development. There are other marriages,
though, and there could be many more, that go in the direction of achieving their full potential. At any rate, they
grow and improve because they know how to do it and we have
to tell them how to do it, except for ten percent for whom

it seems to come natural. The answers for the marriages which
are deteriorating is to get them to counselors, and that is
fine and we want to do that. But the answer for the ones
which are not deteriorating but have potential for growth
and want to grow is to get them to enrichment, because they
will not do their growing effectively unless we deal with
them. So the enrichment zone in offering services to marriage is every bit as important as the counseling zone, but
that is not at all represented in the services we are now
providing for marriages.

SERVICES FOR MARRIAGES

Let us talk about what we should be doing about this and let
us talk about the services we are providing for marriages.
Almost all of the services which we are making available to
marriages today are remedial or corrective. We have not
changed that pattern at all in the entire history of marriage counseling, which goes back about 45 years. I have
been in the marriage counseling movement from its very beginning. I opened the first marriage counseling office in
Europe in 1940. There was an earlier start over here.

It is interesting to realize what our concepts were. We
believed that the great majority of marriages were all right
just because people stayed in their homes and did not break
up. We assumed that behind those closed doors there was
sweetness and light. We did find, however, that a few marriages, a very few, broke up and came out openly to divorce.
It was a very low proportion in those days. We assumed that
we did not have to bother about the all right marriages which
stayed together, the intact marriages as the researchers called them then. What we had to bother about was the small proportion of marriages which got openly into trouble. This
bothered us and we wanted to provide them with help. We
developed marriage counseling with the intention of providing
this service for a limited number of couples who had the mis-
fortune to be different from the majority and get into trouble.
Marriage counseling developed along those lines and has continued to developed along those lines.

MARRIAGE COUNSELING

You do not go to marriage counseling normally, unless you
are a very enlightened person, until you are in trouble and
probably in bad trouble. This means that the thrust of our

efforts to help marriages is overwhelmingly to wait until they
fall down, and then try to pick them up. By the time they
fall down, a lot of damage has been done. These people have
been deeply hurt; they have been alienated. Their motivation to work on the marriage has been eroded, so that marriage
counseling is a tough job.

Marriage counseling is trying to work with people who are
really hurting badly and in a state of almost panic. Of
course we must do it; we must continue to do it. But now with
our awareness that so many marriages need help, ninety percent
of them, it does not make sense to do just that.

THE NEED FOR PREVENTIVE SERVICES

What we need to do today, if we have any sense of working for
stronger families in the future, is to match our remedial
services with corresponding preventive services. What Vera
and I are saying today to communities, with a trumpet call
is, "Look, if you do nothing but pick up people when they
fall down, you will not pick up anything like all of them;
you will have to take care of these people, they will be on
the welfare rolls, they will cost you money. If that is all
you do, you will never emerge from this mess. You have to
go further back and find where the trouble started and stop
it there."

The stream of pathology is coming through, and communities are spending millions providing remedial services for
families which have collapsed, and spending nothing to prevent that from happening. What we are saying is aim as soon
as possible, in your community, to match your services which
are remedial with services which are preventive, dollar for
dollar, worker for worker, day of service for day of service.
When you begin to do that, then the flow of pathology will
die down and the enormous cost of picking up wrecks will
diminish. You can use only a fraction of the money to keep
people out of trouble that you will otherwise have to use to
help them when they are in trouble. Remember that all marriages which are in trouble today were once not in trouble.
They are in.trouble today because no help was given to them
when they were in no trouble; very probably something could
have been done earlier to keep them out of trouble.

We maintain that preventive service is the best way to
develop effective family strength. What do we mean by preventive service? What can we, in fact, do? We can only
answer that question when we know why some marriages succeed
and others do not. That is a very complex question and I
will have to oversimplify it. Some of you may know that

Ernest Burgess was the great father of American family sociology and that he predicted this change in the pattern of
marriage and the family from the traditional pattern to what
he called the "companionship pattern." One of his disciples
was a man called Nelson Foote. Nelson Foote saw it all very
clearly. He wrote a book in 1955, in which he coined an interesting term. The term was "interpersonal competence."
What he said was that large numbers of people today who are
going into marriage do not have a chance of succeeding in
terms of these expectations, unless they are trained in
interpersonal competence, and unless they are given skills
for marriage as they are given skills for any complex job
or vocation. They do not have a chance otherwise. I believe
that to be true. I believe that most of the people whose
marriages are crashing are not failures. They are victims.
They are the victims of an obtuse society which will not
face the responsibility of giving them the tools to do the
job.

What is interpersonal competence? Nelson Foote tried to
spell it out but he could not do so because he did not have
the knowledge in those days. Now we do have the knowledge
coming along fast from the behavioral sciences. Be we have
not been able to get it to the couples out there yet. I
hope we will soon.

WHY SOME MARRIAGES SUCCEED AND OTHERS FAIL

For years, Vera and I have tried to answer this question:
"What is it that makes some marriages succeed and other marriages fail?" For years, marriage counselors were under the
impression that marriages failed because married couples
could not manage their sex adjustment, because they could
not handle their money, because they could not agree about
the raising of their children, and this kind of thing. We
are now convinced that these are not the causes of marriage
failure at all. These are only the arenas in which the
inner failure of the marriage is outwardly demonstrated, and
in which the painful battle takes place which causes the inevitable disruption. These are not the causes of marriage
failure.

We would say emphatically that every marriage which fails,
fails first on the inside. It is the inner relationship
which fails and then all these other things follow as the
expression of that inner failure. So we now see that success in marriage depends, in most instances (there are some
variations here), on the extent to which the couple go into
marriage or achieve in marriage what we call a "primary

coping system." It is their capacity to cope. Some of the
early studies in marriage in this country put great emphasis
on the concept of compatibility. That has dropped almost entirely out of our consideration now. We now realize, with
extreme exceptions, that compatibility is not a state of affairs; it is a job of work. Marriages have to change; the
people have to adapt considerably to each other to achieve a
marriage. It is ridiculous that two people should come together to marry in such a condition that the profiles of
their personalities should exactly match with each other.
They have got to work this out for themselves.

The coping process is what matters; all marriages have
problems. We, for years, have seen the insides of marriages
in serious trouble, and now for sixteen years in marriage
enrichment have seen the insides of marriages not in serious
trouble, and believe me, there is no difference between them.
All marriages have troubles; all marriages have tasks of adjustment; all marriages have pain and conflict, and trouble
and anger. What makes the differences is the couples who
have a coping system can manage to fashion that into a good
relationship and the couples who do not have a coping system
cannot do it.

THREE ESSENTIALS TO MARRIAGE SUCCESS

What is the coping system? We have come to the conclusion
that there are three essentials for a successful marriage.
Given these three essentials, the overwhelming majority of
marriages will succeed; lacking these three essentials, or
lacking two of them or lacking any one of them, the majority
of marriages will fail. The three essentials are discussed
in detail in our recent book, *Have a Happy Marriage*. We will
now take a concise look at each of the three essentials.

Commitment

First, there must be commitment on the part of the' couple
to ongoing growth in their relationship. Growth is the key
word. Every living thing conforms to the laws of growth,
including a marriage. I do not have time to spell that out,
but we have done it very thoroughly and are satisfied about
it.

Growth is something that people have not thought of in
relationship to marriage. We tried asking people at ran-
dom--people out in the street and people we met--what is
your reaction when we talk to you about growth in marriage?
The majority in effect said, "Our minds go blank." They had

no frame of reference in which to think of growth in marriage. Why? Because we have taught people for years that marriage is static. But marriage is a state, a condition; you enter it through a door which is a legal contract and a religious ceremony. Somehow, when you are on the other side of that door everything is different. That is what we told people. We told them there is nothing they need to do about it; in fact, we used the term "marry and settle down." Heaven help us--settle down! But there it is you see; it is a rigid static concept that there is something which exists in these people, and there is some magic in what we call love, romantic love, that will guarantee their happiness, which is just a bunch of complete nonsense.

What we have to realize is that until two people, who are married, look into each other's eyes and make a solemn commitment to each other--that they will stop at nothing, that they will face any cost, any pain, any struggle, go out of their way to learn and seek in order that they may make their marriage a continuously growing experience--until two people have done that they are not in my judgment properly married. So I say a wedding is not a marriage; a wedding is only the beginning of an undertaking which will take years in which a marriage may be achieved. All you have on your wedding day is two disorderly heaps of raw materials which you have to make into one heap and out of it make a marriage. It is like a property lot which somebody has bought; the trucks come and they dump a pile of bricks, and they dump a pile of lumber, and they dump a heap of sand, and they dump cement, and then someone who knows how has to take all that and make a house of it.

A wedding is not a marriage, and the evidence of it is that two million adult persons every year report to the state that they had a wedding but they had not achieved a marriage and they want out. When we talk about growth that implies something else. It implies potential. We have not been talking about marriage potential, but now we are.

Don Jackson was a psychiatrist who studied American marriages intensively at Stanford University. I once spent a day with him there, and I was very impressed with what he was doing. Don Jackson's book, *The Mirages of Marriage*, one of the best books on the subject still, made a startling estimate. He estimated from his very intensive knowledge of marriage that the number of marriages in our American society which have achieved their full potential is not more than five to ten percent. As I told you before, this means that ninety percent of American marriages are short of their potential, and most of them are far short of their potential. They are undeveloped relationships.

It is time we began to talk about potential and we are
doing it. Vera and I have experienced frustration in trying
to get couples to come to marriage enrichment groups. What
they would say was, "Oh we don't need that. Our marriage is
all right." We had no answers to that until we developed the
marriage potential inventory. Now we can say to them, "Fine,
but what you need to do, if we may suggest it, is to come and
find out how all right your marriage is." I cannot take time
to describe this marriage potential inventory to you except
to say it is an extremely helpful thing for any couple to
go through. It was described in a recent issue of the *Family
Coordinator*, and an article in the August, 1979 issue of
the *Reader's Digest* describes how it is used.

We are able now to get two people, who are married to
each other, to do relatively simple exercises, and then get
together on a subjective test in which they can estimate
their probability of the potential for a loving, caring,
happy, tender, warm marriage. They estimate the percentage
of their potential for that sort of marriage, that they have
already claimed, and by deducting this percentage from a
hundred, determine the percentage of marital potential they
have not yet claimed, not yet appropriated. It is there,
like money in the bank, but they have not been there to draw
it out. This transforms the whole perception of many couples;
they suddenly realize they have a whole lot of good things
which are theirs. In all human beings, there is a tremendous
potential for loving, for caring, for warmth, for understanding, for support, for affirmation; yet, in so many marriages
of today it never gets developed. Marriage enrichment is
really saying to people, "Come and join us and develop your
marriage potential. Come and claim the money you have in
the bank."

Effective Communication

The second essential is that the couple must have an effective communication system. I believe that all married couples
try awfully hard to succeed. I think they work at it, but
they fail because they do not know how to work at it. They
must be able to communicate effectively; if they do not communicate they do not know what to work at. Two people can
live together for forty years, sleep in the same bed every
night, and not even know each other as persons. In most
marriages, the couple does not know each other as persons.
Every marriage counselor knows that. The wife tells you
about the husband, and you get a picture of him in your
mind; he then comes in and you just do not recognize him.

The Family Service Association of America made a four-
year study of families in trouble (probably the biggest

study that was ever made) that included an attempt to discover what is going wrong in marriages which are in trouble.
In the course of one week, every worker in every Family Service Association--there were 330 at the time in North Amer-
ica--kept a record of all their cases. Then FSAA tried to
answer some questions about marriage. The question was asked
"What do you see as factors in the marriages of those couples
who are in trouble and seeking your help?" They found sex,
they found money, they found in-laws, they found abuse, they
found disagreements about children, they found infidelity;
they found all these things. But these things were in a relatively low bracket. An average of about 35 to 40 percent of
the couples had these things. The major finding was that 87
percent of the couples experienced deficient communication.
Over and over again, these couples could not communicate with
each other, they could not get through to each other, they
could not hear each other, they could not listen to each
other. No wonder they were in trouble about sex, about money,
and so forth, if they could not communicate. So, communication is of vital importance.

Until a few years ago, we were simply not able to teach
couples to communicate. I made an investigation of 26 of
what I considered to be the best books on marriage, published
between 1930 and 1970, and I found almost nothing about couple
communication in them. This is new. We now have a great
deal of knowledge about communication in marriage. We do
not have space to fully describe it to you, but I will tell
you some of the things that we can teach couples now. We
have to begin by teaching them self-awareness. If you do
not know who you are and where you are, you cannot communicate
it to anybody; you have to begin by learning self-awareness.

Most people are not aware of themselves. There are feelings in them that they deny, that they displace, that they
are ashamed of and guilty of, and if you are not aware of
what is going on inside you then you are not in charge of
your own life; it is just as simple as that. So we teach
them self-awareness. The second thing we have to teach them
is communicating their self-awareness to each other, which
is self-disclosure. We know that the basis for all deep
friendships is not common interests, as we used to think,
but mutual self-disclosure. It is as they open themselves to
each other that they develop relationships, and this is true
of marriage. Large numbers of couples who have never opened
up their inner selves to each other are living far apart
psychologically, though near physically.

The third thing that we can teach couples now is to complete their communication cycles. When couples are taught
to complete their communication cycles, which is very simple
for in a few weeks they can learn the technique, then you

can say to them, "Never again in your married life will you
suffer from misunderstanding." That would be worth thousands
of dollars to many couples, but it is available for free.

The fourth thing that we can do for couples is to teach
them the four stars of communication which were developed in
the Minnesota Couples Communication program. This is a program which every married couple should take. It has trans-
formed the marriages of many.

The final thing which you can learn--there are others but
I picked five of the main things--is the enormous importance
of mutual affirmation. There have been studies and studies
of marriages of families in trouble, but there now have been
some studies of marriages of families who were not in trouble--
they were getting along fine. The studies were conducted to
find why they were getting along fine, and I want to tell you
Nick Stinnett conducted one of these four major studies when
he was in Oklahoma. These studies all basically agree on
what it is that makes great families great families. It is
not something complicated at all; it is something quite simple.
Within these marriages, husband and wife like each other,
and they keep on telling each other. They keep on affirming
each other. They keep on praising each other. They keep
on building each other up, and giving each other a good self-
image. They love each other, and they keep expressing their
love and appreciation for each other with affection, and
warmth, and tenderness; of course because of that they just
love being together. This is true of families too.

You see in the old world--I was raised in Scotland--we
never expressed our feelings to our parents and they never
expressed theirs to us. We believed that they loved us because of what they did for us. But we did not tell them so,
and they did not tell us. Now we have released in families
today the right to express feelings. But have we? In part
we have. What we find when we study the interactions in families is that most of these emotional interactions in families are negative. What we have done is to open up families
to the freedom to say how they are feeling. But what they
share are their feelings when they are feeling bad, not when
they are feeling good. In other words, the average husband
today, when he sees his wife doing something which displeases
him, does not fail to make a remark on it, "Don't do that."
"I don't like you doing that." "You did that wrong." "Why
are you always doing this?" "You are just like your mother."
This is what goes on. But when the husband feels warm and
tender toward his wife it somehow sticks in his throat and
he does not say it. This is because of a taboo in our culture that has been identified by a British psychiatrist and
has been called the taboo on tenderness. It afflicts particularly the males of the species I am sorry to say.

When people have negative feelings about each other in American families today, they let it all come out, but when they have warm, positive feelings, it does not come out and the result is that the expression of feelings in families tends to disrupt the families rather than unite them. You have to say affirm, affirm, affirm. We have to teach them to affirm. We have couples in an exercise we do, which we call Positive Interaction, simply hold each other's hands and look into each other's eyes, and tell each other what they like about each other. We have had couples who say they have been married twenty, thirty, forty years and have never done it before.

Making Creative Use of Conflict

The third essential is to learn to make creative use of conflict. Let us now summarize the three essentials. First, a commitment to growth is necessary, but it is no use to have a commitment to growth unless you know what growing you have to do. Secondly, you need a good communication system so that you know where you are and where you want to go. There are some people who say, "All you have to do for couples is to teach them to communicate and everything will be all right." Not true! The major reason why couples do not communicate in depth, and are afraid to and back away when they try, is because when you communicate in depth, you reactivate old conflicts which you thought you had buried. You experience pain and tension and give up communicating because it is too hard. You have to teach couples to make creative use of conflict.

Conflict is in all marriages. The psychologists tell us now that conflict is an integral part of every close relationship. We do not tell young people that; we say, "Don't get into conflict. That's nasty!" When couples get into conflict, they get scared to death because they think something awful has happened, and so we think of conflict in marriage like the serpent in the Garden of Eden, who comes subtly and sinuously in to spoil it all. That is a total misconception of conflict. Conflict is something inevitable in every close relationship--indeed in every relationship. Conflict is the raw material for significant growth. Until you see conflict positively as an opportunity to grow you do not have it straight. So you see, if people run away from conflict, they run away from vital growth which they need. No wonder their relationship is soon in trouble.

A husband and wife, before they are married, come to each other as if they were strangers to each other. She emerges from that end of the stage, and he emerges from this end of the stage, and they begin to walk toward each other. They

look at each other, and they begin to smile, and they come
closer and closer. This is marriage. Two people coming out
of their own worlds into a common world and trying to get
close to each other. This is the motive of marriage. In
the old days when people did not choose their partners, the
motive in marriage was to have children and carry on the
family line; however, since there is now freedom of choice,
there is a quest for closeness which is obvious physically
because they join their bodies together sexually, and come
as close as is possible for two people to be physically.
They want to also be close emotionally, intellectually, and
in other ways. They want closeness across the whole range of
their life. They want a shared life.

I believe it was Plato who said that God made people as
opposite halves of each other, and you had to find your opposite half. Not so. People come together who are different
from each other. The only two people who would be really
alike are identical twins. Other than that, people are very
different from each other. They bring those differences when
they marry. That is all right. As a matter of fact, the raw
material which you have on your wedding day consists of three
kinds of things. First, there are the things you have in
common, the things you both like. Second are the things in
which you are different, but the differences are complementary.
Studies have talked about the similarities and complementary
factors in mate selection. Third, unfortunately, are the differences between us which are not at all complementary, and
cause us to meet head-on with a big bang. In every relationship between two people, there is a great deal of those kinds
of differences. So when we move closer together to each other,
those differences become disagreements.

A disagreement between two people is a manifestation of
hostile differences between them which are activated by their
coming close. There may be a man walking through the main
street of Lincoln right now with whom I would disagree about
everything. It does not matter. He is welcome to walk there,
and I am welcome to be here, and we are not bothering each
other. But suppose we turned up together at a party, and
we got talking, and we really started disagreeing. I would
go home and say to Vera, "That is a very unpleasant man."
He would say the same thing to his wife. If we were both working with the same firm we would be running against each other
on a number of occasions, and if we were both committed by our
boss to jointly undertake the same task, all hell would be
let loose. The thing is, the closer you come together, the
more painful many of your differences would become.

Disagreement is really difference brought into painful
encounter through coming close. But what people want to do
in marriages is to come close. So when they come close, many

of their differences turn into disagreements, because never
will you find a married couple where both of them want to do
exactly the same thing at the same time in the same way. Of
course, as you remember, that was all taken care of in the
old days by giving the husband power to have his way and telling his wife to knuckle down and accept him. Now, with the
two-vote system, you can see what trouble it causes.

Since these two people now want to come close, in spite
of their disagreements, they continue to push toward intimacy.
Intimacy is the goal. As they do so, look what happens. As
they get closer, the fuel spots turn into tons of flame and
wide explosions, and that into conflict. What is conflict?
Conflict is simply disagreement heated up--heated up by hot
emotions, exasperation, and irritation. But the basic simple
wedge is anger. As two people move toward intimacy and love,
they inevitably generate anger in each other. The sooner we
get hold of this fact the better.

DEALING WITH ANGER

Even in today's books about marriage, you will find very
little about anger. Vera and I have come to the conclusion
that the state of marriage generates more anger in normal
people than does any other social situation. We believe,
therefore, that the root cause of marriages failing is inability on the part of the couple to handle their anger against
each other constructively. For us, anger is the root of the
matter because a married couple cannot achieve intimacy until they have dealt with their anger. Intimacy demands a
price. The price of intimacy is that you make yourself wholly
defenseless to each other. You take down all your defenses;
you keep them up with other people because you want to keep
them at a distance.

Being intimate in marriage is simply a process of having
the courage to make yourself totally vulnerable to the other
person. You cannot, even if you want to, make yourself totally vulnerable to the other person if there were any chance
that the other person might attack you. As long as there is
a possibility of anger breaking out in a marriage, there can
be no real intimacy and no really deep love and tenderness.
People deal with anger in different ways, and most married
couples know of only two ways of dealing with anger--either
to vent it and get into a fight, or to suppress it and pretend it is not there. The idea of married people fighting
in a love relationship is ghastly. Yet it is perhaps better
than suppressing anger. Because if you suppress the anger,
it is there all the time, and at least after a fight you have

the joy of making up. Many couples build their marriage on
the basis of a fight, and antagonism, and then separation--
getting away. It is a process of cooling down, warming up
again, coming back, reconciling, and experiencing a nice
little bit of intimacy until the next fight. We call that
the "yo yo" marriage.

There is a love-anger cycle that happens to some degree
in most marriages. What happens in the love-anger cycle is
that two people come closer and closer seeking love, and then
to their horror, there is conflict breaking out between them.
When they want to be loving each other, they are hating each
other, and this is shattering to young people who have not
been taught what conflict is all about. What happens, you
see, is they feel that everything has been violated. In the
pain of this conflict they can't stand it, and they back away
and go back where they started. Again they repeat it and
feel close, and just as they are getting warm, they have another conflict. The cycle goes on and on, and the average
marriage where this happens finally settles for a compromise,
where you get a certain amount of closeness--with enough
distance that you will be far enough away not to suffer the
acute pain of the next conflict when it develops. These marriages become progressively superficial because of the distance between then, and their superficiality increases until they are empty and meaningless; this is the main cause of
divorce today.

There are other couples who suppress their anger; they
push it down. It is quite possible to do that, but that is
worse because what couples ultimately do is to produce a
continuing state of low-key hostility. We have a word for it;
we call it resentment. In that continuing state of low-key
hostility something happens. In almost 40 years of marriage
counseling, I have noticed again and again that married people
who bottle up their anger become incapable of tenderness.
They destroy their capacity for tenderness. They may outwardly act as if they were tender, but it is not genuine.
Tenderness is destroyed by the suppression of anger in a loving relationship. What it simply means is this--that being
loving and being angry are opposite emotional conditions. Love
and anger are not themselves opposite. The opposite of love
is cold indifference, which is worse than anger. But in terms
of your emotions, being angry and being loving are irreconcil-
able. You cannot be loving when you are angry and you cannot
be angry when you are loving.

There is a third way of dealing with anger, and very few
people know about it; it is something we are only just discovering. What you have to do is to recognize the differences which have to be worked on in your disagreements. You
can clear up disagreements without them becoming conflicts,

but it is hard to do and most people do not always do it.
When your disagreements become conflict, the only thing to do
is to take anger out of it, because when you are angry you
cannot resolve a conflict. You cannot really hear the other
person because you are just waiting to fire your shot. You
cannot be understanding; you cannot be empathic when you are
angry. So you have to take the anger out, and then when you
have taken the anger out, you are back again with a disagreement. The disagreement is still there, and it can cause another disagreement and more anger unless you clear it up.
What you do is to clear up the disagreement. This is all
quite difficult, and it is the price of a warm and loving
marriage. It is the only price and the reason why so many
couples out there are in a mess is because we have never told
them this. We have never given it as a precious gift with
the insights, skills, and the tools that can make it possible.

NEGOTIATION

Negotiation is the key word. All human conflict at any level
is the same basically, whether it is the kids squabbling in
the background, or a husband and wife, or labor and management, or the impending strike, or a war. The process is always the same and the process is negotiation. The parties
must come together and they must work it through. I am
confining what I say to marriage, although the same process
exists between parents and children. The process of negotiation in marriage offers the couple three options. We
have called them capitulation, compromise, and co-existence.
Most married couples only know one of the three options and
do their best with it--the second one.

Capitulation

The first option is capitulation and that does not sound like
a nice word does it? Capitulation is interpreted by most
people as a kind of weak surrender. But that is not what
the word means; it means coming to terms, which is a good
thing to do. We believe that capitulation should always be
the first option the couple should try.

You see David and Vera there, and the distance between
us is the reality of our disagreement. Let's take an il-
lustration of this. Vera comes to me and says she is going to
a meeting next Wednesday, and she is anxious about it. She
has something to do that is not easy; she feels the need of
support and would I please come with her? I say, "But Vera,
I can't. I've got to do something else. I can't come."

Then I see a shadow of pain cross her face, and I realize
that she is my wife and I love her. I say, "What the heck,
I'll come." You see, that is capitulating. If I capitu-
lated because she nagged me, that would not be any good at
all. Capitulation can be caused by coercion. Some couples
are awfully clever at working with each other that way. But
if my capitulation is a loving gift, which it is, that is
quite different. I am giving her a gift of love by going
over to her side and leaving my own side. That is a beautiful thing; it is also a useful thing, because when I go to
that meeting next Wednesday, I am saying to myself, "You
know, this is going to pay off. Sometime soon, I'll be wanting Vera to do something, and she's much more likely to do it
because I'm doing something for her." So you see, there are
couples who get into a very nice kind of interaction in which
they are trying to do nice, positive things for each other.
That is beautiful. So much better than the marriages, and
I am afraid there are many of them, where they are always
trying to work on each other to gain something from each other.
Giving each other a loving gift through capitulation is beautiful; it is better than a bunch of flowers or a box of candy.
Capitulation should always be the first to be tried.

Compromise: A Bargaining Process

The next one is compromise and you see what happens there.
We both reach out toward each other; we try to come together
at a meeting point, and we finally do. This is bargaining
and very little has been written about bargaining in marriage. Yet bargaining goes on all the time in all marriages,
but an awful lot of it is mean and underhanded. It is a kind
of working on the other to gain advantage by withholding
things--withholding sex, withholding money, punishing, and
this kind of thing. This is all very nasty. It is far,
far better, in our judgment, to bring things out in the open,
and say, "Look, here's where I am," and we finally strike a
middle point. We both have achieved something; we both have
surrendered something, and we agree. This is the only way
most couples know in dealing with disagreement, and if they
do it negatively, then it can be a nasty business. If they
can do it positively and constructively it can be far better.

Co-existence

There is a third possibility, and the third possibility we
call co-existence. There are some situations in every relationship where the differences, for the moment, cannot be
reconciled. They have to be accepted. This was not true
in the old marriages because the husband made the decision

and the wife accepted it; it was very simple. But in the marriage of today there must be a willingness to accept difference. Because if I am not prepared to accept Vera being different from me, then the only alternative I have is to use power to make her do what I want her to do. The use of power in an intimate relationship is always destructive to the relationship. Most parents use an awful lot of power to get things done with their children, and they do not understand why they are destroying trust, confidence, and love in the relationship. I am not willing to use power. I want Vera to have her full personhood in our relationship, and if the only way that can happen is for me to live with the difference between us, which is painful for us both, we live with it. From our experience of nearly 46 years of marriage, living with these differences is all right if you have a good relationship, because we find that the hard lines between our differences begin to melt, and over and over again we have found they were reconciled.

WE ARE EMOTIONALLY MOTIVATED

I have told you some of the tools we have, some of the resources we have. We can give these things to couples and they can make a tremendous difference to their lives. I could cite hundreds and hundreds of couples whose marriages have completely changed in recent years because of these things. The question is, "How do we use these insights to give them to couples?" It is possible to have a very serious misunderstanding about this. For a long time, ever since the fourth century B.C., the Greek philosophers' concept that we are rational beings, and that we do what we do because we reason it out first and then do it, has held sway on a very wide scale. It is not true; we are emotionally motivated when it comes to relationships. We use our brains, of course, but our basic motivation is our feelings and emotions. This is going to be painful to many of you, and it has been painful to me but I had to live through it. The simple fact is that you do not change people's behavior by giving them information. Education in the academic sense has very little impact on people's behaviors--even education for marriage and family living. I want to make it as clear as possible to you because there is a more excellent way.

Information is like a cloud when it is raining, and it is raining all the time; all our life we are being rained on--information, information, information! Some of the communication people have worked out the number of pieces of information which assail us in a given day and it runs into

thousands. Most of that information has no impact upon us
at all, not even on our minds. It falls into a kind of basin
which is the mind, and most of it just pours away and is completely lost. We only retain a limited number of pieces of
new information in a given day. But we do retain some, and
the information we retain we process as knowledge.

Our minds are an amazing computer system. The human
mind can retain, I think, 3.1 trillion pieces of information.
But there is a limit. We process information as knowledge,
and that is what you do when you go to college and school.
You get a lot of information, you stuff it into your head,
and you put it in a filing system so that it is available
on instant recall. You are then qualified to go out and do
your job, and when you need a piece of information, out it
comes. Learning for knowing is that process, but learning
for living is something quite different. If you apply the
learning for knowing procedure to get people to learn for
living, you will fail because it is not enough. However,
from the knowledge which you gain from taking a course on
marriage and the family or reading a book, there are a few
bits of knowledge that filter down to the next level, and
that next level is insight. Insight is knowledge which you
have inwardly applied to your own life situation so that
you perceive it can be useful to you and will make life better
for you. All self-help books are used and internalized into
insight. Of course insight is very good. There used to be
a time when a therapist thought that all you have to do is
give the patient insight and it is all done. Not so. There
are many, many people walking around loaded with insight who
never do anything about it. I believe most self-help books,
including the ones we write, have very, very little to say.
We have asked people what happens when they read self-help
books. What happens is that they create fantasies. Insight
and fantasies are very closely related. They create fantasies of themselves having done like the book says, and
they float in that fantasy and it is lovely. But in time,
the fantasy dies away and they are back exactly where they
started.

EXPERIMENTAL ACTION

So insight does not do it; most of it is lost. However, there
are just a few drips which get through the little pipe and go
down to the next level, and the next level is experimental
action--trying it out. That is really getting someplace.
You see that you could be a better person if you behaved
differently toward your spouse, and you get up the courage

to say, "I am aware that I have been doing something that
isn't good for our relationship, and I want to tell you that
I am going to try and do something different from now on."
That is experimental action. Something is really happening
now. It is getting out of the mists of the mind and down into
the sinews. But all of experimental action does not work.
You try out something different, you choose the wrong moment,
and you get a rebuff; it does not have the effect you thought
it would have. As a matter of fact, when people go to encounter groups and see themselves in a new light or capable
of being changed, they go back and find their friends in
effect gang up to prevent them from changing. They impose
on the individual the pre-existing concepts, and it is very,
very tough for an individual to change.

So experimental action is not by any means always successful, and a lot of it is simply given up and lost again.
But there is one other little pipe, and a little bit of
experimental action drops down to the last level, which is
behavior change. Behavior change is possible. The latest
information we have from the major study on aging which has
gone on for years at the University of Southern California,
under the direction of Dr. Jim Peterson, reveals a startling
discovery that old people can change their behavior up to
the day of their death. We have been imposing our beliefs
and practices on old people that they cannot learn new behavior or change, until they believe they cannot change and
do not try.

COMMITMENT TO BEHAVIOR CHANGE

There is no limit to your capacity to change your behavior
given the necessary incentive. The primary incentive is
the motivation to do it, and then the continuing incentive
is that you are sufficiently rewarded for doing it to keep
it up. Given these possibilities, change without limit is
possible in your behavior--not change in your personality
for that is different. The personality cannot change because it is a result of your genetic inheritance and your
other conditioning, but your behavior is the way you use
your personality to achieve your goals, and particularly
in the way you achieve your goals in relationships with other
people. You can change that without limit. In fact, you
change your behavior a dozen times a day. Behavior change,
then, is the end of the process.

Now look what a long way we have come. If you stop short
on information you have achieved nothing; if you stop short
on knowledge you have achieved nothing; if you stop short

on insight you have achieved nothing; if the experimental
action is unsuccessful and discontinued you have achieved
nothing. Only if you have produced a <u>commitment</u> to behavior
change, have you done anything to change the life of that
person, or to change the life of a marriage relationship for
the better. So you see, we are all living in a kind of dream
in which we think that pouring out information is making a
difference to people and it is not. What do we do? The only
thing to do is that we must learn to structure environments
in which change can take place; we do not have any such environments at the moment in our culture but the promise is
tremendous.

Understanding Couple Interaction within the Family Complex

Dr. Jack V. Buerkle, Donald P.
Eckard, Rhonda Jacobs, and
Jay Bolick
Department of Sociology
Temple University

THE DELICATE BALANCE

It grew slowly, almost imperceptibly out of the Philosophy
of Enlightenment of the seventeenth and eighteenth centuries,
this element of individualism which has so affected our lives
today. Certainly, by the time the Pilgrims arrived at Ply-
mouth Rock to exercise their religious freedom, they were
infused with it. Although their humanism seemed muted under
the formalities of a Calvinistic theology, it too, was there.
So, also, was a pragmatic rationalism beginning to intrude
on their sacred view of family life (Calhoun, 1945).

By the time the American colonists had disassociated themselves from Great Britain and created the Declaration of
Independence, the Constitution, and the Bill of Rights, individualism had been asserted widely in the areas of life,
liberty, and property. Although theological concerns, and
their emphasis upon the individual's obligations to the family group, were still strongly evident at the birth of the
United States, the progressive development of individual
rights within the family was evident. While the primary
American founding documents make specific reference to the
rights of "the people," specific intent was applied only to
men in many instances. From this perspective, all Americans
had certain basic rights, but the major rights of individual
choice and leadership were assigned to men. Women and children, by theological edict, were to follow and obey. The
basic rights of action for the family were a man's; his obligations were to protect and maintain his kin.

Those agencies and institutions external to the family,
e.g., the church, the law, and public opinion, supported this
pattern. It is logical to assume that overt family strife
and/or divorce would be at a minimum within such a system.
Generally, with only a few exceptions, men's rights of familial decision making were formally preeminent, and women and
children knew and accepted it. This made a simple and

111

predictable relationship compared to what we experience in
American families today.

Although the seeds of the "democratic-equalitarian" family were being sown within the Colonial family, it took the
Nineteenth Amendment in 1920 to establish certain rights for
women in a democracy. Women's roles in conquering the wilder-
ness, settling the frontier, and the phenomena of urbanization and industrialization have moved us fully into a new age
of family interaction. Several things have occurred which
make the rules and roles different and more complicated than
the patriarchal system of old.

Over the past few years, individualism has impacted upon
the family setting in full force. With the diminution of
external sacred and secular restraints upon family conduct and
form, we have experienced familial disarray, conflict, and
disruption at a record pace.

Today, it is likely that all, or most, members of families will insist upon what they consider to be their "rights."
After long delays, women and children are exercising their
individualist options guaranteed by the Bill of Rights. That
the rights are there for all to enjoy is not being questioned.
But, from an interactional point of view, what is behind this
family turmoil?

To begin with, it is not individualism, as such, which
lies at the heart of the problem. More precisely, we believe
it is the timing and amount of individualistic expression
which can result in either amity or discord.

The pursuit of happiness was a Declaration-of-Independence-
guaranteed right, and researcher Glick (1975) sees this reflected in the fact that married couples are less likely to
remain together today, than in the past, if they see themselves as "unhappy." But rights also imply obligations. When
is my right accepted as an obligation to my mate? When, and
why, is it not accepted? Thus, the communication patterns
of couples and other family members are set in a delicate
balance. Aldous (1977) has stated, "Families are generally
groups whose members trust that their needs will be met, eventually, by someone."

When working with or studying families today, a basic
concern is being sensitive to certain communication patterns
among family members. Whether we are dealing with couples
(married or unmarried), parent-child relationships, or sibling groups, the problem is there. We must assume (at least
the possibility of) a democratic-equalitarian set of expectations within the group, where each member believes he or she
is entitled to have personal rights perceived and acted upon
favorably. Like no preceding age, this condition requires
that group members be sensitive to the expectations of their

partners. Where this is not evident, the family group is weaker, or dissolves altogether.

Later in this article, we will describe how the Temple University Family Study Unit is attacking part of this complex problem, by attempting to understand and predict how and why couple relationships grow stronger or weaker. In order to see the rationale for our present direction, let us first review, briefly, other relevant research efforts in this area.

AVENUES OF RESEARCHING FAMILY INTERACTION

Studies of family relationships have focused upon both process and outcomes, i.e., on what occurs in family interaction versus what results from that process. Looking specifically at married couples, the most intensively studied relationship within the family, we note varying methods of approaching the problem.

Blood and Wolfe's (1960) investigation of Detroit area marriages was a study of outcomes of marital interaction, and it heralded a large number of projects which have used either exchange theory or its derivative, "resource theory," as its base. The general assumption behind these positions deals with the "power one individual has to influence or change the behavior of another." Here, the marriage partner who exhibits the greatest number of resources would have the greatest power within the family (Aldous, 1977).

Apart from problems of assuming an inequality in power relations among couples, a large number of these studies rely upon interviews with only one member of the couple (Blood and Wolfe interviewed 909 <u>wives</u>) to get information concerning the <u>pair</u> relationship.

Further, exchange theory analyses of couple relationships have been justifiably criticized on the assumption that they deal with family couple interaction as though the persons were merchant and customer, or two players in a game where one player must lose (Sprey, 1972). Much of the family or couple decision-making research has made such assumptions (Ekeh, 1974).

Since the later 1950's, an increasing number of family or couple interaction process studies have appeared. Most of these have, understandably, inspected conflict-management processes among family members, particularly married couples. The general belief is that what goes on in the motivational and communication systems of husbands and wives is vital to their marriage relationship, and, consequently, to any wider nuclear family involvement they may have. By attempting to focus upon interaction process, the observer can study the

plans of action of the pair, and seek to determine the likelihood of amity or conflict. When humans interact, conflict
is inevitable, almost ubiquitous. But, what kind of conflict?
Destructive? Constructive? With what kinds of couples?
What kinds of situations?

The critical relationship of marital conflict, and its
resolution, to couples and consequently, family stability,
has not gone unnoticed by family researchers. Many reject
the "outcomes" approach to family interaction, because they
see it as inadequate, "cold-blooded," and having an ex post
factum stance. Often, they conclude that exchange theory and
related positions are of little assistance in understanding
the specific interactive facts of couple and family life.
Turning to interaction techniques, they have utilized, basically, two approaches: (1) questionnaires depicting couple
conflict, and (2) simulated situations, peopled by actors,
or the research subjects themselves.

Although questionnaire techniques have the advantage of
being economical in time, effort, and cost, they are seldom
valid measures of couple, or family, interaction. A common
problem with these devices is that they depend upon the reading skills of the person exposed to them.

There are other difficulties when questionnaires have been
employed in attempts to gauge interaction process. Perhaps
the most serious, common error occurs when virtually all interactional validity and significance are cancelled by the
ways in which collected data are analyzed (Aldous, 1977;
Glick & Gross, 1975). Perhaps the most critical blow happens
when almost all "process" is taken from the analysis by such
techniques as summing individual scores through situations,
or summing "win scores" through situations (Olson & Ryder,
1970).

Human interaction process occurs within situations, not
as some central summative tendency. Role balances and expectations change for people from situation to situation. More
importantly, if interaction process is to proceed smoothly
for people from situation to situation, there must be agreement on frame of reference (agreement on plans of action, or
how to proceed) among the persons in that situation. While
human personality reflects some strong continuity from situation to situation, certainly our understanding of a couple
or familial relationship can be sharpened by recognizing that
individual role demands vary from situation to situation, and
from time to time.

The use of simulated interaction situations becomes a
trade-off between being able to depict somewhat realistic
couple conflict settings under variably controlled conditions versus the problems associated with contrived events
which may not elicit usual or typical responses from the

subjects. We utilize such simulations in our own work because we feel they are more realistic and more adaptable to
actual familial interaction than even questionnaires which
try to capture interaction. With simulated situations, the
subjects can respond to ongoing action sequences as a couple
or family, and discuss potential resolution of conflict, or
they can list their own conflict areas and then simulate attempts at resolution (Glick & Gross, 1975).

The work which is described in the next section is grounded on the research efforts of Buerkle and his associates at
Yale University (Buerkle, 1960; Buerkle, Anderson & Badgley,
1961; Buerkle & Badgley, 1959). Although the Yale project
used questionnaires, it did attempt to deal with married
couples as couples dealing with conflict problems in specific,
realistic situations.

The original work was, to some extent, a reaction to the
Burgess and Locke-type marriage adjustment scales, who base
their assessments upon a summation of traits which had previously been correlated with rates of marital success. By
comparing the responses of 186 couples belonging to religious-
affiliated couples' clubs within the New Haven, Connecticut,
areas to those of couples from the marriage counseling section of the Margaret Sanger Research Bureau, New York, we
were able to develop a technique using couples' scores, where
responses were made to specific role conflict and conflict
of interest situations involving couple or familial interaction.

In short, we found that the New York couples (who pro-
fessed marital difficulties) performed significantly differently on the couple interaction battery than did those who
had claimed no special interactive problems. The "in trouble"
couples displayed considerably less agreement on frame of
reference on the test. Indirect measures indicated that they
were less accurate in role-taking (or empathy) than the New
Haven couples.

Certainly, the findings did help in beginning to establish the validity of the Yale Marital Interaction Battery as
a paper-and-pencil couple interaction test. However, a number of problems remained. In spite of its virtues, the Yale
Battery was a questionnaire, paper-and-pencil test, and it
derived only an indirect measure of one of the most important human communicative facts--role-taking (empathy).

TEMPLE UNIVERSITY STUDIES IN FAMILY INTERACTION

Within the past two years, we have begun an extension of the
Yale work within the Department of Sociology's new Interaction Laboratory at Temple University. The laboratory was

designed to accommodate the widest possible range of small group experiments and set up expressly to expand what we had learned in New Haven.

There is a large experimental room which can be the locus of simulated or real interaction for an entire family. Observations of this room are possible through one-way glass or TV cameras feeding into a master control room. There are twelve smaller experimental rooms, designed for one or two people, and six of these rooms have decision-making equipment. Here, a subject can indicate a response on the equipment which transmits the response to the control room where it is recorded on tape.

All rooms are equipped with TV monitors, and TV cameras are focused on the subjects. A switchboard in the control room allows the experimenter to feed audio and/or video signals to any or all of the rooms. All communications can be recorded on either videotape, or a standard four-track studio recorder. Our present work employs only the smaller experimental rooms, and we generally deal with one couple at a time, although we have the capacity to see three pairs simultaneously.

Although the Yale work utilized only married couples, we have included heterosexual pairs who are unmarried as well. Our definition of a couple is that a pair define themselves as such. Some couples we see have known each other for as short a time as three weeks; others have been together for fifty years. We widened our concept of the couple so that we might be able eventually to make a number of important tests to determine how marital dyads compare in decision-making and communication patterns with those that range from teenage dating couples to cohabiting, non-married adults.

Certainly, the great variability in alternate life styles in America today begs this kind of question. Further, if contributions are to be made to couple and family stability, such information could prove of great value.

Couples who participate in our program spend about forty minutes in the laboratory. They are placed in the small experimental rooms described above. The presence of audio-visual pickups are pointed out, so that the couples are not misled, and to date, we have not experienced a refusal to participate. We are also confident that the experiment is so designed that the equipment does not interfere with or affect the information we are seeking.

The couple is asked to complete a background questionnaire with the usual demographic data, in addition to information about the nature and extent of the relationship they have with each other. These are used as control variables to give us some idea, comparatively, of what "kinds" of people are in these various relationships.

The couples are read a set of standard instructions by the experimenter, which alerts them to the decision-making equipment they will use, and in general orients them to the procedure. The couple, in separate rooms, views a series of seventeen videotaped skits depicting typical problems encountered by people living together. In each skit there is a conflict of interest between the man and woman; however, they are constructed in such a way as to give both some legitimate grounds for argument. The couple is not able to communicate and, therefore, cannot influence or prejudice each other's opinion when called upon to evaluate the merits of each argument.

The skits were filmed in a home setting, and attempt to present as realistic a situation as possible, both in the acting and the content of the conflicts. We are confident that our skits capture the essence of genuine conflicts in couple relationships, as our subjects have repeatedly assured us "they had experienced the same argument last week!" An example of the type of conflict skits we present to our couples is:

Wife: I think we should buy a second car so I can get out more often while you are at work.

Husband: A second car?!! We can hardly afford one car now. My job with the electric company is in jeopardy and the price of gas is supposed to go to a dollar a gallon!

Wife: I realize that, but I'm stuck in the house all day and have to depend on you to take me any place. I can't do anything until you come home!

These sequences, which our subjects view, represent problems which are typically mentioned by marriage counselors, clergy, psychologists, etc., as common in troubled relationships. Our skits involve conflict over money, child rearing, allocation of time in the relationship, insensitivity, and so on. A wide range of problematic behavior in a relationship is covered.

The subject couples are asked a series of questions after viewing each skit. They are unable to hear or see each other's responses. The questions follow:

To each: Suppose you were faced with this problem; with whom would you agree and how strongly?

At this point, each subject can indicate agreement, with two
degrees of intensity, with either the man or the woman in the
skit. Their decisions are recorded on tape in the control
room. The rest of the questions are answered in the same
way:

> To the man: Suppose _____ (his partner's name)
>   was faced with this problem; with
>   whom would she agree and how strongly?
>
> To the woman: Suppose _____ (her partner's name)
>   was faced with this problem; with
>   whom would he agree and how strongly?
>
> To the man: With whom do you suppose _____ (his
>   partner's name) thought you would
>   agree, and how strongly?
>
> To the woman: With whom do you suppose _____ (her
>   partner's name) thought you would
>   agree, and how strongly?

Thus, for every skit, the subjects are each asked three questions. The information which is supplied in every set of
answers can be found in the following interaction matrix:

Male's Response   Female's Response

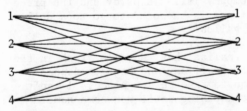

Strong agreement with the man in the skit is indicated by
"1"; "2" indicates agreement with the man in the skit; "3"
indicates agreement with the woman in the skit; "4" indicates strong agreement with the woman in the skit.

With this model, there are sixteen possible interpersonal
combinations, e.g., a "1"-"4" indicates, that in a specific
sequence, the male subject strongly agreed with the man in
the skit, while the female subject strongly agreed with the
woman in the skit. This obviously would be an indication
of a deep disagreement on the frame of reference, or lack
of consensus, in that situation. The second and third question in each sequence establishes the couple's ability to
take the role of the other (empathy) in the specific

situations, while the last questions reveal the extent to which there is an accurate appraisal of the perception of one to the other.

A scoring system is employed to form an overall picture of the couple's interaction regarding the skit. The details need not be presented here; however, we take care not to obscure the dynamics of the interaction with meaningless numbers. To the extent that crucial aspects of scoring systems are abstracted, they lose significance for the researcher and the counselor.

The sequences which we present to our subjects also take into account external factors. We recognize, and build into our skits, the fact that a marriage dyad is not something which exists in isolation. As a couple, they are influenced by pressures originating outside of their relationship. There are frequently varying role demands external to the marital relationship, and these must be present in such skits, if they are to be representative of actual situations. Often, elements of the larger family complex can be important, or intrude upon the couple interaction. Demands of the individual's occupation or friendships are also crucial in the couple's relationship.

The ability of a marriage partner to be empathetic to these various requirements emerges clearly in our series. This element of empathy is increasing in importance as the trend toward individualism in relationships accelerates, and our families begin to look more and more like voluntary associations.

Many studies of family interaction have centered upon either trying to determine the intensity or extent of communication within the family, or attempting to increase it. Yet, in many respects, this misses the point. It is not simply a matter of how much communication, but also the quality and nature of the communication. It is the pursuit of these latter elements which guides our work.

We are not interested in taking a moral posture on specific issues; our program does not attempt to establish a "right" answer to conflicts in couple relationships. Rather, we believe that the techniques we employ can facilitate stability in the relationship, regardless of our particular values. We seek to generate communication within the couple, which allows for a resolution on their terms.

We have begun our present research by inspecting the workings of couple interaction. The couple, typically married, is clearly the cornerstone of family stability; the greater its stability, the greater the chances for a strong family unit. If it were weakened due to poor communication and confusion over roles, the family, as it has traditionally been organized, is headed toward more severe problems. With

fewer and fewer social constraints governing the couple's relationship, it becomes even more critical for them to construct a durable communication pattern from within. To reach
this end, we have attempted to isolate the variables, or constellation of variables, which seem to be associated with
stable, communicative relationships. We need to examine
other pertinent questions, such as what happens in dual career
families when women are no longer content to suppress their
own ambitions? What are the results of these kinds of changes
on the male role, and how is this new role integrated? What
other social characteristics combine to reveal stable patterns of marriage? At Temple, we have begun to organize a
panel study to follow our undergraduates as they enter and
leave relationships, so that our data are not simply cross-
sectional.

Finally, some of the most challenging aspects of this
work concern its utility for the diagnostic and counseling
phases of our interest in family stability. We believe that
our skits can serve as a useful focal point for couple counseling. By presenting these simulated conflicts, the couples
have the opportunity to interact realistically, and at the
same time, avoid the emotional investment inherent in their
own "real-life" situations. Standing "outside" of the situations in our skits allows a troubled couple to discuss conflict in a more objective manner. By focusing on contrived
conflict, seeking agreement between themselves will be much
easier, and at the same time, the lessons can be learned.
Hence, we believe that the Interaction Battery developed at
Temple University can serve as a valuable tool in the hands
of family counselors who are attempting to generate increased and accurate communication.

REFERENCES

Aldous, J. Family interaction patterns. *Annual Review of
Sociology*, 1977, *3*, 105.

Blood, R. O., & Wolfe, D. M. *Husbands and wives: The
dynamics of married living*. Glencoe, Illinois: The
Free Press, 1960.

Buerkle, J. V. Self attitudes and marital adjustment.
Merrill-Palmer Quarterly, 1960, *6*, 114-123.

Buerkle, J. V., Anderson, T. R., & Badgley, R. Altruism,
role conflict, and marital adjustment: A factor
analysis of marital interaction. *Marriage and Family
Living*, 1961, *23*, 20-26.

Buerkle, J. V., & Badgley, R. Couple role-taking: The Yale Marital Interaction Battery. *Marriage and Family Living,* 1959, *21,* 53-58.

Calhoun, A. W. *A social history of the American family.* New York: Barnes & Noble, Inc., 1945.

Ekeh, P. P. *Social exchange theory: The two traditions.* Cambridge, Massachusetts: Harvard University Press, 1974.

Glick, B. R., & Gross, S. J. Marital interaction and marital conflict: A critical evaluation of current research strategies. *Journal of Marriage and the Family,* 1975, *37,* 505-512.

Glick, P. C. A demographer looks at American families. *Journal of Marriage and the Family,* 1975, *37,* 15-26.

Olson, D. H., & Ryder, C. Inventory of Marital Conflicts (IMC): An experimental interaction procedure. *Journal of Marriage and the Family,* 1970, *32,* 443-448.

Sprey, J. Family power structure: A critical comment. *Journal of Marriage and the Family,* 1972, *34,* 325-338.

Personal Major Events and Family Strengths of Retired Couples

Dr. Michael MacLean
School of Social Work
McGill University

INTRODUCTION

Family strengths are an important aspect of successful family development. If these strengths are not created, a couple
is likely to begin life together in a weakened state, and
this will probably lead to the creation of a weak family in
the early years. If these strengths are created but not maintained, it is unlikely that the family will provide adequate
sources of support and growth for its members. In this case,
the family members probably will have little or no commitment to the unit. If these strengths are created and maintained, but not developed throughout the life span of the family, it is unlikely that the family will continue to be a cohesive unit. A family that does not continue to build on
the interaction between members will probably become weakened
structurally or emotionally. Therefore, it is important to
consider the significance of the development of family strengths
in all time periods during the life span of the family.
    There are times during the life span of a family when
its internal strengths are challenged more than at other times.
It could be argued, for example, that in times of crisis, the
internal strength of the family is a major component which
mobilizes forces to keep the unit functioning well enough to
resolve the crisis. It could also be argued that periods of
constant pressure offer considerable challenge to the strengths
of the family. It is probable that the internal strength of
a family is a significant factor in successfully coping with
extended pressure. Therefore, it could be important, from a
practice or research perspective, to focus on specific periods
of family life where there may be more pressures or crises
than at other times.

RETIREMENT AS A CRITICAL PERIOD IN LIFE

One of the critical periods in which the married couple is
faced with many incidents which contribute to considerable
pressure is the time following retirement. During retirement, which itself has been referred to as a crisis (Atchley,
1971; Miller, 1965), the aging couple has to deal with many
significant life changes, such as lower income, declining
physical abilities, increased leisure time, a new role in life,
the possibility of widowhood, and the inevitability of their
own deaths (Kerckhoff, 1964; Lipman, 1961; Streib, 1965).
Four of the ten most stressful life events (death of spouse,
death of a close family member, personal illness or injury,
retirement) can be expected to happen with greater frequency
in the retirement years than at other times in married life
(Holmes & Rahe, 1967). As a result of these events and because retirement tends to focus on the husband and wife relationship more than in earlier years (Troll, 1971), it is
evident that the family strengths of retired couples will be
challenged considerably. The strengths, adaptability, and
individuality of these people may be of critical significance
in helping them cope with these pressures (Bloom & Monro,
1972).

Retired couples who have a strong relationship may be
able to cope more realistically with the traumas they will
face in old age. However, for those without a strong relationship, there may be considerable difficulty in coping with
the stress events typical of this period of life. Therefore,
a significant contribution to practice and research with older
couples would be the development of techniques which retired
couples could use to build their family strengths.

COMMUNICATION IN THE RETIREMENT PERIOD

It has recently been found that one of the eight basic dimensions of family mental health is clear communication within
the family (Barnhill, 1979). It has also been noted that one
important aspect of the older marriage, which has been somewhat neglected in research, is the communication patterns of
older couples (Atchley, 1979). As communication may be an
extremely important element in an intimate relationship, and
as the retired couple probably has more time to talk to each
other than at other points in their marriage, it may be important to develop communication as a family strength to facilitate coping with the stresses of old age.

Communication Patterns

In order to develop communication as a family strength, it is necessary to determine the existing degree of communication within the relationship. There are probably many communication levels within relationships, but for the purposes of this paper, three communication patterns of retired couples will be briefly differentiated: open, neutral, and closed communication patterns.

The open communication pattern is one in which the couple communicates thoughts and feelings about most, if not all, important points. A couple may not necessarily discuss everything they do or think, but this would be because they choose not to talk about something, rather than feeling they could not talk about it. The important criterion of this communication pattern is that a couple feels they can talk about anything they regard as important. Couples who have been communicating in an open way for most of their married life will probably continue to do so.

The neutral communication pattern is one in which the couple communicates relatively well, but primarily about "safe" topics. This couple tends to discuss positive or happy events rather than negative ones. For example, they would more likely talk about a job promotion or a child's accomplishment than about losing a job or a child's failure to achieve.

The closed communication pattern is one in which there is very little communication apart from that on superficial topics. In this pattern, the couple tends not to discuss their feelings or thoughts about important happenings in their life.

Implications of Various Communication Patterns

The family strengths dimension of couples who have an open communication pattern is quite strong. Their strengths will probably continue to develop within the input of researchers or practitioners in the helping professions. They probably will deal with the changes they experience as older couples, and, in all likelihood, these changes will be regarded as challenges. The relationship should grow in even greater intimacy as a result of dealing with these challenges.

The family relationships of couples who have neutral or closed communication patterns could be significantly weakened by the changes old age may force upon them. If these couples cannot, or do not, communicate about such significant changes as retirement, death, or illness, their relationship may deteriorate. Therefore, it seems appropriate for those working with retired couples to try to improve the communication patterns of these couples so that the family strengths which they do have will continue to develop, rather than remain static in the retirement years.

The task of trying to improve the communication patterns of retired couples is a major one, in that it is extremely difficult to change a pattern of communication which has been established over an extended period of time. The purpose of this paper is to present and discuss a model designed to increase the communication level of couples who have developed neutral or closed patterns of communication during their married life. This model focuses on ways which communication can be developed within couples who have not had a strong communication base during their marriage. It is directed towards practitioners and researchers working with elderly couples, as a means of facilitating, through interpersonal communication, the development of greater family strengths of retired couples.

PERSONAL MAJOR EVENTS AND THE COMMUNICATION OF RETIRED COUPLES

The basis of the model of communication for retired couples is the concept of personal major events (MacLean, 1976). This concept focuses on the important events of an individual's life, as he or she sees them, allowing him or her to state which events have been most influential. As these events are individually elicited and therefore subjective, the concept of personal major events is different from the concept of life stress events, which focuses on an established number of stressful events which, theoretically, have similar significance for most people (Dohrenwend & Dohrenwend, 1974; Guttman, 1978).

The personal major events model of communication for retired couples suggests that a couple who can discuss the important events of their past may be able to communicate thoughts and feelings about the personal major events they expect to experience in the future. By discussing these future events, they can, directly or indirectly, prepare themselves in a philosophical, psychological, and practical way for dealing with them. This preparation could lead to greater communication within the couple, which may, in turn, lead to a stronger relationship, and help them face future major events.

It is not an easy task to reach a point where husbands and wives can openly discuss the personal major events of their pasts. As this may be especially difficult for couples who have established a pattern of neutral or closed communication, it would be unrealistic to suggest discussion of these events without offering guidelines. For these couples, it

would be useful to initiate discussion about topics which are
not threatening to them as individuals.

"Remember When" Events

The dynamics of this model of communication are such that
couples begin to talk about events which, in fact, they have
already been talking about for a long time--even couples who
have developed a neutral or closed pattern of communication
(see Figure 1). In this exercise of greater communication,
the first thing that couples talk about is neutral "remember
when" events. These events are those which frequently are
discussed when adult children return to the family home. Such
events tend to be neutral for the couple, because they focus
primarily on topics which are external to them. These tend
to be children-related events, humorous incidents, or minor
incidents which are not too intimate for the couple. Examples of these events are embarrassing statements made by
the children in the presence of other adults, or humorous
incidents related to such occasions as the first boyfriend or
girlfriend of the children. As these "remember when" events
often produce laughter (and perhaps minor embarrassment for
the child who is the subject of the reminiscence), they serve
a therapeutic value for the family during a time when it is
changing from a self-contained unit to one which is becoming
increasingly extended. These events also facilitate conversation between the couple about incidents which are easy and
enjoyable for them to discuss.

Couple-Related Events

By discussing "remember when" events, a retired couple may be
encouraged to discuss more intimate couple-related events.
Couple-related events are those which have influenced the
couple as a unit, in that they may have required some cooperative effort to resolve. These events may have been positive or negative, and could be related to child-rearing incidents, job pleasure or difficulties, or social events in
which both husband and wife were involved. These events could
be relatively minor, thus encouraging the couple to share
past experiences in which both contributed to a satisfactory
resolution of the events. These events should serve as a
stimulus for the couple to discuss examples of mutual support. Hopefully, the couple will be encouraged as such
reminiscences remind them of how they have cooperated in resolving difficult situations in the past. The couple should
also regard discussion of these relatively intimate couple-
related events as an indication that they are developing deeper levels of communication than they had previously experienced.

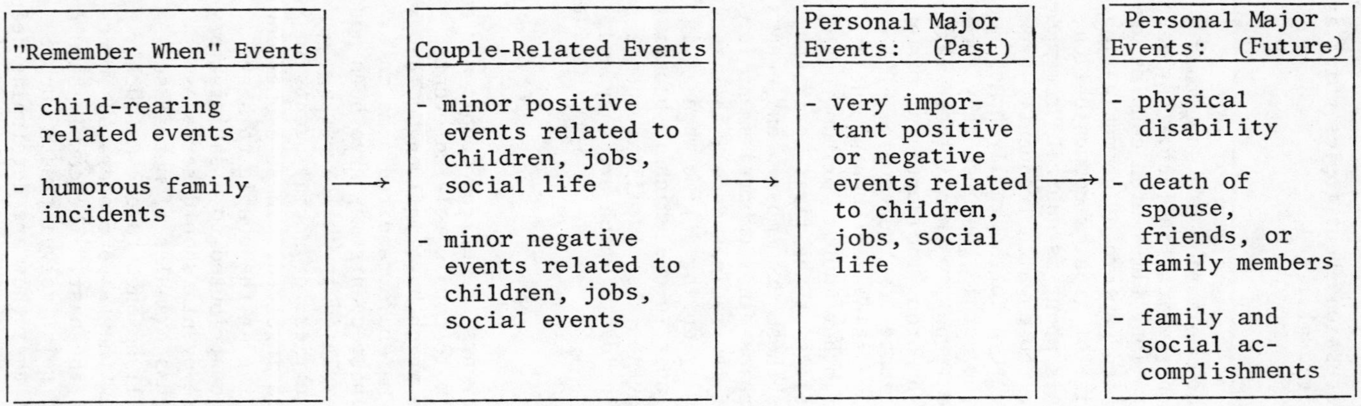

"Remember When" Events	Couple-Related Events	Personal Major Events: (Past)	Personal Major Events: (Future)
- child-rearing related events - humorous family incidents	- minor positive events related to children, jobs, social life - minor negative events related to children, jobs, social events	- very important positive or negative events related to children, jobs, social life	- physical disability - death of spouse, friends, or family members - family and social accomplishments

Figure 1

Personal Major Events Communication Model
of Retired Couples

Personal Major Events of the Past

Having been able to discuss couple-related events, a couple
may be able to talk about some of their personal major events.
While it still may not be easy to talk about these events, the
fact that they have begun communicating about certain aspects
of their earlier life should facilitate discussion of some
of their personal major events. It is not expected that the
individuals will begin immediately to discuss the most important events of their lives. This is extremely difficult,
even for couples with open communication patterns. However,
by focusing on some of the personal major events of their
lives and by discussing them, the couple may develop better
communication patterns than they had previously. This increased communication can contribute to greater family strength
in the retired couple.

Discussion of the personal major events of husband and
wife should allow the couple to realize how much they have
contributed to each other during their marriage. As all the
personal major events of each person will not necessarily
include the spouse, this communication technique also encourages the individual to realize that he or she has managed
to deal with some major life events alone. This realization
may facilitate the development of individual strengths which
come from acknowledging that one can deal with some important
aspects of life alone. The sharing of these personal major
events may also contribute to a couple getting to know each
other more intimately than they had previously. Therefore,
the discussion of personal major events by a retired couple
contributes to building strengths within the individual and
within the relationship, as well as to discovering new knowledge about oneself and each other.

Personal Major Events of the Future

The natural extension of the personal major events of the
past is the discussion of future personal major events, many
of which may be negative as Holmes and Rahe (1967) have indicated (e.g., physical disability; death of spouse, family
members, or friends). This model of communication, through
the progression from family events to couple-related events
to personal events, facilitates the discussion of these negative events. This communication can be therapeutic to both
husband and wife, in that the discussion of such events as
the death of one's spouse or oneself may alleviate considerable fear which each person may have regarding the consequences of these happenings. As a result of this discussion,
practical plans, as well as philosophical and psychological
preparation, can be made for this event. These aspects of

preparation may help the couple think about this and other
events which are likely to occur during the retirement years.

The personal major events model of communication may contribute to building family strengths of retired couples. As
retirement is an important time for couples to have a strong
and supportive relationship, this model may be a significant
contribution to the maintenance and development of family
strengths at a time when this characteristic is of critical
importance to the couple.

RESEARCH AND PRACTICAL IMPLICATIONS OF THE PERSONAL MAJOR EVENTS MODEL OF COMMUNICATION

The personal major events model of communication has implications for research and practice with retired couples. As
the research implications are closely related to practice,
this discussion will focus on the practical application of
this model.

In a practical sense, social workers, medical practitioners, marriage counselors, and other professionals working directly with the retired couple could use this model
to develop greater communication within the couple. Improved communication may lead, in the positive sense, to a
greater feeling of solidarity against, and acceptance of,
some of the difficult aspects of the old age portion of the
life cycle. It could also contribute to the development of
a more philosophical approach to various aspects of past
and future life. This type of professional intervention
could, therefore, contribute to a stronger marriage in the
present and a developing relationship for the future, in
that the retired couple would be able to communicate feelings
and thoughts about what the future may hold for them. Such
an interaction between husband and wife in retirement may
increase the potential for both to achieve the ego integrity
that Erikson (1968) has postulated as an important component
of the final psychosocial stage of adulthood.

An extended aspect of this model is that the couple may
generalize their improved communication to interaction with
their children or other family members. That is, they may
become more open about sharing thoughts and ideas about the
past, present, and future with the important people in their
lives. This may be extremely therapeutic for the couple and
their family, as it may contribute to developing greater family strengths within the family relationships. As the retirement years are a time when the quantity and quality of
family relationships may be affected adversely (Sussman,
1978), this model may be an instrument to influence adult
family relationships in a positive way.

The personal major events model of communication may also serve to facilitate discussion with the very old population-- those people aged 75 years and over (Neugarten, 1974). Butler (1963) suggests that the elderly often use a life review process to integrate various aspects of life. If success- ful, this integration can be therapeutic, in that an individ- ual can face the final years of life optimistically. This model of communication can be used by practitioners as the starting point for the life review exercise. By focusing on the personal major events of life, the individual has a pre- cise and productive way to begin the life review process, as opposed to trying to initiate this process without guide- lines.

It is important to consider a cautionary note about the practical use of the personal major events model of communi- cation with retired couples. In focusing on the major events of one's life, it may seem, to some persons, that their lives have been failures. This could contribute to guilt, anxiety, and depression which may be very difficult for the elderly person to accept. The individual who views his or her life as mostly negative and, therefore, a waste, may need profes- sional help to deal with this self-acknowledgement. This would defeat the purpose for which the communication model was intended. Therefore, the model should be used with dis- cretion. It is most useful with individuals who are rela- tively strong, in terms of mental health, but who are having communication difficulties. If it were used with this kind of elderly couples, it should be of considerable value to them, their families, and practitioners who are trying to improve the quality of their married life in the retirement years.

Apart from this cautionary note, which also applies to the life review process (Butler & Lewis, 1973), the model provides a practical framework for helping couples develop a more open pattern of communication in order to deal with stress in their later years. In this way, the personal major events model of communication contributes to the development of strengths within the family, the couple, and the individ- ual.

REFERENCES

Atchley, R. C. Retirement and leisure participation: con- tinuity or crisis? *The Gerontologist*, 1971, *11*, 13-17.

Atchley, R. C. Issues in retirement research. *The Geron- tologist*, 1979, *19*, 44-54.

Barnhill, L. R. Healthy family systems. *The Family Co-ordinator*, 1979, *28*, 94-100.

Butler, R. N. The life review: An interpretation of remin-iscence in the aged. *Psychiatry*, 1963, *26*, 65-76.

Butler, R. N., & Lewis, M. I. *Aging and mental health*.
St. Louis: The C. V. Mosby Company, 1973.

Bloom, M., & Monro, A. Social work and the aging family.
The Family Coordinator, 1972, *21*, 103-115.

Dohrenwend, B. S., & Dohrenwend, B. P. (Eds.). *Stressful life events: Their nature and effects*. New York:
John Wiley & Sons, 1974.

Erikson, E. *Identity: Youth and Crisis*. London: Faber
& Faber Limited, 1968.

Guttman, D. Life events and decision-making by older adults.
The Gerontologist, 1978, *18*, 462-467.

Holmes, T. H., & Rahe, R. H. The Social Readjustment Rating
Scale. *Journal of Psychosomatic Research*, 1967, *11*,
213-218.

Kerckhoff, R. C. Husband-wife expectations and reactions
to retirement. *Journal of Gerontology*, 1964, *19*, 510-
516.

Lipman, A. Role conceptions and morale of couples in re-tirement. *Journal of Gerontology*, 1961, *16*, 267-271.

MacLean, M. J. *Major life events, life satisfaction and
retirement reactions*. Unpublished doctoral disserta-tion, University of London, London, England, 1976.

Miller, S. J. The social dilemma of the aging leisure
participant. In A. M. Rose & W. Peterson (Eds.),
Older people and their social worlds. Philadelphia:
F. A. Davis Company, 1965.

Neugarten, B. L. Age groups in American society and the
rise of the young-old. *The Annals of the American
Academy of Political Social Science*, 1974, *415*, 187-
198.

Streib, G. F.   International generations: Perspectives
of the two generations on the older parent.   *Journal of
Marriage and the Family*, 1965, *27*, 469-476.

Sussman, M. B.   The family life of old people.   In R. Bin-
stock & E. Shanas (Eds.), *Handbook of aging and the
social sciences*.   New York: Van Nostrand Reinhold
Company, 1978.

Troll, L. E.   The family of later life: A decade review.
Journal of Marriage and the Family, 1971, *33*, 263-290.

III. PARENT-CHILD RELATIONSHIPS

Because most families have children, the parent-child relationship attracts a good deal of attention in any study of family life. Certainly attempts to build family strengths recognize the importance of effective parenting and the mutual satisfaction that arises from a good interaction between parent and child.

Dr. Benjamin Spock's article gives an overview of some of the societal influences on child rearing today. He offers suggestions for parents and for professionals who help children and their parents.

The birth of the first child is a very special time in families. Dr. Donna Sollie and Dr. Brent Miller report on a study in which new parents were asked how the baby had affected their lives. Parents reported emotional benefits and enrichment, as well as physical and emotional strains. Suggestions for parenthood and family life education classes are made.

Dr. David Elkind proposes a model of parent-child interaction based on a constructivist perspective. The parent-child contracts of Freedom/Responsibility, Achievement/Support, and Loyalty/Commitment are examined as they operate in infancy, childhood, adolescence, and between adult children and their aging parents.

Peopleteaching involves helping children gain certain life arts and skills which make them more humane. Dr. Charles Smith explores body awareness, sensory awareness, emotional development, affiliation and friendship, conflict and cooperation, and kindness and affection as arenas for peopleteaching.

Dr. Barbara Forisha presents the thesis that healthy adults combine love, power, and the ability to cope with conflict productively. The theory and research relating childhood environments with adult development are reviewed.

Jean I. Clarke presents *Self Esteem: A Family Affair*, a model designed to invite parents to improve their own self-esteem and to challenge their children to claim high self-esteem. It is based on ideas from Transactional Analysis, Values Clarification, and Andragogy.

What About Our Children?

Dr. Benjamin Spock
Rogers, Arkansas

INTRODUCTION

"What About Our Children?" I would like to begin by saying
I am not one of those who believes that the family is dis-
appearing. It is true that some people prefer nowadays to
live together without the benefits of the marriage ceremony.
I believe this does no harm to society; I think a few people
have always lived that way, but now we are more frank and
accept it more openly. My own view is that those people who
are fearful of getting married, who feel marriage discourages
a good relationship, will find that it is just as difficult
to maintain an unmarried relationship as it is to maintain
a married relationship.

It is slightly more serious that today many people have
decided not to have any children. The statement which I
hear most often is, "I don't want to bring children into a
society that is as sick as this one." In my own experience,
a lot of these people who, at a youthful age, said they were
not going to have children, and a certain number of those
who said they were never going to get married, quietly after
awhile do get married, and then proceed to have a child. It
is not that they were coerced into it; I think it is because
this is our most basic drive--to repeat what happened to us
in our own childhoods. Most of us who had reasonably good
family experiences want most of all to grow up and to have
spouses and children to cherish the way we were cherished.
This is why people have children. It is no longer a financial advantage, as they say it was when so many people lived
on farms, to have large families. The larger the family now
the more expensive it is. Perhaps those who were not too
enthusiastic about having children in the past had them any-
way--partly because their brothers and sisters were having
them, and because it seemed a bit peculiar not to have children. Since we know that children who are not loved do not,

in general, do very well, I think it is good that certain
people who really are not enthusiastic about children are
able to make a decision and to keep themselves from having
children.

I would like now to discuss two more specific trends in
child rearing that I have observed in recent years.

PARENTING HAS BEEN COMPLICATED

The first observation I have to make about child rearing in
recent years is that a great many of our efforts as professionals to help parents have instead complicated the life of
parents--especially the conscientious and highly sensitive parents. It has made them somewhat timid with their children--
hesitant to be firm. They are a little scared of their child-
dren because they feel as parents they are being judged by
their neighbors, relatives, and the world on how well they
succeed. They are scared of doing the wrong thing. Many
will say, "I'm so inexperienced that I'm afraid that I'll
do wrong more often than I'll do right."

Now we professionals did not set out deliberately to mis-
lead parents, but let me give you an example of how we complicated things for parents. At Western Reserve Medical
School, we conducted a child-rearing study, in which twelve
staff members from psychiatry and pediatrics saw families
every two weeks for ten years.

We had read that toilet training was becoming a problem--
not a major one but a problem, especially for college-educated
parents. So, when this first group of babies we were consulting reached the age of two years and three months, we
said, "Now it's time to review the success of toilet training."
We were surprised to find that of twelve babies only two had
made the slightest progress in their bowel training. It was
interesting to us to note that these babies were in the only
two families where neither parent had ever been near a university. I am not anti-education, but it does show that education can produce complicating factors in bringing up children.

We were embarrassed to think that as counselors we had been
no more help than this, so we concentrated more on these parents' difficulty with toilet training. Different parents
expressed their experiences in a variety of ways, but what
it really came down to was that they all started toilet training sometime in the second year. Within a few weeks, they
ran into a certain amount of resistance, and the parent immediately backed away guiltily, fearful of creating hostility
between the parent and the child, or of disturbing the baby's
personality. Then they waited two or three months and very

gingerly tried again. As anybody who has been around children knows, when children get you down on an issue once, and you bring up that issue again, they will get you down even faster the next time. The children immediately resisted re-introduction of the potty on the second and the third tries, and that is why, at two and a quarter years of age, none of them had made progress except for two with the non-college parents.

We urged the parents on. We said, "Don't believe what you've been reading about the possible hostilities between parent and child over an issue like toilet training. Don't worry about distortion of personality. Everybody has to be toilet trained, and we believe that the baby is ready by two years of age. Don't be afraid to persevere a little." We did not say, "get rough with them," or "become overbearing," but "be positive and encouraging."

Two mothers reported that the day on which their children were eventually toilet trained went something like this. On that day, mother was cleaning up a mess and suddenly lost her patience, and said, "I'm sick of cleaning up your mess. Why can't you use the bathroom like me and your father and cousin Janie? You're big enough, you're smart enough." The child looked at her with amazement as if to say, "Why didn't you tell me that in the first place?" Both children became immediately bowel trained and usually urine trained at the same time.

Well, to conclude this example, most of these babies did not get bowel trained until somewhere between two and a half and two and three-quarters years of age. I am not implying that there is anything disgraceful about this, but I do think it was unnecessarily delayed.

As a result of this experience with the college-educated parents, the pediatricians who had been involved talked with a group of parents, most of whom had not finished high school. We asked them, "How do you toilet train?" They said, "It's perfectly easy. You decide it's about time, and you buy a potty, and you say to the child that this is where you do it, and pretty soon the child is doing it." That's an amazing reflection on our society--that, in this situation, we professionals could not help the parents who had been to college, and the parents who had not even finished high school could say it was perfectly easy.

Professional people have the best of intentions in making an understanding of child development available to parents, but I think that we have complicated parenting in the process. I wrote in *Baby and Child Care* that parents do not need to get locked into a knock-down, dragout fight with their children. In fact, it may create unnecessary hostility. I thought I was using my psychoanalytic and psychiatric training

for the benefit of parents--to keep a few parents from getting into real squabbles with their children. I don't know
whether I succeeded or not, but I know one of the results
which I did not anticipate was that I scared millions of
parents who otherwise would not have worried about toilet
training, or any number of other parenting chores.

This kind of timidity, uncertainty, or hesitancy on the
part of parents does not make delinquents or create any serious emotional problem in the children, but it makes "pesky"
children. By "pesky," I mean children who are always arguing
with their parents because they sense their parents' uncertainty. Any time children sense uncertainty, they take advantage of it, because that is the nature of children--to
try to expand their experiences, to expand their control of
the situation if possible. Again, these are not severely
disturbed children. Pesky children do, however, make parenthood more of a chore than it needs to be.

I have been writing in revisions of *Baby and Child Care*
and in *Redbook* magazine, and before that in *Ladies' Home
Journal*, and encouraging parents to be clear and firm with
their children. Actually, children and adults like to have
clear directions. As adults in a job, we appreciate a superior who is absolutely clear about what our responsibilities
are, and who gives the guidance we need. We all feel more
comfortable with somebody who expresses exactly what they
want. It is easier to work with somebody who is clear and
firm. I am not talking about oppressive. I don't think children or adults need oppression, only clear leadership.

PARENTS HAVE MORE TRUST IN CHILDREN

While the efforts of professionals to educate parents about
how children develop have caused some complications, these
same efforts have had some beneficial results, too. An experience I had with a group of medical students led me to
this conclusion. This also happened at Western Reserve Medical School in a course called Clinical Science, for which
I was responsible. This course was begun by students in their
first year of medical school. This particular group of students began in the fall and it soon became apparent that they
were very casual about coming late to class. We were teaching
the class in a room with the only two doors on either side
of where the instructor stood. As the late students would
come in, they would tend to hurry past to their seats. I
found it distracting and disconcerting in the early stages
of my lecture to have students hurrying by. It felt like
standing on a traffic island in the midst of rush hour. So

I said, "You know in this school we don't take attendance.
You don't have to come, but if you come, please come on time."
I thought of course this would make them mind their manners.
Not at all! Just as many came late and a few began bringing their breakfast coffee in cardboard cups. At first they
would take surreptitious sips, ducking their heads so they
could not be seen drinking. Since I made no fuss about it,
after awhile, they would nurse the cup all through the hour,
tipping it up, tipping it down. I decided to raise my voice
and show my irritation. I said, "I meant it three weeks ago
when I said, 'please come on time or don't come at all,' and
don't bring breakfast--have it before or wait until after."
It scared me to hear me shouting in a lecture room, but it
did not make the slightest impact on the students.

Several weeks later I decided to try stony silence. When
a latecomer would come past while I was lecturing, I would
stop right in the middle of a sentence, and scornfully watch
him climb up the side of the ampitheatre, imagining him red
in the face and wanting to duck in the first seat. But not
at all! Latecomers would saunter up gradually, waving to
friends, get to the back, and then turn around smiling as
if to say, "You may proceed." This was not the worst of it.
In January, the class sent an official committee to my office to complain to me that the course I was so proud of,
a course which previous students had loved and subsequent
students loved, had no content. This is the most insulting
thing I think you can say to an instructor. It means the
class is not worth spending the hour. It was my turn to
be intimidated. I had tried unsuccessfully again and again
to intimidate them and got nowhere. I did not want the dean
or the rest of the faculty to hear that the students were
complaining so I shut up. I stopped complaining. I paid
no attention when people came late, and gradually most of
the students were sipping coffee contentedly during the
hour.

Then I began to try to reason out why these students
behaved in this manner. At first I thought they were just
rude. However, I had dealt with the same students in small
preceptor groups, and they were not rude. They were quite
cooperative in attitude. So I decided it was not rudeness.
Maybe, they were not sensitive to the feelings of others--
in this case, me. This was all speculation. I decided this
was because when they were small children their parents did
not intimidate them. It is too late to start intimidating
them by the time they are in a university.

Speculating some more, I thought maybe parents nowadays
have more trust in their children, as a result of what they
have learned from Freud, John Dewey, books like mine, and
other books about how children develop and learn. In a way,

we all stress that children do not have to be compelled to
learn. Children do not have to be scared into being responsible citizens. When parents love the child, this en-
genders love on the part of the child. Then the child wants
more than anything else in the world to grow up to be like
the parents. The child wants to become mature as soon as
possible. This is where good behavior originates.

Of course I was furious when I was a professor and could
not intimidate them, but a couple of years later, through certain circumstances, I became a full-time opponent of the war
in Vietnam. Then I thought that this refusal to be intimidated was wonderful. It was what gave those young people,
who thought that the war was totally unconstitutional, il-
legal, full of war crimes, and disastrous to the best interests of the United States, the courage to disagree with
their parents and with the federal government.

While I changed attitudes depending on which side of
the fence I was on, I still have to conclude that the majority of our young people are unusually mature and independent
in their judgment. I think they are made of good stuff. I
personally would prefer a little more political activity from
them. So many things in our society need remedying. Generally, however, we should be proud of the condition of most
of our young people.

While the majority of our young people are doing well,
we must admit that we do have young people are are suffering various kinds of injustices and who are disturbed. As
I mentioned earlier, many conditions in our society need
remedies. I will elaborate on some of these later as I
mention some goals toward which we need to be striving.

BROADER PERSPECTIVE NEEDED

During the first twenty years in my calling as a pediatrican,
I suffered from a narrowness of viewpoint which is called
child-centered. I thought that all we needed to do was to
find out what forces within the family, and what experiences
within the family disturb children. Then we could educate
parents to avoid these or overcome them, and we would have
happy, well-adjusted children. I still think that all of
these things that I was concerned about and that all of you
are concerned about are right. We do need to help parents.
But I think our society plays an enormous role, and in order
to understand our children and ourselves, the stresses of
modern life, and what makes things go wrong, we need a broader
perspective.

We also need to enlarge our children's viewpoint. When
I revised *Baby and Child Care*, 1968 edition, I introduced

what I called "world view." Back in earlier times, and in
other parts of the world even today, children are brought
up to feel a part of something which is bigger than themselves, and to feel a sense of obligation to it. The parents themselves have a feeling of being part of a larger
community and having a great obligation. Many of the questions of how to rear children back in the middle ages, and
even in Colonial times in the United States, were already
answered. Children were brought up for the glory of God.
This was their major goal, and having identified it gave
direction to parents and to children. In European countries
up until at least the turn of the century, another major
goal was respect for the family. Children were given the
feeling that they were not in the world for their own pleasure. Their duty was to serve the family. In France, it was
recognized that the marriage of the child was of prime importance to the family. So, the family selected the bride
or the groom because anything so important to the family
could not be left to immature people to decide. In countries
like Israel or the Soviet Union, children were brought up
to serve the nation. This goal again gives meaning to everything the child experiences. The authorities in those countries know exactly what the obligation of the citizen is.
This helps them with their children because the purpose of
rearing children is to rear them to serve the country. I
do not think in the United States we will get back to raising children in many families for the glory of God or to
serve the family. We certainly are not going to bring up
our children primarily to serve the state. But I do think
we would make our job easier as parents and help to straighten
out our children who are more disturbed if we could instill
the idea from the beginning that there are tremendous un-
solved problems in our country and in the world. Each person's primary job as an adult is to help solve these problems, so each child's job is to prepare to solve them.

SOCIAL CONDITIONS NEED ATTENTION

Some of the conditions in our society that cry out for more
concern and attention are related to money, or maybe I should
say a lack of it. Consider, for example, our child deten-
tion institutions. In most parts of the country, they are
barbaric. Generally, they have grossly inadequate counseling services. We ought to have free counseling services
for any adult or child who is having trouble. It ought to
be easy for adults and children to get to those services
instead of having to wait so long, as is the case, for instance, in child guidance clinics at the present time.

Especially in our cities, a lot of our housing is dilap-
idated, and recreational facilities are nonexistent. The
schools are poorest in poverty stricken areas where children
need the best schooling in order to overcome the disadvantages
of their background. Instead we have the best schools, of
course, in the neighborhoods where the parents are well-to-
do. I am not saying that those areas should not have good
schools, but we certainly should be fighting for better
schools for all our children.

We have a poor distribution of medical care in the United
States. The well-to-do can get very good medical care because American medical care at its best is the best in the
world, but there are millions of families who see a doctor
only when they are in dire circumstances, and there are many
families who never see a doctor from the day they are born
until they die. We have poverty which I believe is unnecessary in a country as rich as ours. Our country is the rich-
est that the world has ever known. The Scandinavian countries, for instance, long ago legislated poverty out of existence. They said, "It isn't right when a nation can't take care
of those who are, for one reason or another, unable to fend
for themselves; it isn't decent for that nation not to do
this."

TOO MUCH EMPHASIS ON COMPETITION

I do not want to imply that social conditions are only unfortunate for the poor or the people who are disadvantaged
by belonging to minorities who are still discriminated against
in our country. When you get to cities like New York, the
well-to-do are full of ulcers and tensions. I think this
points out the extensive competitiveness in our society. We
take for granted the social conditions in our country. However, in recent years, I have traveled in other parts of the
world, and have observed how much calmer, how much more serene
people are in countries which do not have this excessive emphasis on competition.

There is a philosophy which says that individualism and
competition have made this country great. Well, I think they
have contributed to the rapid progress in this country, but I
think we should calm things down a bit.

One of the things which I value greatly that I learned
from many people with whom I was closely associated during
that phase of opposition to the war in Vietnam was their attitude toward competition. They wondered why, instead of having
such a ferociously competitive society, couldn't we create
a more cooperative society in which the people work together
in a spirit of brotherly love. I endorse that fully.

TOO MUCH MATERIALISM

Another thing which I learned from these young people with
whom I associated during that phase of opposition to the war
in Vietnam was the idea of striving to live simply. That
does not mean removing all the pleasure from life; you can
get pleasure from living simply. I think the ideal of a simple way of living might be a helpful antidote to the harmful
effects of so much materialism in our society.

My feeling is that our country is much too materialistic in its basic convictions. Unfortunately, for many families, religion has lost its inspiration; not for all, fortunately, but for many. Nothing very satisfactory has been
substituted for religion, so "getting things" is in a sense
the highest ambition of many Americans. Perhaps, too, many
people have thought that our knowledge of science nowadays
displaces the need for a religious basis. I do not think
that is true. I think that man is spiritual in his nature,
as well as practical. I think that religious belief in a
family is wonderful.

Another example of the thoughtlessness of the profit
system going kind of crazy is the commercials for cereal for
children. Cereals that are sweet will decay teeth and many
are nutritionally poor. Yet, these great corporations go
right ahead trying to sell the sugar-coated, deprived cereals
because it makes profit. Since many people share my concern
about this kind of advertising, you might wonder why we do
not have a law to prevent such. Part of the reason is, that
in our political system, industry pays the election bill of
Democrats and Republicans alike. This is where presidents,
vice-presidents, senators, and congressmen get a major part
of their contributions for their elections--from industry.
Therefore, they tend to listen first to what industry asks
for.

WHAT PROFESSIONALS CAN DO TO HELP

I was asked recently what I thought should be the contributions of professionals to straightening out some of the things
which are wrong in our society. There are two things I want
to mention here. The first is that I would like to see professionals become more politically involved.

By putting this emphasis on the need for change in our
society, partly through political activity, I do not mean
to belittle or to minimize in any way the other things which
professionals do to help families. I still believe in those
professional activities for myself and for other professionals. I think we ought to broaden our perspective and our

effort, because I do not think we are going to solve the problems of our country just by counseling alone--whether it is
counseling as a pediatrician, as a social worker, or as a
psychologist.

An increased political awareness comes partly from a
recognition of the progressiveness of the problems of our
society. These must be solved if we are to make a really
good, secure life for all of our people. We have to reverse
the demoralization which is constantly going on in the most
troubled areas of our society because if we do not, that demoralization is going to gradually reach the rest of us. I
think this has been shown in one sense in the reports that
crime is spreading from the center city out into the suburbs.
While this may be regarded as a relatively narrow example,
I think in another sense anything that is wrong in a poverty-
stricken and demoralized area will eventually contaminate
the whole society.

I, myself, get more political, and every chance I get,
I bring up the political issue as well as the professional
issue. For example, I have mentioned a need for better social
conditions--better housing, recreational facilities, and medical care--for some of our children. Too often we hear, "It
can't be done because of inflation." Well, I disagree. I
could go on and say, "Let's persuade our president and legislators in Washington to close the tax loopholes which give
grossly unfair advantages to industry and the rich. Let's
reduce the Defense Department budget." The Defense Department
budget will never be reduced by the Pentagon, by presidents,
nor, I am afraid, by Congress, unless they feel they are forced
by their constituents. Otherwise, they can always claim to
be patriotic people by upping the Defense Department budget.
It does not seem to matter that we are spending 130 billion
dollars a year for more arms when we have enough now to kill
everybody in the world plenty of times over. I think our
country would be stronger and more able to stand up to competition from socialist countries if we were proving to the
rest of the world what a magnificent job we can do for all
our citizens within our system.

So I think we should use our influence as professionals
in a broader way. We should also continue to study our professional disciplines, and continue to make that information
and services available to clients. Aside from the technical
knowledge which we use, I think listening, and more important
still, showing that we like our clients, are very important.
I remember when we formed a nursery school in a neighborhood
health center in Pittsburgh a number of years ago. This
nursery school was in a relatively poor neighborhood, where
the parents, in general, were not particularly sensitive to
the needs of children. They loved their children, but none

of them had ever had any glimpse of psychology. Most had
no idea they were influencing their children's personality
every day they lived together. The staff was an unusually
sensitive and wise one. They felt that part of the job in
this particular neighborhood nursery school was to make the
parents welcome. They could come any time of the day, and
stay as long as they liked. There was a coffee urn which
was always percolating. This is the way in America that we
show it is to be partially a social situation is to have coffee ready at all times. The staff noticed something extraordinary as the years went on. The parents, without ever
having been lectured to, or without necessarily having asked
specific questions, were taking on the attitudes of the nursery school teachers toward these children. They were noticing and taking part in observations of the subtle emotional
aspects of these children. The parents took on these attitudes just by a process of quiet identification with the
teachers, without anything ever having been said in the way
of a preachment to them.

The success of *Baby and Child Care* is partly because it
has always been cheap, although it has gone from twenty-five
cents in 1946, to $2.50 now. It is complete and its gets into
the psychological as well as the physical, but I think the
main reason that it has been accepted so well is because it
is friendly. I wrote it to be friendly, although I was not
sure I was achieving this while I was writing it. The first
few sentences say, "You know more than you think you do.
Don't be over-awed by the professionals and the scary things
that your family and friends tell you." Although most of my
mail about children is concerned with the terrible problems
that children are involved in, and asks me to help solve them,
there is a small trickle of fan mail. The theme of it is the
same, whether it comes from Canada, Australia, France, Italy,
or the United States. The words are almost the same. They
say, "It sounds as if you are talking to me, and as if you
think I am a sensible person." I almost weep when I think
that people can be pleased with as little as that. This is
what people want--to be listened to and treated as sensible--
not talked down to, not lectured to. It is one of the hardest
things for professional people to avoid because we work so
hard for so many years developing and acquiring expertise.
After all the years of education and training, it is terribly
hard not to become sort of condescending without ever meaning
to be so.

CONCLUSIONS

In conclusion, let me summarize by saying that I see many conditions in our society which call out for attention. Some of these are poverty-related, such as the unequal distribution of medical care and schools, poor housing and recreational facilities. We need to remedy these conditions for the people involved and for ourselves. Despair and demoralization tend to spread to influence the entire population. Other conditions in our society which affect us are an emphasis on competition and materialism. Two ideals, from my viewpoint, which we should strive for are a more cooperative society, and one in which we try to see how simply we can live.

As professionals, I think we should continue in our professional roles, but strive always to listen to our clients. We must avoid preachment or condescension. I would also like to see professionals broaden their perspective to include political issues, especially where these influence our professional concerns. As parents, we need to help give our children a sense of purpose, and of their involvement as citizens of the world.

The Transition to Parenthood as a Critical Time for Building Family Strengths

Dr. Donna L. Sollie
Department of Home and
   Family Life
Texas Tech University
   and
Dr. Brent C. Miller
Department of Family and
   Human Development
Utah State University

INTRODUCTION

After a negative, crisis-oriented beginning (LeMasters, 1957), there has been an increasing realization that the transition to parenthood has both positive and negative aspects (Russell, 1974). The birth of the first child constitutes an important or critical role transition, necessitating the reorganization of marital roles and redefinition of relationships. Some aspects of parenting are more intense for new parents than during later stages of parent-child relations (Hoffman & Manis, 1978). New parents are likely to experience both tensions, anxieties, and the heavy weight of total responsibility for their infant, as well as intense joy, pride, and closeness to each other (Rossi, 1968).

In Knoxville, Tennessee, we studied couples before and after the birth of their first child, to find out what happened during the transition to parenthood. A large amount of quantitative information was obtained to describe changes in personal and marital qualities from the middle of the wife's pregnancy until the baby was about eight months old. In this paper, however, the more open-ended qualitative responses of new parents are emphasized. Implications for parenthood education, and for family life education in general, are suggested from what the new parents wrote about their experiences.

PROCEDURES

The couples in our study were originally contacted through either LaMaze or hospital-based prenatal classes for prospective parents. At these group meetings we explained the study, asked those who were about to have their first child to volunteer, and passed out separate husband and wife

149

questionnaires which were returned to us in the mail. Wives
were generally about six-months pregnant when the study began. When the baby was about six-weeks-old, and again when
eight-months-old, our second and third questionnaires were
sent out and returned. The 120 new parent couples who participated in the study were mostly young, middle-class East
Tennesseans, although some older couples, working-class
couples, and people from other parts of the country were included.

A major objective of the study was to assess changes in
personal and marital qualities during the transition to parenthood. For this purpose, most of the questionnaire was
standardized and objective. However, in order to obtain a
more complete picture of the transition period, the parents
were also asked to respond to the following open-ended question in both the second and third questionnaires: "Would
you please write just a few things, both positive and negative, about what the baby has meant in your life?" From
the written comments of parents whose babies were six-weeks
and eight-months-old, we have drawn several major themes related to the effects of parenthood. These themes generally
reflect the positive and negative values of children identified by Arnold et al. (1975) in their cross-national study.
The written comments provide insights about the needs of
first-time parents, their life-style changes, and the bonuses
which come with the birth of a child.

POSITIVE EFFECTS

From the comments of the parents, four major positive themes
were identified. The first of these included emotional benefits derived from the child; typical comments included love,
joy, happiness, and fun. The baby was experienced as a source
of affection for both parents and provided happiness and fun
as the parents played with, watched, and participated in the
growth and development of the child. One mother wrote only
one positive comment, and that was "sheer enjoyment of baby."
Another mother commented that her baby "is a pleasure and
joy." Although the responsibility of parenthood was mentioned repeatedly, one mother stated:

The rewards for all the efforts and hard work are
well worth the trouble. The look in a child's
eyes as he or she looks at you makes a warm feeling go through you. Love flows through those eyes
and hands that reach out for Mama or Daddy. A
child can make a drab working day turn into an

enjoyable evening with just a look, a smile, and hurried crawling toward Mama.

A father described his baby as being "cute, funny, and lovable." Another father said, "I get an extreme amount of happiness being with him when he's in a good mood (not crying). Touching him, holding him gives me a great feeling of closeness." Comments by this father indicated an increase in enjoyment of the baby over time: "He has given me some moments of extreme happiness like when he smiled at me for the first time. He does grow more enjoyable each week and I appreciate him more as he develops." Another father said, "I can't fully express the fullness of joy I have with him. It is a magnificent blessing, increasing the love I give and feel that I receive."

Several of the comments reflected a dimension of love not experienced before, including the spontaneity and undemanding love received from the infant, and the love of parent for child. As one mother expressed it: "She's brought a new dimension of love to us. The parent-child love is special and different from others." Another mother said: "I never realized exactly what a mother could feel for a child until having a baby. I love her more than words could ever express."

One mother wrote about the overwhelming responsibility she felt after the birth of her child--feelings which were compounded by her fear, fatigue, and depression. She did not experience the rush of maternal love that she expected to feel immediately:

The flow of maternal love I expected didn't rush over me as I thought it would--I was more in awe of the baby than anything else. As I became less tired and more sure of my ability to take care of him, the more I loved him. . . . Being a mother is such a totally different feeling; I have a special kind of love for my baby that I never knew existed.

The comments made by mothers seemed to reflect the special mother-child love they experienced. Fathers' comments were more likely to indicate strengthened feelings for spouse, and feelings of love as a family unit than a special father-child love. This may be a result of our culture, which does not recognize a special father-child love to the same degree. Several fathers included the word "love" in their lists of positive experiences and feelings, but only one father specified the enjoyment derived from being able to "experience the love of parent for child."

Parents also commented on another aspect of love--being able to spontaneously express their feelings and give of themselves totally to another person. A mother listed positive aspects of parenthood as including "feelings of love and adoration and being able to express those spontaneously to my baby." A father described his child as "someone I can totally love."

The second positive theme was self-enrichment and development, which included being viewed as an adult, becoming more mature and responsible, thinking and planning for the future, becoming less selfish, and experiencing self-fulfillment. This theme reflected the idea that becoming a parent is one way to be recognized as an adult. In our society, it is expected that most adults will, at some point in their lives, assume the parental role. Blake (1974) noted that parenthood is implicit in adult roles as they are societally defined. The Hoffman and Manis (1978) study on the value of children also indicated that parenthood is seen as an important sign of adulthood.

Whereas motherhood has always been stressed, increasing emphasis recently has been placed on the importance of the father in the development of children. Terms such as fathering and parenting have become more prominent, indicating an increased involvement of fathers in child care roles. However, this pattern is definitely not the norm in our society. Parental status is still more crucial in defining a woman's role than it is in defining a man's role. Although fatherhood has been viewed as an expected role for men, males are usually defined more in terms of their occupations than their children.

Both mothers and fathers noted the new meaning of life. Fathers did not comment on fatherhood as specifically as mothers wrote about motherhood; instead, they talked about parenthood in general and the sense of family. Fathers did, however, make frequent mention of the fullness and meaningfulness of life since the birth of their children.

One father said, "The birth of our baby has brought more purpose in my life and has given me an overall greater depth and meaning to my life." Along the same lines, a mother said, "I have never felt more like I had a reason to live."

Several women commented about their sense of fulfillment since becoming a mother. One mother wrote that "all in all I feel a more complete person since becoming a mother." Another wrote: "Personally, motherhood is a wonderful thing. I am fulfilled in this new role and cannot understand anyone who doesn't love having babies."

Both mothers and fathers talked about changes in themselves in the direction of less selfishness. A mother commented: "She has made me mature in the sense that caring for her has made me less selfish and more able to take on responsibilities." Another mother commented that parenthood "requires sacrifices that will, in the long run, be to the betterment of my character." A father said, "I feel like a much more giving, selfless person than before."

New parents also noted the changes in themselves as they became more responsible and mature. These are traits which are associated with adulthood. "Surprisingly, I feel more mature and capable," said one mother. A father commented, "I feel a bit more responsible for the actions I make that determine my future; financially, time-wise, and so on." One father said, "I have grown up more, but by my own choosing," and another wrote that being parents "has added to our maturity." A mother stated, "I really enjoy the fact that I'm a parent with responsibilities."

An orientation toward the future was also apparent in the parents' reflections on their new status. One mother stated:

> I feel she has added some depth in the relation-
> ship I have with my future. By this I mean I
> find myself planning far in advance of what I
> used to do. I have discovered myself to be an
> adult person capable of doing many menial tasks
> for practically a stranger without bitterness
> or remorse. As the days go by my love builds for
> her, I feel closer to my husband and I hope to
> be prepared for what the future may bring.

The orientation toward the future included a change in priorities, expressed more by fathers than mothers. "A greater need to and incentive to succeed and achieve growth," was expressed by one father.

The third positive theme reflected a sense of family cohesiveness. Children were viewed as a bond between the mother and father, adding to the completeness of the family. Some parents noted a stronger bond between themselves, not only as parents, but also as husband and wife. Strengthened relationships with grandparents were also mentioned, along with the happiness of grandparents and greater appreciation by the new parents for their own parents. The sense of family and experiencing the bonds between husband and wife and between parent and child received greater emphasis than the ties between parents and their own parents. The idea of continuing the family name and tradition was not an essential element of the family cohesiveness theme.

A mother stated that parenthood "has brought us closer as husband and wife. . . . I feel very fulfilled as a person and woman. . . . I respect my husband in a new and different

way." Another mother commented on the strong bond created
between her and her husband as a result of becoming parents.
"My husband and I are very close already, but I do feel that
our child still is a strong uniting force between us. I don't
feel that every marriage needs children. When you and your
husband are ready for a child it is wonderful."

Fathers as well as mothers noted the stronger bond between the new parents. One father said, "Since he is part
of both of us, we not only feel very close to him but closer
to each other, especially mentally and spiritually. I feel
closer to my wife because she is the mother of our child and
I respect and appreciate all the attention she gives to him."

New parents also mentioned the changed focus in their
lives. The baby was viewed as the most important part of
their lives. One father emphasized the changes in commitment
to his wife and changes within himself. "I feel a greater
personal commitment towards our marriage. We have become much,
much deeper in our contact. I feel like a more giving, selfless person than before." A mother commented: "The baby
has totally changed our lives--he comes first no matter what.
We are very happy being parents and every time he does something new we're both excited." Being parents was seen as a
shared interest. One father wrote: "The baby is one of the
strongest common interests in our marriage. Using our talents and resources to meet the needs of each other and the
baby will help us to keep our perspective in life and not
get lost in this world." Another father emphasized the depth
that parenthood brought to a happy marriage. "Our little
girl has provided additional fulfillment for an already happy marriage. We both enjoy taking care of her and share the
responsibilities."

One mother talked of the developing sense of being a family.

> It seemed odd at first, to think of us as a family,
> but now that's what I feel we are. Being a mother
> is such a totally different feeling; I have such
> a special kind of love for my baby that I never
> knew existed. And I'm so happy that my husband
> loves the baby and takes such interest in him. I
> feel that our already good marriage has been made
> even better.

One father commented that the baby, "seems to make our family complete."

The transition to parenthood also led to an increased
appreciation of the respondents' own parents. One father
wrote this about his parents: "The baby has made me realize
how important my parents are and what a good job they did."

A mother talked about parenthood in glowing terms: "In rearing our child, we look at our parents with new respect. We feel that parenthood is like an exclusive club to which we have just become joyful members. We have a delightful marriage and baby, which not everyone has." Another wrote, "I certainly have developed a greater understanding and appreciation of my own parents, especially my mother." Becoming a parent often led to increased contact with the baby's grandparents. In some instances, new parents resented the intrusion on their time and the suggestions made concerning the baby. For the most part, however, the increased contact was viewed positively. One mother listed "getting closer to my parents" as a positive effect that her child had on her life. New parents also mentioned their enjoyment of seeing the pride and joy evident in their own parents.

The fourth positive theme reflected a sense of identification with the child, and pleasure from watching the child's growth and development. One aspect of this theme was a future orientation--parents anticipated the joy they would derive from seeing growth, development, and accomplishments in the future as well as in the present.

Watching and participating in the child's growth and development was mentioned repeatedly as one of the pleasures of parenthood. This was viewed as a source of enjoyment by a large majority of the parents.

One father commented, "It has been a great pleasure to watch our son grow and develop. To see first hand the process of 'becoming a person' is an amazing experience." A mother said, "It is hard to describe the personal satisfaction one can derive from watching a baby grow and develop." One father noted that fun and feelings of pride accompany the child's development. "The baby is fun to watch grow and develop. A source of pride and feeling of accomplishment."

Being a parent also provided an opportunity for introducing to and sharing with the child some of the things that the parent enjoyed in childhood. The child provided a link to the parents' past, enabling the parents to re-live some of these past experiences which were so enjoyable. Being a parent seemed to add a new perspective to remembered childhood experiences; the parents could approach them from two points of view--their child's and their own. One father wrote, "Our baby boy has brightened up our lives. It's like seeing a part of yourself you never saw. I will enjoy showing our son the beautiful things in life." Another father said that parenthood "gives me a feeling for the developmental process that occurs in children. Lets me reflect back on my own experiences as a child and put that part of my life in a different perspective." A mother wrote that parenthood "has made me appreciate things anew and look forward to introducing

some of the things I loved as a child to him." Another mother
said, "She is so happy and receptive to the world that it
becomes contagious." One father emphasized the special relationship he had with his son, reflecting the sense of identification between father and son, and that between mother
and daughter. He stated: "He has brought great joy into
my life only a son can bring. As a daughter brings to a
mother."

As noted, the sense of identification and the pride in
the child's accomplishments, growth, and development has a
future orientation as well as a present orientation. One
father wrote, "I look forward to both the good and bad times
with our little one--it will be exciting and interesting, I
think." A mother commented: "Our baby is full of promise.
My husband and I can look foward to the day when he will carry on with part of us, our traditions, our hopes." One father
wrote about the "feeling of anticipation about her in the
future."

The four themes described above reflect positive aspects
of the period known as the transition to parenthood. Additional comments made by parents indicate, in a more general
sense, the merits of this stage in the life of the family life
cycle. A mother exclaimed, "I didn't expect parenting to
be this thrilling." One father said, "The pleasures of having
a child have been greater than I anticipated." A mother said,
"I think parenthood is the most wonderful and difficult thing
to do in my life. I think my family is the most important
thing in my life and I truly enjoy it." One father described
his experience more fully:

> Most of all I have enjoyed the whole process so
> far (pregnancy, birth, development). It has been
> educational, rewarding, and it has brought me
> closer to probably some sort of essence of life
> (the process). Unexpectedly, our marriage has
> become closer and we get along much better. (We
> were aware that this was a reason why some people
> have children--and we were aware that it might do
> the opposite, so we made sure this wasn't our
> reason.) I think that the reason we do get along
> better is that the child is something very much
> in common with both of us.

Another father also noted the advantages of this stage
in the individual and family life cycle:

> I have really enjoyed the past year and feel
> that the whole experience has been good for
> my wife and I. We could never forget what

these times have been like for us. In my opinion
nothing can compare to the birth of our own child
as a great period in our lives.

NEGATIVE THEMES

So far, we have focused on the positive aspects of parenthood, but new parents also described negative feelings. These
negative effects, or disadvantages, had impacts on the individual, the marital relationship, interaction with others,
and feelings for the child. Most parents listed both positive and negative effects.

For some parents, this transition period was extremely
trying, particularly during the first few months of the child's
life. These parents reported mainly deleterious effects of
the child on their lives. However, these effects seemed to
diminish as the child grew older, thus easing the trauma of
the first few weeks or months. This mother described such
an experience:

> The first three weeks were awful. She ate every
> two hours night and day. She cried all the time--
> no matter what we did. The fourth week she didn't
> cry so much, and the fifth week she started
> sleeping much better at night. This gave me more
> sleep and made me less irritable. Now at six weeks
> things are great. But at two weeks I was doubt-
> ing my ability as a mother. I almost stopped
> breastfeeding, and I felt awful.

In some cases, the negative period of time lasted longer.
For one couple, it was several months rather than several
weeks. The mother wrote:

> The first six months has been terrible, colic,
> sick--ear infections, teething, lots of crying,
> and so on. Child cried most of the time--no
> pleasure. At seven months, teeth started pop-
> ping out, tried to walk, play by himself, and
> more lovable. He is very enjoyable now.

A father wrote:

> Before the baby was born there were some
> positive thoughts. Since the birth these
> thoughts have turned to negative ones. This
> is probably because care of the baby has
> been somewhat tiring for both parents. I

expect my thoughts to become positive again
after the baby grows some more; becomes more
predictable, and can be played with.

The preceding quotations reflect both physical demands and
characteristics of the child that can make caretaking even
more demanding and tedious.

Among the most common negative aspects of parenthood are
the physical demands of caring for the child. New parents
report loss of sleep, constant fatigue, extra work around
the house, and the drains in both physical and emotional
strength. A large part of this is the demand made on the
parents' time, particularly the mothers' time. One mother
wrote:

> The first big shock was how weak and tired I was
> after delivery (never having been ill before)--
> I was physically unable to do what I wanted to.
> I had a lot of help after I got home--thank God!--
> but now that I'm physically recovered I find I'm
> unable to do things with a tiny baby. Going to
> the grocery store was a nightmare, for instance--
> she got hungry between "paper goods" and "pet
> food."

Another mother said that she did not get enough sleep
or rest, and therefore was tired all the time, "staying in
a continuous state of exhaustion." Two additional comments
by mothers were: "I really feel mentally and physically
exhausted," and "total exhaustion." Finally, a comment by
a father was, "Too tired for any meaningful statements." The
loss of sleep, accompanying fatigue, and drains on physical
and emotional strength result from the demands made by an
infant. One mother wrote:

> Because an infant is so demanding there are days
> when one wishes the baby did not exist. Knowing
> these things are normal, however, makes coping
> with the day to day routine possible.

Another mother said:

> She takes so much time I find myself going in
> circles most of the time. This isn't so hard
> during the day, but at night I find that I
> can't deal with her as objectively.

A father said that one of the negative aspects of being parents was that the child was "demanding of our time when we
were unwilling or tired."

It is interesting that most of the comments about the physical demands of the child were made by mothers. Most fathers are not the primary caretakers of the child, and they do not take as much responsibility for meeting the child's physical needs. This is not to say fathers do not participate in feeding, diaper changing, and so on. However, their participation in these activities is viewed as "helping" their wife. A few wives noted that they were hesitant to request help from their husbands, who had been working all day. For several other couples, the physical care of the child, as well as the emotional care, was viewed as a shared responsibility. For the most part, though, the mothers assumed the major responsibility for meeting the child's physical and emotional needs. The first several months after the birth of the child were filled with the necessity of meeting these needs, resulting in missed sleep, weariness, increased work around the house, and drains on the emotional and physical strengths of both parents.

A second negative aspect the new parents mentioned centered around strains on the husband-wife relationship. Although the husband-wife relationship can be closer after the birth of the child, there are also strains on marriage caused by less time spent together as a couple, changes in the sexual relationship, and the belief that the child's needs are more important than the needs of the husband and wife.

Time devoted to the infant means less time for spouse and for self. One mother said that she had "little time alone with my husband." Another mother wrote: "Sometimes I feel my husband and I should share more time together--just to talk." Another mother wrote:

> Having the baby has resulted in us being further
> apart based on different personal needs in our
> relationship, due, I think, to changed environ
> ment. However, we are aware of this and while
> working at it will probably end up closer to
> gether.

One mother expressed resentment toward her husband for his continued participation in outside activities, although she could no longer participate in these activities or her own activities. She wrote:

> It seems that we (my husband and I) never have
> any time to spend together anymore. My husband
> continues to go on about his routine and plans
> his evenings for activities as he has always done--
> only now instead of going with him as I had pre
> viously done or making plans of my own--I stay at

home to take care of the baby. I feel resentment
a lot of times but I have always seemed to be able
to cope with my feelings so far.

One husband said that he and his wife, "don't have as much
time for each other."
    The sexual relationship also tended to be negatively af-
fected, both by pregnancy and the presence of the child.
Husbands were more likely to comment on the changes in sexual
activity than wives. One husband listed the "prolonged in-
terruption of normal sexual relations with my wife" as one
of the negative effects of becoming parents. Another husband stated: "Our sexual relations are just now beginning
to normalize (to near before pregnancy) after a year." A
wife referred more directly to a factor leading to disruption of sexual activity. She said that one negative effect
of being parents was "having to plan sex around when baby
is asleep and having her wake up in the middle of the process!"
    A husband-wife relationship may be adversely affected
when the needs of the child must be met first. Several wives
commented that they felt they were neglecting their husbands.
One wife said, "My relationship with my husband is affected
by the baby's demands on me and this can be disturbing at
times. Our spontaneity has been limited." Another wife
confessed, "I have felt guilty for not giving my husband the
attention he needs." Another wife said, "The only negative
part of our life is that, being a mother, I have put that
first when I should have put being a wife first." Interestingly, comments such as these seemed to be less common when
the baby was older. Perhaps mothers began spending more time
with their husbands, or perhaps they became accustomed to
giving their time to the baby and no longer noticed the decreased amount of time spent with their husbands.
    Several other comments were made by wives about dissatis-
faction in the husband-wife relationship. One wife expressed
unhappiness because "my husband does not help me as much as
he should." Another wife was uneasy due to her increased
dependence on her husband. She said, "I depend on my husband
too much and feel dependent like a child." Another wife commented on the balance of power in her marriage: "Equal financial earnings are important to me and I'm now in an inferior
position."
    A third negative theme about new parenthood centers around
emotional costs experienced by the new parents. One emotional
cost is the strain of having total responsibility for the
child. This can be overwhelming when parents view themselves
as totally responsible and consider the length of time that
parenthood will last. Another emotional cost is the feeling

of uncertainty about one's own competence to care for the child. Combined with the lack of time, some new parents feel depressed, frustrated, and resentful toward both their child and spouse.

Responsibility for the child was mentioned repeatedly by the parents in our study. The enormous responsibility was felt intensely. A mother wrote:

The responsibility for supplying and satisfying his emotional and physical needs seems overwhelming at times and this has certainly increased what I consider to be the importance of my life. He has consumed me and now everything in my life revolves around him.

This mother went on to describe her feelings of helplessness, inadequacy, and self-doubts.

I am 29, this is my first child, and I don't think I've ever been so helpless. Having the responsibility for someone else's life is an adjustment that is hard to describe. It has produced self-doubt, the feeling of inadequacy and it has reduced my feeling of "having control" of my life. I often wonder if I have the capacity to meet the tremendous responsibility of being a good parent.

Parents sometimes resented the demands made by the baby. One mother said, "I have and still do feel very tied down and cut off from the outside world." A father said, "I feel more tied down than ever in my life. I occasionally feel resentful of the baby for inconveniences he often causes." Another mother experienced difficulty in adjusting to the lack of control she had:

Besides being more tired, and caring for the baby taking up so much of my day, one of the hardest adjustments for me was the unpredictableness of my day. I couldn't be sure of anything: That I would be able to take a nap after her next feeding, that I would have time to clean the house on a certain day, that I would have time to fix supper later, and so on. Before I adjusted to this, it caused me to be less satisfied with myself, the baby, and my husband.

New parents, particularly mothers, frequently questioned their abilities to meet the needs of the baby. One mother said, "At times I am unable to comfort my baby and am frustrated or resentful towards nature for making the life of an infant difficult." Another mother expressed her "unsureness about some aspects of the baby's personal needs." One mother commented that "the pressure is tremendous, knowing that he is depending entirely on me and that I might do something wrong out of ignorance that can greatly harm him."

One mother stated, "I feel at times he has completely taken over my life, my time, my freedom. I am adjusting to his total dependence." Another mother voiced a similar experience. "There is a loss of time for myself. Every minute seems to revolve around the baby--more than I expected." Yet another mother yearned for "time for myself to just be lazy, to read a book, and so on."

The fourth negative theme we detected included opportunity costs and restrictions. Parents wrote about restrictions on their social life, including recreation, travel, and interactions with friends. There were also financial restrictions, particularly when the wife had quit her job in order to care for the child. Additionally, there were restrictions on careers, especially for the mothers.

New parents were often reluctant to leave their baby with a sitter, unable to find a sitter, or unable to afford a sitter. Fatigue may have prevented parents from pursuing interests or activities they enjoyed before the baby's birth. One father commented that having a baby "decreases freedom to go at will." Another father wrote, "Most of our close friends are childless and it is hard at times to relate to them our experience. Many times I feel that the baby is a nuisance to some when he goes with us to visit."

A mother said, "We've missed our friends and parties, our unscheduled life style, and so on. These are things I've had to postpone because my son's needs come first." Another mother wrote, "Having our daughter has meant staying at home a lot more for me. I do miss those spur of the moment trips to shop or visit with friends." Another mother said, "I find a new baby hard to adjust to as I am a fairly social person. I feel tied down to a great extent." A father commented that there was "less time for hobbies."

Some parents mentioned financial concerns. Since the sample was mostly middle-class, financial worries were probably not as extensive as they would be for parents in lower socioeconomic groups. Interestingly, fathers were more likely than mothers to comment on the financial situation. One father, a student, said, "My wife's job was our major source of income. Now she is unemployed." Another father said that the birth of the child had "caused some financial concerns." "Our incomes were cut in half," stated one father. Another

father said, "My wife's income loss has been significant as
far as having 'extra' money to spend."

There was also concern about the impact of the birth of
the child on the wife's career and about the decisions that
would have to be made about the wife's return to work. One
father expressed this concern in relation to both himself
and his wife:

> The most disruptive aspect of her birth is the
> change we have had to make in our thinking and
> planning for both our careers. Where we could
> previously measure decisions affecting our careers
> in terms of an ideal of equality for both of us,
> now the equation is much more complicated to
> balance because of our decision to avoid day care
> for two or three years.

One mother expressed her dissatisfaction about her career
plans this way:

> The most negative aspect of having a baby for me
> has been giving up my career of teaching. I en-
> joyed my job tremendously and I miss it. At this
> point I do not feel fulfilled in my role as a
> mother. At times I feel frustrated and slightly
> depressed, but I know that I couldn't do a good
> job of handling the many responsibilities that
> go along with being a full-time teacher as well
> as being a good mother and homemaker. I have ap-
> plied to do some part-time teaching on a home-
> bound basis and just knowing that I might soon
> be working has lifted my spirits.

Another mother expressed concern about her decision to continue working. "The only negative feeling I have is, in
returning to work, I will be unable to care for him in the
way I feel is right. I feel pulled between my desire to
care for him and to continue my career. He is the most important of the two, and I do not want to hurt him by my working."

When the child was older, mothers expressed their difficulties in making decisions about their careers. One mother
mentioned that she "wondered about my future career plans--
will I get a job after not working for awhile?" Another
mother expressed her frustrations and discontent that resulted from leaving a career:

> My baby is a new individual in my life whom I
> love dearly, but at this point in my life I am

not personally fulfilled in simply being a mother.
I am finding it difficult to cope with the bore-
dom and lack of intellectual stimulation in my
life. I gave up my career of teaching because
I felt it would be unfair to take my baby to a
day care center or babysitter. I'm very undecided
as to what I should do.

Making a decision between a career and staying home with
the baby is difficult for some mothers. Other mothers indicated that they were happy and thought it was important
and imperative to remain home with the child. Mothers who
had had careers seemed to experience more stress and discontent over being full-time homemakers, in addition to concern
about the effects of their return to work on their child.

RECOMMENDATIONS

In the preceding sections we have related the positive and
negative aspects of the transition to parenthood as described
by new parents. From their comments, we see that at times
the baby was a "bouncing bundle of joy" for his/her parents;
at other times, however, the new parents were anything but
delighted with parenthood. The comments made by the parents
in our study reflect the realities of parenthood--there are
good times as well as bad, advantages as well as disadvantages. One father's total written comments are an especially
pithy summary of what many parents reported: "Joy, pride,
love. Tired, irritable, broke."
     In this section of the paper, implications and recommenda-
tions for strengthening this critical stage of the family
life cycle are suggested. Perhaps our motto for this section
of the paper could be: "Accentuate the positive, try to
anticipate and prepare for the negative!"
     Rossi (1968) noted that, in our society, people do not
learn beforehand how to be parents--we expect that people
will do the right thing "naturally." There is little preparation for parenthood, and prospective parents are usually
confused or uncertain about where to go for advice. There
are many popular books available, but these books are not
infallible. A couple could turn to their own parents for
advice (many do), but the parents might not be readily available or able to help.
     We are, perhaps, living during an era when realism about
parenting has come of age. The early studies of the transition to parenthood painted a picture of severe crisis.
LeMasters (1970) later pointed out many of the myths about
parenthood, noting that the romanticism surrounding parenthood

is probably greater than that surrounding marriage. These myths, which were so prevalent during the 50's and early 60's, were replaced by "hard facts" about the unpleasant realities of parenthood during the late 60's and early 70's. More couples are remaining "childfree." Some parents are openly expressing their dissatisfaction with parenthood. Some of these include restrictions on time, freedom, careers (especially for women). Also, having a child definitely involves responsibility; a child is a responsibility that remains a part of the parents' lives for many years. People are definitely more aware of the impact of parenthood. One of the fathers in our study said, "The disadvantages are about what I expected before the birth. The pleasures of having a child have been greater than I anticipated." Most of the parents included both positive and negative effects in their comments. We seem to be in a period when the picture of parenthood that is presented is more balanced. We are also in a period that provides us, as family life educators, with both an opportunity and responsibility to provide prospective parents and new parents with information and guidance on adjusting to a new phase in their lives.

Pre-parenthood classes are among the best opportunities for teaching skills and educating parents. Such classes are evident throughout the country, but many do not reach their full potential. In our study, the parents were recruited from childbirth preparation classes at hospitals in the area. The major focus of these classes is to talk about changes in the woman's body, prepare the woman, and, in some cases the couples, for the birth, and provide some information about the care of the infant. While these are certainly important topics, so much more could be done.

Pre-parenthood classes have great potential for informing the parents-to-be, not only about labor and delivery, but also about changes in the sexual relationship, feelings that new parents may have difficulty with, and for providing parents with group support. Although each parent will have to work out his/her own adjustments to new roles and to problems that appear, parenthood classes can help by setting up more realistic expectations. If new parents are aware of some of the things they are likely to experience, they will be better prepared to adjust.

Mann, Woodward, and Joseph (1961) reported that many new parents were overwhelmed with what they referred to as the actual phenomenology of infancy. By this they meant the sights, sounds, and smells associated with infants. Hogberg (Zack, 1975) reported that the two factors mentioned most often by parents in childbirth classes were their tiredness and the baby's crying. The newborn may be difficult to adjust to, but this adjustment is compounded by the constant

166

Family Strengths

fatigue of the parents, and especially of the mother. One suggestion for helping parents cope with this is to show films which provide a realistic picture of an infant's activities (Mann, Woodward, & Joseph, 1961), and to bring in real, live babies. This would make prospective parents more aware of what daily life with an infant involves. Of course, the impact would not be nearly as great as the impact of having a child in the home 24 hours a day, but it could serve to provide the parents with more realistic expectations.

One of the negative aspects of parenthood mentioned by the respondents was the physical demand of caring for an infant. Classes should provide more guidance on feeding, diapering, dressing, bathing, and coping with illness. Just as important, these classes can provide emotional support to new parents. Usually, parenthood classes end just before the birth of the child. As Hogberg stated, "This shows where we've left people, right at the delivery table" (Zack, 1975). Actually, the parents need continued information and support during the first few months after the birth of the child. Several parents in our sample reported feelings of helplessness in meeting the needs of their infants. New parents need to have a support system during the first years of the child's life, and parenthood classes could provide an excellent group opportunity for such a support system.

Some of the advantages of continued parenthood classes through the first year of the child's life include:

1. An outlet for feelings that parents may be reluctant to express

2. A chance to watch other parents and gain more knowledge and ideas about interaction with their child

3. An opportunity for both parents to participate, which would foster feelings of togetherness

4. Sharing ideas with other parents on adjusting to the changed marital relationship and the changed role of the wife if she quit work to care for the baby full-time

Generally, the birth of a child means more changes for the wife than for the husband. Women are more strongly socialized toward parenthood, and they learn more unequivocally that it is expected of them. Marriages which were egalitarian in terms of role-sharing frequently change after the birth of the first child. It seems easier to slip into the traditional societal definitions of mother and father, with the mother assuming most of the responsibility for meeting the child's physical and emotional needs, and the father providing the financial support for the family.

There is a need to foster an attitude of mutuality in caring for the child. Both parents can be actively involved in preparation for parenthood classes, childbirth, and care of the child. In fact, when both parents are involved, a feeling of family unity may be more likely to develop. Marital relationships may also benefit from the feeling of "weness" which can develop from shared responsibility. Also, the father gains satisfaction from participating more actively in his child's life.

High school and college classes to provide information and guidelines on parenting could include values exploration, values clarification, and role-playing. The participants could be encouraged to talk about their expectations of parenthood, of themselves, and of their spouses. The use of groups to discuss these topics would provide opportunities for hearing other viewpoints, and an atmosphere which provides support as well as encouragement for self-exploration. The same kinds of activities and topics could be used for preparation for parenthood classes, especially for expectant parents.

Emphasis should also be placed on the husband-wife relationship. New fathers and mothers should be encouraged to spend time together, away from the baby. Hogberg (Zack, 1975) states that time away from the infant can also be beneficial to the infant, since it allows a chance for the infant to develop trust in people other than the parents. In the parenthood groups, support can be given for time alone by other parents, thus helping alleviate the guilt the parents might feel about leaving their baby. Also, parents might take turns baby-sitting, eliminating the cost of baby-sitters, and making it possible for some parents to have some time alone even when they cannot afford to pay for baby-sitters.

Another of the problems reported by the parents was the disruption of their sexual relationship. The couple should be informed of some of the changes which may occur in the wife's sexual feelings and desires. It is important to encourage both husbands and wives to talk with their physician about their sexual relationship, and to try to get individualized advice. In order for this to occur, there is a need to include information about sexuality in the curriculum of medical schools. There is an increasing emphasis on training doctors in communication skills, and one possibility might be to set up workshops in hospitals for both doctors and nurses.

As noted, parenthood classes could be extended beyond the birth of the child. Post-childbirth classes would provide

an opportunity for parents to get more information about child
development, as well as providing a support system. Another
idea is to establish a "Parenting Hotline," which could be
used by parents when they feel unable to cope, or need answers
or ideas for dealing with some of the problems of parenting.
Such a hotline might be staffed by specialists in child development, providing a needed service as well as an opportunity for students to learn and apply their skills.

SUMMARY

The transition to parenthood is a period in the family life
cycle which involves redefinitions of roles and relationships.
There is increasing recognition that this period has both
positive and negative aspects. The purpose of the research
reported in this paper was to generate implications for parenthood education from the responses of first-time parents
who described the positive and negative effects of the baby
on their lives.

Eight themes regarding parenthood were derived from the
comments of parents, written when their baby was six-weeks-
old, and again when the child was eight-months-old. The
positive themes included emotional benefits, self-enrichment
and development, family cohesiveness, and identification with
the child. The negative themes reflected physical demands,
strains on the husband-wife relationship, emotional costs,
and opportunity costs and restrictions. These themes reflect the realities of parenthood; there are both advantages
and disadvantages to this transition period.

In preparing people for parental roles, pre-parenthood
classes have an unrealized potential for providing information and guidance. The continuation of such classes through
the first year of the child's life offers several advantages,
including an outlet for expressing feelings, opportunities
for gaining knowledge, and sharing ideas with other first-
time parents. The needs of the mother and father, as individuals and as a married couple, should not be overlooked.
Those who work with new parents, and those who study them,
must keep in mind the complexities of this period, and the
needs of those who are just beginning parental roles.

REFERENCES

Arnold, F., Bulatas, R. A., Buripakdi, C., Chung, B. J.,
    Fawcett, J. R., Iritani, T., Lee, S. J., & Wu, T. S.
    The value of children: A cross-national study.
    Hawaii: East-West Population Institute, 1975.

Blake, J. Coercive pronatalism and American public policy.
    In R. L. Coser (Ed.), *The family: Its structures and
    functions.* New York: St. Martin's Press, 1974.

Hoffman, L. W., & Manis, J. D. Influences of children on
    marital interaction and parental satisfactions and
    dissatisfactions. In R. M. Learner & G. B. Spanier
    (Eds.), *Child influences on marital and family inter-
    action: A life-span perspective.* New York: Academic
    Press, 1978.

LeMasters, E. E. Parenthood as crisis. *Marriage and Family
    Living,* 1957, *19,* 352-355.

LeMasters, E. E. *Parents in modern America.* Homewood,
    Illinois: Dorsey, 1970.

Mann, D., Woodward, L. E., & Joseph, N. *Educating expectant
    parents: Some observations and recommendations based
    on a research study.* New York: Visiting Nurse Service
    of New York, 1961.

Rossi, A. S. Transition to parenthood. *Journal of Marriage
    and the Family,* 1968, *30,* 26-39.

Russell, C. S. Transition to parenthood: Problems and
    gratifications. *Journal of Marriage and the Family,*
    1974, *36,* 294-301.

Zack, M. Help offered for parents after baby comes. *Min-
    neapolis Tribune,* April 13, 1975, pp. 1E, 4E.

Parent-Child Contracts: A Life-Span Perspective

Dr. David Elkind
Eliot-Pearson Department of
Child Study
Tufts University

FAMILY LIFE MODELS

There are many different ways of looking at family relationships, no one of which is yet able to give a comprehensive
depiction. My own feeling is that it is valuable to have
many different models because each illuminates a facet of
family interaction which may have been left in the dark by
others. And, only when we can see all the many different
sides of family life will we be in a position to construct
a truly encompassing theory of the whole.

It is in this spirit, the spirit of a need for different models of the family, that the present conceptualization
is offered. This model makes no claim to being a complete
portrayal of family interactions nor at providing a full
explanation of family difficulties. What the model does provide is an interactionist or constructivist perspective on
family life. It suggests that just as each child constructs
reality out of his or her experiences with the environment,
parents and children construct realities in consort. These,
what might be called collective realities, play a powerful
role in parent-child relations. This paper will be concerned
with the construction and evolution of these collective realities throughout the human life cycle.

Before proceeding, however, a word about the plan of
presentation is in order. In the first section, a general
description of some major collective realities, namely, parent-
child contracts will be described, particularly with respect
to their contents at successive age levels. Then, in the next
section, some of the dynamics of these contracts will be detailed, especially at fracture points in the evolution of
families. Finally, the last section will attempt to place
the contract position in a somewhat broader theoretical perspective.

PARENT-CHILD CONTRACTS

From a constructivist position, reality is always relative
in the sense that it is a joint product of the individual's
intellectual activity and the materials provided by the environment. In the realm of physical reality, for example,
the child's conception of the conservation of number, the
notion that the number of elements remains the same despite
their physical arrangement, requires both an experience with
objects and reasoning activity. This is true because numer-
ical equality is more than a perceptual judgment.

Although social realities are more complex, because the
stimulus cues such as facial expression and voice intonation
are more subtle, the same premise holds true. Children must
construct out of their mental abilities and their social
perceptions a social reality which enables them to survive
both within the family and outside of it.

There is, however, a sense in which social reality is
different than physical reality. At least initially, the
child's discovery of physical reality is immediate; it is
derived directly from contact with physical objects and events.
On the other hand, the child's discovery of social reality
is always mediated by parents and caretakers. Mediation means,
simply, that parents and caretakers act back upon the child
in such a way that they mediate his or her construction of
social reality. A child who smiles and is smiled back at
acquires a different social reality than does a child who
receives a different reaction. The physical world, by and
large, does not act back differentially upon the child; the
social world always does. Hence from their first moments
of life, infants' social experiences are mediated by the particular caretakers in the environment.

The fact that social reality is mediated by particular
caretakers does not mean that its construction is totally
capricious. There are constancies in the construction of
social reality much as there are constancies in the construction of physical reality. These constancies exist in the implicit expectancies which both parents and children carry
with them and which result in collective realities that have
some commonalities from family to family. These collective
realities, constructed anew with each child and having commonality across families, are what I call parent-child contracts.

Freedom/Responsibility

One of these common constructions is what might be called
the freedom/responsibility contract. Parents, borrowing from

their own experiences as children (more about social trans- mission will be said later), expect that children will pro- gressively begin to take responsibility for their own be- havior. And they, in turn, expect to provide the appropriate freedoms commensurate with the child's level of intellectual, social, and emotional development.

It is important to emphasize that as children mature, the freedom/responsibility contract is rewritten again and again. In effect, parents and children construct and recon- struct their collective realities. Indeed, as we shall see in the next section, when this is not done, significant inter- personal damage can occur. On the other hand, when there is a reasonably healthy match between parental expectations and child performance, and between child expectations and parental performance, reasonable familial harmony is likely to prevail.

To illustrate how the responsibility/freedom contract operates, consider the following examples. In infancy, par- ents do not expect a great deal in the way of responsibility and they grant few freedoms. Infants are closely monitored. But parents do have some expectations which emerge as soon as the infant wants to do things for himself or herself. When, say, an infant wants to take his or her own food, par- ents are likely to permit this so long as at least some of it gets in the baby's mouth, as well as on the floor, walls, and kitchen counters.

In early childhood, children become mobile and want to take liberties for which they may not be ready. A young child may, for example, want to lift a glass or plate which the parent feels sure will be dropped. What is critical here is that the parent adequately assess the child's competencies. Often this involves a little trial and error and a few broken plates. So long as children understand that they will have more chances later, withholding freedoms can help children assess the limits of their own competencies of the moment.

During infancy and to some extent during early childhood, the parent-child contract is generally communicated absolutely. The parent decides whether or not a particular freedom should be allowed and the child has little recourse other than an emotional reaction. In childhood proper, however, thanks to the school-aged child's language facility and reasoning powers, contractual arrangements become more relative. Children, for example, will often not accept a unilateral judgment by the parent and will argue their case for a particular freedom, such as staying up late, with considerable vehemence.

It is at this juncture that parenting styles come into play. Actually one can define the typical categories of parenting--democratic, authoritarian, *laissez faire*--with respect to their treatment of contracts. The democratic parent

listens to the child's argument, gives his or her own reasons
and makes a judgment which takes the child's position into
account. The authoritarian parent will not entertain the
young person's arguments for a particular freedom and continues to make unilateral judgments. The *laissez faire* parent,
in contrast, grants children freedoms without demanding any
responsibility in return.

In adolescence, parent-child contracts reach a new level
of complexity. Contracts now become abstract or general, and
merge with moral and ethical principles as well as with the
laws of the larger society. The use of the family car, for
example, is controlled in part by the parents' assessment
of the young person's responsibility, but also by his or her
age, and the obtaining of a driver's license. Smoking mari-
juana or consumption of alcohol likewise is regulated, to
some extent, both by parents and by society. In short, what
seems to happen is that in adolescence the freedom/responsi-
bility contract becomes one between the child and society,
as well as one between the parents and their offspring. Put
differently, the freedom/responsibility contract prepares
the young person to become a responsible member of the larger
society.

Achievement/Support

A second type of reality that is constructed between parents
and children has to do with achievement and support. In general, parents have certain expectations regarding children's
achievements, which they then support cognitively, affectively,
and materially. Again, these contracts have to be rewritten
as children mature, and as the kinds of achievements of which
they are capable begin to broaden. Parents, too, have to
broaden the types of support they provide.

A few examples may help to make the evolution of this
contract more concrete. During infancy, the achievements
parents expect of their offspring are largely sensori-motor
and the supports are largely affective. When an infant holds
his or her head up, or stands up in the crib, or says a recog-
nizable word, the parents respond with hugs and cries and
other affective signs of approval. In such a way, the child
learns quickly that achievements, attempts at mastery, are
rewarded by parents.

During the preschool years, sensori-motor achievements
are coupled with symbolic achievements, and affective supports
on the part of parents are coupled with symbolic rewards.
Young children not only begin to master their bodies but also
their clothing, their eating, and their toileting. They also
begin to master language. Parents, who could not wait for
the child to speak, now cannot wait for him or her to be still.

Parents, in addition to the affective supports of infancy, add the symbolic supports of the preschool period. Such phrases as "very good," "nicely done," and "look at that" are frequent.

In childhood proper, the achievements become more differentiated as children enter school. Now achievements are evident in three domains--the academic, the interpersonal, and the extracurricular. Unlike the achievements of infancy and the preschool years, these achievements have a social dimension and involve interaction with teachers, peers, and other adults. At this stage, the child is not as totally responsible for his or her achievements as in the years of infancy and early childhood. It is important that parents appreciate this interaction, and that they recognize a child's success or failure in these domains is not entirely his or her doing.

Parents in turn expand the range and nature of the supports that they provide. There is, for example, an increase in the amount of material support as children get clothes and supplies for school, and the money and equipment for extracurricular activities. Among middle class parents, at least before the energy crisis, parents showed support by driving their children about to friends' houses, for lessons, and so on. Parents also show support by their presence at certain activities, particularly when the child is performing at some school or extracurricular event. In other words, as children's achievements become more social, they expect parental support to be more public.

In adolescence, accomplishments in the same three domains are expected. Young people are expected to achieve academically, interpersonally, and extracurricularly. Parents, however, become more particular in these domains. They may expect adolescents to do well in certain courses but not all; they are not pleased with any and all adolescent friendships; and some extracurricular activities may be frowned upon. In adolescence for the first time, parents and their children may not agree on what sorts of achievements are most valuable.

The parental support system changes, too. Adolescents are much less concerned than children about public parental support for their achievements, and may even resent it as embarrassing. Indeed, adolescents seem to want only one type of support from parents, namely, material support in the way of money for clothing, records, and so on. This is deceptive, however, and adolescents still want affective and symbolic rewards as well. When their children become adolescents, therefore, parents must learn how to provide support in diplomatic and tactful ways that will not offend the young people to whom it is directed.

Loyalty/Commitment

A third collective reality constructed by parents and children has to do with implicit expectations regarding loyalty and commitment. In general, parents expect a certain amount of loyalty from their children in return for the time, energy, effort, and expense the parents expend in their upbringing. As in the other contracts, however, the realities have to be reconstructed as children and parents mature. Indeed, the parents come to expect new loyalties consistent with the child's expanding sense of self and world.

During infancy, for example, children progressively construct a world of permanent objects conceived as existing when no longer present to the infant's senses. At the same time, the infant also begins to construct a notion of self as existing in time and in space. Not surprisingly, parents come to expect that during infancy their offspring will be loyal to them as objects, showing attachment, fear of separation, etc. Indeed, while much has been written about separation anxiety as a sign of attachment, for parents it is an expression of loyalty. Likewise, the infant who refuses to respond to strangers gives the mother or father or both an important and gratifying sign of loyalty to them.

During early childhood, children begin to construct a world of signs (conventional representations, such as language), and symbols (personal representations, such as dream images) to signify and extend their control over the object world. Consequently, the child also constructs a notion of the symbolic self associated with the words "I," "me," "mine," with his or her name, and with the family name. Parents at this stage begin to expect, in addition to loyalty to themselves as persons, a loyalty to symbols which they represent. Parents, for their part, show commitment in the amount of time and concern they put into child rearing.

As this point, something should be said of siblings. The birth of a sibling causes, in a real sense, a crisis in the loyalty/commitment contract. This is true because with pregnancy and the birth of a new sibling, the parents' commitment clearly becomes divided. Indeed, one way of looking at sibling rivalry and at birth order effects on personality is to consider the ramifications of siblings on the loyalty/commitment contract. We shall explore this issue in a little more detail in the last section, but it was necessary to raise the point here to avoid the impression that loyalty/commitment progression is linear and straightforward.

In childhood proper, children construct a world of rules that results in what might be called a lawful world. At the same time, they construct a "lawful" concept of self as a rule maker, follower, and breaker. Again, the parental conception of loyalty expands to include these new constructions and children's loyalty is now measured in terms of the extent to which they abide by the rules. One reason parents get so angry when school-age children lie and take things is that they see it as a kind of disloyalty to them. Just as parents expect children to be loyal to the symbols they represent, so do they expect their children to be loyal to the rules which they espouse.

When young people reach adolescence, they become capable of new, higher-level modes of thought and new conceptions of the world and the self. The new world that is constructed is ideological in the sense that young people become capable of dealing with abstract ideas and that they become enamored of them. But they also construct a concept of the reflective self which can think about itself, as well as about the thoughts of others. Not surprisingly, the kinds of loyalties parents expect change, too. Parents now want young people to be loyal to their beliefs and values, as well as to them as persons, to family symbols, and to moral values. For example, during adolescence parents may take it as a sign of disloyalty if the young person dates someone from an ethnic or religious group of whom the family disapproves.

To be sure, the kinds of commitments parents are expected to show change, too. At all age levels, commitment is measured in the amount of time and concern parents show children. That is the bottom line. But it has to be shown differently at different age levels. This is true because children expect parents to be committed to the same things which they are committed to. Children expect parents to be committed to family symbols, to moral rules, and to the ideologies they espouse. Children, then, expect parents to broaden their commitments in keeping with the parents' broadened expectations with respect to loyalty.

This is a brief description of the kinds of realities that I believe parents and their offspring construct in the process of living and growing with one another. It is just a framework and needs a lot of filling in to be meaningful in specific cases. I want to turn now to another issue and to suggest what happens to contracts across the life cycle.

CONTRACTS ACROSS THE LIFE CYCLE

How, one might ask, do contracts come to be transmitted across generations? More specifically, one might ask how a child, who has been at one end of the freedom/responsibility, achievement/support, and loyalty/commitment contracts, gets to be at the other end when he or she becomes a parent? Although

a simple modeling of parental behaviors can provide part of
the answer, it really does not suffice to tell the whole story.
This is true because contracts involve a whole series of implicit expectancies which may never be modeled directly, and
which are communicated in complex and subtle ways. Modeling
is too simple to account for the intricate transformations
which take place.

It seems to me that one has to look at the interpersonal
patterns which evolve in childhood and adolescence for the
answer. Relationships to parents tend to be unilateral in
the sense that parents expect responsibilities in return for
which they grant freedom. Children are not in the position
to demand that parents act responsibly or to give freedoms.
This is one reason I find it difficult to believe that children learn to use contracts as parents by modeling their own
parents' behavior. They are always on the receiving, never
the giving, end of things.

I believe that children learn the other side of contracts
with other children and siblings. Here the relationship is
one of mutuality and is not unilateral. In playing and working with other children, young people can begin to expect
certain behaviors in return for certain favors. In childhood, the rewards for obeying contracts are most often personal acceptance. If, for example, a child shows that he
or she is willing to abide by the rules of the game, then
permission to play is given. It is with peers, therefore, that
children learn the reciprocal nature of contracts, and how
to be on the giving as well as the receiving end.

This is perhaps most clear in adolescence when strong and
abiding friendships are formed. In such friendships, one
can discern contracts which have mutuality as their basis. In
true friendships, for example, each friend supports the other's
achievements. For example, on a football or hockey team,
everyone embraces the player who gets the winning point--
but they would embrace any player who did it. This is a clear
case of reciprocal achievement support.

In close friendships loyalty/commitment is also apparent.
Commitment is shown by working at the relationship, trying
to be together, and loyalty by defending it against those who
would break it up. In the same way, good friends may advise
one another about their actions, or about the responsibilities inherent in certain freedoms. In summary, I hold with
Sullivan (1953), and Piaget (1965) that friendships during
childhood and adolescence are critical to the attainment of
adult competencies, particularly parenting skills.

When young people marry, the contracts of freedom/re-
sponsibility, loyalty/commitment, and achievement/support
have to be mutually accepted and understood if the marriage
is to survive. One advantage that young people coming from

similar backgrounds have over those who do not is a certain commonality with respect to their contractual expectations. Although we cannot go into the matter here, one approach to understanding marriage and marital breakdowns is from the standpoint of the contractual understandings each person brings to the relationship.

It is thus through the intimacy of friendships and marriage that young adults become capable of assuming the parental role, in this context, of administering contracts. Once a couple has a child, the consequences of the couple's upbringings and personalities become apparent. For example, some young parents, most often men, may refuse to enter into contracts with their children, or may want the children to be on the giving end. Sometimes too, the parents may disagree on what to expect from the children, so the contractual expectancies are confused and conflicting. One reason parents often do a better job with later children than the first is that they know more of what to expect and can establish more clearly defined contracts.

Sometimes parenting difficulties arise from sources other than the parents themselves. Television is a case in point. One problem with new technological innovations is that society has had no previous history with them. The same was true with radios and cars. The problem for parents was, and has been, to determine what is responsible television watching, and how much freedom children should have in this regard.

Again, my feeling is that second generation television parents--those who grew up with television but whose parents did not--have a better sense of responsible television watching than their own parents did. In other words, my guess is that contemporary parents are more careful about their children's television watching than their own parents were. Clearly, this is not a case of modeling their parents' behavior. Rather, it is probably a matter of drawing upon their own experience as a television watcher. It is my contention that only when a young person has grown up with a technological innovation can he or she write adaptive contracts about it with children. Most likely the problem of excessive television watching by children will diminish as children who have grown up with television become parents.

Earlier, I suggested that siblings pose a special problem to parent-child contracts. Not only do new children challenge the loyalty/commitment contract, but also the freedom/responsibility and the achievement/support contracts. It is in the administration of contracts with children at different age levels that parenting skills and sensitivity become most evident. Only a few examples of some of the complications introduced by siblings can be offered here.

With respect to loyalty/commitment, it is clear that older siblings naturally feel a younger sibling is a breach of a parental contract of commitment. The young child's early sense is that parental commitment is absolute, and it comes as a little shock to discover that this is not the case. Some of the regressive and angry behavior shown by older siblings, for example, can be understood, in part at least, as a reaction to a sensed breach of contract. The child feels that since the parents are not committed to him or her, there is no need for loyalty to them. When siblings arrive, it is important for parents to demonstrate their abiding commitment to older siblings as well.

Siblings also produce complications for the freedom/responsibility contract. Clearly, older children are allowed freedoms which are not permitted younger children. They can stay up later, stay overnight at friends' houses, and so on. The younger children want these freedoms, too, and have difficulty understanding what the requisite responsibilities are for their attainment. They feel that there should be no differential treatment, and that freedoms granted to one should be granted to all. Successful handling of this situation requires a clear articulation of the freedom/responsibility contract.

Finally, the achievement/support contract can also pose problems when there is more than one child in the home. This is true because not all children achieve in the same domains or equally well. Parents must learn to support these differential achievements without showing preferences, and by working hard to show that children's different achievements can be valued and supported equally. When this is not done, difficulties often ensue.

Consider a family in which the daughter is training to be an Olympic ice skater. All the family's resources and much of the mother's time is devoted to this enterprise. The younger son is bright and is a good athlete and musician. But clearly, much more support is given to the daughter's achievements, which are much more valued. The result is a somewhat immature, whiny boy who feels undervalued and undersupported. My guess is that he will always resent his parents for the unfair treatment he received.

What I am suggesting here is that, when parents break contracts in the sense of not holding up their part of the bargain, serious difficulties can result. Elsewhere (Elkind, 1979), I have suggested that juvenile delinquency can result from broken parental contracts. Here, I am suggesting that contractual violations on the part of parents can help to account for a wide variety of childhood problems. Stated differently, the frustrations and anger children feel when their expectations from parents are unfulfilled contribute,

I believe, a great deal to a wide variety of behavioral difficulties children manifest--from learning disabilities to
aggressive acting out.

Before closing this section, brief mention should be made
of the other end of the life cycle, namely, aging. As parents
age and their offspring leave the home, their contractual
responsibilities are really not at an end. What often happens is that they must re-engage in contracts with their own
parents, but from the opposite direction. They must now write
responsibility/freedom, achievement/support, and loyalty/
commitment contracts with their own parents, which are remin-
iscent of, but quite different from, the contracts written
with their own children.

Consider the elderly parent who insists on living alone,
but who cannot really care for himself or herself. At this
point, the children must decide the parent cannot have this
freedom because he or she does not demonstrate the requisite
responsibility. It should be said that, more often than not,
not all of the siblings share in such decision making. Usually one sibling, the one who felt most fairly treated by
the parents, is likely to take charge.

Similar reversals occur with respect to achievement and
support. Offspring encourage their parents to get into a
variety of activities, and support such endeavors as trips,
cruises, etc. They encourage their parents to take courses,
and even to work if work has been a mainstay of a person's
life. Such support can, by the way, be financial as well as
psychological. Some children do underwrite their aging parents' activities, much as their own achievements were under-
written.

Finally, the loyalty/commitment contract also comes into
play. Children who are devoted to their parents, and who
show commitment to them by calling, visiting, writing, and
by financial support, expect some form of loyalty in return,
although in many cases it is done out of genuine affection
and caring, as a result of fulfilled contractual obligations
on the parents' part. But aging parents can break contracts,
too, and can favor a sibling who has neglected them over one
who has given and devoted much to their care and well being.
Of contracts and breaches of contracts--real and imagined--
there is no end throughout the whole life cycle.

GENERAL CONSIDERATIONS

In this paper, I have sketched in broad strokes a contract
theory of family relationships which is largely cognitive in
origin. Contracts are cognitive constructions, collective

realities--shared by children and parents--that express mutual
expectancies about behavior, thought, and feeling. Contracts,
in this view, help to regulate the day-to-day and long-term
interactions of family members. Breaches of these contracts
can, I have argued, help to account for a wide variety of problem behaviors on the part of children.

Although the contract notion is still very descriptive
and has a clinical rather than a research base, something
should be said of its relationships to other theories. My
own belief is that there is much of value in the dynamic
theories of Freud, Jung, Sullivan, and Erikson. Contract
theory is not offered as a substitute or alternative explanation for family interactions. Rather, it is offered as a
sort of complement to these theories which, however, valuable, are not really informed by a knowledge of the cognitive development of children and parents. Only when we begin to incorporate that knowledge into our theories of family interactions can we hope to have a comprehensive theory
of the family. It is in that spirit, the spirit of moving
towards a theory of the family that is at once cognitive, developmental, and dynamic, that the present conceptualization
has been offered.

REFERENCES

Elkind, D. Growing up faster. *Psychology Today*, 1979,
    38-47.

Piaget J. *The moral development of the child*. New York:
    The Free Press, 1965.

Sullivan, H. S. *The interpersonal theory of psychiatry*.
    New York: Norton, 1953.

Parents as Peopleteachers: The Prosocial Skill Enhancement of Children

Dr. Charles A. Smith
Extension Specialist,
 Human Development
Kansas State University

INTRODUCTION

In order to fully understand the concept of family strengths
our focus could go beyond the more descriptive qualities
which underly family life satisfaction and characterize strong
families (Stinnett, 1979). Such characteristics as "good
communication patterns," "spending time together," and "high
degree of religious orientation" are actually the means toward
some end which an effective or strong family strives to attain. Thus, the emphasis on family strengths could be broadened to include those individual and interpersonal outcomes or
skills which emerge as the result of these types of important
family interaction patterns. The questions which examine the
heart of the family strength issue are, "What kind of person
are you becoming as the result of the family's influence?"
"How are other family members influenced by your involvement
with them?" "Are you and the rest of your family basically
satisfied with their directions of personal growth and interpersonal relationships?"

The emphasis of this paper will be on examining the personal and interpersonal outcomes which may emerge from effective family interaction. Furthermore, these outcomes will
be organized into a matrix model which could be used to develop and evaluate skill development programs. This model
will be applied more specifically to parent-child relationships. This specific emphasis affirms our convinction that
parents can have a powerful influence on how children perceive and deal with their social reality.

Children are not born with an understanding of life.
They have no concept of themselves or their family. But
through experience, observation, and feedback, children gradually develop concepts of how their world does and should
operate. They also begin to form ideas of how they should
behave in relationship to that world. For example, through
the experience of physical contact, the infant begins to

differentiate between self and non-self; through observation he or she learns to recognize that self; and if the parent should make such comments as, "Oh, what a beautiful body you have; I think you are beautiful!" the child begins to form certain attitudes toward that self through feedback from others whose opinion is valued. These ideas about one's physical self then influence the child's use of his or her body in dance, play, and all forms of movement. Similarly, children begin to acquire a broad range of knowledge about themselves and others in a predictable, age-related manner (Damon, 1977).

The pursuit of social understanding serves two important functions. First, young children have a great need to resolve the uncertainty which is generated in their experiences with people. The impersonal environment is much more predictable than their social reality. A piece of paper will nearly always tear, a glass dropped on a hard surface will nearly always break. But what will happen when the little girl in the next desk has her hair pulled, or the child quietly building something nearby has his or her tower pushed over? By experimenting with their ideas of social cause and effect, children gradually discover that people respond differently from each other even under similar circumstances. Over time, the uncertainties of children diminish as the behavior of other people becomes more familiar, more predictable, and less mysterious.

A second critical function which social experiences serve is to enable children to gain a measure of self-definition.

> Every person wants to know his outstanding characteristics, the traits that define self-as-object to the self-as-person. This desire is the essential component of the wish to gain information about the self, to know what one is . . . . Some questions about the self can be resolved without anyone else's help. But in most cases the only way to evaluate one's self is to be with others. (Kagan, 1971, pp. 49-50)

How are young children to know if they are worthwhile unless others respond favorably to them? How certain could children be of their own gentleness unless others affirm the presence of this characteristic in their relationship with them? Conceptions of one's self must be socially validated in order to be accepted as true. The desire to relate to others is an important aspect of the continually unfolding pursuit of self-knowledge.

In my work as a preschool teacher of four-year-old children, as a director of a university child development center,

and now as an extension human development specialist at
Kansas State University, I have found parents to be very interested in the personal/social development of their children. However, they are confused and frequently misinformed
regarding the nurturance of prosocial skills in their children. For example, parents rarely appreciate the importance
of non-destructive conflict in sibling relationships. The
petty arguments which are so frequent among children are certainly irritating to adults but are vitally necessary for
the weakening of egocentrism in children. By emphasizing
impersonal skills, schools fail to help parents understand
the educational significance of personal/social development.
New models exploring competence in the "life arts" may provide guidance to better understand their children.

THE MODEL

The Peopleteaching Approach

Several innovative approaches to early childhood and parent
education have emerged over the past decade. Now known by
a variety of terms--confluent education, filial relationship
enhancement, transpersonal education, peopleteaching, social
problem solving (Brown, 1971; Coufal, 1978; Hendricks &
Fadiman, 1976; Smith, 1974; Spivak & Shure, 1974)--
these approaches herald the emergence of an educational
renaissance in programs for children and their parents.
All share a common concern on establishing some type of
program which will enable children and their parents to
become more aware of themselves personally and to become
more effective socially.

The peopleteaching model is one significant and comprehensive approach to fostering life skills in families. The
term peopleteaching refers to any effort which helps children
and adults learn more about their humanity and acquire the
skills necessary to live harmoniously with others. Parents
who would like to give their children a sound beginning on
these skills can focus on two parallel goals. First, parents can try to reach out to the minds of their children and
try to help them better understand and organize their thoughts
about their personal and interpersonal experiences. Second,
parents can try to nurture behaviors which promote personal
and interpersonal relationship development. The central focus
of peopleteaching is people and their relationship to each
other.

Within the PT model, this dual emphasis of reaching out
to the child's mind and fostering behavioral change is applied
to six content or subject matter areas: body awareness,

sensory awareness, emotional development, affiliation and friendship, conflict and cooperation, and kindness and affection. Some of the skills are the result of parental efforts to create a learning environment which leads the child in certain directions--instructional effects--while others are simply "caught" from living in the environment--nurturant effects (see Table 1).

Body awareness involves learning the names and functions of various body parts, accepting one's self and others' physical traits, understanding the changes associated with growth, and expressing one's self through movement. Sensory awareness is the establishment of real contact with and awareness of one's environment, as well as the sharing of these experiences through language. Emotional development involves the development of an affective vocabulary, a recognition of emotional experiences in others, and the growth-promoting expression of feelings. Affiliation and friendship refers to the development of an understanding of human groups, achieving social contact and forming friendships. Conflict and cooperation signifies the development of conflict awareness, cooperation, and nonviolent resolution of conflict. Finally, kindness and affection involves understanding the meaning of kindness, and developing such "good Samaritan" skills as task-oriented help, compassion, affection, compensation, and sharing.

Body Awareness

Families have an impact on how children view and feel about their bodies. How do parents deal with such issues as racism, sexism, and age bias? How are such issues as birth, life, and death presented? What kinds of comments are made regarding the child's body? What kinds of restrictions are placed on the child's movement and spontaneity?

Body awareness involves a constellation of skills which relate to a person's understanding of and attitudes toward his or her own body. The three basic body awareness skills which parents can nurture in themselves and their children are: (1) an accurate body concept, (2) physical acceptance, and (3) body integration.

One important objective for peopleteaching is to help children develop an age-appropriate understanding of their physical structure, an accurate body concept. Parents can help their children learn the names and functions of various aspects of their body; they can help them learn how they change over time--that life begins at birth, that people grow and change over time, and that death gives meaning to life and is an event we can discuss and explore. Furthermore, parents can teach their child the meaning of sickness and the

Table 1

Instructional and Nurturant Effects of the Peopleteaching Model

Nurturant Effects

- Self-acceptance
- Self-actualization
- Prosocial values
- Positive feelings

The Peopleteaching Model

Instructional Effects

Themes (Subject Matter Areas):

1. Body Awareness
2. Sensory Awareness
3. Emotional Development
4. Affiliation and Friendship
5. Conflict and Cooperation
6. Kindness and Affection

Processes:

A. Understanding (self/social cognition)

B. Behaving (personal/social behavior)

significance of the body's healing capabilities. When they
do not receive support from parents in their attempt to understand these life issues, children will reduce their uncertainty with their own misconceptions. For example, the author
once had an adult student who revealed that for many years
he thought he was filled with tar. He came to this conclusion
after hearing his parents tell him many times, "If you don't
stop doing that I'm going to beat the tar out of you!" He
made up for his lack of sound information by accepting the
literal meaning of his parent's remarks. All children, no
matter what their age, need experiences and adult support which
help them better understand themselves.

A second important life-skill related to body awareness
involves self acceptance of one's physical characteristics
and a willingness to accept physical differences in others.
This concern would reflect the parent's commitment to eliminate racism, sexism, rejection of physically stigmatized individuals, and other forms of prejudice.

Parents can promote this type of acceptance by showing
their pride in their children's bodies and by demonstrating
a willingness to discuss their children's concerns. Parents
can also affirm the value of physical differences in others.
But self-acceptance is made difficult by our prevailing cultural aspect of the ideal body. Children are socialized into this cult of the "beautiful body" by television images
(especially the commercials), some children's books (as in
the physical perfection of Sleeping Beauty), and toys (especially the well-developed teenage dolls like Barbie and
Ken). Parents can refuse to legitimize these influences by
commenting on what television portrays and selecting books
and toys which do not emphasize a stereotyped view of beauty.

The third critical skill which contributes to body
awareness is body integration--the ability to productively
channel energy throughout the body, to become aware of body
tension, and to express creative and graceful body movement.

The healthy infant who has nurturing parents is a balanced, centered being. Energy flows naturally and is not held
back and confined to a specific area of the body. For example, when they are angry or sad, infants allow their energy
to flow by crying, and when happy they express energy by
laughing and making gleeful sounds. Children who are centered dance and run with joy and abandon. They are having
a romance with their bodies.

Parents can nurture this skill by helping children to
express energy in nondestructive ways, by encouraging and
showing pleasure in the child's movements, and by participating with them in joyful movement activities. Every parent can help create the conditions which nurture the feeling

in children that they are truly "at home" in their bodies,
which is what body awareness really is.

For reviews of various body awareness issues see Fisher
(1974), Lifton and Olson (1974), Porter (1971), and Ward
(1969).

Sensory Awareness

Families also have an effect on how children use their senses
in making contact with their world. Do parents encourage
sensory play? Do they provide experiences which nuture all
their child's sensory capacities? Do parents help their children use language and the arts to communicate and enrich sensory experiences?

Sensory awareness involves a balance between two complementary skills. The first--sensory contact--is primarily
experiential, while the second--sensory expression--intro-
duces a cognitive element.

Sensory contact is a skill parents can strive to maintain rather than teach their children. Physically healthy
infants are very skilled in sensory contact. Infants become
totally absorbed in their experiences; they are neither preoccupied with concerns related to the past nor distracted by
the anticipation of what will happen tomorrow. They are totally absorbed by the "now," by what is happening to them as
it occurs. When they eat, for example, infants involve as
many of their senses as possible--they touch their food,
taste it, look at it, smell it, sometimes to the consternation of their parents. Because so many of their experiences
are new, infants and young children eagerly strive to investigate everything as thoroughly as possible. This absorp-
tion in immediate sensory experiences is the foundation for
all pleasure in life.

But sensory contact may become a casualty to other developmental gains. The child's acquisition of language and
associated conceptual skills may intrude in sensory experiences. While they are preoccupied in thinking, children
and adults cannot also appreciate the experience of making
contact. Instead of experiencing the texture/sight/smell/
taste of an object, the child or adult may simply call it a
"rock." In one sense, familiarity may breed contempt. However, this loss of contact is not inevitable. Parents can
legitimize sensory experience. For example, one parent gives
a rock to his child and says, "Wow, Janie, look at this! What
do you see? Feel it; find out what its texture is. Find
out what kind of smell it has." Another parent gives his
child a rock and says, "Mike what is this? What color is
it? Is it bigger than this other rock? Is is round or
square?" The first parent encouraged the child to come closer

to experiencing the rock, while the second was asking the child to think about the rock. If this thinking about things is over-emphasized at the expense of experiencing things, then the child will grow into an adult who has lost the child-like ability to enjoy a sense of wonder in life.

Sensory expression involves the creative use of words and the arts to portray sensory experiences. Parents can nurture a conviction in their children that words can convey a sense of wonder. In their use of language, young children are very much in touch with the poetic. A child points to an umbrella and calls it a "rainbrella," while another asks her parent to "unzip the present." Another child around seven years old writes, "The wind is soft. I felt it kiss my cheek." These are examples of words which promote rather than inhibit contact with the sensory world. As parents we should do all that we can to encourage this poetic use of language.

Additional information on sensory awareness can be found in Brooks (1974), Gunther (1968), and Liepmann (1973).

Emotional Development

Families also influence children's attitudes toward emotions and fantasy. How do family members express love and affection? How do they deal with anger, fear, and sadness? Do the parents talk about their own feelings? Do they encourage children to listen and learn from their own emotions? How do family members relate to fantasy and imagination? Are dreams and nightmares discussed? Children are eager to make sense out of their emotions in the same way they are trying to understand their own physical growth and sensory experiences.

The skills of emotional development involve the ability to (1) be aware of and identify emotional experiences, (2) communicate emotional experiences to others; (3) demonstrate an awareness of the feelings of others; and (4) understand and appreciate the usefulness of fantasy and imagination.

Emotions provide information about how we are really responding to our world. Emotions emerge from ideas or beliefs about something. For example, a child who believes that snakes are dangerous will experience the emotion of fear, while a younger child who has not acquired this belief will show no hesitancy in approaching a snake. These two children react differently because they believe differently. One sees a snake and perceives something threatening, while the other sees a snake as something interesting.

When they are encouraged to listen to the messages underlying emotions, children will gradually begin to understand better how they perceive their world. For example, when they become frightened, children can be encouraged to identify and understand what is threatening them; when they are sad, children can be encouraged to explore the significance of what they have lost or think they may lose; and when they are happy, children could be encouraged to become familiar with experiences which they value and find pleasurable. Emotional awareness can contribute to self-understanding.

Once they become aware of their feelings, children can learn to communicate their experiences to others. Parents can encourage their children to talk about their feelings. Parents can try to convey the belief that every feeling, no matter how strong, can be discussed, and that talking about a feeling does not mean it will necessarily be acted upon. Sadly, many of us have learned that emotional experiences are supposed to be hidden. We have learned rituals like the "How are you . . . I'm fine" exchange which occurs so frequently in our everyday life. No matter how lousy our feelings, we will always say, "Oh, fine!" Instead of hiding behind these psychological masks and rituals, children can learn to make emotional contact with others.

As children become aware of and communicate their own emotional experiences, they can also learn to identify emotional expressions in others. Identifying feelings in others serves two useful purposes. First, this empathy will suggest how one should respond to the other. For example, a five-year-old could try to comfort her brother when he begins to cry. Second, communicating this empathy will enhance the relationship of those involved. For example, in the previous situation the sister might also say, "Oh, Bill's sad. His truck broke." An expression of empathy such as this would help her brother to feel understood and closer to his sister. Emotional development depends on awareness, communication, and empathy.

A fourth issue which relates to emotional development is an awareness of fantasy and the imaginary--the appreciation of intuitive, nonrational, creative ways of thinking and solving problems. Parents can gradually help their children realize that even though imaginary events and fantasies are not "real," this faculty is enjoyable and worthwhile. The mind's capacity for engaging in fantasy and other forms of mental play is a critical element in creative thinking.

Additional information on emotional development in children can be found in Borke (1973), Deutsch (1974), and Gilbert (1969).

Affiliation and Friendship

The fourth theme emphasized by the peopleteaching approach is affiliation and friendship. This particular concern is the first of three (along with conflict/cooperation and

kindness/affection) which examines interpersonal relationships. These themes parallel Schutz's (1979) work on in-
clusion/control/affection as basic dimensions in interpersonal
orientations. Affiliation (or inclusion) refers primarily to
the desire to be included by others. Achieving social contact is the first step in developing relationships. Everyone needs to be recognized. Without social contact, we feel
isolated, abandoned by others.

How well do parents include their children in their life?
Do they give their children the attention they need? Do they
provide opportunities for their children to make contact with
their peers? How do they respond to their child's rejection
or shyness? These questions focus on the affiliation theme.
Affiliation skills include: (1) developing a perspective on
human association, (2) initiating social behavior, and (3)
forming and negotiating relationships.

Developing a perspective on human association means helping children to form a rational orientation to their social
world which will enable them to reach out confidently to
others. During their early years children begin to form a
set of beliefs about people and groups to whom they belong.
Because of their experiences with their parents and others,
some children may conclude that people are to be mistrusted
and avoided. Conversely, others may decide that, although
there are exceptions, people are generally interesting and
worthwhile.

These ideas tend to influence how children initiate social behavior. A child who perceives others as potentially
dangerous will hesitate to make contact. Another who views
others as sources of gratification, though, will show eagerness in initiating social interaction. Parents influence
this decision-making process by what they do and say to their
children. For example, parents can encourage their children
to be friendly and courteous to strangers but avoid going
anywhere with them. Parents can also try to help their children understand the "give and take" of friendships. The objective here would be to build the child's confidence in initiating social contact.

In addition to facilitating the development of a positive cognitive framework regarding social behavior, parents
can also exert influence on the child's ability to initiate
contact and form friendships. Competence in this socializing skill means establishing a comfortable level of with-
drawing from social contact. For example, two four-year-
old children meet each other for the first time in their preschool class. After a brief period of "checking each other
out," they begin to play. Successful contact has been made.
The skills of social contact are very subtle, including such

behaviors as reciprocal eye contact, gestures of invitation, and supportive verbal comments.

On the other hand, solitary play is also an important capacity. A parent might also notice that there are times when two children drift away from association with others and engage in some satisfactory form of solitary play. By doing so, they are demonstrating they are neither compulsively social nor antisocial. Enjoyment in their initiating social contact is matched by their comfort in solitary behavior.

Parental influence over a child's social relationships is somewhat limited. No adult can make one child be liked by another. The child has to do the "work." He or she must want to become involved and be willing to make the effort to establish contact. Friends can be won only at the risk of rejection. Parents can help the process by bringing children together and creating opportunities for them to learn about each other--their names, preferences, and other characteristics.

For additional information on affiliation, see Ferguson (1971), and Gottman, Gonso, and Rasmussen (1975).

Conflict and Cooperation

Once the affiliation concern is resolved, relationships will inevitably move to resolve conflict-related issues. The focus now is on control and influence. For any relationship to develop and deepen, those involved must learn how to resolve conflict and share power to the satisfaction of each. Each person in the relationship must believe that he or she has some influence over what happens. These concerns are important for both parent-child and peer relationships.

The child's ability to resolve conflict and acquire a satisfying sense of influence begins with his or her relationship with the parents. How do parents resolve conflict? Do they listen to their children, or do they maintain control by use of coercion? Do parents include their children in the decision-making process? Is competition consistently emphasized over cooperation? These questions relate primarily to the issue of conflict or control.

Conflict-related skills include the following: (1) forming a rational perspective on conflict and cooperation; (2) developing assertive skills; (3) acquiring a balance between competition and cooperation; and (4) resolving conflict nonviolently.

Parents help their children form an effective perspective on conflict and cooperation by making household rules clear and understandable, and making punishment, when necessary, relevant to misbehavior. Furthermore, they can try to

convey the idea that conflict without violence is something
to face rather than to avoid, and that best effort is more
important than winning.

In order for interpersonal relationships to be satisfying, those involved must feel free to state their own needs
and work actively to have them satisfied. Individuals must
feel they have the power to successfully influence their own
development and avoid destructive interference by others.
This type of social influence might be called self-assertion.
Children respond assertively when they refuse to eat a particular food, ask their parents for a certain kind of toy,
ask another child to play a particular game, and insist that
a bully stop teasing. In each case, the child is attempting
to make his or her opinion or need known to someone else.

Self-assertion will sometimes lead to conflict when the
other person does not accept the child's point of view. For
example, parents may insist that a child eat Aunt Martha's
spinach cake, and refuse to purchase a requested toy; friends
may not want to play a particular game; and the bully may
continue teasing despite pleas to the contrary. This clash
of wills and definitions of what is right are not uncommon.
However, conflict is an important part of life because it is
the process of two or more people accommodating their needs
to each other.

Conflict between parents and their children is inevitable.
But in regard to some issues, parents may have to insist on
some conformity while still giving their children an opportunity to make their own desires known. Parents can be firm
in their limit setting while allowing their children the right
to dissent. Whenever possible, expectations could be negoti-
ated.

Parents can also emphasize a balance between competition
and cooperation. Competition can be useful because it provides an opportunity for children to be challenged by another's skills. The emphasis should, however, still be on
best effort rather than winning. In contrast, cooperation
emphasizes the shared use of power to the benefit of all.
Parents who involve their children in cooperative activities
like building something or working on puzzles are teaching
their children that ability can be mutually shared to reach
a common goal.

By talking about their anger and exploring ways of resolving problems, parents can demonstrate to their children
that conflict can be resolved nonviolently. Success in dealing with conflict is an important skill since all interpersonal relationships involve some degree of conflict. Children who typically use force to end conflict will either find
themselves isolated from others or victims of counterforce.

In contrast, children who learn more peaceful means of re-solving disagreements are likely to attract and keep friends. For additional information on conflict and aggression, see Feshbach (1970), Fromm (1973), and May (1972).

Kindness and Affection

Affection is the last phase to emerge in the development of interpersonal relationships. With affiliation, the individual obtains a sense of belonging and significance; with control, the individual develops a sense of influence and competence; and as the relationship continues, affection bonds emerge and the individual obtains a sense of closeness and feeling of lovability. Thus, children cannot truly respond affectionately to a parent until they feel fully recognized as a person who has influence in the relationship. Before this time, affection is accepted but not fully reciprocated.

It is possible for parents to be effective in helping their children develop skills in the affiliation and conflict areas but find difficulty with the affection issue. How do parents convey affection to their children? Do family members accept and request kindness from others? How do family members react to expressions of affection between others within the family? These questions focus primarily on affection issues.

The skills for this particular theme include: (1) forming a constructive attitude toward kindness and affection; and (2) offering/accepting/requesting help, compassion, caretaking, affection, and sharing. This last series of behaviors collectively comprises what might be referred to as "kindness."

What are some of the important ideas regarding kindness and affection parents can try to convey to their children? First, parents can emphasize that displays of affection are not "unmanly." Honest forms of affection are a legitimate way to bring people together in a more satisfying relationship. Similarly, asking for kindness is also acceptable. Second, parents can try to communicate the idea that real kindness is freely offered, accepted, or asked for without expectation of ulterior reward. Third, parents can try to help their child realize that one's self-worth does not depend on being liked by everybody.

Parents can also create conditions which actually encourage offering/accepting/requesting kindness. They can demonstrate by their own helping behavior that receiving and asking for this form of kindness is acceptable. They can also allow their children to help them whenever possible. Children can also be encouraged to respond to the suffering of another by providing some form of psychological support.

A child who approaches and gives his or her crying mother a
hug would be demonstrating compassion. Children can also
learn how to respond to another's distress to resolve a problem. Children who put a band-aid on a friend's cut, run to
get a parent when someone is hurt more seriously, and bring
a cool washcloth for a mother's headache are demonstrating
caretaking skills.

Children can also learn to express gentle affection or
appreciation both verbally and nonverbally. The tenderness
of young children does not have to be replaced by mock fighting and other forms of aggression so frequently displayed by
men in our own culture. Finally, children can gradually learn
to share their material sources with others without being coerced by parents. Their generosity is in response to another's
need and their reward can be found in experiencing the pleasure of another.

Additional views of altruism can be found in Bar-Tal
(1976), Staub (1971), and Yarrow and Waxler (1976).

CONCLUSION

The acquisition of these life arts is an awesome but critical
task. Researchers who are examining prosocial development
(see Smith, in press) are beginning to trace the both gradual
development of these skills beginning in infancy on and the
relative influence of parents. The focus on prosocial skill
enhancement in children as a family strength is a relatively
new endeavor.

Ultimately, the strength of any family which includes
children depends on the ability of that unit to nurture optimal development in the younger generation. Parents can
discover that childrearing is much more than just overcoming
problems, for effective parents confidently reach out to
their children in an effort to nurture the kinds of prosocial
strengths identified above. The ultimate happiness and satisfaction of their offspring depends on the mastery of these
critical life arts.

REFERENCES

Bar-Tal, D. *Prosocial behavior: Theory and research*. New
    York: John Wiley, 1976.

Borke, H. The development of empathy in Chinese and American
    children between three and six years of age: A cross-
    culture study. *Developmental Psychology*, 1973, *9*,
    102-108.

Brooks, C. V. *Sensory awareness*. New York: Viking Press, 1974.

Brown, G. I. *Human teaching for human learning*. New York: Viking Press, 1971.

Coufal, J. D. *Filial relationship enhancement: Leader's manual and parent home sessions*. Unpublished manuscript, Texas Tech University, Lubbock, 1978.

Damon, W. *The social world of the child*. San Francisco: Jossey-Bass, 1977.

Deutsch, F. Female preschooler's perception of affective responses and interpersonal behavior in videotaped episodes. *Developmental Psychology*, 1974, *10*, 733-740.

Ferguson, L. R. Origins of social development in infancy. *Merrill-Palmer Quarterly*, 1971, *17*, 119-137.

Feshbach, S. Aggression. In P. H. Mussen (Ed.), *Carmichael's manual of child psychology*, Vol. II. New York: John Wiley, 1970.

Fisher, S. *Body consciousness*. New York: Jason Aronson, 1974.

Fromm, E. *The anatomy of human destructiveness*. New York: Holt, Rinehart, & Winston, 1973.

Gilbert, D. C. The young child's awareness of affect. *Child Development*, 1969, *40*, 629-640.

Gottman, J., Gonso, J., & Rasmussen, B. Social interaction, social competence and friendships in children. *Child Development*, 1975, *46*, 709-718.

Gunther, B. *Sense relaxation below your mind*. New York: Macmillan, 1968.

Hendricks, G., & Fadiman, J. *Transpersonal education: A curriculum for feeling and being*. Englewood Cliffs, New Jersey: Prentice-Hall, 1975.

Kagan, J. *Understanding children: Behavior, motives, and thought*. New York: Harcourt Brace Jovanovich, 1971.

Liepmann, L. *Your child's sensory world*. Baltimore: Penguin Books, 1973.

Lifton, R. J., & Olsen, E. *Living and dying.* New York: Praeger, 1974.

May, R. *Power and innocence.* New York: W. W. Norton, 1972.

Porter, J. D. R. *Black child, white child.* Cambridge: Harvard University Press, 1971.

Schutz, W. *Profound simplicity.* New York: Bantam Books, 1979.

Smith, C. A. *Developing personal-social skills in young children.* Palo Alto: Mayfield Publishing, in press.

Smith, C. A. Peopleteaching: A personalized approach to teacher education. In B. Spodek (Ed.), *Teacher education: Of the teacher, by the teacher, for the child.* Washington, D.C.: N.A.E.Y.C., 1979.

Spivak, G., & Schure, M. G. *Social adjustment of young children.* San Francisco: Jossey-Bass, 1974.

Staub, E. A. The child is distress: The influence of nurturance and modeling on children's attempts to help. *Developmental Psychology,* 1971, *5*(1), 124-132.

Stinnett, N. In search of strong families. In N. Stinnett, B. Chesser, & J. DeFrain (Eds.), *Building family strengths: Blueprints for action.* Lincoln: University of Nebraska Press, 1979.

Ward, W. D. Process of sex-role development. *Developmental Psychology,* 1969, *1*, 163-168.

Yarrow, M. R., & Waxler, C. Z. Dimensions and correlates of prosocial behavior in young children. *Child Development,* 1976, *47*, 118-125.

The Role of Love, Power, and Conflict: Socialization for Creativity or Alienation?

Dr. Barbara L. Forisha
Department of Psychology
University of Michigan-
Dearborn

When the cultural mythology departs from the experienced reality in the lives of most individuals in the culture, increased tension and anxiety are the result. The tension and anxiety can lead to the conflicts resulting in alienation or precede the integration achieved in creativity (May, 1977). The tension and degree of uncertainty are even greater when the mythology of the culture is inherently contradictory; one is not only concerned about how to get from "here to there," but also how to know where "there" is. In our mythologies of "optimal functioning" and "optimal socialization" procedures, we have reached a time of contradiction; the mythology of the two-parent tranquil home (with a working father and home-based mother) not only does not fit for the majority of Americans, but also contains contradictions in which stability is substituted for vitality, dependency usurps self-reliance, and alienation overrides creativity.

It is important, therefore, that we begin to shape new belief systems which are more consonant with our experiences. In an age of working parents and single-parent homes, we need not suggest that healthy individuals only result from the more traditional two-parent, single breadwinner ménage. Moreover, when we review the results from homes in which this mythology does prevail (the father works, the mother remains at home, and harmony is paramount), we find that such homes may not produce the creative, self-reliant, change-adapted characteristics valued by the American belief system, but produce rather alienated, dependent, and somewhat rigid characteristics generally devalued by the mythology itself. It is becoming imperative we now take a closer look at our reality and produce a mythology of child rearing and adult living more suited to the late-twentieth century American experience.

We have available both the theoretical support and the research evidence to make a beginning in this task. This paper is a preliminary attempt to sketch what might be an optimal procedure for socializing creative, productive,

loving human beings, and addresses the integration of love,
power, and conflict in the individual's experience as well
as the family's behavior. This is a preliminary, and perhaps
but one possible, alternative. However, Douglas (1977) stated
in her critique of American culture: "We induce people to
alter partly by urging them to think, and to think from a different perspective than the one they normally adopt" (p. 198).
The view of process-oriented living described below is one
such perspective which integrates both recent theoretical ex-
positions with relevant research on socialization and development.

THEORETICAL FORMULATION: THE PROCESS-
ORIENTED INDIVIDUAL

Throughout psychological literature, the definition of health
has revolved around the ability to work creatively and to
love. One must be able, as an individual, to find satisfaction and meaning in productive work, and then to join with
others in a full relatedness and communion. In a context in
which these two variables alternate with each other, in which
one variable does not exclude but enhances the other, I have
come to define such individuals as process-oriented (Forisha,
1978).
    The process-oriented individual, therefore, combines both
power (to be and to work) and love (the capacity to relate
to others in a fully caring fashion). In so doing, process-
oriented individuals blend other dichotomies; they are both
assertive and sensitive, strong and tender, able to work and
to play, to be alone and also together with others (Fromm,
1941; Maslow, 1970; May, 1969; Rogers, 1961). They are able
to incorporate the best of the traditionally masculine and
feminine characteristics and, in that sense, are androgynous.
    From their own strength, process-oriented individuals find
security within themselves rather than in the world without.
From their capacity to care, process-oriented individuals
reach out to others and meet with others in relationships which
are not bound by the dependencies of each. Process-oriented
individuals enter into full commitments in the world (commitments to the process, not the end goal), since their capacity
to say "yes" is balanced by the ability to say "no." The
security of the yes/no balance gives process-oriented individuals the strength to live from their own value base rather
than having to cling to a structure which is external to
themselves.
    The security and inner strength of process-oriented in-
dividuals, however, are not won easily. As they come to unite
in themselves both power and love, they also experience the

inner (and sometimes outer) conflict which occurs in the process of self-discovery and in the achievement of a new integration. In such a venture, process-oriented individuals are willing to allow dissonant awareness of self to surface, to tolerate and live with the ambiguity that they are complex and often not harmonious within, and then out of the tumult of their complexity to achieve a new integration.

The process of coming to terms with oneself, involving spiraling cycles of differentiation and integration, is one which applies to all learnings, whether they be large or small. In our overall development, for example, we proceed from the undifferentiated infant to the differentiated young adult to the new and unique integration of our later years (Loevinger, 1966; Perry, 1968; Werner, 1948, 1957). In the process, we struggle with our own limitations and those imposed by the outer world, and from our struggle wrest new meanings for our lives. The journey from integration to differentiation has generally been paved by others before us. The passage from differentiation to personal integration is, however, one which is more risky and perilous, as we must let go of our previous organization in order to await the achievement of a new.

This period of letting go, of seeking a new integration, is termed a crisis in the language of developmental psychology. We must let go in order to reshape ourselves in a way which best suits the new growing self and the new changing situation. We must venture out in order to return again. The subjective experience of crisis, however, is heightened by the sense that the return is never guaranteed, the new integration is never a sure thing, and the experience of diffusion and of chaos may appear without conclusion (Barron, 1963; Forisha, 1978; Perry, 1968). The risk is indeed not negligible, but the alternative, that of remaining on the differentiated trail shaped by others, leads only to eventual alienation from self. Kierkegaard (1941) reminds us, "By not venturing at all, we risk losing ourselves" (p. 52).

Process-oriented individuals, then, are at home with both love and power, and have learned to profit from ensuing conflict rather than to disintegrate in its grasp. In the process of achieving integration from the recognition of apparent opposites, such individuals have learned to overcome dichotomies, to live in a world where often their experience is both/and rather than either/or. Such individuals are, by definition, androgynous in their sex-role orientation and creative in their life style. They are allowing their own experiences to guide the way to their own personalized integration.

What does all of this mean in terms of describing family settings which foster the development of the healthy individual? First, it implies that parents can in no way guarantee the future "success" of their children. They can in no way assure a positive outcome of their child-rearing efforts, for the eventual welfare of the child depends only on the child as our welfare does upon us, and we cannot trade one for another. Secondly, however, it suggests that a home in which two process-oriented individuals raise their children will most likely have certain characteristics, even though those characteristics cannot guarantee the outcome of the lives of children in the home. We shall take a moment to explore these characteristics.

The process-oriented family would be one in which each individual combines both power and love and is tolerant of conflict and dissonance. (The level and quality of "constructive" conflict, as opposed to that which we know to be damaging, will be discussed later.) Individuals within the home would be described as strong in themselves and from that strength able to care for others. Husbands and wives would not exist solely to meet each other's expectations. Children would not be raised in order to fulfill the unmet needs of parents. From their own strength, parents would provide firm guidelines for children, but also allow them the experience of choosing their paths in ways consonant with their age levels and personal inclinations. This means that children would be allowed their own mistakes, as well as their successes. They would learn to test themselves and learn from that testing both their own strengths and their limitations. In such a way, children would develop their own sense of power and competence.

Moreover, such explorations of their power would be carried out in an atmosphere which is warm and supportive, and respecting of the individualities of each person. From the warmth and support, from the experience of love, children would also learn to love. In addition to fostering individual power and love, however, children would also learn to live with conflict--the conflict which always arises when strong individualities live in juxtaposition with each other--and would learn that the conflicting desires, needs, and wants of all parties, when recognized and respected, can lead to a new experience of understanding of each other, of negotiation and compromise, and a new harmony of the group experience.

Other authors have also concurred with this theoretical formulation by supplying similar descriptions. Satir (1972) talks of aliveness, genuineness, honesty, and love which characterize homes in which rules are shaped to the individual and communication is free and open. Rossi (1964) also describes what would be a process-oriented home when she outlines an ideal androgynous upbringing, in which both boys and girls would experience warmth, discipline, responsibility, and a

full exploration of their unique talents--regardless of gender.
Such homes combine power and love.
   In the research literature, these characteristics are
generally translated into the dimensions of warmth and control. Turning now to the research, do we find that such homes
exist, and if they do, is the outcome similar to that proposed by the theoretical formulation? Specifically, does
the literature support the role of conflict in full human
development? Does the opportunity for full human development differ for males and females?

RESEARCH FINDINGS: PARENTS AND THEIR CHILDREN

Much of the research appears to have been done in homes in
which one parent is dominant (at least in the eyes of the
researcher), rather than in homes where each individual balances power and love. What researchers find in these homes
is that children of the same sex as the dominant parent tend
to be more independent and responsible than children of the
less dominant parent (Douvan, 1963; Moulton, Burnstein,
Liberty, & Altucher, 1966; Nye & Hoffman, 1974; Siegal &
Hass, 1963). It appears that in homes in which parents are
not equal in power--and love--children of the two sexes are
also not equal. When power and love are unequally apportioned
among the parents, they are also unequally apportioned among
the children. As the imbalance of power and love within individuals leads to a separation of power from love, children
learn that those who are strong have power, and those who
are weak are loving (Kagan & Lemkin, 1960; Kagan, Hosken,
& Watson, 1968).
   Other data show that achieving boys tend to come from
warm and controlling homes in which at least the father represents both power and love. The role of the mother, it may
be inferred, exists primarily in terms of the love dimension.
In the same homes, girls become docile rather than assertive,
responsive rather than achieving (Bronfenbrenner, 1961). On
the other hand, achieving girls come from only moderately
warm and permissive homes; boys from these homes tend not to
achieve in as directed a way (Nye & Hoffman, 1974).
   Another body of research, specifically investigating the
background of creative individuals, indicates a slightly more
encouraging picture. In the homes of creative high school
boys and girls, researchers indicate that one of the chief
reported characteristics was a respect for the individuality of
the child of either sex (Anastasi & Schaefer, 1969; Dauw,
1966; Domino, 1969; Schaefer & Anastasi, 1968). In such
homes, moreover, the child had the attention, interest, and
encouragement of the parent of the opposite sex. Particularly

in the case of the creative male, there appears to have been
a competent as well as loving mother in the background. In
one study of the mothers of creative high school boys, Domino
(1969) states that mothers are "highly independent and capable" women who can "adapt to change and variety" and in fact
tend to represent a "balance between contrasting dynamic
forces" (pp. 181-183).

However, the literature on creative individuals, positive
as it may appear in a process-oriented sense, is sparse compared with the number of studies which document homes in
which one parent is dominant and in which only the same-sexed
child appears to demonstrate both assertive and caring charac-
teristics--more assertive if male and more caring if female.
With this in mind, let us turn to another body of literature,
that which specifically examines the childhood antecedents
of personality characteristics in young and not-so-young
adults.

Research on Androgyny and Socialization

In a longitudinal study, Block, von der Lippe, and Block (1973)
have studied the sex-role development and overall level of
maturity of individuals whose development had been followed
for a number of years. These results are also reviewed in
a second article by Jeanne Block (1973). In interpreting
their data, they rely heavily on Bakan's (1966) definition
of the two fundamental modalities of human existence: agency
and communion. Agency represents the masculine principle,
and is concerned with the self-protection, self-assertion, and
self-expansion of the organism (this is similar to our definition of power). Communion represents the feminine principle,
and is descriptive of the individual existing as part of a
larger unit, and existing in relationship with others (this
is similar to our definition of love). The height of maturity
occurs when the two modalities are integrated with each other.
At this point, for men, the self-assertiveness learned earlier
is tempered by considerations of mutality and interdependence,
whereas, for women, the early learning of harmonious group
skills is amended to include self-assertion and self-expression.
Jean Block (1973) points out, however, that this level of
integration is achieved only by a few, since our current socialization practices emphasize masculine machismo and feminine docility, and thus "impede the development of mature ego
functioning."

For this particular study, the researchers divided 65 men
and 68 women, aged 30 to 40, into four groups determined by
their scores on the California Psychological Inventory. The
groups were divided into those high and low on socialization
(ability to govern thought and behavior in accordance with

cultural expectations) and high and low on sex-role differentiation (a continuum with initiation-oriented at one pole
and conservation-oriented at the second pole). The result
was four groups each of males and females, composed of those
high on both dimensions, those low on both dimensions, and
those high on one and low on the other.

Socialization appeared to be a more salient variable than
sex-role orientation. Men who were high on socialization
were competent, confident men who were comfortable with themselves and their roles. The men who were high on sex-role
differentiation had a more masculine emphasis in their personality and job choices than did those who were low on sex-
differentiation. However, the difference was not startling
nor pronounced in terms of other variables. Block (1973)
concludes that "both masculine and less masculine men in the
highly socialized groups appear to have incorporated positive
aspects of both the masculine and feminine sex roles, both
agency and communion. They were productive, effective, dependable, and conscientious."

Women, on the other hand, who came from highly socialized
homes, regardless again of sex-role differentiation, were con-
tented and conventional, although the more masculine women
were less passive than those in the other group. Block (1973)
sums up the impact of socialization on women by saying:
"Characteristics that are essential for individuation and
self-expression have been defined by the culture as 'masculine,' and so, progressively, these must be relinquished in
the case of female socialization." Socialization for women
results in the renunciation of achievement and autonomy.
Whereas socialization for men expands their life options, for
women it narrows them. This difference is largely attributable
to differential expectations which the culture holds for women and men. In Block's (1973) words, "the achievement of
higher levels of ego functioning for women is more difficult
because individuation involves conflict with prevailing cultural norms." These findings are not dissimilar to those
found in other studies.

What about individuals low on socialization? Men who
were low in socialization appear to have introjected the least
appealing characteristics of the masculine sex role in highly
sex-differentiated homes or the feminine role in less-
differentiated homes. Women, on the other hand, also became
exaggeratedly masculine or exaggeratedly feminine. However,
the exaggeratedly masculine woman was staunch in defense of
her autonomy--the only representative of that value among
the females. Moreover, career women tended to come from low
socialization homes but career mobility (upward) was associated
not with socialization but with masculinity, whatever the
degree of socialization had been.

The major implication in terms of development from this study is that none of the groups of women represented process-oriented or androgynous individuals. Those who are masculine tend nonetheless to adopt a relaxed feminine life style unless they are also low on socialization, in which case they may develop their career opportunities but at the cost of interpersonal growth. Moreover, all of the factors which we associate with healthy child rearing, warmth, and control, or in our terms power and love, appear to produce docility and responsiveness in women, and communal traits alone rather than an integration of agency and communion. The reason for this is most likely attributable to a culture which does not value feminine independence, so that independence for women is bought at other costs and does not occur in those who accept the cultural norms.

The well-socialized men, on the other hand, appear to be androgynous, more or less. They are basically agentive in orientation, but their agency is tempered with respect for others. For a man to be loving in our society is apparently not as disastrous as for a woman to be powerful. Men are given the option of emotional expressiveness within the home if they choose to make that choice. Women have no arena in which they can, with full social acceptance, be overtly powerful. Hence, socialization for men may be a blessing but a curse for women; however, lack of socialization is not a better alternative.

Finally, in terms of the process-oriented model of human development, there is some support for, but little emphasis on, the role of conflict in healthy development. Block's (1973) article relies heavily on Loevinger's (1966) model of growth, and hence does see the later stages as requiring an awareness of conflicting elements of the self and the achievement of an individually defined self-concept. Yet, the process of conflict and conflict resolution is not explored in any depth, although it is suggested that conflict is more essential for women than men (Block, von der Lippe, & Block, 1973). Further, nowhere in the portrayal of their sample do the Blocks and von der Lippe mention the terms "creative," "exciting," or "enthusiastic." It may be that these terms are appropriate to some subjects but not to an entire grouping. One may infer that this study does not shed much light on the development of individuals who are challenged and excited by the complexities of life, and utilize this challenge to create new forms. Rather, this longitudinal study does tell us that the road to maturity, the integration of agency and communion, begins with warm and competent parents--but for men only. We shall look elsewhere for further information on the potential for creative process-orientation in men--and also women.

Other Developmental Studies

Several other studies originating in the same Berkeley Institute add footnotes to the information gleaned from the Block,
von der Lippe, and Block study. Their findings indicate that
we can raise androgynous men, but perhaps not men who are
challenged or excited by life in the process-oriented modality.
Warmth and control, or power and love, do lead to the development of men who are in many ways mature and well-integrated,
although this is not the case with women. Moreover, the
studies reviewed here suggest that warmth and control may not
be enough. In order to grow in a process of differentiation
and personal integration, we need the stimulation provided by
conflict.

MacFarlane (1938, 1964), who initiated one of the longitudinal studies at Berkeley, noted that of the 166 persons
in her Guidance Study, many were able in time to overcome and
grow from early conflict and developmental crises. In fact,
many of the most outstandingly mature in adult life were those
who had overcome very difficult situations, which their own
behavior had magnified in childhood and adolescence. Contrary to expectations, predictions made in childhood and
adolescence about adult mental health were contraverted by
the later evidence. In two-thirds of the cases, early predictions were wrong. In fact, many of those who had grown
up under the "best" circumstances became unhappy, strained,
and immature adults who had difficulty coping with adult
problems.

A later reanalysis of these data, however, concluded that
it was possible to derive general outlines for socialization
procedures leading to optimal development (defined, in part,
as insight and mastery). Siegelmen, Block, Block, and von
der Lippe (1970) state that optimal adjustment is facilitated
by open and direct democratic homes with free interchange
of feelings and an emphasis on intangible cultural values as
opposed to materialistic ones. They state also that the
mothers, especially, demonstrated both a greater openness and
greater intellectual acuity than mothers of those subjects
showing lower adjustment.

This study again bears out the necessity of the integration of love and power--particularly in the mother in this
case, who was in the 1930's (and generally is still) the more
salient parent figure. There is no explanation of the variance with MacFarlane's conclusions. One might suggest that
the predictive variables first selected in the 1930's were
those more in accord with the model of a "tranquil home
mythology" and did not include the openness and "freer interchange of problems and feelings," including the direct expression of anger by the father, which are seen as the salient

variables in the more recent analysis. Is it just hindsight which allows us to see the antecedents of healthy development, or are we, indeed, on the way to revising our belief system and hence our predictions of what leads to optimal adjustment?

We may be moving closer to a recognition that conflict, along with love and power, are better antecedents of all development than we thought in the 1930's. Other studies done by some of the same researchers (Block, 1972; Haan, 1971; Haan, Smith, & Block, 1968), which examine the backgrounds of students in the 1960's, tend to reinforce this view. Haan (1971) prefaces her article by stating that "harmony would defend society against both disequilibrium and progress" and finds that college activists, as compared to non-activists, reported experiences of disequilibrium within their families, but in the context of a maintained family unit with shared decision-making by both parents. Block (1972) found that student activists, who were not alienated from their parents, had grown up in homes in which they were encouraged "by both parents to confront dilemmas and to arrive at their own conclusions." Parents of these young people are described as both responsive and limit-setting, which can be interpreted as both loving and powerful, in addition to encouraging the resolution of conflict.

These conclusions are emphasized once again in the study of principled, conventional, and non-principled students in the study of Haan, Smith, and Block (1968). Once again, in viewing principled students (defined by Kohlberg's scale, 1964), these researchers found that the parents were "actively involved and conflict-producing," and that they insisted on their own rights as people at the same time as they respected those of their children. However, it is noteworthy that for women there were fewer indications of personal self-satisfaction than there were for men. The authors suggest, once again, that moral growth is perhaps a "more arduous task for girls than for boys and one that is not accomplished with comfort by this age group."

In contrast, the coventionally-moral students were raised in homes which were characterized more by harmony than conflict. The researchers state:

> . . . when harmony is an ultimate value, individuals are prone to base their decisions on the approved solutions. Furthermore, conflictless experiences are probably inconsistent with both moral and cognitive growth. (Haan, Smith, & Block, 1968, p. 200)

Thus, the argument is made that, for high levels of moral growth, "the role of conflict and disagreement seems central." This conflict, however, must not be accompanied by either neglect nor overindulgence as in the homes of the non-principled youth, nor must it attain chronic nor affectively disabling levels. Rather as Seligman points out, "controllable stress may be better for a child's ego development than good things that happen without any effort on the child's part" (Skolnick, 1978, p. 60).

The conclusions which we can draw from this body of work are that conflict plus warmth plus moderate control tend to lead to the development of young people who are principled and morally mature. Neglect and over-indulgence, on the other hand, are conducive to the development of neither principle nor autonomy, whereas continuing evenness and equilibrium tend to lead to conventional personalities in persons who do not seek out higher levels of personal integration. The conclusions also suggest that the above results are more true for men than they are for women. In fact, the data point in the direction of suggesting that women require more conflict than men in order to fully develop, a view contrary to the traditional view of female children as "fragile." Keniston (1971) suggests the same when he comments that individuation requires women to come into conflict with their social environment, since social expectations tend to inhibit their development. Another series of studies sheds further light on this view.

Identity and Family Backgrounds: James Marcia

In the last ten years, James Marcia has developed empirical measures of Eriksonian identity achievement, and he and his colleagues, using these instruments, have contributed considerable new evidence on the process of identity formation (Marica, 1967, 1976).

Erikson's (1950) theory, on which Marcia builds his work, centers around the achievement of "identity" which occurs in adolescence or later, and presumes an integration of personal attributes with some contributing function to the larger society. The formation of identity, according to Erikson, is the prerequisite for intimacy and the capacity of love. Having attained both identity and intimacy, the capacity for constructive work and mutual love, one would suppose that one has also achieved a balance of agency and communion in Bakan's sense.

Erikson does not, however, deal with differential development for males and females in an unbaised manner. In general, he has based his theory on male development and generalized his findings to "people." In recent years,

however, Erikson (1968) has stated that women generally do
not form an "identity" until after marriage, and never develop the internalized standards for behavior by which men
guide their lives. Women, rather, learn responsiveness to
others, and mold their identity in terms of significant males
in their lives, rather than as independent individuals. As
in Block's paradigm, one might assume that well-socialized
men blend agency and communion, whereas well-socialized women primarily demonstrate the characteristics of communion.

     Marcia (1967), however, has conducted empirical studies
on both men and women, and adds greatly to our knowledge about
higher levels of development in both sexes. His empirical
measures encompass two dimensions as do Block's, but draw
upon rather different concepts. These two dimensions are
"crisis" (the fact of having thoroughly thought through one's
own perceptions due to internal conflict) and "commitment"
(the capacity to devote oneself fully to beliefs, occupational goals, and, eventually, relationships). He divides
his subjects into four groups: those high on both characteristics he terms "identity achievers"; those high on crisis
and low on commitment he defines as "moratoriums"; those high
on commitment and low on crisis are "foreclosures"; and those
low on both dimensions are termed "identity diffusions."

     Among young men, Marcia finds that identity achievers
are capable, self-confident, and flexible, and suggests that
they come from homes in which parents are both warm and controlling. Identity achievers and their parents tend to see
each other as separate people who have decided independently
on their own life patterns. Moratoriums, on the other hand,
share many of the achievement-oriented, flexible characteristics of the identity achievers but are not content, happy,
dependable, nor predictable. Their lives are in crisis,
and they have not fully separated themselves from parental
authority figures; however, they tend to defy such figures
rather than comply with them. One could postulate that the
homes from which these people come are powerful homes, but
more stressful and less accepting than those of the identity
achievers.

     Foreclosures, on the other hand, tend to be rigid and
authoritarian, still attached to their parents' value systems. Marcia finds foreclosure men are defensive and stereotyped. Such defensiveness is most likely a reaction to options presented to them by university life, which must be shut
out in order to remain faithful and committed to the ideology of their parents. The parents of these men are warm,
child-centered, accepting, available, and companionable. Marcia
comments that perhaps the control dimension (which I suggest
precipitates conflict) is missing in these homes so that
there has never been any need (or at least, a recognized need)

for these young men to define themselves. Marcia (1976) finds, in fact, too much love and too little power in such homes: "If parents and their children are, in fact, different people, then there is no reason to expect them to be quite as en- amored of each other as the foreclosure ménage seems to be."

Finally, those labeled as identity diffusions are un- committed, unquestioning, and drifting, seeking merely to maintain their own survival and a basic level of security. Some identity diffusions reveal their shallowness in later life, others manage to "skim the surface throughout life, making few lasting commitments" because if they "don't just skim the surface then they will drown" (Marcia, 1976). Iden- tity diffusions tend to have parents who are emotionally ab- sent or hostile, and thus lacking in both power and love.

In viewing the development of men, it is apparent that, as assessed by other measures of emotional well-being, the more crisis in one's life, the more health. In this schema, crisis plus commitment leads to the highest level of maturity; crisis without commitment comes closest to this level. How- ever, one more point needs to be made: Block's well- socialized men tended to be content and self-confident, sug- gesting perhaps less than a full measure of excitement with living. Marcia (1976) adds weight to this point of view. In speaking of identity achievers he says, "There can be, as with some well-psychoanalyzed persons, a certain lack of ex- citement about them." On the other hand, moratoriums are frequently described as creative and enchanting. If we value creativity, perhaps we have to define maturity somewhere in between these two identity statuses; such an "identity" would include a well-thought out commitment, but one which remains flexible enough to allow for the change, the creativity, and some of the turmoil which marks a growth-oriented path.

In turning to the women, however, Marcia (1976) finds different patterns. Where male identity achievers and male moratoriums appeared to be the most healthy on other measures, for women, identity achievers and foreclosures scored high- est on other measures of mental health. The unifying thread of identity achievement and moratorium is crisis; that of identity achievement and foreclosure is commitment or stabil- ity. Moratorium and identity diffusion women were similar; neither had a stable frame of reference for making decisions, and this tended to impede their functioning much more than for men.

The development of a stable frame of reference thus ap- pears to be very important in the psychological lives of wo- men. Foreclosure women take this frame of reference from their parents and are content. Identity achievers develop an internal frame of reference which gives them similar sta- bility. However, it is notable that anxiety is higher in

identity-achieving women than in foreclosures. The implication is that the formation of identity for a woman is <u>not</u>
socially approved, and therefore is accompanied by a greater
internal conflict. On the other hand, foreclosure women,
unlike their male peers, appear to manage remarkably well.
Marcia (1976) remarks:

> My suspicion is that Foreclosure women look as
> good as they do because of the social props sup-
> porting their child-likeness. I think that if
> these props begin to disappear, if social support
> moves away from a Foreclosure solution and towards
> an Identity Achievement solution for women, that
> Foreclosure women will have to become as defensive
> and rigid as Foreclosure men in order to maintain
> their position.

Just as in Block's study, we find that well-socialized men
expand and personalize their options; well-socialized women adapt to whatever system is handed to them. Once again,
the prognosis for women, in a society dominated by masculine values, is poor.

<u>Identity</u>, <u>Androgyny</u> and <u>Self-Esteem</u>: <u>Jacob</u> <u>Orlofsky</u>

Orlofsky (1977), who formerly worked with Marcia in his study
of identity, has contributed a very recent study which further
clarifies our knowledge of growth in men and women, and which
expands further upon the tentative conclusions already presented. Orlofsky measured identity achievement, androgyny,
and self-esteem in college-age men and women, and found again
a bias toward more advanced masculine development.
     Males who developed an identity were either masculine
or androgynous in their sex-role orientation (this is similar to the finding of Block, von der Lippe & Block that sex-
role orientation is less important than socialization in
highly developed men). Orlofsky's (1977) finding that many
masculine males were identity achievers contraverted his
hypothesis that identity achievement and androgyny would be
highly related. He interprets this unexpected finding in
the following way: the traits needed to achieve an identity
are primarily autonomy, independence, and assertiveness, and
hence men who possess these traits, whether in the presence
or absence of more feminine, communal, or nurturing traits,
have the necessary personality characteristics needed to develop an identity in our culture. In addition, those men
who were masculine and those who were androgynous were equally
high in self-esteem. Once again possession of masculine

characteristics is conducive to a psychological health along other dimensions.

Women, on the other hand, who were sex-typed tended to be either foreclosures or moratoriums. Once again, even for women, those who possessed masculine characteristics, whether predominantly masculine or androgynous, were more likely to be identity achievers, and also more likely to have high self-esteem. However, Orlofsky points out the disturbing nature of these results. Since slightly over half of college females are sex-typed, and most of these females are foreclosures, the prognosis for identity achievement--and high self-esteem--in the majority of women is nearly nil. Moreover, Orlofsky points out that it is most difficult for foreclosure women to break the parental mold, since there is little reinforcement for such from society. He points out that these findings (once again) "call into question the socialization process which requires that girls suppress or fail to properly learn the very behavior (assertive, instrumental) that leads to high self-esteem in males (and in masculine and androgynous females)." These results again augur poorly for women.

Orlofsky (1977) also sheds some light on another issue of concern in this paper. He emphasizes in his conclusions the role of crisis for both men and women. He argues that early identity achievers tend to level off at less high levels of development, whereas those who have a sustained moratorium, or an extended period of crisis, tend to develop higher levels of differentiation, tend to balance sex-typed characteristics in an androgynous orientation, and tend also to higher levels of moral growth.

His study, therefore, confirms the necessity of crisis as well as the duration of crisis in development, but once again emphasizes that the beneficial results of crisis are more often to be found in men than in women. His study also illuminates the questions raised about the Block, von der Lippe, Block, and Marcia findings: within the groups of identity achievers there are varied levels of maturity and growth. Some are highly principled; some are not. Therefore, those who experience less crisis, less questioning, perhaps remain at a lower developmental level. They may indeed lack the excitement of process-orientation. Those who experience a prolonged moratorium may be those who achieve integration at the higher levels of human potential.

IS CRISIS NECESSARY FOR HIGH LEVELS OF DEVELOPMENT?

We have hypothesized, and found some empirical support for, the view that warmth and moderate levels of control lead to more integrated development in both men and women. However, the outcomes of this development are differentiated by sex; the men more often rise to the higher levels of development, perhaps accenting agency but incorporating communion, and women more often remain at lower levels of development, accenting communion but to the exclusion of agency. There is also some evidence for the theoretical supposition that a crisis is necessary in order to promote the highest levels of growth. In fact, a crisis may be a misnomer, but a series of reevaluations throughout life may indeed lead to continuous growth. Orlofsky's (1977) conclusions nail down this theoretical viewpoint: those who experience more crisis move further ahead than their more content peers.

We now turn to a recap of the role of crisis in male and female development, and an assessment of the cultural norms which lead in this direction.

All theories of development postulate some self-searching which may or may not be termed a crisis. Block (1973), in her model of development, speaks in turn of an "examination of self as a sex-role exemplar," "coping with conflicting masculine-feminine aspects of self," and finally, the "achievement of an individually defined sex role." One might suppose that such a pattern of self-examination leads through an internal crisis. Erikson's theory, and Marcia's development of it, focuses on an "identity crisis," and further emphasizes the crisis stage, by finding that the healthiest men have self-perceptions of a crisis of self-definition whether or not that self-definition has been achieved.

In these developmental theories, at least in those which have been researched at any length, it is clear that the developmental pattern involving crisis pertains mostly to the male and not the female. Developmental theorists postulate several crises for the male, beginning with his need to detach himself from his early feminine environment and the later adolescent need to define himself in terms of internal standards and societal expectations. On the whole, most theorists (Block, 1973; Douvan, 1963; Erikson, 1950; Marcia, 1976) find such a crisis stage lacking in female development. Female development proceeds more smoothly (Lynn (1969) states such development is comparable to a "lesson", whereas boys' development is more analogous to a "problem") without a crisis stage, and possibly without either high ego development or maturity. Women, Marcia tells us, tend to value stability over self-exploration and for this they are reinforced by society.

Speculating further, in comparing male development (with crisis) and female development (without crisis), and comparing also the relative heights of personal development which appear to favor males, one is led to the conclusion that crisis is a necessary part of full human development. In terms of our current societal structure, which is highly sex-role stereotyped, such crises will necessarily involve a re-examination of sex roles and a confrontation with masculine and feminine dichotomies. At the highest levels of development, these dichotomies will be integrated.

However, in viewing the role of crisis in human development, and seeing it most clearly in male development, we are reminded also that male development is generally more difficult than female development. More pressures are placed on the growing male, and in the process more young males go astray, developing various physical and psychological disorders. It would appear that for women who also reach their full potential there is a high level of crisis marked by heightened anxiety and an exaggeration of assertive tendencies. Moreover, the female "identity crisis" is not socially accepted as is the male's, so the female is operating without the support and encouragement of peer groups and institutions. Thus, in observing development, the female "identity crisis," when it occurs, appears more critical and more filled with turmoil. Such women are not only fighting within themselves, but fighting social expectations without. One might expect also that as women come to search themselves, and call themselves into question, that some of the liabilities of being male will accrue to the female gender, for crisis in general tends to wipe out the middle road and one is forced either to integrate the conflicting elements or to drown in them. Historically, this has been the experience of more men than women. In addition to buying into achievement and its attendant identity crises, women may find also that they must either sink or swim and the comfortable road of second class citizen is no longer available.

STABILITY IN ADULTHOOD: BARRIERS TO DEVELOPMENT

Yet, regardless of the sex-differentiated disparities in developmental paths, only a few reach the highest levels of development (Block, 1973). Most remain at the early stage in which they have first achieved an identity, however unintegrated or societally given. There is a tendency after "achieving an identity," to remain there rather than continuing a growth process throughout life. Our society does not tend as a whole to view adults as constantly changing, but to see them in a more static way, defined in terms of occupation and marital and parental status. Once these commitments are made, they become institutionalized and bar the path to further development which, in the process-oriented model, requires periodic crises and renewed commitments.

Therefore, most men fail to achieve the integration of agency
and communion proposed by Block, but remain at more conventional agentive levels, just as women have remained historically at more conventional communal levels.

Therefore, although it is socially acceptable for men to
undergo crisis in adolescence, men and women both tend to
value stability over crisis in their adult years. What this
means in terms of our views of child rearing is suggestive:
Do we project our adult desire for stability backward onto
our past and onto our children? Are we unwilling to accept
the uncertainties and the outright chanciness of the experience of bringing children into this world? Is the perpetua-
tion of our mythology of the tranquil two-parent home founded
in our own search for stability?

If this is so, then we not only do our children a dis-
service but ourselves as well. If we refuse to accept the
process-oriented requirement of continual (or periodic) self-
evaluation, we allow ourselves to become stagnant and in-
flexible; the result of this, in a constantly changing society, is alienation from society and eventually from self.
We then project upon our children the same expectations of
stability, since we ourselves have not maintained the ability
to meet new challenges and create new forms. We tend to overlook the importance of crisis and self-questioning and to
seek the middle road. Yet, for those who allow themselves to
experience the complexity of living, there is no middle road--
only a detour to the low road of insecurity and alienation.
Is this what we choose for ourselves and for our children?

If we face these questions squarely, then we must look at
our own lives closely before we examine those of our children.
Bettleheim (1965) and Erikson (1976) have both suggested that
the example of our adult lives gives our children small reason
to grow up. Only if adults accept periodic times of self-
questioning and new integration, will they have the strength
and the acceptance to find their children's search both tolerable and growth-promoting. Only if they provide desirable
models of adulthood, will the young choose to grow up, will
the young choose to emulate adults, and to strive against and
with adults in their own search for self-definition. So,
if we wish to improve the chances for our children, we must
first find ourselves. If we wish to make growing up well
a positive value we must first grow up ourselves. We dare
not ask of them what we are afraid to ask of ourselves.

CONCLUSION

We have suggested that creative children are raised in warm
and moderately controlling homes by powerful and loving

parents, and that such homes must allow for the conflict which
occurs between highly individuated persons. The role of productive conflict cannot be minimized. Moreover, the outcome
of conflict, the outcome of crisis, cannot be predicted. Thus,
we cannot place our hopes in the hands of children who ultimately, in carving out their own sense of personal definition,
will do exactly as they please. We must instead turn to ourselves and, in so doing, provide a model of healthy adult
living which is a spur and motivation for young people to
grow up. Instead, we so often live our adulthood as a shadowy
half-life which encourages our children, initially so much
more lively than we, to remain forever young and to cling,
as do so many American adults, to the irresponsibility, the
shallowness, and the youthful appearance of the young.

The process of self-definition, however, has been and
is still more difficult for young women in our society than
for young men. But past the stage of youth, both sexes have
allowed adulthood to stamp their images in concrete. Both
sexes have given up the hope of a satisfying middle and old
age, and still cling to the traces of youth; being no longer
young and refusing to grow older they become caught in a
limbo which erases their sense of power and their capacity
for love. What we must do instead is to emulate not the
form of youth, but the spirit of youth. As adults, we must
accept change, allow for process, and remain throughout life
on an exciting and exhilarating journey. In so doing, we
will give our children, whose fate we cannot control, a reason
to grow up. We will provide models of creative living instead of the resignation of alienation from ourselves and our
world.

Finally, if it were true that the disjuncture of reality
and mythology can be an impetus for creativity, we must also
remember that such is a primary cause of anxiety and neurosis.
From the cultural disparities, the creative may wrest a mythology which more suits the experience of lived lives; for
those who cannot individually make this integration, a new
mythology better suited to current experience will reduce
the tension caused by the separation of belief and reality.
A mythology which replaces the views of the tranquil two-
parent home with one which urges openness and tolerance of
differences would be one such possibility. Such a view of
child rearing would, very possibly, provide the guidelines
for socializing our young for creativity rather than alienation, although the outcome of that socialization can never
be guaranteed.

REFERENCES

Anastasi, A., & Schaefer, C. E. Biographical correlates
of artistic and literary creativity in adolescent girls.
Journal of Applied Psychology, 1969, *53*, 267-273.

Bakan, D. *The duality of human existence*. Chicago: Rand
McNally, 1966.

Barron, F. Diffusion, integration, and enduring attention
in the creative process. In R. White (Ed.), *The study
of lives*. Englewood Cliffs, New Jersey: Prentice-Hall,
Inc., 1963.

Bettleheim, B. The problem of generations. In E. Erikson
(Ed.), *Challenge of youth*. New York: Anchor, 1965.

Block, J. Generational continuity and discontinuity in the
understanding of societal rejection. *Journal of Per-
saonlity and Social Psychology*, 1972, *22*, 333-345.

Block, J. H. Conceptions of sex role: Some cross-cultural
and longitudinal perspectives. *American Psychologist*,
1973, *28*, 512-526.

Block, J., von der Lippe, A., & Block, J. H. Sex-role and
socialization patterns: Some personality concomitants
and environmental antecedents. *Journal of Consulting
and Clinical Psychology*, 1973, *41*, 321-341.

Bronfenbrenner, U. Some familial antecedents of responsi-
bility and leadership in adolescents. In L. Petrullo &
B. Bass (Eds.), *Leadership and interpersonal behavior*.
New York: Rinehart & Winston, 1961.

Dauw, D. C. Life experiences of original thinkers and good
elaborators. *Exceptional Children*, 1966, *32*, 433-440.

Domino, C. Maternal personality correlates of son's creativity. *Journal of Consulting and Clinical Psychology*,
1969, *33*, 180-183.

Douglas, A. *The feminization of American culture*. New York:
Avon Books, 1977.

Douvan, E. Employment and the adolescent. In F. E. Nye &
L. W. Hoffman (Eds.), *The employed mother in America*.
Chicago: Rand McNally, 1963.

Erickson, E. *Childhood and society.* New York: W. W. Norton, 1950.

Erickson, E. *Youth: Identity and crisis.* New York: W. W. Norton, 1968.

Erickson, E. Memorandum on youth. *Daedalus,* Spring, 1976.

Forisha, B. *Sex roles and personal awareness.* Morristown, New Jersey: General Learning Press, 1978.

Fromm, E. *Escape from freedom.* New York: Holt, Rinehart & Winston, 1941.

Haan, N., Smith, M. B., & Block. J. The moral reasoning of young adults: Political-social behavior, family background and personality correlates. *Journal of Personality and Social Psychology,* 1968, *10,* 183-201.

Haan, N. Moral redefinition in families as the critical aspect of the generation gap. *Youth and Society,* 1971, *3,* 259-283.

Kagan, J., & Lemkin, J. The child's differential perception of parental attributes. *Journal of Abnormal and Social Psychology,* 1960, *61,* 440.

Kagan, J., Hosken, B., & Watson, S. The child's symbolic conceptualization of the parents. *Child Development,* 1968, *39,* 625-636.

Keniston, K. *Themes and conflicts of "liberated" young women.* Papaer presented as the 19th Annual Karen Horney Lecture to the Association for the Advancement of Psychoanalysis, New York, March, 1971.

Kierkegaard, S. *Sickness unto death* (1849). (Walter Lowrie, trans.) Princeton, New Jersey: Princeton University Press, 1941.

Kohlberg, L. Development of moral character and moral ideology. In M. Hoffman & L. Hoffman (Eds.), *Review of child development research.* Vol. 1. New York: Russel Sage Foundation, 1964.

Loevinger, J. The meaning and measurement of ego development. *American Psychologist,* 1966, *21,* 195-206.

Lynn, D. *Parental and sex role identification.* Berkeley, California: McCutcheon, 1969.

MacFarlane, J. W. Studies in child guidance. I. Methodology of data collection and organization. *Monographs of the Society for Research in Child Development,* 1938, *3*(6), 1-254.

MacFarlane, J. Perspectives on personality consistency and change from the guidance study. *Vita Humana,* 1964, *7.*

Marcia, J. Ego identity status: Relationship to change in self-esteem, "general maladjustment" and authoritarianism. *Journal of Personality,* 1967, *38, 249-263.*

Marcia, J. *Manuscript in preparation for publication.* Simon Fraser University, 1976.

Maslow, A. *Motivation and personality* (1954). New York: Harper and Row, 1970.

May, R. *Love and will.* New York: W. W. Norton, 1969.

May, R. *The meaning of anxiety.* New York: W. W. Norton, 1977.

Mouton, R. W., Burnstein, E., Liberty, P. G., & Altucher, N. Patterning of parental affection and disciplinary dominance as a determinant of guilt and sex typing. *Journal of Personality and Social Psychology,* 1966, *4,* 356-363.

Nye, F. K., & Hoffman, L. W. (Eds.). *Working mothers.* San Francisco: Jossey-Bass Publishers, 1974.

Orlofsky, J. Sex-role orientation, identity formation, and self-esteem in college men and women. *Sex Roles,* 1977 *6,* 561-566.

Perry, W. G., Jr. *Forms of intellectual and ethical development in the college years.* New York: Holt, Rinehart, & Winston, 1968.

Rogers, C. *On becoming a person.* Boston: Houghton-Mifflin, 1961.

Rossi, A. Equality between the sexes: An immodest proposal. In R. Lifton (Ed.), *The woman in America.* Boston: Beacon Press, 1964.

Satir, V. *Peoplemanking*. Palo Alto, California: Science & Behavior Books, 1972.

Schaefer, C. E., & Anastasi, A. A biographical inventory for identifying creativity in adolescent boys. *Journal of Applied Psychology*, 1968, *52*, 42-48.

Siegel, A. E., & Haas, M. B. The working mother: A review of research. *Child Development*, 1963, *34*, 513-542.

Siegelmen, E., Block, J., Block, J. H., & von der Lippe, A. Antecedents of optimal psychological adjustment. *Journal of Consulting and Clinical Psychology*, 1970, *35*, 283-289.

Skolnick, A. The myth of the vulnerable child. *Psychology Today*, 1978, 55.

Werner, H. *Comparative psychology of mental development*. Chicago: Follett, 1948.

Werner, H. The concept of development from a comparative and organismic point of view. In D. B. Harris (Ed.), *The concept of development: An issue in the study of human behavior*. Minneapolis: University of Minnesota Press, 1957.

Jean Illsley Clarke
Consultant
Minnesota State Depart-
ment of Education
St. Paul, Minnesota

INTRODUCTION

"I love you," "you can do it," "ask me if you need help,"
are the essence of self-esteem inviting messages. These
are simple messages; messages easy for any parent to deliver. However, sometimes parents become estranged from their
ability to give these kinds of nurturing signals to their
children and to themselves. *Self Esteem: A Family Affair*
is an invitational education model designed to encourage
people to claim their positive self-esteem, to accept their
innate loveableness, and to claim their inherent capableness.
It also offers a variety of tools which people can use to
invite other people, young or old, to claim their positive
self-esteem. The book, *Self Esteem: A Family Affair* (Clarke,
1978) can be used for an individual study program, or as
part of a group meeting model.
  Cognitive materials on developmental stages, communication, responsibility, and self-esteem are presented in the
framework of family stories in the book. The worksheets in
the book are designed for individual study. This book, as
a text, and the *Leader's Manual for Self Esteem: A Family
Affair* (Clarke, 1979) are used by groups. The theoretical
base for the process in both the individual study and the
group meetings is based on a growth (rather than therapy
or medical) model, and follows a five-step process evolved
from a combination of transactional analysis (Berne, 1963),
andragogy (Knowles, 1970), values clarification (Simon,
Howe, & Kirschenbaum, 1972), and the personal beliefs of
the author.

UNDERLYING BELIEFS AND THEORIES

Whenever I read a book, I spend my first energy identifying
the frame of reference of the author. Once I have decided

where that person is coming from and, by implication, what parts of the book I will be inclined to believe or to discount, my energy is free to attend to the subject matter at hand. For this reason, I shall first list the beliefs underlying *Self Esteem: A Family Affair*. Although this model can be used by any adult who is interested in improving the quality of nurturing and self-esteem inviting which he or she delivers to self and other people of any age, in this paper I shall use the word "parents" to symbolize all adult care takers. The underlying beliefs and theories are as follows:

1. Parents and children are important and both deserve healthy, loving places in which to live and grow.

2. All parents have inside of them a person who is capable of being a good (or better) parent.

3. Parents know what they need, so the model offers opportunities and options, rather than "right answers." This philosophy of adult education is developed in Knowles' (1970) book, *The Modern Practice of Adult Education*.

4. Child rearing takes place in families. Therefore, rather than presenting developmental information in isolation, as if the only thing in a mother's life is an infant, information and problem-solving techniques are presented within the framework of family systems.

5. Since families are wherever people live, and since it is impossible to know what forms the family will take in the future, the model recognizes that a variety of family types are OK places for people to claim positive self-esteem. It avoids negating labels like "broken family." It suggests the inclusion of people of different ages, from different family types (nuclear, single parent), and with different focuses (infant, teenager, retarded child, foster child) in one group which emphasizes that all families have joys and problems.

6. Children learn more from modeling than from admonition. Therefore, the model focuses on the development of the self-esteem of the parent. Children watch and choose for themselves how much of their own self-esteem to claim. Parents cannot "make" children have positive self-esteem.

7. People learn in different styles, so visual, kinesthetic, and auditory experiences are offered.
The model provides for both deductive and inductive
preferences.

8. Unstructured discussion is of little value. If it
were, parenting problems would long ago have been
solved over coffee or gin. Therefore, opportunities
to share thinking are offered within the structure
of data gathering, practicing new behavior, comparing
ideas and beliefs, or clarifying values and wishes.

9. All adults and children are inherently powerful, and
the people in any family can improve the quality of
the living experiences they offer to each other and
to themselves.

PROCESS

Individual Model

The methods in the individual study model, *Self Esteem: A
Family Affair*, include a combination of reading, comparing
values and ideas with the author, rewriting content to fit
the reader's value system, collecting data on how the reader
behaves in his or her family, writing, practicing aloud, and
trying out new behaviors in the family. The reader also has
the opportunity to update personal values, and to compare
them with the values of other people either by comparing
lists with a friend or with the updated list reproduced as
an example in the book.

The Group Model

The methods presented for the group model, *Leader's Manual
for Self Esteem: A Family Affair* (Clarke, 1979), are a
series of exercises designed to provide auditory, visual,
and kinesthetic involvement in experiences which allow and
encourage participants to discover how their own values and
behaviors enhance or discourage positive self-esteem. Enhancing behaviors are celebrated and alternatives are offered
to the discouraging behaviors.
    The underlying framework for the exercises is a five-step
process by which a participant can enhance or redirect behavior. These are to identify specific problems; to honor
the old frame of reference which produced the no longer wanted
behavior; to consider, practice, and evaluate optional

behaviors; to identify a new frame of reference which will
support the new behavior; and to reinforce the new frame of
reference.

Step 1

A specific behavior to be improved or problem to be solved
is identified. The assumption is that adults are more apt
to achieve permanent changes in behavior if they isolate a
specific behavior problem, than if they try to solve multiple-
faceted problems all at once. For example, the goal, "I
want to improve the way I communicate with my child," is
broken down into specific areas: How do I let her know I
love her? How do I tell her she did something well? How
do I tell her she did not do well enough? Do I send confusing positive/negative messages? Do I send "don't live"
messages? What will I do instead?

Step 2

The frame of reference which produced the old behavior is
honored, but is not necessarily identified to the group. The
assumption is that dysfunctional behavior is being used,
because at some time in the person's life that behavioral
approach appeared to work better than others. Consequently,
the dysfunctional behavior came from a frame of reference
that is now archaic rather than "bad." The book points out
that the people in the stories behave in ways which somehow
in the past made sense to them, even if the behavior does not
seem to work now. The group model uses a ground rule which
states that everyone's attitudes, opinions, and beliefs are
respected, because they represent the best effort of that
person to make sense out of life so far. That ground rule
protection, plus other people's sympathy toward a particular
problem, produces acceptance of the old frame of reference.
When a parent says, "My folks hit me and even though I didn't
like it, sometimes I feel like hitting my kids; I need something to do instead," the parent is usually greeted by heads
nodding up and down, and several "me, too" messages. "Twenty-
six Things to Do Instead of Hitting" is an exercise which
invites everyone in the group to think of things to do instead of hitting. This reinforces that it is important not
to hit, and that it is also important to take care of one's
anger. It does not deride the person for having had an old
frame of reference about violence that he or she now wants
to change.

Step 3

Opportunity to consider and practice one or more new types
of behavior is repeatedly offered. The underlying assumption is that the individual presenting the problem has a more

accurate perception of what is needed than anyone else, and
that the solution is more apt to work if the individual has
thought through and selected that solution, than if it were
selected by someone else. The individual model describes
families exploring options, and offers work sheets at the
end of each chapter to encourage the reader to think through,
write down, try out, and evaluate options. In the group
model, participants practice alternative behaviors, and make
their own judgments about which ones to continue, explore
further, or discard.

In response to individual problems, the groups frequently
use "Suggestion Circles" which sharpen ability to collect
data and to consider, try out, and be responsible for behaviors. Also, "The Four Parent Exercise" presents four alternative ways of responding to any problem which involves
one's own or another person's behavior or one's own feelings.
Suppose a parent says, "I need information about teenagers.
Last year my daughter seemed so grown up and competent. Now
she is 13 and sometimes she acts like a baby. Sometimes I
feel irritated at her and sometimes I feel scared. Have
other parents in the room had that experience?" The facilitator might say, "The recycling theory explained in *Self
Esteem: A Family Affair* suggests that thirteen-year-olds
are recycling the first developmental stage in which they
decide how much to trust themselves and their world to get
their needs met. Would you be interested in hearing a 'Suggestion Circle,' in which people offer different ways you
might assure your daughter that you care about her basic
supply lines, such as love, food, clothing, shelter, transportation, that you will care for her, and focus on those areas
in ways which are satisfying to her and appropriate for a
thirteen-year-old? Or would you like a 'Four Parent' exercise
about how to take care of youself when you feel irritated or
scared?" The following meeting the parent will be invited
to tell what behaviors were tried out and their effectiveness.

Step 4
A new frame of reference that will support the continuation
of positive self-esteem reinforcing behavior is identified.
The assumption is that a person does not carry over a new
learning from one concrete experience to future different
experiences, unless some symbolic frame of reference for the
new behavior has been identified and claimed. Often parents
make the generalization themselves. In addition, *Self Esteem:
A Family Affair* offers a general frame of reference for inviting positive self-esteem at each developmental stage. The
messages which make up the positive frame of reference are
called affirmations. Affirmations are things we say to people,
ways we treat them, or things we say about them which indicate

how we expect them to act and to view themselves. Although adults need all of the affirmations from time to time, parents of particular age children often recycle the developmental tasks their children are learning, and therefore take comfort from the same affirmations that are appropriate for their children. The theory of recycling is presented by Levin (1974) in her book, *Becoming the Way We Are*. The affirmations are adapted with her permission from the "new messages" in that book. Specific affirmations for each developmental stage are listed later in this paper.

Step 5
Once the new frame of reference has been identified, it is reinforced to support the continuation of positive self-esteem supporting behavior. The assumption is that reinforcement, support, and celebration will help the person move from "tried new behavior once" to "new habit." This last step in the process of inviting and supporting changes in behavior is woven throughout *Self Esteem: A Family Affair* by repetition, permission, and invitation to celebration. Each group meeting agenda includes the invitation to share celebration, and has general celebrations built in. The individual model includes repeated invitation to start now, assess growth, claim competence, and celebrate wins. The problems stemming from lack of adequate external support for family systems are addressed repeatedly. Some groups continue as support groups after the *Self Esteem: A Family Affair* group meetings are concluded, and the invitation to do so with a suggested model is included in the last meeting.

BUILDING FAMILY STRENGTHS

The central theme of *Self Esteem: A Family Affair* is the belief that parents are powerful people; they can improve their own self-esteem and can invite and challenge children to do the same. The strengths which parents are encouraged to reconize and accept in themselves include identifying areas in which they have been doing a good job of parenting, and claiming their power and ability to improve the areas they want to change. While it is difficult or impossible to force change in other people, parents learn ways to challenge others to change. They also invite changes in others as they shift family systems and model new behaviors by changing themselves.
The methods which are used to encourage people to identify areas in which they are proud of their parenting vary from name tag exercises to celebrations, to listing ways they take good care of self and others, and to offering suggestions for other people in "Suggestion Circles" or the "Four Parent Exercises."

Activities which encourage people to identify what they are doing now and indicate what behaviors they want to keep and what to change are direct tools for inviting parents to claim their power. The developmental information presented offers some parents a new vantage point from which to evaluate the suitability of their parenting. The power people have to change themselves is embraced by the deliberate way in which the design encourages data collection and options evaluation, and the way in which it avoids offering specific problem solutions which could encourage adaptive rather than autonomous behavior on the part of the parents.

Specific techniques for challenging destructive behavior in other family members include constructive hassling, encouraging responsibility, dealing with redefinitions, and offering affirmations (Clarke, 1979). The affirmations listed below are skeletal sketches of the self-concept ideas which children need, starting at various ages, to help them feel loveable and capable; that is, to perform the tasks and to accept the responsibilities which are suitable for their age.

Affirmations for Being-Deciding to Live: Birth to Six Months

You have every right to be here.
Your needs are OK with me.
I'm glad you're a (boy, girl).
You don't have to hurry.
I like to hold you.
(I'm glad you're here.)

These affirmations for being are particularly important from birth to six months, for early teenagers, for people who are ill, tired, hurt, or vulnerable, and for everyone else.

Affirmations for Doing-Starting to Do Things on Our Own: Six to Eighteen Months

You don't have to do tricks to get approval.
It's OK to do things and get support at the same time.
(Try things, initiate things, be curious, be
   intuitive.)
(I'm glad you're here, and I see you are
   doing things.)

The affirmations for doing are particularly important for six to eighteen-month-old children, for thirteen and fourteen-year-old children, for people starting a new job or a new relationship, for people starting to learn any new skill, and for everyone else.

Affirmations for Thinking-Deciding It's OK to Think and to Separate: Eighteen Months to Three Years

I'm glad you're growing up.
I'm not afraid of your anger.
You can think about what you feel.
You don't have to take care of me by thinking
    for me.
You can be sure about what you need and want
    and think.
(I'm glad you're here, I see you are doing things,
    and I expect you to start learning about cause-
    and-effect thinking.)

These affirmations for thinking and separating are of
special importance to children who are eighteen months to
three-years-old, to young people in the middle teens, and
to everyone else.

Affirmations for Separating-Learning Who We Are: Three to Six Years

You can be powerful and still have needs.
You don't have to act scary (or sick or sad or
    mad) to get taken care of.
You can express your feelings straight.
(I'm glad you're here, I see you are doing things,
    and I expect you to start differentiating feel-
    ings and actions and to ask for your needs to
    be met straight.)

These affirmations for learning who we are have special
importance for children who are three to six-years-old,
for middle teenagers, for people who are owning their power
to be who they are and to ask straight for what they need,
for people who are giving up old, inadequate ways of dealing
with life, or who are giving up crutches and are incorporating healthier ways, and for everyone else.

Affirmations for Structure-Learning to Do Things Our Own Way: Six to Twelve Years

You can think before you make that rule your own.
You can trust your feelings to help you know.
You can do it your way.
It's OK to disagree.
You don't have to suffer to get what you need.
(I'm glad you're here, I see you are doing things,
    and I expect you to continue learning about

cause and effect. I expect you to differentiate
between feelings and actions, and to ask to get
your needs met straight. I also see that you
are trying out, thinking about, altering, and
claiming your own way of looking at things, and
doing things in order to take care of yourself.)

These are structure affirmations. They are particularly
important for six to twelve-year-old children, for people in
the late teens and early twenties, for people of all ages
who are entering new social settings (such as organizations,
businesses, recreation groups, families, and retirement),
and for everyone else.

Affirmations for Sexuality-Working Through Old Problems with Sexuality Added and Separating from Parents: Thirteen to Nineteen Years

You can be a sexual person and still have needs.
It's OK to know who you are.
You're welcome to come home again.
I love you.
(I see that you're recycling and going over old
    needs and problems with an added dimension of
    sexuality. It's OK to work through, to separate,
    and to assume responsibility for your own
    needs, feelings, and behavior as a grown-up
    person in the world.)

These affirmations for sexuality are important for
thirteen to nineteen-year-old human beings, for any older
persons who are making relationship separations, and for
everyone else.

Adults need various sets of these messages as they recycle earlier developmental tasks in more sophisticated ways.
The individual and group models contain numerous ways for
parents to examine, evaluate, and incorporate into family
life the affirmations they want to use for their children
or themselves.

OBSERVATIONS

The group model has been used with parents, educators, nurses,
social workers, clergy, and college students. It has been
facilitated by more than 40 different people with groups
which have included parents of children of all ages; foster
parents, adoptive parents and adopted people; parents of
children who display behavior problems, physical disability,

or mental retardation; grandparents; day care delivery
people; teachers; nurses; and clergy. It can be offered
wherever adults collect to share and learn. Currently, it
is being offered in three states, in settings as diverse as
college classrooms and family living rooms. The responses
to it are varied:

> A foster parent said: "I learned how to take
> care of myself and my children better."

> A young mother said: "In our group we are up-
> dating our own parenting concepts so we will be
> better equipped to invite growth in all the
> children we know."

> A father said: "That was a sensible class. I
> learned more than I expected to."

> A counselor said: "I see so much pain in family
> systems. And I see *Self Esteem: A Family Affair*
> as a way of preventing problems before they
> develop."

> A grandmother said: "I tried all those positive
> ideas on my husband and he loved it. Now he
> treats me better too."

> A teenager said: "I joined this group to help
> me in my day care job but it helped me with my-
> self even more."

IMPLICATIONS FOR THE FUTURE

I believe it is important to offer people the permission to
explore new ways of making or letting family systems work
better for growing and loving people. The implications in
my own life are exciting. My family is supportive of me as
we all claim more of our own power and positive self-esteem.
As a group facilitator and as a leader of workshops for
people who are learning facilitating skills, I have moved
from the position of helper-fixer-problem solver to co-
learner.

I have learned to trust parents to take what they need,
and to move at their own speed. I have even learned to trust
parents when they "misuse," according to my value system,
tools which I invented, as they adapt those tools to their
own values in their family system. The freedom from the burden of being an expert allows me the freedom and excitement

to meet with any group of parents anywhere, and learn with and from them as we move toward more humane family systems.

I am currently interested in exploring with people the need for new family vocabulary. For example, what are the implications for helping blended families become new forms of positive, supportive, extended families by finding new names for stepparents? How would it change the relation- ship in blended families if there were words which mean to everyone in the culture, "that new loving woman or man who is going to be responsible for part of my nurturing," to replace the words stepmother or stepfather and the images from Hansel and Gretel and Snow White?

Finally, I believe it is important to explore ways to create new and healthier kinds of support for family systems. I am interested in moving beyond the concept of "prevention," which implies staying away from something negative, to the concept of "becoming," which implies moving to something positive. I believe people need support during that journey. Support systems which have grown out of the *Self Esteem: A Family Affair* model are currently being observed and reported in a newsletter for support groups (*Newletter for Support Groups*). The newsletter also contains suggested activities. The author is an active member of a group which has been functioning for more than two years.

REFERENCES

Berne, E. *Structure and dynamics of organizations and groups.* New York: Grove Press, 1963.

Clarke, J. I. *Leader's manual for self esteem: A family affair.* Minneapolis: Winston Press, 1979.

Clarke, J. I. *Self esteem: A family affair.* Minneapolis: Winston Press, 1978.

Knowles, M. S. *The modern practice of adult education.* New York: Associated Press, 1970.

Levin, P. *Becoming the way we are: A transactional guide to personal development.* Berkeley: Transactional Publication, 1974.

Newsletter for support groups. J. I. Consultants, 16536 9th Avenue North, Wayzata, Minnesota 55391.

Simon, S., Howe, L., & Kirschenbaum, H. *Values clarifica- tion.* New York: Hart, 1972.

IV. PARENT-ADOLESCENT RELATIONSHIPS

The period of adolescence is recognized as a critical transitional stage involving major physical, emotional, and
social changes. It is often a difficult time, not only for
adolescents but for parents and teachers as well. Adolescence is also a period filled with opportunities for growth
and positive development. The articles in this section
address these as well as other aspects of adolescence.

Dr. Sol Gordon discusses various aspects of human sexuality that are of particular concern to adolescents.
His article offers suggestions for parents and family life
education teachers.

The article by Cheryl Polson and Dr. Anthony Jurich
discusses the conflict that often occurs between parents
and adolescents. They explain the conflict in terms of
the natural development that adolescents and their parents
are experiencing. Suggestions are offered for improving
parent-adolescent communication and the parent-adolescent
relationship. Because adolescents and parents can generally communicate in the area of career choice more successfully than in many others areas, career choice might
be used as a beginning point to establish a good parent-
adolescent relationship.

Dr. Dorothy Martin reports the results of a study of
father-daughter pairs concerning the perceptions of how
expressive the fathers were to their adolescent daughters.
The daughters recalled receiving less nurturance than the
fathers recalled giving to them. The article concludes
that fathers may need help in expressing affection and
caring for their daughters.

The article by Dr. Jerry Bigner, Judith Miller, and
Dr. R. Brooke Jacobsen reports the results of a study
comparing the levels of aspiration among farm and nonfarm
parents concerning their youth. They provide suggestions
for alleviating the conflict which may arise when parents
and youth have disparate aspirations.

Sexual Concerns of Adolescents: Implications for Sex Education

Dr. Sol Gordon, Director
Institute for Family Research
and Education
Syracuse University

INTRODUCTION

Occasionally when I am asked to speak, I receive a call from the vice-chancellor of a university. "We are very proud to have you come to our community," and I respond by saying, "Why did you decide not to have me?"

"How did you know?" "Well," I said, "I read minds." "Oh, but we decided to have you, but we wanted you to know that you are coming to a conservative community." I reply, "Aren't you lucky, I speak only to conservative communities."

"But, but, but, but, you are very controversial." "Well, if you are not controversial you have nothing to say." Spread that around as a rumor, because if you tell people the truth, they won't believe you.

We have a lot of problems in this country, and one of the most tragic ones is that we have one million pregnancies among teenagers each year. This number is growing by leaps and bounds--10 percent each year. People are saying, "If you tell kids about sex, they will do it." They already are doing it. Why so much promiscuity? There are two reasons given that really are myths.

One, it is said, is because there is sex education in the schools. Name all the school systems in the country that have superb sex education programs. Most of the sex education classes we have in schools are programs in plumbing, a relentless pursuit of the Fallopian tubes. There are isolated, brave people who are doing good programs, but please don't tell anyone who they are. Did you know that virtually all opposition to sex education in this country is based on the assumption that knowledge is harmful? Please think about it. Virtually all opposition to sex education in this country is based on the assumption that knowledge is harmful.

And the other reason (myth) is that it is the Pill which is making girls promiscuous. Less than 20 percent of sexually active teenagers are regularly using the best

contraception. If they were using contraception, how could
we have a million pregnancies?

Before I talk about sex education, I want to help you
come to terms with your own sexuality first. This shouldn't
take too long. Mind you, I said come to terms; I didn't say
get comfortable, because my first premise is that nobody is
comfortable about anything any more, and certainly not sexuality.

SEXUALITY

Nobody is comfortable with their sexuality. Sexuality is
an area of excitement, of mystery, and there is no reason
to ask anybody to be comfortable about it. I say you don't
have to be comfortable. That doesn't mean you have to be
paralyzed either. You can come to terms with it, with the
excitement, with the uncertainty of it, and with the mystery
of it.

There are some areas of sexuality that are more difficult
to understand and cause more concern than others. This is
especially true for adolescents. Much misinformation takes
place in regard to most of these areas. Let's examine those
more closely--maybe more calmly and sensibly.

Masturbation

One area of great concern to many people is masturbation. As
you know, it is the latest thing, and everybody is into it
these days. When I was growing up there was no problem.

From masturbation you got acne, tired blood, mental illness, blindness. I mean, that is why I wear glasses. We
thought we were pioneers in those days. Now nobody believes
any of that stuff. Everybody knows that it is okay to masturbate, but why is it still a dilemma in the United States
today?

Because we have been told it's okay to masturbate if you
don't do it too much. And nobody in the United States knows
how much is too much. Once a year, twice a week, after every
meal? Nobody knows. This is the dilemma. How much is too
much?

The medical literature will tell you if you masturabate,
it is all right, but if you do it too much, you have a tendency to be shy, retiring, narcissistic, and you may have no
friends. I am asking you, why should masturbation interfere
with friends?

What is this nonsense about masturbation? Masturbation
is a normal expression of sexuality at any time, at any age.

It is a problem only if it is guilt-ridden. Once is too much if you don't like it. If you don't like it, don't do it.

Female Orgasm

Another major source of concern is the female orgasm. The female orgasm is the topic of our time. It has reached the point of such absurdity that if a man and woman have sex, the first thing he asks her is, "Did you have one?" What kind of conversation is that? Is there no tomorrow?

Before Freud, women weren't even supposed to have orgasms, and then Freud came along and said they could have vaginal ones. Women enjoyed vaginal orgasms for 50 years, and then Masters and Johnson came along and said the clitoral ones were better, and women switched.

Now somebody has come along and said that only one is not good any more. You have to have thousands of them. So we have reached the age of multiple orgasms and soon someone will come along and say those are not good any more either. You need to have them simultaneously with your friend. So we are approaching the age of multiple, simultaneous orgasms.

What have we come to? Where is love? Where is the caring for another human being? We have forgotten that. We have allowed sexuality to degenerate into a kind of gymnastics. We need to pioneer and reintroduce love into our concern and thinking.

We somehow must help people to realize what we mean by sex education. We don't mean how to have sexual intercourse. We know that one of the few things young people do know is how to do it. I wish they didn't know unless I told them. We are talking about caring, about intimacy, about love. This is why Shere Hite's work, *The Hite Report: A Nationwide Study of Female Sexuality*, is so important.

Some people say it is not scientific. I say it may be more scientific than anything Freud or Erickson ever did. Sure, it is not scientific in a strict sense, but it is one of the great breakthroughs of our time, because she discovered and popularized the idea that what women care about more than anything else is intimacy, is love, is conversation.

What Is Most Important in an Intimate Relationship?

If I were to think of the ten most important things in a relationship, I would say number one is love and caring for another human being, and number two is a sense of humor. Without a sense of humor, you cannot survive in this grim world. You cannot be a teacher, you cannot be a parent successfully. It is very important that you develop a sense of humor, and the way to do it is to just look at somebody who is laughing at things that are funny, and when they laugh, you start to laugh. Practice that for a year, and you will develop your own sense of humor.

The third most important thing in a relationship is communication; talk to each other. They say if you are at a resort or fancy restaurant and see two people of the opposite sex, and they are not talking to each other, they are married. Learn to communicate; talk to each other.

The ninth most important thing in a relationship is sexual fulfillment, and number 10 is sharing household tasks together. Those are among the ten most important things in a relationship.

If you think about it, of the multitude of important things in a relationship, sex is still one of the top ten--not bad. Let's spread the rumor that sex is number 9 in any relationship, and if it is creeping up to number one in the relationship, it is because of some problems.

I acknowledge that sex might be number one the first week and number two in the second week of a relationship, but after awhile, it becomes number nine. It remains number nine for the rest of your life if it is a mature relationship.

We have this absolutely absurd notion about the role of sexuality in our lives, even in the broadest definition of love and caring and intimacy. Sexuality is not the most important thing in a relationship. People say, "If you have sex before marriage, you'll have nothing to look forward to." I say if that is the only thing to look foward to in marriage, don't marry.

Teens and Sex

There are good reasons why young people shouldn't have sex. I happen to be a conservative in this field. I don't think a teenager should have sexual intercourse at all.

I don't think they should have sex because they are too young; they are too inexperienced; they are too vulnerable; they don't have ready access to birth control. Parents have a right to say, "We don't want you to have sexual intercourse." Parents have that right, and it is incumbent upon us as adults to say, "We don't think you should have sex because there are good reasons: You are too vulnerable; you are too readily available for exploitation; you don't know that the first experiences of sex are usually pretty grim."

A lot of young people think that the first sex is going to be bells ringing and fire crackers sounding, but it is usually pretty grim. Why can't we tell young people that! Almost no teenage girl who has sex has an orgasm. Teenage boys often are impotent or have premature ejaculation. Sexually active teens are usually unsure of themselves and each

other; they must often be furtive in the relationship. This
is not a pretty picture. However, in the 25 years I have
been working in this field, no teenager has ever asked me
my consent. If they asked, I would say no. I would not say,
"Well, it depends on your level of maturity and your value
system." I would say no. The fact is they are not asking
counselors or health workers. They are not asking their parents. They are having sex whether we like it or not, and
whether they like it or not.

How do you like that, whether they like it or not? The
peer pressure in sex is so enormous. On the other hand, quite
a large number of young people have asked me if it is normal
to wait until marriage. That is what they want to know. They
are not asking us if it is normal to have sex; they are asking us if it is normal to wait until marriage.

I say, "Yes, it's normal," and I could stop there. But
I add, "Listen, I hope if you wait, you don't expect simultaneous orgasms on your wedding night, because then you might
ask yourself the question, 'For this I waited?'"

Lustful Thoughts

A young man came to see me, and he said, "Can I trust you?"
I said, "No." He said, "You're supposed to be trusted." I
said, "Trust comes at the end of a relationship. All meaningful relationships involve risk. Without risk, nothing happens. If you can't risk my not helping you or helping you,
liking or not liking you, then there is no relationship between us. All meaningful relationships in life involve risk."

He said, "Okay, I will risk it." He continued, "I am a
homosexual." "Do you want to be a homosexual?" "Of course
not," he said. "Have you ever had a homosexual experience?"
"Certainly not, what do you take me for?" I said, "I don't
know yet. Have you ever had a heterosexual experience?" "Of
course not, I'm a homosexual."

I said, "So far the diagnosis is antisexual. Tell me
your life history; you have five minutes." He said, "Ever
since I was 12 or 13, I have had these dreams of making it
with other guys. I knew there was something wrong with me,
and the more I thought about it, the more it repeated itself,"
and here he is at 20, a confirmed homosexual.

I said, "Idiot! Don't you know that all dreams, all fantasies, all wishes, all thoughts are normal? If you feel
guilty about a thought, you will have that thought over and
over again, because guilt is the energy for the repetition
of unacceptable thoughts."

That is the most dynamic concept in psychology. If you
want to do something to reduce anxiety and tension and

dysfunction by perhaps 50 percent, promote the concept that all thoughts, all dreams, all wishes, all fantasies are normal.

Behavior can be abnormal, but not dreams, not wishes, and not fantasies. What do you think, only Jimmy Carter has lustful thoughts? All the rest of us have lustful, sadomasochistic, maybe even murderous thoughts.

I walk down the street, and I see a pretty girl; I have a fantasy about her. Now, she doesn't know it. My wife does not know it. I enjoy my walk; all thoughts, dreams, wishes, and fantasies are normal.

Guilt is the energy for the repetition of unacceptable thoughts. If you have guilt about a thought, you will have that thought over and over again, because guilt is the energy for the repetition of unacceptable thoughts.

Latent Homosexuality

What does the intellectually-minded young man do to search out his identity? He goes to the index of a psychiatric textbook, and he looks up homosexuality. He finds that it doesn't exactly fit him, so he goes to an advanced psychiatric textbook, and he finds latent homsexuality.

There he is, fully diagnosed, and he hasn't even done anything yet. I say, listen, latency is the figment of a psychiatric imagination. You might as well say all women are latently pregnant for all it is worth. We could all be described as latent homosexuals, and we are latent heterosexuals.

Why can't we help people understand that the best definition of homosexuality is a person who in his or her adult life has and prefers relations with members of the same sex? A few homosexual experiences don't make a person homosexual any more than a few drinks make a person alcoholic. Do you know that this can be lifesaving? In yesterday's paper I read of a suicide center visited by one young boy, 17 years old, who had a single sexual experience with another young boy. He thought he was homosexual, and he wanted to commit suicide. He actually made the effort.

We have allowed young people and others to self-diagnose themselves, because we haven't provided them with the information they need. A few experiences, thoughts, and fantasies don't make a person homosexual.

Every time I talk about this on TV or radio, some young man will call me and say, "I am 22 years old. I had this homosexual experience when I was 13. I thought I was going to be homosexual the rest of my life. I like women. I have wanted to marry, but I thought if I did, all my children would be homosexual." He adds, "Now, now I know. I wish somebody had told me this years ago. Now I know. I understand. I

am going to marry." That wasn't five years of psychoanalysis.
That was three minutes of Sol Gordon.

Homosexuality

Perhaps no aspect of sexuality is associated with more fear and
anxiety than is homosexuality. We don't know why people become homosexual. We have no idea. We used to know. We knew
that if you had a strong mother and a weak father, you'd be
homosexual, until we discovered that 80 percent of the American families consist of weak fathers and strong mothers. The
only thing we know for sure is that the homosexual is probably born to a heterosexual couple.

Why should our society be overly concerned that three or
four percent of the men and women in it are homosexuals? Why
should sexual preference be anybody else's business? I suspect most of the problems arise because of our fears about
homosexuals. Some people say if you are frightened of homosexuals, you must be a latent homosexual. Nonsense! I say
if you are frightened of homosexuals, you are somebody who
is frightened of homosexuals. If you are afraid of dogs,
does that make you a latent dog?

However, we need to come to terms with our fears. We
cannot allow the fear to do our thinking. For example, people
are still saying, "If a faggot ever approaches me, I will
kill him." Why do you have to <u>kill</u> him? Why can't you
say, "No thank you? I am going steady already?" There are
so many things you could say.

Another area of concern is about homosexual teachers in
our schools. We hear, "We can't have gay teachers because
they are role models." In a school with a hundred teachers,
only three or four would be homosexual. Why do we assume all
the children would flock to the gays as role models? What
about the 96 or 97 heterosexual teachers? Maybe heterosexuals should also be concerned about the kinds of role
models that some <u>heterosexuals</u> present.

Perhaps the other fear about homosexuals involves sexual
assaults on children. Virtually 95 percent of all cases of
child molesting involve a male heterosexual molesting a girl.
Arrest figures may differ because, in many cases, authorities
are not willing to prosecute fathers or stepfathers who mo-
lest their own female children.

Penis Size

It is unfortunate that so many men have misconceptions and
undue concern about penis size. Freud spoke about penis envy.
He said all women had penis envy. Frankly, I never met a
single woman who had it. The only people I know who have
penis envy are men.

Undue concern and problems arise because the man with a
small penis knows that when his penis is erect, it extends to
five or six inches, and he erroneously assumes that the larger ones undergo a comparable change, and he feels inferior
or inadequate. He doesn't know that you <u>cannot</u> tell the size
of the penis from observing its nonerect <u>state</u>. A nonerect
penis that appears small may extend to six inches when erect;
while a nonerect penis which appears larger may extend to
only five inches when erect.

Many problems related to sexual dysfunction have some
connection with the assumption that the male has a small penis
or that there is something wrong with it. It's the height
of absurdity that we cannot talk about these things. When
the physician examines a young boy, what does he do? He
says, "Your knuckles are okay, your toenails are okay, your
eyebrows are splendid." Why can't he just say, "Your penis
is normal"; just a little remark, and the boy might say, "Oh,
is it?" The physician has an opportunity immediately to say
what I just said; you can't tell the size from looking at its
nonerect state.

SOME THOUGHTS ON SEX EDUCATION

We have just discussed many issues of sexuality which are
sources of concern and problems for many persons--especially
adolescents. Sex education provides an opportunity to deal
with these concerns and to help adolescents come to terms
with their sexuality in a positive, responsible manner. In
the sections which follow, we want to turn our attention to
such issues as changing family styles and teenage pregnancy
as they affect the content of sex education. We will also
discuss strategies for helping teens deal with peer pressure
and develop responsible sexual behavior.

A Scenario

We know what kids want to know. How do we find out? Can
you imagine a setting like this? We have, let's say, an
inner-city high school with a thousand kids in the assembly--
the only subject which is compulsory in that school. Paper
airplanes are flying about; the students are shouting and
screaming. The principal comes to the microphone, and he
says, "Boys and girls, we have a famous speaker from Syracuse
University," and the entire audience erupts into boos. "Boys
and girls, he has written a lot of books." Pandemonium
breaks out. The walls begin to tremble. "Boys and girls,
the honor of Central High School is at stake." Disaster!

I grab the mike, and I say, "Hey, wait a minute, everybody. All I need is one minute of your time." Somebody in any audience of a thousand (you can count on it) will stand up with a watch and say, "You have one minute." By this time, I have distributed index cards and pencils. And I say, "Listen everybody has questions about sex. If you don't have any questions about sex, you're either stupid, you have a limited imagination, or you don't feel well today, so pretend you are writing and nobody will know there is anything wrong with you." Then I say, "Spelling doesn't count, the handwriting doesn't count, and write it in the language you understand, because I know all the obscenities."

In a couple of minutes I have a thousand index cards, 950 questions, and 50 obscene remarks. I then proceed immediately to answer the questions; you know, in this audience of a thousand you can hear a pin drop. Not that they are anxious for their questions to be answered, but they are so fascinated about what their friends are asking, because in this society people don't talk truthfully to each other about sex. They rap, they boast, they lie. But here is an opportunity that is so dynamic, and it can go on for hours.

Don't go into a school and give your birth control lecture. Circulate index cards, and ask them for their questions. You know what the questions are going to be, because we have put them in our comic book, "Ten Heavy Facts with Facts."

Where do you suppose we got those questions? We got them from our collection of some 20,000 questions. Adolescents want to know about masturbation; they want to know about homosexuality; they want to know about their thoughts. These are the things people want to know about, and that is what is specifically excluded in most health and family life classes.

Egalitarian Families

Tomorrow's family will consist of a husband and wife of similar education who marry for love, and they will both spend most of their lives working outside of the home. They will have 1.8 children, a color television, and a dog.

I see tomorrow's family as being more stable, more healthy than ever before. In the good old days, even as little as fifty years ago, we had compulsory pregnancy, and women died of childbirth; longevity was 45 years; and they didn't have a choice of divorce or separation. Is that the good old days that we are hankering after--the traditional family life? I say, "Never, never again back to the traditional family!"

We have to emerge toward the egalitarian family. We have
to work towards women's liberation, and we have to bring it
right down to the high school, the junior high school, and
the little kids. We need to define what we mean by the women's movement.

Those who oppose it say women are aggressive. Women
don't want to have babies any more; they don't want to stay
home any more.

Women are assertive these days, and if they don't get
their legitimate rights, they become aggressive. Women are
assertive, and the real meaning of the women's movement is
equal rights, equal pay for equal work, equal opportunities
for career choice and leisure, and equal responsibilities.
That's the meaning of the women's movement. It has nothing
whatsoever to do with whether a woman stays at home with the
kids or works outside the home. You can be an unliberated
woman and work outside the home, and you can be a perfectly
liberated woman and stay at home with the kids.

We'd better stop putting guilt trips on women who work
outside the home. Do you know that in this country, we have
one million cases of child abuse; 100,000 of these children
are so brutalized that they are hospitalized, and 4,000
children are murdered by their parents. Do you know most
child-abuse parents are at home with the children?

When I first got married more than 25 years ago, I used
to think that women were born cleaning ladies. I married a
professional woman; she worked full time, and I worked full
time. But she did all the cooking and the cleaning and the
shopping and took care of the kid; I was busy. Until one
day, my wife came to me and said, "I am busy too. How would
you like a divorce?" It took me five minutes to rearrange
my schedule.

I realized for the first time I had an assertive wife,
and I didn't want her to become aggressive. Now I do some
of the cooking and the cleaning and the shopping, and I don't
like it. I know now that women don't like to clean, and men
don't like to clean; even cleaning ladies don't like to clean.

The women's movement is a main hope in society today.
We have to stop exploiting each other and playing games with
each other. We have to get these messages across to young
kids.

Pregnant Teens

Among teenagers, we had one million pregnancies, and 50,000
pregnancies were among children under 15 years of age last
year. A teenage girl who gives birth has 90 percent of her
life's script developed for her. Most of them will drop

out of high school. Many of them will never marry. Most
of them will remain on welfare, and there is a big connection between every index of pathology and being born to a
teenage mother, whether it's alcoholism, depression, or being
a victim of child abuse.

We know there is a connection between poverty and racial
discrimination and teenage pregnancy. We have to, somehow,
in the crisis that we are in, stop glorifying teenage pregnancy, stop thinking about alternatives to abortion, and
think more about prevention. That is where it's at. We
must try to prevent the teenager from becoming pregnant in
the first place.

We have to stop all these fantasy interpretations as to
unresolved oedipal complexes. I say a teenager gets pregnant because she has sexual intercourse. We have to understand that we live in a sexist society. Boys are supposed
to have sex, and the girls are not supposed to have it until
they are married. How do we get a million pregnancies?

The girl is seduced, overwhelmed, raped, but mainly isn't
prepared for sexual behavior. We have to say that sex itself
is not romantic. Love and caring are romantic. Holding hands is romantic. Looking into each other's eyes is
romantic, but the actual sexual experience is not romantic
unless you use birth control.

We have to announce that both boys and girls are sexual.
The girl then has some questions to ask. "Am I ready?" "Do
I want to have sex with somebody I don't even know?" "Do
I want to wait until marriage?" "Will we use birth control?"
"What will happen to me and my future if I get pregnant now?"
"Am I ready to be a mother?"

The Best Contraception

Don't we know that the best oral contraceptive is still "no?"
Sex is never a test of love. The boys say, "If you really
love me, you will have sex with me." That is why I developed
the book called, *You Would if You Loved Me*. It's a collection of lines that boys use to seduce girls, and if a girl
read it, she would be able to say, "Hey, that is a line I saw
in the book." All she has to do is hesitate for 30 seconds,
and say, "That's a line."

We have to help the girls with some replies. I asked my
college students, who are now 21 and 22, what they would have
said in retrospect. They came up with some honeys: "Oh
darling, if you really loved me, you would have sex with me."
"Oh, sweetie, I really love you, but if you really loved me
you wouldn't put this pressure on me." Why is it always the
woman who must defend herself? "Oh, darling I will go crazy
if I don't háve sex." Why can't the girls say, "Go!" "Oh

honey, would you like to get in the back seat of the car?"
"Oh, darling, I would much prefer to sit up front with you."

Girls are going to have to play rough sometimes, because as far as we know, only girls get pregnant. I have
never heard of any male dying from an unresolved erection.
Until people begin to communicate with each other, talk to
each other, respect each other, the girls are going to have
to get good at some of the games the boys have been playing for thousands of years.

What Shall We Call It?

First of all, we have lost the term "sex." It no longer belongs to us. The vocal opponents of sex education have sufficiently introduced into the minds of the public that sex
means doing it. We have to declare we have lost that battle. We had better talk about family life education, because that is really what we mean anyway.

We better talk about preparation for parenting, because
that is what we are about anyway. We had better let people
know that we are pro-life and pro-family. We lost one skir-
mish, and we had better not lose the family because we are
the ones who feel children should be wanted, and children
should be born to couples who care about them and want them;
that is the very essence of family life.

We have to introduce programs into our schools which
talk about self-concept and self-affirmation, because people
who feel good about themselves are not available for exploitation and do not exploit others. That is what we are talking
about. We have to have psychology courses, parenting courses,
and family life courses which focus on self-affirmation, on
equality of the sexes, and talk about such things as love.

You have to leave the plumbing for biology, and not introduce plumbing into family life, because it is another subject. You know how terrifying it is to encroach on another
subject. I would like the biology teachers to say, "We want
to teach the plumbing. This is ours." I would give it to
them, but tell them to do it in an interesting way, and include birth control. Our subject-matter is love, communication, caring for another person, and morality.

Teaching Values

We cannot introduce any subject in the schools without its
moral components. I would like to see a social studies
teacher talk about the social systems of our time without
introducing values: "Oh, boys and girls, we have four main
systems in the world today: communism, fascism, democracy,

and anarchy. Choose one; they are all equally good." The
kids will choose anarchy, and where will we be? No, we say
democracy is the best. Communism is evil; fascism is evil;
anarchy is evil. That's what we say.

Values are part of every subject. We don't say in civics,
there are two kinds of people; there are those who litter and
those who don't litter, and the litterers are just as good as
the nonlitterers. We don't say that. We say it's no good
to litter the streets. And you know what we say in family
life education? It's wrong to exploit another human being.
It's wrong to become pregnant as a teenager. It's wrong to
spread venereal disease. But when we come to other subject-
matters which are sensitive, we make a distinction between
being moral and moralistic. Moralistic means you try to impose your point of view on everyone--your religious or idio-
syncratic point of view on everyone. That is being moralistic. That violates separation of church and state. It
is unethical.

But there is nothing wrong with being moral. We know
that there are some issues which are very sensitive, like
abortion. We know we cannot say in a classroom, abortion is
murder. We have to say this is a sensitive issue, and that
people are entitled to their own points of view about it.
There are many diverse religious and ethical groups in this
country; some are opposed to abortion and some favor it.

Am I in Love?

I want to talk briefly about love, because that is the
subject-matter, the heart and the essence of family life education: how we can tell if we are really in love. Can you
imagine a class not being interested in that subject?

Well, you can tell if you are in love. In one sense,
if you feel you are in love, you are. It's not fair to say
it's puppy love, or you will get over it. But, unfortunately,
there are two kinds of love. There is good love and bad love;
or if we talk to a professional audience, you have to say
mature and immature. There are two kinds of love--a mature
love, that emerges, and an immature love, that is exhausting. You have seen people who have immature love affairs.
They go around saying, "I am in love, I am in love, I am in
love." It's exhausting even to watch them.

People who have an immature love affair are too tired to
shower. They are too tired to do their schoolwork. They
have what we call a hostile/dependent relationship. They
can't stand to be with the persons they are supposed to be
in love with, and they can't stand to be without them--"I
miss him, I miss him, I miss him"; "I miss her, I miss her."

When they are with the person they are supposed to be in
love with, they are fighting, they are arguing, and they are
jealous. One of them usually says to the other, "Do you really
love me, do you really love me, do you really love me?" I
advise the other person to say, "No." You will have your
first conversation that way. On the other hand, the person
who is really in love, is energized. They have time to shower.
They have time to do their schoolwork. They have time to
help with household tasks. When they are with the person they
are supposed to be in love with, they enjoy it most of the
time. Now some of you know why you are tired most of the
time.

Can you imagine a group of young people not being interested? We must discuss topics like love and finding a mate,
communicating. We must deal with their feelings and concerns.

IN SUMMARY

Now I would like to conclude by reading to you one of my poems
from the *You* book. The *You* book is my favorite book. It's
got the world's longest title. It's called, *The Psychology
of Surviving and Enhancing Your Social Life, Love Life, Sex
Life, School Life, Work Life, Home Life, Emotional Life, Creative Life, Spiritual Life, Style of Life, Life*. You know,
there is nothing else. It's got all the famous comic books
in it, and it's got a lot of slogans and pictures; it's very
exciting for young people, especially those who don't like
to read much.

It says: Life is not a meaning. Young people come to
me and say, "Life has no meaning." I say, "I hope not. Life
is not a meaning; life is an opportunity. The people who
have found the meaning in life are usually the ones who are
so hostile and so angry that they are willing to take you
and throw you against the walls with the meaning they have
found in life."

Life is not a meaning; it is an opportunity. It's an
opportunity for meaningful experiences. Sometimes young
people come to me and they say, "Life has no meaning. I have
to go off and find myself." "Where are you going to go? With
whose money?" You have to find yourself right where you are,
and then go off and have a good time. The poem is called
"Random Thoughts" and it reads as follows:

We all have some areas of vulnerability. Not
everything in life can be understood or resolved.
I feel that just about everything worthwhile in
life involves some risk and some sacrifice of
time, energy, and patience.

I suspect that really meaningful experiences are
of brief duration, albeit repeatable, and rarely
occur on schedule.   Even tragic events offer us
opportunities for review and renewal.

Some people are strange.   If they don't understand something they haven't heard about, they
think it either doesn't exist or isn't worthwhile.   If God wants to test you, what will you
do?

Using Adolescent Occupation Development to Strengthen the Parent-
Adolescent Relationship

Cheryl J. Polson
and
Dr. Anthony P. Jurich
Department of Family and
Child Development
Kansas State University

INTRODUCTION

Adolescence is a product of social invention of Western in-
dustrialized culture. It was created to define an artificial
period of development between childhood and adulthood. Adolescence is a time of rapid development. The adolescent is
reaching sexual maturity, defining values, and discovering a
vocational and social direction (Ambron, 1975). The adolescent period leads to adult maturity. Adolescence in the
United States usually begins at or after the age of 10, but
not later than 13, and ends by age 18 for some and by the
mid-20's for almost all individuals.

Adolescents are often put into the role of playing the
"marginal man" in a society where they have no clearly defined script (Landis, 1952). This undefined role is confusing, in that one is often treated like a child, but is
expected to perform as an adult. Adolescent development does
not occur overnight. The adolescent develops through interactions with society, and the significant people in his or
her life (Jurich, in press). Through interactions with
others the adolescent sees the reflection of self through
the perceptions of significant others. Therefore, the adolescent discovers self-identity. If these interactions are
of a positive nature, the adolescent will develop a good
self-concept. Should these interactions be negative, they
may result in growth, during this time, being particularly
painful.

Adolescents have limited resources to assist them through
this difficult time. Society offers little support to lessen
the intensity of the adolescent experience. Most of the peer
resources of the adolescent have limited skill in helping the
adolescent to cope with the dilemmas of the teen years. Consequently, it is extremely important that parents be supportive

253

of the adolescent. Parents have the opportunity to play a
critical role in the adolescent's life. Adolescents often
seek independence from their parents but still want the comfort of knowing that mom and dad are there in case of an
emergency. The parent-adolescent relationship often takes
on an "approach-avoidance" aspect, giving rise to parent-
adolescent tensions.

Many researchers choose to focus entirely on the negative
experiences which occur during adolescence. Moreover, parents and practitioners are given few guidelines by which they
can establish positive parent-adolescent relationships. The
remainder of this paper will focus on a task of adolescent
development which has the potential to become an area in
which parents and adolescents can become closer to one another.

LATE-ADOLESCENCE

Adolescents begin to play a more clearly defined role as they
move from the "marginal man" status to the young adult during
late adolescence. This transition usually extends from the
period of time after high school, until the adolescent
achieves full adult status. This would include those youths
in college. The way in which the late adolescents are able
to cope with the changes they are experiencing during this
stage is directly related to their adjustment made in previous stages (Crites & Semler, 1974). Munley (1975) found
that students who had made well-adjusted vocational choices,
and had developed mature career attitudes, successfuly resolved the first six psychosocial crises outlined by Erikson
(1959), including the fifth stage (identity versus role confusion). The ease with which the adolescent is able to define career goals is directly built upon successful completion of developmental tasks required in other stages outlined
by Erikson (1959). The necessary skills to cope with the
crisis at one stage are built upon the successful completion
of tasks at preceding stages. It is through these stages
that the adolescent must gain preadult experience, in order
to be able to deal with the tasks confronted during adulthood. For example, an adolescent, who has not been able to
move away from the peer group in order to form close one-to-
one relationships, may experience dilemmas during late adolescence. Such an adolescent may choose a career which will
hold high prestige within the peer group, rather than defining
a career which will be personally fulfilling.

Crystallization of the adolescent's identity should be
accomplished during late adolescence. Identity formation
is a process that is unique for each individual. Identity

is like a solution to a jigsaw puzzle, where each person has different pieces to create a unique puzzle. Included in the process of "fitting the pieces together," the late adolescent decides how to relate to society. The late adolescent may have different values from his or her parents, but in late adolescence, instead of rebelling, is able to take his or her value system into a realistic perspective (Keniston, 1970). Adolescents may no longer view their parents as adversaries. Erikson (1959) defines one aspect of identity formation as the delineation of a vocational direction. Adolescents are involved in a process of defining the career they are best suited for. They are continually trying on new faces to reach a maximum comfort.

OCCUPATIONAL AND EDUCATIONAL DEVELOPMENT

One of the primary developmental tasks of this period is exploration of alternative career choices. Late adolescents should be able to measure their capabilities against the objective reality of work and the subjective reality of interest (Ginzberg et al., 1956). For example, an adolescent girl, who desires to be a model but is only five feet tall, must look realistically at the physical characteristics required for modeling. In another situation, an adolescent boy may disappoint his parents, who would prefer him to be a doctor, by actively pursuing a career of plumbing. After exploring a number of occupational alternatives, there is finally a reduction of alternatives to a smaller number of feasible choices, from which a final career choice is made. The adolescent who has explored these various alternatives will have a healthy outlook on a chosen career, and will most likely be fulfilled in that occupation. If forced into a particular career through parental pressure, the adolescent may resent the career, and may also be very unhappy in the job.

While attending college, the adolescent encounters a variety of values, behavior codes, and opinions through interaction with teachers and other students. During college, an adolescent has contact with many individuals holding different values and varied experiences. With this contact, adolescents can broaden perspectives and incorporate parts of other lifestyles into their own way of living. This enables adolescents to separate themselves from the past, especially the family, and to use the contacts made in college as a foundation upon which to build a personal value system. Over the course of the college career, the late adolescent will combine past experiences with the new experiences. This provides new avenues of personality development and solidifies identity. Freedman (1960) observed substantial personality changes between freshman and senior years of college attendance, such as the amount of independence elicited. For example, a freshman may be more inclined to follow parental wishes instead of following personal preferences, as opposed to a senior who may evaluate parental desires, but will make a final decision based upon his or her own judgment.

Sanford (1967) found that the majority of students experience their greatest changes during the first two years of college. These experiences may not have occurred if they had remained in the home setting. The student faces new challenges and adjustments to a new environment (Bloom & Kennedy, 1970). Adjustments, which the late adolescent makes towards the college environment, reveal assumptions about self and others which have been protected from challenge (Madison, 1969). Many times, the adolescent feels secure in the web of roles which are reinforced by family, friends, and community. Once adolescents enter college, the friends and professors, who make up this new personal environment, will not accept old roles as easily. Therefore, adolescents are asked to redefine themselves based upon the input from these new surroundings. Furthermore, the competition for choice roles in the college environment may be stiffer than that in a previous community setting. Students become aware of the fact that others cannot make their decisions. Each adolescent is responsible for his or her choices, behavior, and the consequences. Through this awareness, self-confidence grows, more responsibilities are accepted, more risks are taken, and new experiences are sought.

THE ADOLESCENT'S FAMILY

It is crucial to remember that the changes the adolescent is going through do not occur in a vacuum. Changes occur within the context of the family, and have an impact on family functioning (Ginsberg, 1971). The family experiences the greatest amount of change when a family member is entering new roles and relationships, such as when the adolescent enters college. Once the late adolescent enters college, parental self-doubts, as to whether they have fulfilled their parental roles, are accented. The parents question how and if they have prepared their adolescent to become independent, and to stand alone in the "real" world. Parents may evaluate whether or not they have over-protected their child. In addition to examining their effectiveness as parents, they may also be experiencing a problematic time of life. They are reexamining their own life goals. Through

this process, each parent will realistically appraise where
he or she has been and where to proceed in life. For example, a father may question his career choice or may have
to face the fact that he did not achieve the career goals
that he set for himself. A mother may feel the pressure of
menopause, as the childbearing portion of life draws to a
close. Adjusting to her son or daughter's leaving the home
only serves to compound the changes she is experiencing during this transition. Both parents encounter a sense of emptiness, in that there is often an absence of the goals which
motivated them through their child-rearing years (Anthony,
1975). They may also feel a sense of failure in achieving
their own life goals at a time when their adolescent is beginning adult life with idealistic expectations. Equally as
well, parents have to adjust to declining physical energy,
which prevents them from doing the things they were once able
to do. Whereas they may have been able to work all day and
then exercise recreationally for an hour or two, they may
now find themselves needing to rest and relax during the evening. These parents are now confronted with an adolescent
who is in prime physical condition, and who is just beginning
to explore his or her sexuality. The adolescent is also just
beginning to map out life goals in the context of idealistic
expectations.

With emotional enthusiasm and recently acquired cognitive
goals, the adolescent may tend to be overly idealistic. Part
of the growth process throughout the remainder of adolescence
will be tying organizational aspirations to reality. Furthermore, not only are both late adolescents and their parents
forced to deal with internal conflicts and frustrations, but
the adolescents' developmental tasks are often in direct conflict with the developmental needs of the parents. "Many
times, what will please the adolescent is diametrically opposed
to the parents' needs and fulfillment and the parents' needs
will frustrate the adolescent's development" (Jurich, in
press). In this manner, the problems and developmental tasks
of parents and adolescents interlock (Scherz, 1967). How
these conflicts are resolved has an impact on the future development of the adolescent in becoming more independent and
mature (Katz et al., 1968). Therefore, necessary adjustments
are required of both the parents and the adolescent or the
unity of the family may be threatened (Ginsberg, 1971).

The tensions may escalate stress in other areas of the
parent-adolescent relationship (Bettelheim, 1962; Hess, 1970;
Keniston, 1962). Unresolved dilemmas from the parents' past
may resurface because of the developmental tasks the adolescent must accomplish during this stage of life. For example, parents and the adolescent may have previously been
able to talk freely about dating. However, at this time of

rapid change for both the parents and the adolescent, this becomes an area of controversy. Parents refer to their own dating behaviors and may want to tighten the strings on the adolescent. At the same time, the adolescent is experiencing a greater need for independence, and needing to make personal decisions about dating.

COMMUNICATION IN THE FAMILY

If the level of stress gets too high, parent-adolescent communication may be inhibited. Although both parents and the adolescent desire to share the adolescent's experiences, their conversations are often short circuited. The highly volatile nature of such crucial issues as sexuality forces both the adolescent and parents into a defensive posture, which greatly hinders constructive communication. This type of behavior often leads to a "conspiracy of silence," in that both the parents and the adolescent choose not to communicate. The adolescent fears a restrictive response by parents to his or her activities. The parents want to avoid looking at the behaviors of their adolescent which will make them feel guilty about their effectiveness as parents. Also, both parents and adolescent conspire with each other to keep silent. This communication gap increases the parent-adolescent stress and inhibits the achievement of developmental tasks for both the parents and the adolescent.

The quest of adolescents to complete the developmental tasks of independent identity help to create a generation gap. Therefore, some adolescents seek to reduce family tension by delaying or avoiding this crucial task of development. Josselson (1973) found that adolescents, who foreclose their development, have no generation gap, but they also stop growing. This indicates that adolescents may not want to lose the sources of love from parents. Instead, they choose to remain dependent, and give up the autonomy which accompanies independence. This suggests, perhaps, that late adolescents and their parents should be encouraged to talk about their differences and try to lessen the degree of anxiety experienced. Through such steps, miscommunication can be avoided. Adolescents should be prompted to talk about their feelings, while the parents should listen carefully and try to see the situation through the eyes of an adolescent. This does not mean that the parent will or should agree with the adolescent, but that an attempt has been made to understand the adolescent's feelings and perceptions. Parents should also expect to be included in this process. They should request the adolescent's attention to their perspective. This enables the adolescent to better understand his or her parents.

Moreover, the adolescent should be able to share experiences without fearing the loss of parental acceptance. Often parents and college students cannot agree on the nature of their communication. Sistrunk, Fretwell, and Kennedy (1972) found that two-thirds of the students sampled experienced a change in communication between themselves and their parents. However, 80 percent of the parents said there were no changes. The students experienced feelings of being distant from their parents, and talked less about significant experiences than their parents realized. This may be largely due to the fact that adolescents, facing the developmental task of establishing their own independent identity, tend to emphasize the differences between their parents and themselves. Parents, on the other hand, often feel threatened by the thought that their adolescent has changed, and the quality of their relationship with the adolescent has changed. In addition, adolescents tend to overestimate the differences between themselves and their parents in attitudes; parents tend to underestimate the differences between themselves and their adolescents' attitudes. This is largely due to the parents' need to feel close and the adolescents' need for independence. Parents find it difficult to let go of their adolescents. They are afraid of no longer being needed and, as a result, attempt to keep their adolescents close. In direct opposition to this, adolescents are pursuing an independent life; this often requires a "pulling away" from parents.

PARENTS VERSUS PEERS: WHO ARE THE EXPERTS?

Adolescents, feeling a need for independence from their parents, still need to belong to their peer group. Adolescents tend to look to their peer society for much of their status and identity. Brittain (1963) found that adolescents look to their peers for choices with immediate consequences, such as areas of fashion, style, and dating customs. Whereas parents may view these areas as trivial, to the adolescents they are of paramount importance. Consequently, parents may discredit the degree of importance placed on these areas by adolescents. The parents often view adolescents as being similar to themselves, because many of the areas in which adolescents rebel are areas of minimal importance to the parents. Parents can experience difficulty in communicating with adolescents if they do not acknowledge the extent and magnitude of such issues. The parents who cannot appreciate the level of adolescents' feelings may find communication blocked. Propper (1972) identified five major areas of parent-adolescent conflict, with the primary area concerning

the adolescent's social life and customs. The focus of these
arguments is not usually on major value issues, but over small
matters such as specific time of curfew, date selection, and
church attendance (Kinloch, 1970). Because of the conspiracy
of silence, neither the parents nor the adolescent want to
fully discuss volatile issues, such as morality. Issues are
discussed when the necessity of the moment dictates an immediate decision. Therefore, the parent-adolescent conversations are characterized by situation-specific topics and incomplete discussion.

In order to narrow the communication gap between parents
and adolescents, attention may be focused on those areas in
which adolescents refer to their parents for their expertise.
Researchers concentrate on parent-adolescent conflicts, and
the continuous struggles which are going on during adolescence.
They too often fail to examine those areas where parents and
adolescents can and do have positive interactions. Brittain
(1973) discovered that when parents and adolescents are questioned about such areas as life goals, career choices, and
general home situations, their answers are very positive.
He also found that adolescents look to their parents in making
decisions with long-term effects, such as defining a career
goal. Studies have found the area of career exploration to
be one which the late adolescent freely discusses with his or
her parents, seeking opinions and information. This is also
an area in which parents have expertise (Brittain, 1963).
They have been involved in the search of an occupation themselves, and have experienced the various aspects of career
decision making.

For most parents, the adolescent's career selection is
not an area in which they feel that they should make the final
decision. Rather, they attempt to assist the adolescent in
any way they can. The threat level is low, in that the issues involved are not of a volatile nature, and the parents and
adolescent do not take adversary roles. The late adolescent,
in essence, does a complete turnabout in this area. He or
she may have leaned heavily as a subordinate on parents for
support, pulled away from them as an adversary, and returned
to seek their guidance in an exchange between equals (Jurich,
in press). Ultimately, this leads to better understanding
between the parents and adolescent. The adolescent must break
the initial subordinate bond of childhood in order to re-
approach his or her parents as an equal adult. The adolescent comes to view parents with respect instead of directly
opposing them. Perhaps, with the new perspective, the adolescent can refer to them for advice in other areas of concern.

PARENTAL INFLUENCE ON CAREER DEVELOPMENT

The adolescent progressing through the teen years narrows
the number of career alternatives and becomes decisive about
career choices (Gesell, Ilg, & Ames, 1956; Ginzberg et al.,
1951, 1956; Hershenson & Roth, 1966). At this time, parents
become sensitive to the fact that their adolescent will soon
decide upon a career. With this awareness, the parents are
anxious to supply the adolescent with their opinions and
values about careers.

Opening Up the Discussion

In most cases, the parents will have to approach the adolescent to initiate a discussion about careers. If parents wait
until the adolescent is already in college, they may have to
work against a family expectation of little parent-child discussion about careers. Therefore, parents should try to establish a pattern of career conversation during early adolescence.
However, for the early adolescent, the choice of an occupation seems far in the future. Consequently, in most cases,
the parent will have to initiate any discussion about careers
and occupations. No special time need be set aside for discussion. Such interaction may arise spontaneously from television shows, the nightly news, or day-to-day interactions.
Questions about occupations may arise from the adolescent.
Whenever a question is asked, parents should attempt to answer
it to the best of their abilities. If the parents do not
know the answer, they should explore the situation with the
adolescent. Such mutual exploration serves to give the adolescent information, and also presents the parent as a good
model for exploring career alternatives.

Keeping Horizons Open

Parents may have a tendency to become threatened by their
adolescent's career explorations and often inhibit the growth
which can occur during this time. At the same time, the parents can stifle the adolescent's creativity in job exploration if they do not take the time to examine what the adolescent's interests and capabilities are. Instead, parents
may push their own individual goals onto the adolescent. If
the adolescent decides to pursue the goals parents have laid
out, he or she may be frustrated by an inability to successfully accomplish these goals. In addition, resentment of
not having ownership of a career choice can arise. Therefore, it is important that parents treat their adolescent
as a mass of potential. Exploring this potential, the adolescent must have freedom to try on new faces. Some of the

roles the adolescent tries on may be alarming to parents. On first impulse, the parents may want to cut off such exploration, and "sell" the adolescent on the career of which they approve. Parents must remember the price the adolescent must pay, for an unclear definition of personal and professional self is far too high to risk.

Not only must parents be aware of the direct messages which they give their adolescent, but they must also monitor the indirect messages they send about careers. In the case of career education, what the parents do and how they act is a much more powerful influence on the adolescent than what they say. Parents influence the adolescent's career aspirations in ways of which they are totally unaware. For example, an adolescent who sees a parent come home from work every evening complaining about a manual job, may be indirectly influenced by that parent to continue his or her education in order to find a fulfilling position upon graduation.

Providing an Example

If the adolescent can observe parents as they work in their own careers, they can serve as models in the world of work, and open a new resource to the adolescent. Parents can be a sounding board for the adolescent's career explorations. The parents can gain this position through demonstrating their competency in the area of careers. This can be initiated by talking about their jobs. They may also directly share their jobs with the adolescent by having him or her spend time on the job.

In essence, parents do play a critical role in the adolescent's career decision making. The amount of influence appears to vary, depending upon such factors as the parents' education, socioeconomic status, and the amount of parental encouragement the adolescent is given. Through direct or indirect influence, parents allow adolescents to see their attitudes, opinions, and sometimes their preferences about occupational aspirations.

Going Beyond Occupational Development

Parents should utilize the areas in which the adolescent sees them as experts as a bridge to other areas of adolescent concerns. This enables the adolescent to see parents as competent role models. In addition, the adolescent is able to experience a positive interaction with his or her parents. By creating a positive interaction in these areas, such as career selection, there can be a rippling effect into other areas. The adolescent may begin to feel secure enough and give parents enough credit for their expertise to make an attempt to seek information on other matters, such as sex and drugs. These areas are of particular concern to parents, and many parents would like to be consulted on these issues. If the adolescent is impressed by parental expertise in the area of careers, he or she is more apt to seek out parents' advice in areas which are less in their domain. Hopefully, when consulted by the adolescent, the parents will feel less urgency to "hard sell" their values and will allow time to explore these values with their adolescent.

CREATING A TOOL FOR THE PROFESSIONAL

Professionals working with adolescents in a number of different capacities often fail to realize the potential resource that lies within the adolescents' parents. All too often, the parent is assumed to be an adversary to the adolescent and, therefore, of minimal use in helping the adolescent work out problems. Professionals who work with adolescents in the area of career decision making fail to recognize and utilize the parents as a natural resource in career guidance of the adolescent. Instead, the adolescent is often supplied with vast amounts of material on various occupations, and then given the task of defining his or her choice of occupation. As an alternative to this, the professional can arrange situations where the adolescent and his or her parents share in the experience of career exploration. Many parents do not know their adolescent's thoughts, feelings, and dreams about careers. By the same token, many adolescents are unaware of their parents' knowledge in the area of occupations. By presenting information to both parents and adolescents at the same time, professionals can promote discussion which will enlighten both parents and adolescents to the resource each has in the other.

Once professionals working with adolescents and their parents become aware of the natural credence adolescents give to their parents in the area of career development and occupational choice, they can build upon this aspect of the parent-adolescent dyad. Moreover, they can utilize this situation as a leverage point to open up other areas of communication. With career development as a starting point, the professional can help parents progress to more sensitive topics, and establish a more effective system of parent-adolescent communication. In this way, parents and adolescents can better respond to each other as equal partners within the family. They can create a vital family environment which can withstand the divisive impact of the generation gap.

REFERENCES

Ambron, S. R. *Child development*. San Francisco: Rinehart Press, 1975.

Anthony, E. J. The reaction of adults to adolescents and their behavior. In *Contemporary issues in adolescent development*. New York: Harper & Row, 1975.

Bettelheim, B. The problem of generations. *Daedalus*, 1962, *91*, 68-96.

Billings, J. E. Are parents irrelevant? *Journal of the National Association of Women Deans and Counselors*, 1970, *33*, 112-117.

Bloom, E., & Kennedy, C. E. The student and his parents. *Journal of the National Association of Women Deans and Counselors*, 1970, *33*, 98-105.

Brittain, C. Adolescent choices and parent-peer cross pressures. *American Sociological Review*, 1963, *28*, 385-391.

Brown, R. D. Relationship between parent and student perceptions of campus life. *Educational and Psychological Measurement*, 1972, *32*, 365-375.

Crites, J. O., & Semler, I. J. Adjustment, educational achievement, and vocational maturity as dimensions of development in adolescence. In Z. N. Cantwell & P. N. Svajian, *Adolescence: Studies in development*. Itasca, Illinois: F. E. Peacock Publishers, 1974.

Crookston, B. S., Keist, R. T., Ivey, A. E., & Miller, C. P. A study of attitudes concerning university relations with students. *National Association of Student Personnel Administrators Proceedings*, 1967, *5*, 134-139.

Erickson, E. Growth and crises of the healthy personality. *Psychological Issues*, 1959, *1*, 50-101.

Freedman, M. B. *The impact of college: New dimensions in higher education* (No. 4). Washington, D.C.: U.S. Government Printing Office, 1960.

Gesell, A., Ilg, F. L., & Ames, L. B. *Youth: The years ten to sixteen*. New York: Harper, 1956.

Ginsberg, B. G. *Parent-adolescent relationship development: A therapeutic and preventive mental health program.* Unpublished doctoral dissertation, Pennsylvania State University, 1971.

Ginzberg, E., Ginsburg, S. W., Axelrad, S., & Herma, J. *Occupational choice: An approach to a general theory.* New York: Columbia University Press, 1956.

Ginzberg, E., Ginsburg, S., Axelrad, S., & Herma, J. *Occupational choice.* New York: Columbia University Press, 1951.

Hershenson, S. B., & Roth, R. M. A decisional process model of vocational development. *Journal of Counseling Psychology,* 1966, *13,* 368-370.

Hess, S. Listening to youth: A less traveled road and on being young, down and out in the American system. *Congressional Record,* 1970, 13512-13515.

Hurst, J. A., Munsey, W. L., & Penn, J. R. The effect of college attendance on student parent attitude congruence: Enlargement of a generation gap. *Journal of College Student Personnel,* 1971, *12,* 340-346.

Johnson, S. W. Freshman student parental values: Similarities and differences. *Journal of College Student Personnel,* 1969, *10,* 169-173.

Josselson, R. E. Psycodynamic aspects of identity formation in college women. *Journal of Youth and Adolescence,* 1973, *2,* 3-52.

Jurich, A. P. Parenting adolescents. *Family Perspective,* in press.

Katz, J. et al. *No time for youth.* San Francisco: Jossey-Bass, 1968.

Keniston, K. Social change and youth in America. *Daedalus,* 1962, *91,* 631-654.

Keniston, K. Youth: A new stage of life. *American Scholar,* 1970, 631-654.

Kinloch, G. C. Parent-youth conflict at home: An investigation among university freshmen. *American Journal of Orthopsychiatry,* 1970, *40,* 658-664.

Landis, P. *Adolescence and youth.* New York: McGraw-Hill, 1952.

Madison, P. *Personality development in college.* Reading, Massachusetts: Addison-Wesley, 1969.

Munley, P. H. Erik Erikson's theory of psychosocial development and vocational behavior. *Journal of Counseling Psychology,* 1975, *22,* 314-319.

Propper, A. M. The relationship of maternal employment to adolescent roles, activities and parental relationships. *Journal of Marriage and the Family,* 1972, *34,* 417-421.

Sanford, N. *Where colleges fail.* San Francisco: Jossey-Bass, 1967.

Scherz, F. H. The crisis of adolescence in family life. *Social Casework,* 1967, *48,* 209-215.

Schuh, J. H., & Francis, R. L. A comparison of student and parental attitudes. *Journal of College Student Personnel,* 1976, *17,* 376-379

Sistrunk, J., Fretwell, A., & Kennedy, C. E. *Windows into student life: Growth and change during college years.* Manhattan, Kansas: Kansas State Agricultural Experiment Station Project, Kansas State University, 1972.

Expressiveness in the Father-Adolescent Daughter Relationship Measured by Their Perceptions and Desires

Dr. Dorothy H. Martin
Extension Specialist
Department of Human Development
and Family Studies
Colorado State University

INTRODUCTION AND DEFINITION OF TERMS

How do fathers perceive their expressive relationship with their adolescent daughters? In later years do fathers wish they had been more nurturant? How do daughters describe their fathers' expressiveness with them when they were in early adolescence? In later years, do daughters wish their fathers had been more nurturant, less rejecting? These and other questions about the father's expressive relationship with his adolescent daughter were explored in a 1978 study at the University of Northern Colorado.

For the purposes of this research, the expressive role was defined as behaviors and attitudes which were loving, approving, affectionate, undemanding, and provided psychological support or security. Nurturance was defined as emotional closeness involving acceptance and help demonstrated by physical and nonphysical expressions of love, caring, and positive regard. Nurturance is closely aligned with expressiveness.

Rejection was defined as emotional distance involving physical and nonphysical expressions of denial of love, care, and positive regard. It was considered a negative type of expressiveness. In view of these definitions, expressive behaviors were considered on a nurturance-rejection continuum, with nurturance a positive dimension and rejection a negative dimension of the expressive domain.

The term early adolescence refers to the time when the daughter was in seventh or eighth grade.

REVIEW OF THE LITERATURE

A review of the theory, research, and opinions concerning the father-adolescent daughter relationship, with emphasis

on the expressive nature of the roles, reveals some basic
ideas and assumptions.

Theoretical Frameworks

Freud (1959) and Parsons (1955) provided two major theoretical frameworks concerning the father-daughter dyad and the
expressive domain. Within the Freudian framework, daughters
aged five or six developed hostility toward their mothers
when they discovered they lacked a penis. The daughter responded to her consternation by seeking to develop a relationship with her father, a form of retaliation directed at
her mother. Freud hypothesized that daughters never fully
resolved the Oedipal conflict.
     The daughter may have wished to replace her mother in
her father's affections, and thus feared her mother's rejection. This fear, although not as strong as the son's fear
of castration, never quite allowed the daughter to resolve
the Oedipal complex through identification with her mother.
Freud (1959) concluded that the female's conscience never
becomes fully developed, due to the lack of that motivating
fear of castration.
     A second, related Freudian assumption concerned the de-
velopment of the superego, the conscience. In Freud's theory,
the parent was responsible for development of the child's
superego as a moral control over the child's behavior; however, the Oedipal complex prevented the complete development
of the superego for the female. Therefore, the male parent
was the only possible moral ideal to serve as a model for
his daughter, because the female parent never completed the
superego development. A neoanalytic position presented by
Forrest in 1966 suggested that the "daughter's experiences
with the father from early infancy are related to the daughter's
later ability to trust other males, and the ease with which
the father and daughter can accept her fuller sexual development in adolescence" (Hamilton, 1977, pp. 80-81).
     A second theoretical development came from Parsons in
1955. His explanation of the expressive-instrumental role
function was built upon the Oedipal extension of identification. It was at the Oedipal stage that Parsons believed the
father was established in the instrumental parent's role,
while the mother's expressive role continued in a less dominant manner.
     Later, Heilbrun (1976) disagreed with some of these ideas.
Heilbrun indicated that sex-role development is not so easily
differentiated as to the parental source because children
model behavior of both parents, because parents are not pure
sex-role types, and because boys and girls may behave quite
differently from each other in their modeling behavior.

Father-Daughter Research

According to Biller and Meredith (1974), "Less than 10 percent of the scientific studies of parents have taken the
father's role into account, in spite of the fact that half
of all parents are fathers" (p. 345). When we consider the
daughter half of the father-daughter dyad, we find a similar
rate. Lynn (1974) comments on research with children, "Unfortunately, most of the relevant research has been done with
male subjects only" (p. 160). The father-daughter dyad may
well be the most neglected relationship in the family in terms
of scientific investigation. Heilbrun (1976) indicates the
father-daughter relationship remains "unexplored."

Recently, the father-infant relationship, including the
father-daughter dyad, has attracted increasing research attention (Stone, Smith, & Murphy, 1973). Child development
researchers have studied the father-daugher relationship in
the preschool and elementary school years (Lynn, 1974). Yet,
when one begins to look at the father-daughter interaction
during her adolescence the findings are sparse, especially
in regard to the nature of the expressive relationship between the two.

Only a few studies have dealt with some aspects of the
expressive-instrumental function in the father's relationship with his adolescent daughter (Heilbrun, 1965; Lang,
Papenfuhs, & Walters, 1976; Straus, 1967; Weaver, 1969).
A brief summary of some of their findings follows.

In 1965, Heilbrun asserted that "fathers are more capable
of responding expressively than mothers are of acting in-
strumentally" (p. 796). His assertion was based on Parsons'
contention that both males and females learned the expressive role in the early relationship with their mothers, but
only males later learned the instrumental orientation. "Thus,
boys retain the capacity to respond in either an expressive
or instrumental manner, whereas girls can behave only expressively" (Heilbrun, 1965, p. 790).

In the study by Lang, Papenfuhs and Walters (1976), it was
found that "delinquent adolescents perceived their fathers as
cold, rejecting and uninvolved" (p. 481). Subjects were 175
incarcerated females aged 13 to 18 in Georgia and Oklahoma.
On the *Itkin Attitude Toward Parents Scale (Form F)*, chi-
square analysis revealed the Georgia and Oklahoma groups were
not significantly different in their lack of closeness to
their fathers.

Straus (1967), in a study of 64 families, found that
fathers were predominant in both instrumental and expressive
roles, especially in the middle class. Expressive role performance of parents was measured by counting supportive acts
initiated by each parent during a problem-solving session

involving a laboratory task. Father-to-child supportive acts
were 5.8 for male children, 6.8 for female children (p < .05).
Mother-to-child supportive acts were 2.9 for male children,
4.3 for female children.

Zelditch (1955), in a cross-cultural comparison of ethno-
graphic reports, found the father's role primarily instrumental in 48 of 56 societies, and the mother's role primarily
expressive in 50 of the 56 societies.

Winch (1950) was perhaps the first to indicate the positive effect of close father-daughter relationships on long-
term romantic relationships. When 502 female students in
midwest coeducational institutions were asked which parent
loved them more, of those females who responded either father
or mother, there was a disproportionately high proportion of
high courtship women who responded father (p < .01). Of
those women who responded either father or undecided, there
was a disproportionately high proportion of high courtship
women who responded father (p < .05).

Biller and Meredith (1974) also found a "strong association" between the daughter's perceived relationship with her
father during childhood and her marital adjustments. This
study reported that divorce, separation, and unhappy marriages
were more common among women whose father had been absent,
or those who indicated poor or infrequent interactions with
their fathers.

According to Green (1976), girls who had an "open-minded
and loving relationship" with their fathers would be successful in male-female and marital relationships in later life.
Lamb (1976), summarizing several studies, concluded:

> Nurturant fathers may . . . contribute greatly to
> the psychological adjustment of their daughters
> and facilitate their happiness in subsequent heter-
> osexual relationships. (p. 21)

Weaver's (1969) study tested the hypothesis that "girls
who were very instrumental reported a different pattern of
father-daughter interaction than girls reported who were less
instrumental" (p. 49). In her questionnaire, Weaver used 38
items to measure instrumentalness, and five items to measure
expressiveness. The five items measuring expressiveness asked
about being comforted by or talking things over with a parent.
A correlation (p < .001) was determined between closeness
and expressive scores. Her findings indicated the importance
of verbal communication between father and daughter, in that
"closeness" tended to be associated with those factors which
included much helpful understanding and "talking over" of
personal concerns.

In 1973, Fish and Biller asked 106 female undergraduates to assess the quality of their relationship with their fathers when they were children. Fifteen items were selected from Schaefer's (1965) parent perception questionnaire. Five items were used to assess nurturance, five items to assess positive involvement, and five items to assess rejection. Personality adjustment was scored using Gough and Heilbrun's (1965) *Adjective Check List*. Fish and Biller (1973) found significant interrelationships involving perceived degree of paternal nurturance and positive involvement (p < .001), nurturance and rejection (p < .001), and positive involvement and rejection (p < .001).

In regard to nurturance and positive involvement, significant main effects were found when these factors were related to high personality adjustment. In terms of the rejection variable, analysis indicated subjects in the high rejection group received much lower personality adjustment scores.

PROCEDURES FOR THE STUDY

Subjects

A preliminary inventory was made available to all female students in the introductory psychology classes at the University of Northern Colorado, Greeley, Colorado, during May, 1977, and was mailed to the fathers of the female students. The University of Northern Colrado is primarily a teacher education institution under the auspices of the State of Colorado. The final inventory was offered to all female students enrolled in the introductory psychology classes at the University of Northern Colorado, in April of 1978, and was mailed to their fathers.

Apparatus

The preliminary expressive-relationship inventory used in this study was designed by the author, after reviewing existing instruments. A total of 58 items were written for the preliminary instrument, taking into consideration the definitions of nurturance and rejection.

Subjects were first asked to respond about the relationship as it had been when the daughter was in early adolescence. Inventory items one through 58 represented that perspective. Items 59 through 116 requested responses in terms of how each subject would like the relationship to have been. The inventory items for the father were identical to the items for the daughers, with the exception that different pronouns

were used (I for fathers, My father for daughters). Father-
daughter inventory pairs were keyed with the same numbers.
The Kuder-Richardson Formula 20 (Guilford, 1954) was
used to assess internal-consistency reliability. For the
desired expressiveness items, the internal-consistency reliability score was .99.

Following the administration of the preliminary inventory, several modifications were made. Three psychologists
made an item evaluation of the content validity of the original 58 items. They assessed the relevance of each item
to nurturance, rejection, lack of involvement, or having
no relationship to caring behavior or attitudes. In the
final analysis, 18 items were judged as measuring rejection,
and 32 items measured nurturance.

Demographic data on the final inventory included fathers'
and daughters' ages, fathers' and daughters' marital status,
family income, race, ordinal position, and number of siblings
of the daughter.

Method

Each female student in the introductory psychology classes
was offered a daughter form of the final expressiveness inventory with an answer sheet to complete and return to the
psychology office or to the instructor. In addition, each
female student was given the father's form of the inventory,
an answer sheet, a cover letter, and a stamped, return envelope for her father. Then the student was asked to address
an envelope containing those items to her father. The student was asked to seal the envelope and return it to the
principal investigator, who mailed all the envelopes. The
females were asked not to discuss their responses with their
fathers until both had completed the inventory.

Statistical Analysis

Differences between father and daughter perceptions and differences between father and daughter desires were analyzed
using a t-test for correlated samples in order to determine
the significance of differences between paired fathers and
daughters. Multiple regression was used to analyze the influence of the independent variables on the perceived and
desired expressiveness scores.

Product-moment coefficients of correlation were used to
test the strength of the relationship between rejection and
nurturance scores of individuals. The .05 level of significance was adopted as the minimum criterion for acceptance
of a difference as a real difference rather than a chance
difference.

RESULTS

Returns

Of the 434 inventories distributed, 302 were returned. Father-daughter pairs submitted 116 of the returns. The 116 matched father-daughter pairs who returned answer sheets represented 53.5 percent of the total subjects who received inventories. Responses came from 153 of the fathers, while 149 of the daughters responsed.

Reliability

The Kuder-Richardson Formula 20 for internal-consistency reliability yielded .81 for the first 50 items, which were concerned with perceived expressiveness, and .96 for items 51 through 100, which were concerned with desired expressiveness.

Statistical Analysis

Perceived Nurturance and Rejection
When the 116 father-daughter pair scores were analyzed, highly significant differences were found in the perception of the nurturant dimension of the father's expressiveness. Daughters' scores indicated they recalled receiving significantly less nurturance than their fathers recalled having given them (p < .001).

Desired Nurturance and Rejection
Although the differences were not statistically significant, fathers and daughters both desired less rejection and more nurturance than they recalled. An average score indicating that nurturance was "OK as it was" would be 96. The fathers' desired nurturance scores had a mean of 106.61, and the daughters' desired nurturance scores had a mean of 105.57.

An average score indicating rejection was "OK as it was" would be 54. The fathers' desired rejection scores had a mean of 60.56, and the daughters' rejection scores had a mean of 60.16. Due to the reverse scoring of rejection items, this indicated both fathers and daughters desired less rejection than fathers remembered giving and daughters remembered receiving.

Daughters' Nurturance and Rejection Correlations
Responses from 149 daughters were analyzed with the product-moment correlation test. Daughters who perceived their fathers as more nurturant also perceived them as less rejecting (p < .001). Considering the reverse scoring of

rejection items, this is consistent with Fish and Biller's (1973) finding of a negative interrelationship between the daughter's perceived degree of paternal nurturance and paternal rejection.

Correlations indicated that daughters who desired more nurturance from their fathers also desired less rejection ($p < .001$). When daughters recalled more nurturance, they desired less nurturance ($p < .001$) and desired less rejection ($p < .001$). As the daughters' perceived rejection scores increased, their desired nurturance scores ($p < .001$) and desired rejection scores ($p < .001$) both decreased significantly.

Fathers' Nurturance and Rejection Correlations
When the scores of 153 fathers were treated statistically, fathers who believed they were more nurturant also believed they were less rejecting ($p < .001$). Fathers also desired to have been more nurturing and less rejecting ($p < .001$).

Independent Variables
A multiple regression analysis with the demographic variables yielded no significant effects on any of the father or daughter expressive scores. These results are consistent with the Fish and Biller (1973) findings, in which age, social class, family size, or ordinal position were not significantly related to expressiveness and personal adjustment.

Demographic Data
The sample was predominantly Caucasian (85.6 percent). At the time the daughters were in early adolescence, their fathers were usually in their first marriage (90.8 percent), had family incomes of $10,000 to $19,999 (55.6 percent), had a mean age of 41.92, were most often employed in professions (31.6 percent) or business fields (34.2 percent), and had finished high school, had some college, or had a bachelor's degree (69.8 percent). For the daughters, the mean age was 18.29, the birth order mean was 2.24, and the mean number of siblings was 3.394. Most daughters were single at the time of the administration (94.1 percent).

DISCUSSION

While the data in this study cannot explain why fathers and daughters perceive and desire as they do, several hypotheses can be proposed. Why do fathers remember being more nurturant than their daughters recall that they were?

First, it is possible that fathers preferred to believe they were more nurturant than they actually were. Most fathers would want to believe they had done well with their daughters.

Second, it is possible that the time perspective was responsible for the discrepancy. The maturity and experience acquired by the subjects in the interval which existed between the time of the direct experience and the time of reporting their perceptions could have had a bearing on changes in their recalled perceptions. It is also possible that the college-student daughters experienced some longing for the fathers' nurturance in their present environment, and were not able to distinguish this from the realities of the relationship during early adolescence.

Yet another explanation is possible. Such differences could mean that the level of nurturance changes in the adolescent stage of the daughter's development. It is possible that fathers interacted in expressive ways with their daughters until the daughter reached early adolescence when she began to display physical sex characteristics. At this time, the father may have responded to the societal incest taboo, and withdrew any expressive responses that had sexual connotations in his mind. If the father equated his expressions of love with his expressions of sexual feeling in his relationship with the adult female in his family (his wife), then when the daughter began to become a sexual, adult female, he may have withdrawn much of his nurturing behavior from his daughter.

There are societal messages which attest to the changes in the father-daughter relationship at this time. A recent magazine advertisement depicting a young adolescent female sitting on her bed indicated she was "too old" to sit on her father's lap. In this research, one father subject indicated this attitude when he refused to respond to an item stating, "I touched my daughter in loving ways." He responded he "wouldn't touch that one . . . ."

This causes some concern on the part of this author. If the daughter notices this change and perceives her father's withdrawal at this time as a rejection of her budding female sexuality, she may become overly concerned with her sexual self-concept, a behavior which could provoke difficulties in establishing a healthy heterosexual relationship with adult males outside the family.

The hypothesis that fathers withdraw physical nurturance when their daughters begin the physical sexual development of puberty should be rigorously researched. Certainly, such research would not promote incestuous relationships. Biller and Meredith (1974) answer those who fear that such paternal nurturance would not be healthy. They indicate flirtations

and physical attractions between father and daughter are natural, and are a problem only when overdone by people who have
"serious psychological problems."

Fathers indicated that when they desired to have been more
nurturing, they desired to have been less rejecting. Some
fathers may not have known how to give their daughters such
non-sexual nurturance, and may not have known how to be less
rejecting.

The negative correlation between the daughters' perceived
and desired nurturance indicated that when the daughters remembered receiving higher levels of nurturance from their
fathers, they also desired less nurturance. Perhaps when the
need for nurturance was met, the daughters felt no need for
further nurturance. It may also be possible that there is
such a thing as "too much nurturance." Daughters who perceived little rejection also desired less rejection, and those
who recalled little nurturance also desired little rejection.
Perhaps a "leave me alone" attitude prevailed in these low
nurturance relationships.

RECOMMENDATIONS

Future Research

As mentioned earlier, the dynamics of the father-adolescent
daughter dyad have received little research attention. While
this study represents an attempt to clarify some aspects of
the father-adolescent daughter relationship, it does have
limitations. One limitation of this study was the exploratory
method used to investigate the problem. Another was the *ex
post facto* design which precluded experimental applications.
Limitations in the development of the expressiveness questionnaire included lack of convergent validity data on the
nurturance and rejection factors, and lack of subject identification which would have enabled test-retest reliability
analysis, as well as analysis with non-respondents.

Because of demographic restrictions in this sample, it
would be advisable to draw samples from different race, income, education, and marital status groups. Two interesting
research possiblities would be a sample of incarcerated juvenile females, or a sample of homosexual females and their
fathers. Certainly not an issue in this research, but one
in need of exploration is the nature of the expressive relationship in father-daughter pairs when incest is involved.

Cross-generational and cross-sectional study of father-
daughter pair relationships involving samples from different
developmental stages would also generate important data.

Obviously, the optimum research design would be a longitudinal study of father-daughter pairs through the daughter's
first 30 or 40 years of life.

Education and Counseling

If, in fact, there is a need for fathers to be more nurturant
with their adolescent daughters, our society may have to
teach and support the concept of non-sexual caring between
sexually mature human beings. It is this author's position
that there is a great need for such skill development, not
only in father-daughter relations, but also in sibling relationships, same-sex peer relationships, and to some extent,
in the husband-wife dyad.

Biller and Meredith (1974) suggest: "The next time your
child does something you admire, tell him. The next time you
feel especially loving toward the child, tell him you love
him; demonstrate it by hugging and kissing. . ." (p. 139).
Should this concept change when the child--especially the
female child--becomes an adolescent?

Including fathers, as well as mothers, in child psychotherapy provides an opportunity for fathers to have expressive involvement with their daughters, and perhaps learn
nonsexual expressiveness. Perhaps families can plan schedules to maximize the time a father can spend with his adolescent daughter, both of whom frequently have busy schedules
at this stage of life.

While available data seem to warrant attempts to engage
fathers in treatment programs if their daughters exhibit
psychological problems (Biller & Weiss, 1970), it seems even
more appropriate to develop preventive programs in which
fathers are educated and encouraged in the non-sexual, nurturing dimension of the expressive role function with the
daughters. This is so critical to the daughters' future
heterosexual relationships. Biller and Weiss (1970) believe:

> Most men seem to want to be good fathers, but
> many have not had the opportunities to learn
> about the psychological needs of children and
> do not seem to be aware of what functions they
> can perform beyond being providers for their
> family. (p. 89)

REFERENCES

Biller, H. B., & Meredith, D. *Father power*. New York: David McKay Company, Inc., 1974.

Biller, H. B., & Weiss, S. D. The father-daughter relationship and the personality development of the female. *The Journal of Genetic Psychology*, 1970, *1*, 79-93.

Fish, K. D., & Biller, H. B. Perceived childhood paternal relationships and college females' personal adjustment. *Adolescence*, 1973, *8*, 415-420.

Freud, S. *Collected Papers*. Vol. II. New York: Basic Books, 1959.

Gough, H., & Heilbrun, A. B. *Joint manual for the Adjective Check List*. Palo Alto, California: Consulting Psychologists Press, 1965.

Green, M. *Fathering*. New York: McGraw-Hill Book Company, 1976.

Guilford, J. *Psychometric methods*. (2nd ed.) New York: McGraw-Hill Book Company, 1954.

Hamilton, M. *Father's influence on children*. Chicago: Nelson-Hall, 1977.

Heilbrun, A. B. An empirical test of the modeling theory of sex-role learning. *Child Development*, 1965, *36*, 789-799.

Heilbrun, A. B. Identification with the father and sex-role development of the daughter. *The Family Coordinator*, 1976, *25*, 411-416.

Lamb, M. E. *The role of the father in child development*. New York: John Wiley & Sons, 1976.

Lang, D. M., Papenfuhs, R., & Walters, J. Delinquent females' perceptions of their fathers. *The Family Coordinator*, 1976, *25*, 475-481.

Lynn, D. B. *The father: His role in child development*. Monterey, California: Brooks/Cole, 1974.

Parsons, T. Family structure and the socialization of the child. In T. Parsons & R. F. Bales (Eds.), *Family, socialization and interactional processes.* Glencoe, Illinois: Free Press, 1955.

Schaefer, E. R. Children's reports of parental behavior: An inventory. *Child Development,* 1965, *36*, 413-424.

Stone, L. J., Smith, H. T., & Murphy, L. B. *The competent infant.* New York: Basic Books, 1973.

Straus, M. A. The influence of sex of child and social class on instrumental and expressive family roles in a laboratory setting. *Sociology and Social Research,* 1967, *57*, 7-21.

Weaver, F. J. Selected aspects of father-daughter interaction and daughter's instrumentalness in late adolescence (Doctoral dissertation, The Pennsylvania State University, 1968). *Dissertation Abstracts International,* 1969, *29*, 3690A-3691A. (University Microfilms No. 69-5592)

Winch, R. F. Some data bearing on the Oedipus hypothesis. *The Journal of Abnormal and Social Psychology,* 1950, *45*, 481-489.

Zelditch, M. Role differentiation in the nuclear family: A comparative study. In T. Parsons & R. F. Bales (Eds.), *Family, socialization and interactional processes.* Glencoe, Illinois: Free Press, 1955.

Aspirations for Farm-Nonfarm Youth: A Multivariate Analysis and Implications for Farm Family Life

Dr. Jerry J. Bigner, Judith A.
Miller and Dr. R. Brooke
Jacobsen
Department of Human Development
and Family Studies
Colorado State University[1]

No one doubts the transition of farm families away from their
historic ties to the land and the resulting question of farm
youths' adaptation to suburban life. In fact, fewer than
five percent of American families own and reside on farms.
In general, the pattern has been for farm youth to migrate
into suburban and urban areas, with the family farm eventually becoming part of a commercial conglomerate. Thus,
from both parents' and their offsprings' viewpoint, youth
must adopt the appropriate values, education, occupation,
and life style to be successful in the urban world of work.
This transition process is doubly important. Even existing
farm families must adopt efficient technology to compete
successfully with farm commercialization. The basic issue
for farm parents, then, is to socialize their children into
extended education and a competitive occupational attitude,
regardless of whether the children remain on the farm.

The fundamental problem was addressed a quarter-century
ago by sociologist Seymour Martin Lipset (1955), who formulated what has come to be a commonly-studied explanation
regarding the life-chances of rural youth. He pointed out
that since children in large cities have access to greater
educational opportunities, farm children would tend to achieve
less mobility, due to their lowered occupational/educational
aspirations. For example, many studies have documented mobility aspiration differences between rural and urban and
male and female children (Haller, 1958, 1960; Haller & Sewell,
1957; Middleton & Grigg, 1959), and for low income out-
migrants (Schwarzweller, 1964). In particular, certain individual and family factors have been related to differences
in upward mobility values; Straus (1956) studied personal
characteristics in choice of farming as an occupation. Likewise, Schwarzeller (1959) investigated individual value orientations in educational/occupational choice. However, few
studies have been based on a multivariate analysis--an

analysis of how several family factors combine to affect a
youth's mobility aspiration.

The problem addressed in this paper was an investigation
of the combined effects of three basic family variables--
age and sex of parent, and number of children in the family--
in terms of their relative effects on mobility attitudes of
children. Specifically, we compared two samples of farm and
nonfarm parents, and also compared parent mobility attitudes
held for both boys and girls. Thus, the investigation in
effect retested the aforementioned Lipset (1955) hypothesis
of lowered aspirations for farm boys.

DATA AND METHOD

Selection of Samples

It should be noted from above that the majority of aspiration studies comparing farm vs. nonfarm populations analyze
data from high school students. The assumption researchers
make is that adolescent responses accurately reflect long-
term occupational decisions.

Other researchers have taken the opposite viewpoint by
investigating the actual family sources of adolescent aspirations. For example, Payne (1956), in a study of 438 twelfth-
grade southern boys, points out that the family plays the
major influencing role on the child regarding occupational,
educational, and migration alternatives. Likewise, family
sociologist Straus (1956), in studying a rural farm sample,
points to the pervasive familial influence on occupational
choice for farm youth. In fact, most contemporary family
theorists take essentially this point of view: Research
should be based on data collected from all family members,
in order to accurately reflect each person's attitudes.

It was decided to collect data retesting the Lipset
(1955) hypothesis by comparing a sample of farm parents
with a sample of nonfarm parents in the late 1970's.

The Farm Sample
First, our farm sample was composed of 52 parents (34 mothers
and 18 fathers), residing in a small high plains rural community, where each family lived and derived its livelihood
directly from farming and ranching. Thus, we expected that
parental attitudes toward their children's future were
strongly influenced by values involving rural life; for example, most of the parents were very concerned about the
children's education as it related to the agricultural life
style.

The Nonfarm Sample
The authors had the opportunity to collect aspiration data
from a parent group attending a conference at a land-grant
university, in the summer of 1978. The sample was a Voluntary Association Group of 69 parents (35 mothers and 34
fathers) studying misuses of alcohol. While having diverse
backgrounds, all respondents resided either in downtown urban areas or in typical suburbs. These respondents derived
their livelihood as employees, and not directly from agricultural pursuits.

The Dependent Variable--Upward Mobility

All respondents completed a paper and pencil questionnaire,
including standard familial background data (marital status,
age, education of parents, number, and sex of children).

The parents responded to an inventory containing a number of items most adults feel are important attributes for
both boys and girls to develop. They represent social competencies which society regards as important for the child's
future. Respondents were asked to state the degree of importance (from "minor" to "very important") on a seven-point
Likert scale for all 50 items. This was to be done separately
for boys and girls, so as to assess sex differences, if any,
in future aspirations. This inventory constituted the dependent variable, the source of aspiration data from all parents.

A factor analysis performed on the collected data revealed three main independent values parents hold for children's future development: (1) upward mobility--parents wish
the child to achieve success in education and the world of
work (it is here that parental aspirations for education and
occupation were directly measured); (2) aesthetic--the child
should learn to appreciate and understand fulfilling life
experiences; and (3) civic--the child should be aware of the
several responsibilities of citizenship. There were ten items
on each subscale, hence the range of attitude scores was 10-
70, for each of the three values. It is the first attribute--
mobility--that is the subject of all analyses below.

The Independent Variables

The age of parent may influence parental mobility attitudes
for children. We expected that older parents would hold quite
different values for children than would younger parents, due
to the continuing decline in numbers of farm families.

Likewise, sex of parent was an important factor, in that
the farm mother had always been employed in farm-related jobs.

Only in recent times have nonfarm mothers taken gainful employment in large numbers.

The number of children in a family was an important variable, since historically farm families have been larger, and parents thus have had longer-range educational responsibilities.

The Multiple Regression Equation

The analyses are organized in terms of viewing parents' mobility attitudes as a function of the causative factors of age and sex of parent, and number of children in the family. The regression equation used for each computation is:

$$Y = a + \beta_1 X_1 + \beta_2 X_2 + \beta_3 X_3$$

| (Parent Mobility Value) | (Age of Parent) | (Sex of Parent) | (Number of Children) |

where Y = the stated mobility value for a child
a = constant of origin
β = standardized partial regression coefficients, measuring the relative influence of each independent variable.

The standardized beta usually is computed, since it rests on a dimensionless scale, hence allowing direct comparison of causal effects of all predictor variables.

A standardized multiple regression analysis was performed using the SPSS (Nie et al., 1975) prepackaged computer program. The logic was to decompose the dependent variable (mobility value for child) in terms of the relative influence of each independent variable (cf. Blalock, 1972; Gordon, 1968).

FINDINGS

The farm-nonfarm comparison for youth has been the basic strategy used previously in testing the aspiration. We also replicated this method to obtain the data shown in Table 1. This table contains the complete multivariate analyses of the effects of all predictor variables on the mobility value for the child. The basic farm-nonfarm dichotomy is organized by columns in the table. Within each column, the analysis for boys is separated from that for girls. The results are thus presented for four multiple regressions, showing the beta coefficients, the multiple R^2's, and tests of statistical significance (any coefficient not significant at the .05 level or less was rejected).

Table 1

Summary of Constants for Upward Mobility Values

Nonfarm (N = 69)			Farm (N = 52)		
Mobility for:	Variable	(β)	Mobility for	Variable	(β)
Boy	Sex	.08	Boy	Sex	.12
	Age	-.24*		Age	-.17
	# Children	.30*		# Children	.36*
	$R^2 = .07$			$R^2 = .12$	
Girl	Sex	.13	Girl	Sex	.07
	Age	.28*		Age	.23
	# Children	-.26*		# Children	.21
	$R^2 = .07$			$R^2 = .15*$	

*F-test significant at $p < .05$ level.

Mobility for Nonfarm Boys

The upper-left hand cell of Table 1 presents the analysis for
the nonfarm boys. It can be noted that parents' age and
number of children are significantly related to the mobility
value. For example, the younger parents held higher mobility
values for boys (β = -.24); similarly, in larger families
(β = .30) high mobility for the boy was expressed by parents.

Mobility for Farm Boys

In contrast to results above, it was only large farm families
(β = .36) which revealed high aspirations for boys. Apparently neither parents' age nor sex significantly affected aspiration attitudes for the farm boy. However, it should be noted,
that while not statistically significant, the multiple R^2
(indicating the percentage of explained variance) was considerably higher for the farm sample.

Mobility for Nonfarm Girls

Most of the research cited earlier indicated no patterns when
considering future mobility of the girl. The lower-left
cell in Table 1 presents a striking contrast to this research.
Both the older parents (β = .28), as well as the smaller family (β = -.26) had significant effects on the nonfarm girls'
future aspirations. Further, these results are exactly the
reverse of those for the nonfarm boy (see upper-left hand
cell, Table 1).

Mobility for Farm Girls

The final analysis investigated mobility aspirations for farm
girls, and again, in contrast to earlier research, the overall
regression equation was statistically significant (R^2 = .15).
However, no pattern was evident when the independent factors
of age and sex of parent, or number of children in the family,
were compared. The higher level of explained variance for
this subsample should be noted.

DISCUSSION

The data analyses clearly show that a number of family factors
were operating jointly when the question of the future of the
farm child was addressed. Age and sex of parents, as well
as size of family, apparently cannot be considered as having
isolated effects on the child's future aspirations. The

regression analysis, therefore, makes it possible to pinpoint certain important factors apparently operating within the farm family.

The analyses show, first, that the hypothesis which postulates farm youth have lowered future aspirations is apparently no longer accurate. Farm parents held high aspirations for both sexes, especially girls. Apparently they recognized the continuing transition of farm youth to suburban life. Thus, the relatively high mobility of values held by these parents may be seen as an expression of their awareness of change among farm families. The fact that farm girls were seen in this context suggests the simple recognition of the increasing likelihood of females entering a full-time occupation.

The data imply that the roles of parents in a farm setting were themselves in a state of transition. Historically, many children were educated toward the farming life by on-the-farm experiences; increasingly, however, parents are encouraging youth to obtain extended educations, hence enabling them to take over competitive suburban occupations.

We suggest that the changing roles for farm parents may be a two-edged sword. On the one hand, parents, in effect, push the child toward the competitive occupational world; on the other hand, parents have limited knowledge and experience in the suburban world of work. They may not provide appropriate family-models to teach their children. From the children's point of view, then, they are in an ambiguous family setting, not fully socialized either to farm or nonfarm occupations and values.

The foregoing line of reasoning implies certain negative consequences for farm youth entering the suburban life. The so-called marginal-man hypothesis--used in industry to explain the situation of the shop foreman--may be appropriate for farm youth in transition. The marginal man (Roethlisberger, 1945; Schneider, 1969; Wray, 1949) is neither part of management nor labor, existing in an anxiety-producing setting. His future is never secure, since neither management nor labor claim him as their own.

Farm youth exist in a very similar situation, albeit a family setting. They are neither members of a farm-oriented family, nor hold a guaranteed promise of future success in a competitive occupational world. Thus, a certain amount of alienation may emerge between farm youth and their parents. Children are subject to conflicting pressures from parents who encourage occupational/educational achievement, but who may not be able to fulfill these expectations. Therefore, if our data analyses are correct, they point very clearly to the need for strengthening the farm family. This is especially important since there is no indication of a reversal to the trend away from rural-based family life.

IMPLICATIONS FOR STRENGTHENING FARM FAMILIES

It is clear that the entire family should be the focus of any efforts at defending against implied parent-youth conflict. It is the social relation between parents and children that is the key issue.

Many junior high and high schools maintain a guidance and counseling program oriented toward the child, the family, and the school system. These programs coordinate a student's educational career in order to meet the needs of all parties. We suggest that in the case of farm families, such programs focus specific attention on this pattern of conflicting pressures. Equal attention should be given to farm girls in school, as parents clearly held high aspirations for them. It was the older parent, as shown by the data, who held high aspirations for girls, and the younger parent who did so for boys (this was also the case for nonfarm families). This familial difference should also be recognized in the guidance and counseling relationship.

The rural extension specialist serving the farm family may also focus directly on the potential for parent-child conflict. Through the use of family workshops, for example, the specialist may bring out and discuss means of identifying any conflicts and alternative solutions. This may take the form of informing parents that the child may be in a so-called "marginal man" situation. Parents may view their encouragement efforts positively; through the workshops they may become more aware of potential negative consequences. Through such experiences, both parents and children may come to a deeper understanding of how movement into the suburban life can affect the entire family.

Lastly, 4-H has always been part of rural family life. During meetings where many families are in attendance, the 4-H youth agent, the extension specialist, or family members may bring out and discuss many of the issues noted above. Since the whole family usually attends, this is an ideal time for everyone to participate, to learn, and to understand. It is here that children may examine in-depth parental expressions of encouragement and how they relate to children's career explorations. By such interaction, lines of communication may be kept open between parents and children. Such family-based experiences will serve to broaden knowledge, and to facilitate the successful transition to the suburban life.

NOTES

1. The data collection and analysis were supported through the Western Regional Project W-144, Colorado State University Experiment Station. The Index of Children's Competencies used in all analyses was developed and tested by Dr. D. Bruce Gardner, Department of Human Development and Family Studies, Colorado State University, Fort Collins, Colorado.

REFERENCES

Blalock, H. M. *Social statistics.* (2nd. ed.) New York: McGraw-Hill, 1972.

Gordon, R. A. Issues in multiple regression. *American Journal of Sociology,* 1968, *73,* 592-616.

Haller, A. O. Research problems on the occupational achievement levels of farm-rural people. *Rural Sociology,* 1958, *23,* 353-362.

Haller, A. O. The occupational achievement process of farm-rural youth in urban industrial society. *Rural Sociology,* 1960, *25,* 321-333.

Haller, A. O., & Sewell, W. H. Farm residence and levels of educational and occupational aspirations. *American Journal of Sociology,* 1957, *26,* 407-411.

Lipset, S. M. Social mobility and urbanization. *Rural Sociology,* 1955, *20,* 220-228.

Middleton, R., & Grigg, C. Rural-urban differences in aspiration. *Rural Sociology,* 1959, *24,* 347-354.

Nie, N. H., Hull, C. H., Jenkens, J. G., Steinbrenner, K., & Bent, D. H. *Statistical package for the social sciences.* (2nd. ed.) New York: McGraw-Hill, 1975.

Payne, R. Development of occupational and migration expectations and choices among urban, small town, and rural adolescent boys. *Rural Sociology,* 1956, *21,* 117-125.

Roethlisberger, F. J. The foreman: Master and victim of double talk. *Harvard Business Review,* 1945, *23,* 283-298.

Schneider, E. V. *Industrial sociology*. New York: McGraw-Hill, 1969.

Schwarzweller, H. K. Value orientations and educational and occupational choices. *Rural Sociology*, 1959, *24*, 246-256.

Schwarzweller, H. K. Education, migration, and economic life chances of male entrants to the labor force from a low income rural area. *Rural Sociology*, 1964, *29*, 152-167.

Straus, M. A. Personal characteristics and functional needs in the choice of farming as an occupation. *Rural Sociology*, 1956, *21*, 257-266.

Wray, D. G. Marginal men of industry: The foreman. *American Journal of Sociology*, 1949, *54*, 298-301.

V. THE MIDDLE AND LATER YEARS

Aging is inevitable and individuals change as they grow
older. So, too, the family changes as the children grow
up and leave home, and eventually parents may find themselves
being cared for by their adult children. Change at this
period in the human and family life cycles offers possibilities for positive growth.

Dr. Karen Arms examines theories of middle age. She
discusses changes in the husband-wife and parent-child
relationships, as well as occupational and emotional shifts
in mid-life. With understanding, middle age becomes more
an opportunity and less a crisis.

The care of elderly parents is a concern to many middle-
aged persons. Dr. Diane Levande summarizes the dynamics
of filial responsibility and how those interact with traditional sex-role expectations. She urges close examination of what the caretaker role means to women and their
own nuclear families.

Dr. Mary Jane Van Meter urges a change in our attitudes
about dependency. Each of us is dependent at some time
in life. Dependency gives others the opportunity to show
love, be nurturant, and meet another person's needs.

The alienation and enrichment myths which pertain to
older people and their families are summarized by Dr. Jay
Mancini. He also lists research frontiers. Programs to
enhance the quality of family life among older persons
will likely be more effective as these research frontiers
are addressed.

While funerals are sad times in families, they also
are times when kinship ties are reaffirmed and memories
are shared. Ruby Gingles discusses how funerals may
provide positive interactions in families.

Dr. Joan Weisman discusses programs such as Teaching,
Learning Communities (TLC) and U.S. Fostergrandparents
which bring older persons and children together for
mutual benefit. Suggestions for expanding similar programs to Head Start, Senior Citizens Centers, etc. are
made.

Dr. Karen G. Arms
School of Home Economics
Kent State University

What is strength? It is the power to resist strain; it is mental power, force, or vigor; it is moral power, firmness, or courage; it is vigor of action, language, and feeling. In other words, strength can come from the personal conviction of being right, of knowing what one is doing, and being prepared.

Enrichment, goal orientation, assessment of one's self and circumstances, and planned progression within the context of the realities can all be considered features or characteristics of strength. If one were to consciously progress in one's life career, one must develop a cognizance of personal goals and accurately assess personal and concrete resources. Only then is it possible to achieve true stature and life satisfaction through one's own eyes, or, in other terminology, through the feeling of inner strength and personal conviction that all is right with the world.

This paper will address the meaning of the middle years in terms of one's total life career and discuss the reassessments and reorientations likely to occur during this time if one has the strengths in hand to do so. The middle of the adulthood years will be the central focus of this writing because, if for no other reason, it is the middle. Heed must be taken, however, to the caution by Lidz (1976) that there are relatively few intensive and careful studies concerning the middle years as compared with childhood and adolescence, and even old age.

DESCRIPTION OF MIDDLE YEARS

The adult years, and more specifically the middle years, have been defined many ways. Simplistically, it could be the period between when the children leave home and the breadwinners leave their jobs. Kerckhoff (1976) summarized the developmental marriage characteristics during the early years of middle age as having terrible pressures and competing demands, and the later years of middle age as smug complacency and

293

comfortable rot. One theorist (Denton, 1978) paralleled
middle-aged development to the stages of death and dying as
detailed by Kübler-Ross (1969). LeShan (1973) called it
the time to "do you own thing," "to sing your own song."
LeShan further expounded upon the importance of friendship
in the marriage partnership that would at this time encourage
individuality and the seeking of self-fulfillment.

Chronological age has been one descriptor of an adult,
since one reaches the age of legal adult majority in most
states by age 18 or 21. However, dependency, whether financial, physical, psychological, or otherwise, may deter or
defy the chronological age and necessitate the replacement
of this form of definition with an index of individual maturity. Such an approach to definition was attempted in a survey for self-classification, which, though it may be reality
for some, contains impracticalities for researchers. Eisendorfer and Lawton (1973) found that only people over 80 clas-
sified themselves as old; this group comprised about half of
those surveyed in this age category, with the other half of
the people over 80 seemingly claiming that they were middle-
aged.

One of the greatest of the controversies is the mid-life
crisis theories which have been described as parallel to the
identity crisis of adolescents. Brayshaw (1962) referred to
the identity crisis as centering around the philosophical
questions of "Who am I? "What is the purpose of my life?"
Prior to middle age these questions were answered in terms
of occupation held (I am a teacher), parent role (I am the
mother or father of John Doe), and sometimes spouse role (I
am Paul Jones' wife or I am Kay Jones' husband). The philosophical questions were considered to become acutely personal
during middle age when contemplating the second half of one's
life and the roles one would shed or assume. McMorrow (1974),
in comparing the identity crises in both periods, characterized middle age as a reverting to the bizarre, irrational,
sexually confused status of adolescence. Continuing during
the years 1974-1976, developmental theorists (Gould, 1975;
Levinson et al., 1974; Sheehy, 1976) emphasized the "crises"
or major anxiety times.

Levinson et al. (1974) used the term "transitions" in
place of "crises" in describing the developmental stages for
men. In depicting the Early Adult Era between the ages of
22 and 40, separations included entering the the adult world,
the age 30 transition, and settling down. Beginning at 40,
the mid-life transition was described as leading to the Middle
Life Era, which was separated by entering middle adult, the
age 50 transition, and the culmination of middle adulthood.
Described at age 60 was the beginning of the late adult transition into the Late Adult Era.

Gould's (1975) research included men and women. He separated seven age-graded groups. The first age group was the 16- to 18-year old who was described as attempting to "escape from parental dominance." The second age group was 18 to 22 years, the age of substitution of friends for family. The third group was 22 to 28 years, the "now" generation. Now was the time to live; now was the time to build for the future, both professionally and personally. But the downward swing of marriage satisfaction had begun. The 29- to 34-year-olds were frequently questioning what they were doing and why they were doing it, a time for self-reflection. Marriage satisfaction reached its lowest ebb at the end of this time, then began a slow recovery which was reached about age 52. The fifth group, the 35- to 43-year-olds, was continuing the expansion of the personality and life structure begun in the early thirties, but began experiencing a quiet urgency, with the nagging feeling time would one day run out. Guilt about mistakes in rearing children increased from ages 35 to 42, then remained constant. At 43 to 50, the adult came to terms with time and with self as a stable personality. Children of these adults were becoming adults, and the circle was closing. By age 50 and on, the last age group, a mellowing of feelings and relationships had occurred. The adult focused on what had been accomplished; the sense of urgency earlier in life was relaxed; and there was an eagerness for "human" experiences--with family, children, and friends. Death became a new presence. These findings by Gould convinced him of a developmental sequence in the early and middle-adult years.

McLeish (1976), however, quarreled with these developmentalists as being too limiting, and he combined selected pieces from several theorists to support his philosophy of the achievable and continued creative contributions throughout existence. Neugarten (1973) used the term "awkward" in relating developmental theory to aging.

The thrust of this writing will be to agree philosophically with McLeish and to reinforce those who have chosen to dispute the crisis theorists. Lowenthal and Chiriboga (1972) reported an intensive study of 54 middle and lower-middle class men and women whose youngest child was about to leave home. For the most part, they found the departure of the youngest child was generally anticipated with a sense of relief. Cooper (1977) specifically addressed the question of crises in a study and did not find support for a mid-life crisis theory. Costa and McCrae (1978) reviewed the research available on the crisis hypotheses and interpreted the results as not supportive.

The conclusions of Neugarten (1973) reconfirmed the complex interaction of biological, social, and psychological

factors on developmental theories. She stated that the older
one becomes, the more variables in terms of one's past experiences are inextricably interwoven.

Here, too, the wish is not to totally refute the knowledge being gained by the efforts of those attempting to
trace steps and stages of developmental growth during the
middle years (which is why considerable space has been given
to them in this writing). Nevertheless, one can accept some
theories, such as the crises theories, as informational but
not necessarily basic truths. If that stance can be accepted,
crises need not necessarily occur. To some extent, one then
could call upon the old adage, "To be forewarned is to be
forearmed."

REASSESSMENT AND REORIENTATION

Concerns unique to the adult years can then be addressed with
the intention that, being alerted, one can plan for his or
her resolutions so they need not become of crisis propor-
tions, which in itself would dispel the crisis theories. Included would be readjusting the central focus of one's life,
reconciling one's perceptions of personal success or failure
in the role of parent, and adapting to the role-reversal of
adults as parent to older parents.

The refocusing of one's life at middle-age appears paralleled to children leaving home, the peak of career dreams
or realization that career dreams will not be fulfilled, and
for some the leveling off or decreasing of financial pressures.

Husband-Wife

Sheehy (1976) simplified the middle-aged conflicts of the
forties by stating that men are wanting to learn how to be
responsive while at the same time there is a surge of initiating behavior in most women, two possibly opposing forces
which could create conflict. The conflict comes, according
to Sheehy, in the passage to mid-life, when the source of
identity moves from outside ourselves to inside ourselves.
In other words, the identity for the man begins to transfer
from his work (that outside image) to himself and his reflection on his family. Sadly, this is at a time when his children are struggling for independence from the family and will
not welcome his approaches. The husband has by this time
spent years in the work force and may well be realizing his
ultimate career dreams will not be reached; he is feeling
uncertainties about his formerly proud self-image. The wife
is completing the perceived extensive responsibilities to
the children and her projection of identity through them is

shifting to the exploration of who she personally really is
and what she will do with the second half of her life; that
is, unless she already has begun increased commitment to a
career of her own. This newly-found independence implies an
essential aloneness which gives us security within ourselves
and a feeling of confidence in our own capabilities, according to Jung (1933). This personal security (or self-image)
permits us a greater involvement to become more loving and
devoted.

This expression of philosophy is not possible for the
dependent wife if her husband loses his career dream or if
a divorce ensues; she then loses that identity doubly, for
it may be the only one she has had. Even if his career dream
does come true, if she has borrowed her husband's self-image
without developing one of her own, she will be known only
as his wife and not a person in her own right.

Stated another way, a dependent wife must remove the
parental authority she has permitted her husband and assume
responsibility for herself if she is to continue to grow
developmentally. The conflict or basis for anxiety, then
(for Sheehy follows the crisis theory), comes in the couple's
acknowledging and allowing the healthy expression of the
wife's increasing assertiveness and the release of the husband's suppressed tenderness. Sheehy's advice is that a
couple must renegotiate the marriage contract. Restated in
more temperate fashion, a process or series of readjustments
in the relationship over a period of years can occur through
discussions requiring close communication and real effort.
If productive, this process will permit the growth for greater
independence and assertion for the wife and greater expressions of worth and tenderness (that feeling of closeness he
needs with family and friends) by the husband. Each needs
to grant these types of licenses to the other. Not everyone is capable or willing to make such accommodations.

Erikson (1959) believed the path to replenishment in
mid-life was through nurturing, teaching, and serving others.
This seems to be true for men at this age; however, the
woman has usually already been doing that through child-
rearing or typical choice of career, and she is ready to cul-
tivate talents left half-finished and may feel a creativity
not possible when the option of having more children was
viable.

Employment

For many adults of today the time of middle age and the chil-
ren leaving home prompts a reassessment of employment for one
or both marital partners. Women on the whole still face a
pay differential for a variety of reasons. Twenty percent

of working wives now bring home a paycheck as large or larger
than their husbands (Smith, 1978), an increase from seven
percent only about three years ago. The decision for a wife
to begin outside-the-home employment or renew career efforts
may bring frustrations unrelated to the employment and not
anticipated. In addition to the feelings of uncertainty in-
duced by entry or re-entry into the job market, she is likely
to find unequal expectations of husband and wife in the home.
The average American wife typically spends seven and one-half
hours a day on household chores if she is not employed outside
the home, and an average of five and one-half hours a day if
she is employed. Her husband, on the other hand, makes a
contribution which is most likely to be under two hours a
day, whether or not his wife has a job and regardless of the
number of children in the family (Smith, 1978). Stated another way, working wives have only 60 percent of the free
time of their working spouses. Yet in 1975, the Department of
Labor indicated that even if a woman marries, she can expect
to work 25 years. With the extensiveness of that commitment,
an argument could be made for the importance of careful selection of work which could be considered a career rather than a
job.

Ways of assisting families to establish a pattern compatible with their values and styles of life can benefit the
nation's children. Jean Young (1979), Chairperson of the
United States Commission on the International Year of the
Child, indicated that of the 66 million United States children under age 18 in 1978, one million were runaways; one
million were abused; 10 million had no medical care; 20 million had no dental care; 10 million were living in poverty;
and 13 million were not immunized against childhood diseases.
Knowledge and availability of alternatives for families can
provide a direction for action when frustrations or lack of
resources appear overwhelming.

Considerations for those contemplating dual careers could
be selection of careers compatible with rearing children, or
avoidance of having children; support of each other's career
by sharing of responsibilities at home; hiring of live-in
help, or at least cleaning help; selection of housing close
to work or school, bus service, and library; meeting children
for lunch if work is located near home and where the children
go to school; taking children on a rotational basis on out-
of-town business trips; consideration of the need for one
parent to quit if the situation becomes intolerable; and development of a neighborhood cooperative for assistance during
trying times.

A paradox apparently exists for the adult striving to
accomplish or, in fact, strengthen the middle years. The
person who does not expect much from life or from himself or

herself is less likely to be disappointed. This "simple" person tends to seek protection from the environment, avoid stress, and not strive for much. The "complex" person has a high share of resources, is "growth motivated," and accepts stressful situations as part of the price one must pay for an adventurous, stimulating life. A study by Lowenthal et al. (1975) revealed that from middle age onward, the "simple" person tended to be happier. However, the "complex" person tended to achieve more and adapt better in early adulthood. Interestingly, occupational concerns entered the picture strongly for the complex person, and were especially stressful and a complication for women. Women with strong self-concepts and a firm sense of competence were more apt to meet satisfactorily the challenges of the home-work conflict; however, middle age was, in general, the least satisfactory stage of life for these complex women, often because of career obstacles and not necessarily the family.

Parent-Child Reflections

The Art of Living, Day by Day, by Wilferd Peterson (1972) illustrates modeling as a critical learning theory, and addresses to parents the guides for their behaviors:

> . . . . When we encircle them with love
>   they will be loving.
> When we are thankful for life's blessings
>   they will be thankful.
> When we express friendliness they will be
>   friendly . . . .

Although these goals are noble, the burden of responsibility on the parent is unrealistic. Any time an adolescent is not thankful for sacrifices parents have made, it becomes the parents' fault; when an adolescent becomes unfriendly or rejecting in the striving for independence, it appears the parents have not set a good model. Thus, parents begin to doubt their contribution as parents. For those who have devoted their lives as a value to the important full-time job of rearing children (and even for those who have not), the realization that their offspring may not achieve any more, or appear to be any more worthy than other children, can be an invalidation of them and their entire value structures. In other words, the self-image has lost its foundation of worth.

The realistic parent is aware of the many outside influences on the behavior of children, and yet, to validate one's procreation to the universe, a sense of influence on the direction of choices the adolescent will make needs to be

balanced with an ego separation which permits and encourages
increasing independence. The parent who feels confident in
the parenting role, and gains pleasure in the end product
of child-grown-to-adult, is fortunate. It is this parent
who can look forward to pleasant family interaction in the
years ahead.

Adult-Adult Parent Relationships

Strength comes from planning. If one does not make a choice,
a choice has been made which is as emphatic as consciously
making a decision. It is a choice of default by choosing
not to make a choice. Therefore, if one makes plans or establishes directions for one's life before specific instances
occur, the necessity to make a pressure decision is abated,
the feelings related to the decision have been contemplated
and resolved, at least theoretically, and the control one
then has at the "time of action" is likely to result in good
choices being made. If one does not preconsider the major
events likely to occur in the future, one can be put in a
situation which is not compatible with future decisions that
will need to be made.

There are questions common to every family which deserve
consideration and contemplation for the governing of decisions that, without thought, appear unrelated. What do I
want for the remainder of my life; what are my goals? What
do I yet want to do; what are the priorities?

What is my present relationship with my parents? The
phenomenon of retirees with retired parents came only with
the increased longevity of life of the last couple of generations. Do I want to retire to Florida and leave my parents
behind, if in fact they now live close to me? Do I want to
maintain a house; to maintain their house? The majority of
care for older people is done by family members; nursing
home residency is the exception, not the rule.

What about pets? Is their companionship worth the confinement, effort, and expense? Do I want to live alone into
widowhood? If not, do I know how to initiate group living?

What is my relationship with my own children? What interactions support my children's involvement with me? Is
it a friend relationship? A parent-authoritarian relationship? One must ask the question, "How realistic is the
statement, 'I do not want to be dependent on my children'?"
Some day, the dependencies will be reversed. How do I help
my children help me? Am I prepared to be an asset if
placed within my child's family unit (Ritchie, Note 1)?

CONCLUDING COMMENTS

The middle-aged adult in present society, in responding to relevant questions for the future, is serving the unique responsibility of being a model for future generations. Even those who derive less satisfaction from the life decisions they have made are performing the function of holding society together, and permitting those who will follow to learn from their experiences (Kastenbaum, 1979).

A more exhilarating approach is the prospect outlined by McLeish (1976), where selected, vibrant and creative adults, who age well and continue to contribute to the enrichment of life for others, can serve not only as models but as case studies. Others may then glean the secrets of environmental conditions which are optimal for living the fullest life.

Neugarten (1973, 1977) credited the middle-aged person with considerable proficiency through experience, and a greater capability to apply this proficiency than those who are younger. Society has long credited adults with the characteristics of maturity (time of full development or perfected condition) and wisdom (knowing what is true). Let us now add "strength" to the list: Strength from the knowledge of our capabilities, creativity, and contributions, and strength from our vigor, interest in life, convictions, and solidarity in resisting the strain of crises.

REFERENCE NOTE

1. Ritchie, S. Personal communication, March, 1979.

REFERENCES

Brayshaw, A. J. Middle-aged marriage: Idealism, realism and the search for meaning. *Marriage and Family Living,* 1962, *24,* 358-364.

Cooper, M. W. *An empirical investigation of the male midlife period: A descriptive cohort study.* Unpublished thesis, University of Massachusetts, Boston, 1977.

Costa, P. T., & McCrae, R. R. Objective personality assessment. In M. Storandt, I. C. Siegler, & M. F. Elias (Eds.), *The clinical psychology of aging.* New York: Plenum Publishing Corporation, 1978.

Denton, W. Middle age grief process. *Intellect,* 1978, *106,* 355.

Eisendorfer, C., & Lawton, M. P. (Eds.). *The psychology of adult development and aging*. Washington, D.C.: American Psychological Association, 1973.

Erikson, E. Identity and the life-cycle. *Psychological Issues*, Monograph I. New York: International Universities Press, 1959.

Gould, R. L. Adult life stages: Growth towards self-tolerance. *Psychology Today*, 1975, *8*, 74-78.

Jung, C. G. *Psychological types*. New York: Harcourt, Brace, & World, 1933.

Kastenbaum, R. *Humans developing: A lifespan perspective*. Boston: Allyn & Bacon, Inc., 1979.

Kerckhoff, R. K. Marriage and middle age. *The Family Co-ordinator*, 1976, *25*, 5-11.

Kübler-Ross, E. *On death and dying*. New York: Macmillan, 1969.

LeShan, E. *The wonderful crisis of middle age*. New York: David McKay, 1973.

Levinson, D. J., Darrow, C. M., Klein, E. B., Levinson, M. H., & McKee, B. The psychosocial development of men in early adulthood and the mid-life transition. In D. F. Ricks, A. Thomas, & M. Roff (Eds.), *Life history research in psycho-pathology* (Vol. 3). Minneapolis: University of Minnesota Press, 1974.

Lidz, T. *The person*. New York: Basic Books, 1976.

Lowenthal, M. F., & Chiriboga, D. Transition to the empty nest. *Archives of General Psychiatry*, 1972, *26*, 8-14.

Lowenthal, M. F., Thurnher, M., & Chiriboga, D. *Four stages of life*. San Francisco: Jossey-Bass, Inc., Publishers, 1975.

McLeish, J. *The Ulyssean adult: Creativity in the middle and later years*. New York: McGraw-Hill Ryerson Limited, 1976.

McMorrow, F. *Middlescence: The dangerous years*. New York: Quadrangle, 1974.

Neugarten, B. L.   Personality change in late life: A developmental perspective.   In C. Eisendorfer & M. P. Lawton (Eds.),
The psychology of adult development and aging. Washington, D.C.: American Psychological Association, 1973.

Neugarten, B. L.   Personality and aging.   In J. E. Birren
& K. W. Schaie (Eds.), *Handbook of the psychology of
aging.* New York: Van Nostrand Reinhold Company, 1977.

Peterson, W. A.   *The art of living, day by day.* New York:
Dell Publishing Company, 1972.

Sheehy, G.   *Passages: Predictable crises of adult life.*
New York: E. P. Dutton & Company, Inc., 1976.

Sheehy, G.   The crisis couples face at 40.   *McCalls,* 1976,
103(2), 107, 155-162.

Smith, L.   Average American facts.   *Akron Beacon Journal
Newspaper,* Akron, Ohio, January 27, 1978.

Young, J.   *Speech given to the United Methodist women.*
New York, April 29, 1979.

Sex-Role Expectations and Filial Responsibility

Dr. Diane I. Levande
School of Social Work
Michigan State University

FILIAL RESPONSIBILITY AND CARETAKER SELECTION

The obligation or duty of adult children to meet the needs of their aging parents is referred to as filial responsibility (Schorr, 1960). Blenkner (1965) discusses the related concept of filial maturity as a state of development which occurs after the resolution of a filial crisis in such a way that adult children become sensitized to the fact that their aging parents are becoming dependent upon them. This process is dramatically illustrated by a serious illness or accident which leaves the parent weakened for a lengthy period, with the possibility that he or she may never regain former abilities to manage the events of daily living. Other filial crisis events might include widowhood, the discovery of terminal illness, or retirement with subsequent decline in financial status.

In discussing the older family in crisis intervention, Kuypers and Trute (1978) note that adult children, who are usually in the middle years of life, may anxiously observe their older parents for signs of crisis, trying to judge whether the situation will worsen or be self-corrective, and measuring what the cost of their potential involvement as caretakers will mean economically and emotionally. Stereotyped fears associated with aging can distort these assessments, making it nearly impossible for children to consider positive outcomes, and a scenario develops in which the children visualize ever-increasing dependency and resource drain. Under these conditions it is difficult for some adult children to commit themselves to action; a denial of an impending or actual crisis is often an initial reaction.

Little evidence exists to explain the process by which one child in a family of several siblings becomes the primary caretaker for aging parents. Silverstone (1978) indicates

305

that complex behaviors characterize a family in the process
of "electing" a caretaker or where "self-election" of a family member to do something about a parent in crisis is in
progress. It is further suggested that the child who ends
up in the caretaker role may ironically be the one who has
been least loved and is trying to reestablish a once-desired
special relationship with the parent. Aldous (1978) notes
that the responsibility for parental care, especially "seeing
parents through their last illnesses," is often taken on by
those siblings with fewer family of procreation obligations,
such as a bachelor uncle or married aunt without children.

Informal observations and discussions with caretakers
by the writer in a limited number of intimately-known situations suggest additional factors which may influence the
process of electing a primary caretaker. A case can be made
for the adult child who assumes the caretaker role out of
deep affection and compassion for his or her dependent parents. It is also possible, although not as prevalent, that
the caretaker role will be shared equally by two or more
siblings, either at the same time, or in a sequential manner.
In the case of a small family, where there would only be a
few children, the "election" of a caretaker is seriously influenced by a lack of alternatives. In addition to those
children who are not married or who are childless assuming the
caretaker role, as Aldous has suggested, there seems to be a
number of cases where a divorced child is elected to this
role, thus reinforcing the idea that often it is the child
who has in some way deviated from traditional norms who provides primary aid. As noted by Weihl (1977), the child who
ultimately serves as caretaker may be able to offer only
scarcely adequate help, often because the child lacks financial resources. This situation would seem to have special
significance for divorced women with children of their own
to support. A brief summary of factors involved in the caretaker selection process is offered by Treas (1977): "Assistance to aging kin rests on delicate sentiments such as affection, gratitude, guilt, or a desire for parental approval"
(p. 490). Clearly, this is an area for further investigation
as Weihl (1977) suggests: "One would like to know more about
the distribution of help to parents among siblings and about
the differential use of available familial resources" (p. 124).

Although scant evidence exists about the caretaker selection process, it is becoming increasingly evident that the
sibling who is ultimately "elected" by other family members,
or who is "self-selected," is more likely to be female than
male, especially for the time-consuming, long-term filial
responsibility commitments. Thus, "It is daughters who take
widowed mothers into their homes, run errands, and provide
custodial care" (Treas, 1977, p. 488). There also seems to

be a sexual division of labor in the care of aging kin. In
a Chicago-area study of widows (Lopata, 1973), it was found
that sons were more likely to be helpful in managing funeral
arrangements and financial matters, while daughters were more
likely to be involved in providing services and social/emo-
tional functions. In one of the strongest statements to date
summarizing this sexual division of labor in filial responsibility, Treas specifies: "Devoted though sons may be, it is
clear that the major responsibility for psychological sus-
tenance and physical maintenance of the aged has fallen traditionally to female members of the family" (p. 488).

The remainder of this paper explores the needs of dependent
parents as definers of caretaker functions according to sex-
role expectations and available resources. Implications for
helping professionals attempting to support and strengthen
the family system are also discussed.

NEEDS AND EXPECTATIONS

In the past decade or so, numerous studies have seriously
challenged the once-popular theory of the isolated nuclear
family, which leaves elderly kin lonely and separated from
their adult children. Research on this issue has revealed
not only patterns of mutual aid between aging parents and
their adult children, but also clear evidence that most dependent elderly kin do receive help from their adult children. This includes frequent contact, financial assistance,
help in times of crisis, shared living arrangements, and aid
with various tasks of everyday living, such as household
maintenance, cleaning, laundry, meal preparation, shopping,
and transportation (Sussman & Burchinal, 1962; Shanas, Townsend, Wedderburn, Friis, Milhhoj, & Stehouwer, 1968; Adams,
1970; Troll, 1971).

Other studies of parental expectations related to filial
responsibility indicate that aging parents state they will
turn to their adult children as caretakers of first choice
to provide social and affective support, financial assistance,
physical care in times of health crisis or extended illness,
and assistance with tasks of daily life (Gurian & Cantor,
1978; Seelbach, 1978).

Thus, the evidence suggests that elderly parents assign
the caretaker role to their adult children, and that these
children respond to actual needs according to parental expectations. According to Brody (1970), adult children do
internalize the belief that they are responsible for their
parents, and, in turn behave very responsibly with regard
to their parents' well-being.

Certain qualifications of these data on the seemingly
"good fit" between parental expectations and the actual behavior of adult children related to filial responsibility are
necessary. First, aging parents do not want to be a burden
to their children or to interfere in their lives. This is
especially true with the financial and shared living assistance (Troll, 1971; Robertson, 1978). The fact remains, however,
that for a significant number of elderly and their adult children, the caretaker role becomes a salient part of the family
life process, and, for most families, this mode of support
is preferable to institutionalization.

Another element of the filial responsibility question
which needs clarification concerns the quality of care given
to dependent parents. For example, the finding that an elderly
parent receives a telephone call or personal visit from an
adult child at least once a week does not explain the emotional or psychological significance of this event. Whether
this interaction is satisfying for the parent and child, or
fraught with hostility and unresolved conflict, is left un-
answered. As has been noted many times, the support which
middle-aged children give to their aging parents is the con-
summation of a deferred exchange process entered into earlier
in life. Not much is known about the part which tension and
anxiety may play in this exchange process, although it is
difficult to imagine a family system which has not experienced
some conflict over years of interaction. Harbert and Ginsberg (1979) indicate that guilt over past family functioning,
on the part of both generations, may be a pervasive element
in the exchange.

A further limitation of the current data is the relative
absence of information on filial expectations and behavior
from the perspective of those in the caretaker role. Seelbach (1978) calls for further research on how filial responsibility expectations are formulated, and how the expectations
and behaviors of both generations interact and influence each
other. Streib (1972) also draws attention to this lack of
focus on the care providers. He states:

> Gerontological studies have tended to overlook the
> rights and needs of the adult children and have
> seemed to blame them if they do not work out an
> arrangement that keeps the aged parent happy and
> comfortable. There has not been enough attention
> to the needs of the adult children when a crisis
> extends for ten or fifteen years. (p. 14)

The fact that this extended or long-term care of aging parents seems to be assigned to daughters leads to the exploration

of a sexual division of labor in filial responsibility and its subsequent consequences.

SEX-ROLE EXPECTATIONS

The concept of sex role refers to the expectations assigned on the basis of whether one happens to be born female or male. In the United States, the ideas of masculinity and femininity traditionally assume a dichotomy between a number of human characteristics, behaviors, and attitudes. Although it is frequently recognized that such a division exists more as a belief system than reality, it is also apparent that such stereotyped notions have an overwhelming influence on human actions.

Studies of the origin of sexual differences, sex-role expectations, and role performance are numerous in the contemporary literature. There is considerable agreement that common ideas of masculinity include being strong, aggressive, interested in things rather than people, analytical, skilled in leadership, and courageous. On the negative side of the masculinity coin, men are seen as unexpressive, unemotional, and inept at interpersonal relationships, social, and domestic affairs. In complementary fashion, positive aspects of masculinity reflect negative aspects of femininity. Thus, traditional stereotypes of women hold that they are inferior to men in affairs of the world, irrational, lacking in scientific and mathematical ability, and submissive. More positive aspects of femininity include interest in others, interpersonal skills, nurturance, empathy, and social competence (Forisha, 1978).

It seems clear that the needs and expectations of aging parents for social and emotional support, assistance in domestic matters, and nurturance and physical care fall into the categories traditionally defined as women's work. With the exception of financial assistance and help with household repairs, the definition of the caretaker role, based on expectations of elderly parents, is more feminine than masculine. There is some documentation that parents expect more from their offspring in the way of social and affective support than in the area of instrumental and economic assistance (Seelbach & Sauer, 1977). In addition, the increase in government programs related to the financial aspects of elderly support, in the form of social security payments and health insurance, has served to decrease the economic resource drain on adult children. More appropriately stated, these programs have served to institutionalize the allocation of income between generations, thus removing this function somewhat as a direct factor in filial responsibility (Kreps, 1977).

It should be noted that the caretaker tasks assigned to
women are usually more time consuming and location specific
than those assigned to men. It takes more time to see to
the domestic affairs of everyday life, such as cleaning, meal
preparation, laundry, and physical care, than it does to make
an occasional household repair. A check may be written from
hundreds of miles way, but it is impossible to give a bath
from such a distance. The feminine tasks may also be seen as
more emotionally draining, particularly those expectations
involving care and support during a serious or terminal illness. Treas (1977) reports one study which revealed that
two-fifth of children caring for aged parents in their homes
spent the equivalent of a full-time job in this custodial
activity. Moroney (1976) further summarizes evidence showing
that the caretaker role can have a serious effect on the caretaker's own physical well-being, as well as on relationships
with his or her spouse and children.

If resources are conceptualized, as Foa and Foa (1974)
propose, to include not only money, but also love, services,
goods, information, and status, then a reasonable hypothesis
suggests the care of dependent parents can and often does
involve a serious resource drain, especially in those areas
involving the affective and service domains which are traditionally assigned to women. Some recent recognition has been
given to this issue in the literature, especially in view of
current population projections and changing roles of American
women. Treas (1977) reports that the ratio of persons 60
years and over to those in the 20-59 year-old category has
grown from a low of 13 per one hundred 20-59 year-olds in
1900, to 29 per 100 in 1975; there is a projected ratio of
44 to 100 in the year 2030. Combined with the increasing
participation of young and middle-aged women in the labor
force, a future shortage of women as caretakers of aging parents seems a possibility.

Questions of equality and justice have also been tenta-
tively raised concerning the expectation that women who carry heavy responsibilities for the economic and emotional support of their own nuclear families should further extend
their resources to aging parents (Rosenmayr, 1977), or that
women in mid-life who are just becoming free from their own
parenting functions, and beginning to think in terms of self-
development after many years of investment in family matters, should be asked to forego this period of potential
personal growth and concentrate their energies once again
on the caretaker role (Robertson, 1978).

It is assumed that growing numbers of middle-aged women
are now being asked, and will increasingly be asked, to make
decisions related to filial responsibility which involve
greater costs than benefits for their own quality of life. As

Seelbach (1978) speculates, "Filial duties may have marked effects upon the nature and quality of husband-wife and parent-child relations within the nuclear unit. Other family members may feel neglected, deprived, bitter, jealous, or resentful, depending on how they view the caretaker's responsibilities" (p. 347). In addition, there may be individual resentment, guilt, or anxiety related to having to forego career opportunities, social activities, and self-development possibilities in order to fulfill the caretaker role. Seelbach (1978) summarizes:

> There may, perhaps, be some positive outcomes from filling the caretaker role, e.g., feelings of self-satisfaction from helping others and achieving a feeling of worth. But overall, it appears that the potentially negative consequences of the role far outweigh the positive ones, especially if the role is of long duration. (p. 347)

What implications do these potential costs of the caretaker role, especially for women, have for the helping professionals concerned with family strengthening and support?

IMPLICATIONS FOR INTERVENTION

The current debate about whether the family is more viable as a short-term, crisis-oriented care provision unit for elderly members (Ward, 1978), or as a long-term care provision alternative to institutionalization with additional new roles such as mediation (Sussman, 1977), should be carefully reviewed and analyzed for the impact of both proposals on the family unit. While it seems true that most families do find at least one caretaker among their members, usually a daughter, public policy recommendations by helping professionals, which support family responsibility for filial care, may have unforeseen consequences. In Great Britain, where policy statements recognize the shared responsibility of the State and family for care of dependent elderly, it is clear that, once a given family accepts the responsibility for filial aid, the State takes for granted this commitment, and offers little by way of support to the family system. It is primarily in those situations where no offspring or other close family member exists, or where the family cannot or will not accept filial responsibility, that the State takes on this function. Thus, the State may become a substitute rather than a support system for the family (Moroney, 1976).

Public professional support of measures which attempt to strengthen the filial aid commitment on the part of families could serve to decrease resources available for alternative modes of care, as well as further depress the already limited attempts to define the problem and seek appropriate solutions. Such a position might also make the decision to institutionalize an aging parent--a situation which Silverstone (1978) has described as one of the most unhappy times in the life of any human being--even more difficult for the families who do not have the resources for filial care.

As life expectancies increase and the population balance continues to shift toward an older society, the declining number of family members available to assume the caretaker role presents yet another resource problem.

On the other hand, it is evident that most families accept filial responsibility obligations and attempt to meet the needs of aging parents, although the cost of this commitment to the individual care provider and the nuclear family unit may be considerable. Some existing programs can help lessen the cost of this type of aid, such as homemaker services, day care centers, and provision for meals. Availability of these services, however, varies from community to community, and in many places it is extremely difficult to find competent individuals to care for dependent elderly, even when financial resources are available. This situation is not likely to be improved by plans which provide some funding for health care and other services unless greater value is placed on work which involves physical and emotional care for the aged. Appropriate training programs for such care providers need to be an integral part of any such plan.

The argument can be made that care of the elderly, because it has been defined primarily as women's work, is not highly valued in the United States. Thus, the economic rewards for this kind of work are often minimal, as are the skill requirements. It is almost as if being born female automatically qualifies one to perform both the necessary nursing care and the complex and frequently stressful emotional support functions. Whether or not this situation is likely to change with the current emphasis on more liberated sex-role functioning, which encourages assertiveness for women and freer emotional expression for men, remains to be seen.

In the meantime, it is evident that many women, usually in the mid-life years, are being asked to make filial aid commitments as primary caretakers of aging parents. These individuals need help. Information about realistic alternatives and supplementary community-support systems should be readily available. Knowledge about the mental and physical state of the dependent parent, and what this may mean in terms of support, is a necessity. Ideally, the implications of such a commitment should be openly discussed with spouses, children, extended family members, and friends; their instrumental and emotional support should be enlisted. The primary caretaker, especially in a long-term situation, needs caretakers of his or her own to listen empathically to negative feelings and discouragements, to mobilize substitute providers when time away from the role is needed, to obtain information about services and resources, and, in general, to see that the physical and emotional health of the filial aid giver is maintained. Spouses, children, siblings, and friends may all serve in this intimate support role, although some sensitivity to the situation may need to be developed, and actual instruction in appropriate support behaviors may be necessary.

A major effort in the area of prevention remains to be actualized. Programs which encourage parents and adult children to communicate about filial expectations and make tentative plans prior to a filial crisis seem a meaningful place to begin. Parents often say they do not want to be a burden on their children in their aging years. Yet, just as often, no plans are made which would lessen the impact of a crisis when it occurs. Educational programs which specify and actually demonstrate appropriate supportive behaviors, in the provision of filial care for an increasingly dependent elderly parent, could help both men and women by promoting realistic assessments of the filial responsibility commitment, and by allaying fears which stem from feelings of inadequacy and helplessness.

Much knowledge abounds in the area of supportive care for dependent elderly from those who have actualized the caretaker role over time, and from the analysis of other situations within the life cycle which require similar skills. However, there is still a need to compile what is known, and disseminate this information in a sensitive and effective manner. Continuing efforts to define what is and to propose what ought to be in the area of filial responsibility are of prime importance.

REFERENCES

Adams, B. N. Isolation, function, and beyond: American kinship in the 1960's. *Journal of Marriage and the Family*, 1970, *32*, 575-597.

Aldous, J. *Family careers: Developmental change in families*. New York: John Wiley & Sons, 1978.

Blenkner, M. Social work and family relationships in later life with some thoughts on filial maturity. In E. Shanas & G. F. Streib (Eds.), *Social structure and the family: Generational relations*. Englewood Cliffs, New Jersey: Prentice-Hall, 1965.

Brody, E. M. The etiquette of filial behavior. *Aging and Human Development*, 1970, *1*, 87-94.

Foa, U. G., & Foa, E. B. *Societal structures of the mind*. Springfield, Illinois: Charles C. Thomas, 1974.

Forisha, B. L. *Sex roles and personal awareness*. Morristown, New Jersey: General Learning Press, 1978.

Gurian, B. S., & Cantor, M. H. Mental health and community support systems for the elderly. In G. Usdin & C. J. Hofling (Eds.), *Aging: The process and the people*. New York: Brunner/Mazel, 1978.

Harbert, A. S., & Ginsberg, L. H. *Human services for older adults: Concepts and skills*. Belmont, California: Wadsworth, 1979.

Kreps, J. M. Intergenerational transfers and the bureaucracy. In E. Shanas & M. B. Sussman (Eds.), *Family, bureaucracy, and the elderly*. Durham, North Carolina: Duke University Press, 1977.

Kuypers, J. A., & Trute B. The older family as the locus of crsis intervention. *The Family Coordinator*, 1978, *27*, 405-411.

Lopata, H. Z. *Widowhood in an American city*. Cambridge, Massachusetts: Schenkman, 1973.

Moroney, R. M. *The family and the state: Considerations for social policy*. London: Longman Group Limited, 1976.

Robertson, J. F. Women in middle life: Crisis, reverberations, and support networks. *The Family Coordinator*, 1978, *27*, 375-382.

Rosenmayr, L. The family--A source of hope for the elderly? In E. Shanas & M. B. Sussman (Eds.), *Family, bureaucracy, and the elderly*. Durham, North Carolina: Duke University Press, 1977.

Schorr, A. L. *Filial responsibility in the modern American family*. Washington, D.C.: U.S. Department of Health, Education, and Welfare, Social Security Administration, Division of Program Research, 1960.

Seelbach, W. C. Correlates of aged parents' filial responsibility expectations and realizations. *The Family Coordinator*, 1978, *27*, 341-350.

Seelbach, W. C., & Sauer, W. J. Filial responsibility expectations and morale among aged parents. *The Gerontologist*, 1977, *17*, 492-499.

Shanas, E., Townsend, P., Wedderburn, D., Friis, H., Milhhoj, P., & Stehouwer, J. *Older people in three industrial societies*. New York: Atherton Press, 1968.

Silverstone, B. Family relationships of the elderly: Problems and implications for helping professionals. *Aged Care & Services Review*, 1978, *1*, 1-9.

Streib, G. F. Older families and their troubles: Familial and social responses. *The Family Coordinator*, 1972, *21*, 5-19.

Sussman, M. B. Family, bureaucracy, and the elderly individual: An organizational/linkage perspective. In E. Shanas & M. B. Sussamn (Eds.), *Family, bureaucracy, and the elderly*. Durham, North Carolina: Duke University Press, 1977.

Sussman, M. B., & Burchinal, L. Kin family network: Unheralded structure in current conceptualizations of family functioning. *Marriage and Family Living*, 1962, *24*, 231-240.

Treas, J. Family support systems for the aged: Some social and demographic considerations. *The Gerontologist*, 1977, *17*, 486-491.

Troll, L. The family of later life: A decade of review. *Journal of Marriage and the Family*, 1971, *33*, 263-290.

Ward, R. A. Limitations of the family as a supportive institution in the lives of the aged. *The Family Coordinator*, 1978, *27*, 365-373.

Weihl, H. The household, intergenerational relations, and
social policy. In E. Shanas & M. B. Sussman (Eds.),
Family, bureaucracy, and the elderly. Durham, North
Carolina: Duke University Press, 1977.

Seeing Dependency as Strength from Generation to Generation

Dr. Mary Jane S. Van Meter
Department of Family and
Consumer Resources
Wayne State University

INTRODUCTION

Declines in both the birth rate and mortality rate have changed
the structure of the contemporary family such that the shrink-
ing nuclear American family has a lengthening living lineage.
Whereas the average family in 1910 had an average of 4.5
children (Troll, 1979) and the average life expectancy was
approximately 47 years (Kalish, 1975), the contemporary expectation is that of 2.5 children per every married mother
(Glick, 1977) with life expectancy in the 70's. Thus, while
family density has decreased within generations, membership
has been extended over three, four, and five living generations.

To consider family strengths, the physical, emotional,
and social ties which are the lifeline between generations
in the contemporary extended family must be taken into account. Creating and maintaining a satisfying life for each
generational level is an important aspect of family life today. Shanas (1979) has argued that it is the family which
is the first resource of both its older and younger members
for emotional and social support, crisis intervention, and
bureaucratic linkages.

Family strengths in this paper are defined as an intergenerational adaptation of the features of the "energized"
family as conceptualized by Pratt (1976). These characteristics are regarded as resources and skills which affect the
family's perception of potential stressor events (Hill, 1958).
Specifically, the adaptive capacities influence the family's
attitude toward critical developmental changes throughout the
individual's life span. The developmental changes in the
dependency-independency continuum throughout life will be
the particular focus of this paper.

The acceptant manner in which the family views and re-
sponds to normal, developmental dependency as manifested by
all of its various-aged members will be viewed as a strength

317

of the intergenerational family. Implications and suggestions
for building this strength are included.

Dependency as a concept appears frequently in the psychiatric literature as unnatural and generally viewed in negative terms (Gavalas & Briggs, 1966). Developmental psychologists view dependency as a necessary corollary to infant attachment or as an interchangeable term (Bee, 1978; Hetherington & Parke, 1975). Though some evidence indicates that dependency is not a unitary process, the term is used to describe a series of behaviors capable of eliciting social responses in others. In the perspective taken in this paper,
a normal range of dependency is seen as a changing need oc-
curring across the life span between family members (Lowenthal, Thurnher, & Chiriboga, 1975). A special emphasis is
given the later years of the life span at which time the
normal dependencies are often misunderstood by younger family members.

From the vantage point of stress theory, a life-span
range of normal developmental dependency behaviors will be
viewed as potential stressor events with the specified family strengths characterized as resources which influence the
family's perception of the stressor determining whether or
not a crisis reaction occurs.

REVIEW OF LITERATURE

Stress Theory

According to the crisis formulation (Hill, 1958), A (the
event) interacting with B (the family's crisis-meeting resources) interacting with C (the definition the family makes
of the event) produced X (the crisis). As he developed this
conceptual framework, Hill built on findings of Angell and
others who had pointed to qualities of family integration
and family adaptability as critical to the well-functioning
family. These are characteristics of family functioning
noted by Pratt (1976) in the energized family; by Barnhill
(1979) as a dimension of healthy family functioning; and by
Otto (1963) as family strengths. These characteristics,
seen here as family strengths, comprise an important part
of Hill's B factor of family resources.

Though the objective resources of a family might be adequate to meet the hardships or difficulties of the change,
if the family defines the event as insurmountable, the likelihood of strain or crisis is much greater. The interpretation of a stressor event (C) may reflect the value system
of the family which in itself is a product of cultural influences. The experience of the family in meeting crisis,

and in part, the mechanisms utilized in previous definitions
of crisis play a part in the interpretation process. Further,
the definition of the family as to whether the event is seen
as a challenge or as a crisis-provoking occurrence depends
on its belief in the ability to mobilize its strengths (integration, flexibility, adaptability) in solving the presenting problem. Pratt (1976) refers to this as the family's
active coping effort. Whether the stressor event refers to
natural disasters such as floods or tornadoes, or to the normal developmental shifts in life such as marriage, parenthood,
or retirement, the key to its impact appears to be in what
Hill (1958) refers to as the meaning dimension.

The family's view of dependency across the life span can
be viewed in just this perspective.

Family Strengths

One view of family strengths is that of Pratt (1976) who regards certain family structural variables as influencing functioning. While her study is concerned with the effect of
these characteristics on health and health behavior, she presents much evidence to suggest that such functioning influences positive emotional and psychological health as well.
Pratt's (1976) analysis conceptualizes the energized family
as one whose structure allows it to perform personal care
effectively.

> Energized refers to the sheer energy or exhange
> that occurs between family members who interact
> a great deal, the stimulation that comes from
> interacting with outside groups, the generation
> of new ideas and problem-solving effort that re-
> sults from family interaction and the freeing of
> people to develop themselves. (p. 4)

Those family structure concepts which were found to
have an association with health practices were: the ability
to provide a high degree of autonomy and supportiveness for
individual needs of family members; the regular and varied
interaction among family members, especially husband-wife
and father-child; the active effort directed toward problem
solving; the participation in other social systems beyond
the family; and the flexible division of tasks and equaliza-
tion of power between the spouses.

Among the criteria which Otto (1963) has delineated as
appropriate for assessing family strengths are: the ability
to provide for the physical, emotional, and spiritual needs
of a family which includes providing love, understanding,
and trust in an environment of honesty and integrity; the

ability to communicate effectively including sensitive listening as well as verbal expression; the ability to provide support, security, and encouragement; and the ability to perform
family roles flexibly. Of particular interest to this perspective were the strengths of an ability for self-help and
the ability to accept help when appropriate, the ability to
use a crisis or traumatic experience as a means of growth,
and a concern for interfamily cooperation.

Barnhill (1979) has isolated eight dimensions of healthy
family functioning which include: flexibility vs. rigidity,
individuation vs. enmeshment, and mutuality vs. isolation.
He points out that these are interrelated qualities and processes within the family system.

Across the three perspectives of Pratt, Otto, and Barnhill, common denominators of the well-functioning family are
conspicuous. Each names flexibility, it is more than the
"filling the role of another," and it is the capacity to be
both adjustable and resilient in response to varied conditions. The idea that the family has the capacity to problem
solve, to help itself or to seek help when necessary, attests
to its functionality in good times as well as in meeting more
stressful situations. The ability to communicate support also
is an important predictor for effective functioning according to these authors. While Otto is alone in seeing a strength
in the family's ability to use crisis constructively as a
means of growth, implicit in the suggestions of the other
two authors seems to be the foundation for such strength.

Dependency

One common way of viewing dependency is to define it as the
reliance on others for help, approval, and attention. Such
behaviors in children have been further analyzed to suggest
two types of dependency: emotional dependency which involves
seeking affection, approval, and the proximity of others,
and instrumental dependency which involves seeking help and
attention (Hetherington & Parke, 1975)

Throughout life, a range of all these behaviors is appropriately viewed as dependency. However, the number of
these separate behaviors and the extent to which each is
manifested influence whether the dependency is viewed as
normal or pathologic. The interpretation of such behaviors
is in the eye of the beholder. Families vary in the intensity
and range of dependency behaviors which they will encourage
and accept. The tolerance for dependency is influenced by
several factors, among which are the cultural expectations,
the developmental level and the sex of the individual actor.

America, as "land of the free and home of the brave,"
characterizes how we see ourselves as a nation and as a

people. The idea of making one's own way in the New World was a very important expectation of countless thousands of pilgrims and later immigrants to America. It was also essential for the American pioneers who pushed the frontier westward to be very self-sufficient and free from the control of others. Such ideologies and necessities of life for earlier Americans have helped to enculturate the expectancy of independence as the American way of life. In fact, the whole notion of democracy implies the freedom to self-determination.

Americans, it appears, strive for independence in all relationships. From earliest childhood, there is evidence of early training in independence. This is in contrast to many other cultures which tolerate and encourage early dependence in the form of submissiveness, restraint, and protection.

Erikson (1963) suggests that Americans encounter the psycho-social crisis of autonomy at about the age of two. Independence at the earliest possible ages has become so enculturated that dependence at any time or at any age is anathema.

Berardo (1970), in reporting the needs of aged widowers, has pointed out that there is a general societal expectation that males should fend for themselves and avoid taking on a dependency status. While it may be perfectly acceptable to display the same dependence needs within the marital dyad, it appears unacceptable to do so across other familial bonds. This may be one explanation for the fact that widowers remarry at a much greater rate than do women.

Thus, not only a cultural but a stereotypic sexual expectation appears to exist in which males must be independent and self-reliant, while females may be dependent on others, passive, and more easily influenced. However, current research does not show consistent sex effects in dependency-related behaviors (Maccoby & Jacklin, 1974). This has led some writers (Frieze et al., 1978) to conclude that females in actuality are not necessarily more dependent than males.

Unlike other animal species, human beings are biologically and socially programmed for a long period of dependence on others after birth. Typically, families expect to provide the necessary care for the helpless infant. Nonetheless, the crisis of parenthood often occurs due to the unanticipated extent of that care and its effects on the parenting couple.

Early in life a healthy attachment to parents is expected to increase trust so that the growing individual may subsequently develop other social relationships. Some degree of dependency--emotional dependency in this case--is a necessary foundation for mature affectional relationships.

Much of the battering and abuse of infants and young children has been attributed to the unrealistic parental expectations for behavior which is actually not appropriate to the particular developmental level of that child. Such parental attitudes and behaviors which convey rejection and hostility appear to be significantly associated with dependency (Steinmetz, 1979). For those children who are punished for exhibiting dependency in such behaviors as clinging to the mother or attention seeking, a continuous cycle of dependency is thus created.

A study by Lowenthal et al. (1975), in which self-concepts across four periods of life were analyzed, found adolescent girls emerged with perceptions of themselves as helpless and dependent, and questioning their ability to lead an independent life. Their feelings of powerlessness, and a belief that direct action and independent achievement were not within their reach, contributed to very negative self-concepts at that age. High school boys were most troubled by their absent mindedness and dependency.

In adolescence and young adulthood, the emancipation process, from confident dependence on parents to confidence in one's own ability to cope with various situations, is the primary struggle. Adams (1971) has suggested that, in this emancipation process, the relationship between high confidence and dependence on parents and high confidence and dependence on self is curvilinear, with a low point in midstream. This period of uncertainty or low confidence comes at a time in adolescence when peers are available, and are sought for support and assurance. Typically, the struggle for independence is important to the individual, as it means proof of adulthood and self-worth from which self-esteem results.

In young adulthood when intimate relationships with another person develop, the relationship implies a mutuality of giving and taking and a balancing of power. The individual has attained adulthood, achieved a measure of self-sufficiency, and enters into what may best be described as an interdependent relationship with a partner. It requires each to recognize his or her own and each other's moments of independence, as well as dependence or need for help in some form. Not only is this interdependency and mutuality typified by the marital relationship; it is evident also in the new relationship intergenerationally between child and parent who discover each other more objectively on an adult-adult basis, perhaps for the first time.

In spite of children's desire to be grown up and independent, once in adulthood, few remain in a totally "free" state very long, as most people eventually marry. To do so implies a willingness to acknowledge dependency--physically, emotionally, and socially--on another person, and to accept the other person's dependence as well.

Therefore, the high point of confidence, which comes with dependence on the self in late adolescence or early adulthood (Adams, 1971), is not necessarily synonymous with total independence. Rather, it may be viewed as a long plateau extending throughout adulthood, in which interdependence with spouse as well as children and parental generations is the case. Throughout the marital career, the changing dependency needs of the two spouses, and the manner in which they are fulfilled, though generally unstudied by researchers, undoubtedly create new experiences demanding adjustment. Lowenthal et al. (1975) report that older women felt their spouses were overdependent, whereas newlywed men were more likely to express such feelings.

When one reaches old age, a number of normal dependencies can be expected (Blenkner, 1969; Clark, 1969). As with infants and young children, these derive both from the age itself, and from the cultural expectations for the age. Economic dependency occurs when the worker is no longer employed and must rely on the income transfers from the currently working generations. These may come through taxes or Social Security payments, but also through contributions of children and other younger members. Physical dependency arises from the aging process itself, in which muscle strength diminishes, reflexes are slower, coordination is poorer, sensory acuity is decreased, and the general level of energy is lower. Thus, the everyday routine of living becomes more taxing, and may one day become impossible to perform without assistance.

A social dependency comes about, particularly because of the variety of losses the individual experiences in the deaths of meaningful others, especially the spouse, close friends, and siblings. Also, Blenkner (1969) points out that the loss of roles which are the basis of power, status, and avenues of social participation, coupled with a loss of contemporaneousness in values, expectation, and knowledge bring about the need to rely on others.

Emotional dependency is a human need throughout life. Infants need tender, touching, and loving care, as do children and adolescents, adults of all ages, and even old people. Scientific research and institutional observations have taught us what loving contact with another human means to the well-being of infants and young children. Often, however, the needs of the lonely, the isolated, and the institutionalized elderly for the same quality and quantity of human contact are forgotten. Thus, across the life span there exists need for emotional support and understanding.

Atchley (1977) reports that independence is probably most influenced by finances, housing, and mobility. Lack of financial resources is the most frequent reason the elderly cite for having to rely on others, and becoming dependent upon them. The prevalent norm and expectation of older people is a desire to maintain their own living arrangements--to gain household independence. Maintaining mobility is another vital aspect of independence. When one can no longer afford to drive, or finds it impossible physically to do so, severe limitations are put upon one's freedom and ability to live an independent life.

Having money and good health are fundamental routes to independence in American society. Johnson (1978) found the variables of health and finances had an indirect influence on both the living environment and one's attitude toward aging. Living environment and attitude toward aging were the predictors of the quality of the relationship between the elderly and their adult daughters.

Although mental dependency does not occur for all old people, the isolation from the mainstream of society for many old people, because of illness, strokes, drug use, or poor nutrition, may require the help of others in decision making and problem solving. Unpredictable personal crises, such as the loss of spouse, a critical accident, or a severe illness, may have a special impact on one's dependency needs at any point in the life span. However, the grieving and depression caused by such crises may necessitate a dependency viewed as a mental dependency of old age, rather than the crisis dependency which it more accurately may be. The fact is that most older people do retain mental self-sufficiency.

The experience of financial, personal, and social losses in old age may bring about a decrease in confidence in the self, until support is provided by others, and high levels of confidence can be placed in them. The resurgence of confidence occurs when the family can be counted on to be supportive and dependable. Once again, the curvilinear relationship of confidence levels to the dependence of self and others appears, this time at the end of life.

The elderly usually turn to their kin first for help. If the older person is heavily dependent on children, great strain is placed on the relationship, perhaps in part due to the prevalent negative attitudes about dependency. If an interdependent relationship can be maintained, the chances are much better for a good relationship.

The family's role in fulfilling dependency needs is established by the adult children in relation to their elderly parents. When the normal dependencies of later life occur, and the elderly turn to their adult children for support, a role reversal does not occur (Blenkner, 1965). Being dependable is one of the adjustments of the middle years. Indeed, it is one of life's crises in itself, as this marks what Blenkner terms "filial maturity." To have an attitude that one must be "parent to his or her own parent" is distasteful, and must in itself cause resentment toward the aged parent. On the other hand, if the individual, with high confidence in his or her own ability, can accept the parent's need for help as normal and reasonable for an aged individual, the supportiveness expressed will strengthen the relationship.

There are, to be sure, instances in which undue and unreasonable demands are made of family members by their aged parents. In many cases, this may be a pattern of behavior established much earlier in life, which has persisted and possibly become more blatant in the later years. Also, the behaviors may be part of the depression which may accompany other illness or loss the individual has suffered. It is not intended here to suggest that such cases of dependency be overlooked, nor that it be handled by the family. Therapeutic intervention is necessary and appropriate under such circumstances.

VIEWING DEPENDENCY AS AN OPPORTUNITY FOR STRENGTHENING GENERATIONAL TIES

In the following section, the components of Hill's (1958) stress theory are analyzed, according to a view in which dependency is seen as a potential stressor event. However, with specific family strengths which color their perception of dependency, the event is not regarded as a crisis. Such a point of view allows the family to respond with greater sensitivity to individual needs.

The Stressor Event

Just as young children seek reassurance from loving caretakers, and adolescents check out their parents' attitudes and values on current issues, so too do elderly parents seek advice in decision making, and help in routine tasks of daily living from their competent family members. Individuals of all ages seek support and guidance from parents, peers, siblings, and their own children. Such dependency behaviors are normal and variable throughout life, as they may accompany age-related changes, social losses, and psychological shifts; to be dependent is part of the human condition.

The Family Resources

1. An understanding of human development. One of the most
   important resources to meet dependency needs is a fundamental understanding of what can be reasonably expected
   at every stage of human development. Parents are not as
   likely to respond irrationally when the ten-month-old
   child does not eat with a fork if they understand that
   such coordination and manual dexterity cannot be expected
   at that early age. Although the 15-year-old may complain
   about curfew times, or inability to do what "everyone
   else is going to do," because of consistent parental
   limits, inwardly that teenager may be grateful that his
   or her parents are caring and supportive. Such parents
   realize that adolescents need dependable limits, not only
   to protect them from poor judgment and the lack of con-
   sequential thinking, but also as steadying and secure
   supports. In adulthood, when job transitions occur, in-
   terspousal understanding and supportiveness can help ease
   the adjustment to inevitable transfers, promotions, being
   by-passed, or even demoted or unemployed. For the aged,
   sympathetic recognition by the family of the variety and
   impact of economic, social, psychological, and physical
   losses is likely to help the individual function better.

   These, as well, as numerous other developmental changes,
   are potential stressors in the life of the individual.
   If the family understands and can accept normal developmental sequences, and the demands of each, it is more
   likely to be able to respond appropriately.

2. Flexibility. One of the fundamental requirements of family interaction over time is that it be flexible and able
   to adapt to individual needs. As each family member changes
   over time, old patterns must change when new demands are
   created. Each age and stage through which individuals
   grow call upon varied resources and different supportive
   techniques. When a flexible division of tasks and decision making exists, even in the multigenerational family, the adjustment to change is likely to occur with
   greater ease.

3. Community participation. Regular links with the broader
   community provide opportunities for expanded social experience. For example, when young children go to nursery
   school, or are involved with their peers in formal community groups, their parents inevitably become more than
   observers to the scene; they learn about community resources, and they may achieve a measure of social competence

in dealing with a network of community resources. This
experience should additionally increase their knowledge
of the age group, and give them greater tolerance for
individual differences in development, in addition to
an increased ability to handle their own parental responsibilities. The consequences of familial ties to
the community constitute an important part of the family's resources.

4. Active coping effort. The active coping effort of a
family can best be seen in the way in which they creatively develop solutions to suit their changing needs,
and how they proceed through a rational decision-making
process. Although a variety of programs exist today
which are aimed at helping families better understand
their members (e.g., Parent Effectiveness Training,
Marital Enrichment, group sessions for adults with elderly parents), the vast American public has not engaged
in either informal or formal course work or lessons to
develop new ideas or skills in interpersonal relationships. The extent to which family members understand
developmental needs, and can apply that knowledge to
the problem-solving process, surely lessens the impact
of normal dependency needs as they first appear or re-
appear in a new guise. Further, families who feel they
have some ability to control their lives, and who seek
and get information are more likely to utilize community resources to alleviate stressful circumstances.

5. Ability to communicate effectively. Through its interactions, the family must be able to reflect acceptance
and a respectful recognition of each other's developing
self. In communicating this acceptance, trust and understanding develop and are sustained between members. Interpersonal needs may be mediated best by being able to
discuss them with family members free of disdain or
ridicule.

6. Ability to learn from past experience. Being able to
look back on previous attempts to meet members' needs
for dependency, to evaluate that experience, and then
to move on constructively, seeing it as a means of growth
for the entire family, may also be seen as a criterion
of strength.

The Family's Interpretation of the Stress Event

The family's definition of dependency is a reflection of its
value system, its experience in meeting previous dependency

needs, and the mechanisms it has employed in previous definitions of these needs. If the family defines needs for dependency as instigators of other family hardships, conflicts
and crises are likely to ensue. The accumulation of these
tensions may be destructive to intergenerational relations.

On the other hand, if the family sees the dependency as
normal, and can utilize its resources effectively to meet the
needs, it will not interpret the event as a crisis-provoking
demand. In such cases, the proneness to crisis, the X factor
in Hill's (1958) model never occurs.

IMPLICATIONS

The ability to see dependency needs as normal and varying
throughout life can be achieved by families. For them to
do so creates an intergenerational strength in which greater
opportunities are available for supportiveness by more generations. The following suggestions would help strengthen
this trait.

1. More formal and informal educational programs about
   human development need to be available. At the present
   time, many high school programs are including child development courses. There seem to be no valid reasons
   why such courses should not be changed to human development courses which would cover the life span. In today's world, men and women need to understand about
   growing old, as well as about child care.

2. Good attitudes toward all age groups need to be expressed
   within the family. There is evidence that attitudes concerning the aged and aging are learned very early in life.
   Robertson (1975) has pointed out that parents act as
   mediators between grandchildren and grandparents. The
   positive or negative attitudes which parents express
   about the aged, or the older person's need to be dependent, will be taken on by children.

3. Role modeling of filial maturity needs to be provided
   by adults. In addition to positive attitudes, adult
   children of elderly parents need to behave toward their
   parents in ways which express support and understanding.
   Younger generations observe and imitate the behavior
   toward the elderly which they themselves will use toward
   the present elderly--perhaps their grandparents--and
   the future elderly--their own parents.

4. Communication and planning is a family affair. Good communication facilitates understanding at all ages and stages of family life. When an old person expresses dependencies, it is important the family does not completely assume decision making and planning for that person. Younger generations can provide information on alternative solutions and consequences, and offer to stand by the elderly person when a decision is made; however, the elderly must be able to participate in and understand the reasoning behind specific plans. The aged person, as well as others, can initiate discussion of contingency plans for debilitating illness or terminal care, his or her own death, specific desires about funeral arrangements and burial, and property settlement or disposition. These discussions, carried on in advance of need, may help families feel more comfortable about "doing the right thing" for aged members when the time arrives.

5. The family should facilitate interaction of aged persons with their peers. Dependency on children is a loathesome experience to aged persons (Atchley, 1977). An important way to avoid or lessen the feeling of dependency on children is to maintain or develop peer friendships. Constraints are often placed on the elderly person's ability to see age-mates, due to mobility, health, or housing factors. The role of adult family members can be to facilitate such opportunities by providing transportation, arranging get-togethers, or taking the aged person to a Senior Citizens' program. Opportunities for them to be with friends may lessen loneliness, and help build self-esteem, both of which are likely to diminish the dependence on children for social stimulation.

Thus, the ability of the family to perceive the changing character of dependency across the life span, and to view dependency as normal and acceptable is seen as a strength of both the nuclear family in its own family career, and across the generational family in its life cycle as well. The achievement of this strength is derived, in part, through structural flexibility and interactional exchange.

REFERENCES

Adams, B. N. *The American family.* Chicago: Markham, 1971.

Atchley, R. C. *The social forces in later life* (2nd ed.).
Belmont, California: Wadsworth, 1977.

Barnhill, L. R. Health family systems. *The Family Coordinator,* 1979, *28,* 94-100.

Bee, H. *The developing child* (2nd ed.). New York: Harper
& Row, 1978.

Berardo, F. Survivorship and social isolation: The case
of the aged widower. *The Family Coordinator,* 1970,
19, 11-25.

Blenkner, M. Social work and family relationships in later
life with some thoughts on filial maturity. In E.
Shanas & G. F. Streib (Eds.), *Social structure and the
family: Generational relations.* Englewood Cliffs,
New Jersey: Prentice-Hall, 1965.

Blenkner, M. The normal dependencies of aging. In R. A.
Kalish (Ed.), *The dependencies of old people.* Occasional
papers in Gerontology No. 6, Institute of Gerontology,
University of Michigan-Wayne State University, August,
1969.

Clark, M. Cultural values and dependency in later life.
In R. A. Kalish (Ed.), *The dependencies of old people.*
Occasional papers in Gerontology No. 6, Institute of
Gerontology, University of Michigan-Wayne State Uni-
versity, August, 1969.

Erikson, E. *Childhood and society* (2nd ed.). New York:
W. W. Norton, 1963.

Frieze, I. J., Parsons, J. E., Johnson, P. B., Ruble, D. N.,
& Zellman, G. L. *Women and sex roles.* New York: W. W.
Norton, 1978.

Gavalas, R. J., & Briggs, P. C. Concurrent schedules of
reinforcement: A new concept of dependency. *Merrill-
Palmer Quarterly,* 1966, *12,* 97-121.

Glick, P. Updating the life cycle of the family. *Journal
of Marriage and the Family,* 1977, *39*(1), 5-13.

Hetherington, E. M. & Parke, R. D. *Child psychology.* New York: McGraw-Hill, 1975.

Hill, R. Social stresses on the family: Generic features of families under stress. *Social Casework,* 1958, *39,* 139-150.

Kalish, R. A. *Late adulthood: Perspectives on human development.* Monterey, California: Brooks/Cole, 1975.

Johnson, E. S. "Good" relationships between older mothers and their daughters: A causal model. *The Gerontologist,* 1978, *18*(3), 301-306.

Lowenthal, M. F., Thurnher, M., & Chiriboga, D. *Four stages of life.* San Francisco, California: Jossey-Bass, 1975.

Maccoby, E. E., & Jacklin, C. N. *The psychology of sex differences.* Stanford: Stanford University Press, 1974.

Otto, H. A. Criteria for assessing family strength. *Family Process,* 1963, *2*(2), 329-338.

Pratt, L. *Family structure and effective health behavior.* Boston, Massachusetts: Houghton Mifflin, 1976.

Robertson, J. F. Interaction in three generation families, parents vs. mediators: Toward a theoretical perspective. *International Journal of Aging and Human Development,* 1975, *6*(2), 103-110.

Shanas, E. Social myth as hypothesis: The case of the family relations of old people. *The Gerontologist,* 1979, *19*(1), 3-9.

Steinmetz, S. K. Disciplinary techniques and their relationship to aggressiveness, dependency and conscience. In W. R. Burr, R. Hill, F. I. Nye, & I. L. Reiss (Eds.), *Contemporary theories about the family* (Vol. I). New York: The Free Press, 1979.

Troll, L. E., Miller, S. J., & Atchley, R. C. *Families in later life.* Belmont, California: Wadsworth, 1979.

Strengthening the Family Life of Older Adults: Myth-Conceptions and Investigative Needs

Dr. Jay Mancini
Department of Management, Housing,
  and Family Development
Virginia Polytechnic Institute
  and State University

OUR GRAY POPULATION

One of the more marked trends on the American scene is the "graying" of the population. It has recently been suggested that this demographic evolution could be "as sweeping a transformation as the opening of the frontier, the industrial revolution or the tide of European immigration after the Civil War" (The Graying of America, 1977). A fair amount of concern regarding this population trend relates to the economic costs of caring for a disproportionate number of older Americans. However, of equal importance is the nation's quality of life as reflected in the well-being of its older adults. These two considerations provide the orientation for this paper. In particular, the focal point of inquiry is the quality of family life, and how it can be strengthened among older Americans. The questions to be addressed are as follows:

1. What do we know about the importance of family life for older adults?

2. Are the research findings "translatable" into programs designed to build family strengths?

3. What more do we need to know about family life and life quality among older adults?

This issue-raising exploration seeks to examine the "fit" between what research tells us regarding family life in old age, and what we probably need to know to effectively build family strengths among this age group. An initial issue involves some common misunderstandings about the family life of older people.

MYTH-CONCEPTIONS ABOUT OLD AGE

As a group, older adults are assigned numerous characteristics
that are not reflective of reality. Older people supposedly
have a declining interest in sex, become more religious, feel
miserable most of the time, are socially isolated and lonely,
and are unable to learn anything new (Palmore, 1977). Family-
related myths pertain to the amount of contact with family
members, especially children, and the end result of interacting with one's kin. The alienation myth would have us
believe that older adults are isolated from other family members, and are, in effect, neglected (Shanas, 1979). This myth
is rooted in sociological musings of the 1940's (Linton,
1949; Parsons, 1949). During the World War II era, there was
considerable concern about loss of family functions in general, and about isolation from kin in particular. The enrichment myth suggests that the lives of older adults are
necessarily bettered by interaction with family members. No
doubt this misconception stems from notions concerning family life in past times, what Goode (1963) has termed "the
classical family of Western nostalgia." In the classical
family, everyone interacted with everyone else, and both
families and individuals were happy. Each of these notions
about old people and their families is contradicted by research. The average older adults interacts with kin on a
regular basis, but the result of interaction is not always
productive for either the older person or for his or her kin.

KIN CONTACT IN OLD AGE

How much do older adults interact with their children and
other relatives? Are they socially alienated? When examining
interaction, one must consider contact via telephone and letter, as well as personal visits. A study I conducted in 1976
revealed that the average number of weekly visits between
older parents and their adult children was slightly fewer
than two; phone contacts per week were slightly fewer than
six (Quinn & Mancini, 1979). Unpublished data from a 1977
study, conducted by the author on role competence and well-
being (Mancini, 1977, 1979a), also suggest the regularity
with which older parents and adult children interact. Thirty
percent of the sample saw their children several times a
year, 13% saw them about once a month, and 49% saw them at
least once a week. Regarding contact via telephone, 25% interacted in this manner on a monthly basis, and 50% did so
at least once a week. Contact via letters or cards was somewhat less common, with 25% indicating they never received

letters from their children, and another 30% reporting this type of contact occurred several times a year. The findings from numerous researchers are consistent with those of this author. In most cases the major proportion of older parents have weekly contacts with their children (Hill et al., 1970; Shanas, 1973; Shanas et al., 1968; Troll, Miller, & Atchley, 1979; Watson & Kivett, 1976). Apparently, older parents and adult children who live in relatively close spatial proximity see each other often, and where distances are greater other contact patterns, especially through the telephone, are maintained.

The data base on contact with other relatives is severely limited. Most researchers, for example, ignore sibling relationships beyond those in childhood. There is even less known about contact with non-child, non-sibling kin. A number of studies report that the proportion of older adults with living siblings, on the average, is about 80% (Clark & Anderson, 1967; Harris & Associates, 1975; Shanas et al., 1968; Youmans, 1963). Compared to the data on contact with children, the amount of interaction with siblings is about half. Our own data report an average of less than one visit and about three phone calls per week between the sample and relatives other than children (Quinn & Mancini, 1979).

There is considerable evidence to suggest that the perception which maintains aged people are isolated from children and other kin is in error. Most elders are in regular contact with members of their family. What are the implications of having contact? Are the lives of older adults enriched by interaction with their family? These questions bring us to a second major myth concerning the family in aging.

PROXIMITY, ENRICHMENT, AND MORALE

Another misunderstanding about the family life of older adults concerns the outcome of family interaction. Does interaction always lead to enrichment? It is this myth that can be most troublesome if we are attempting to strengthen or improve family life. An interesting relationship is posited between physical proximity and psychological closeness. This suggested linkage is essentially a positive one; that is, the greater the physical closeness, the greater the interpersonal bond between the two individuals. In the case of older parents, it is thought that interacting with children on a regular basis bonds one to the other, and necessarily contributes to greater happiness. An outcome variable which has been examined considerably is morale (also called life satisfaction or well-being). Numerous investigators have

attempted to determine the extent to which family interaction
increases morale, and therefore have focused upon both visiting, as well as less direct patterns of family interaction.
Most studies which have examined the amount of contact
and morale have found these two variables to be unrelated
(Edwards & Klemmack, 1973; Mancini, 1979a; Martin, 1973;
Quinn & Mancini, 1979). Apparently morale is not directly
influenced by personal visits, phone contact, or regularity
in letter writing. Several examinations even more strongly
refute the enrichment myth. Kerckhoff (1966) reported that
those older parents who were more distant, and who had a
limited mutual support relationship with children, exhibited
higher morale. Bell (1976) found lower morale to be related
to a greater amount of time invested in the family.

Contact with one's children, per se, in most cases has
little impact on well-being. Of course, in some families
contact and interaction do facilitate or debilitate the older
adult's sense of well-being. Notions which suggest a necessary link between family interaction and well-being are in
error. It is apparent that investigators have neglected to
specify important conditions under which family contact does
influence life quality.

PROGRAM NEEDS AND THE ROLE OF RESEARCH

In suggesting how professionals and programs could potentially
strengthen the family life of older adults, one is confronted
with the lack of empirical data on which to draw. Despite
some major efforts to collate the available data on family
life in the later years (Berardo, 1972; Brubaker & Sneden,
1978; Troll, 1971; Troll, Miller, & Atchley, 1979), there
is relatively little to guide those professionals in the delivery of services sector. Numerous research studies would
have one believe that interacting with family members at best
has no impact on the older adult's well-being, and at worst
has a negative influence. If such is the case, professionals
should implore families and their older members to limit their
contact. However, the amount of contact as a meaningful
measure may be weak. Up until now, we have probably been
asking the wrong questions about older people and their families.

A second issue, one which will linger even when our knowledge base is considerable, concerns the probability of trans-
lating research findings into community programs to enhance
family life. There has long been a "gap" between practice
and research in the family studies field. Are the respective
methods of research and practice sufficiently diverse, as

to insure the severest of difficulties in applying empirical findings?

The social scientist desiring to investigate family life in the later years can choose from a considerable array of research frontiers. Following is a list of potential research questions, the answers to which should provide meaningful information for strengthening the older adult's family life quality.

The Roleless Role

What are the expectations for older family members held by those who are younger? Some years ago, Beard (1949) asked, "Are the aged ex-family?" If the major expectation about the older family member's behavior is one of non-involvement, we might surmise less satisfaction with family life, especially if the older adult desires more involvement.

Use of Time in a Family Context

The social-psychological implications of how time is used is an emerging focus in the social sciences. I have found that older adults, who were more satisfied with their leisure and recreational pursuits, reported higher life satisfaction levels, regardless of their health or economic status (Mancini, 1978). What is the contribution of family-related time use patterns to well-being? Are there specific styles of family leisure interaction which are more conducive to adjustment in old age? Perhaps aged people who spend time with family members in pursuits pleasurable for both are more satisfied with life.

Parental Dependence-Independence

Most older adults feel the forces of dependence and independence simultaneously pulling at them. On the one hand, increasing physical infirmities and economic constraints require further reliance on other family members, particularly children (Seelbach, 1978). However, at the time, human needs for having control over one's own life are operating, as evidenced in the research of Kuypers (1972) and Mancini (1979b). How are these requirements for independence and dependence reconciled in a family, and what implications are there for well-being? Can the average family fill both needs for independence and dependence?

Family Size

Several recent reports have indicated a negative relationship
between the number of living children and the older person's
morale level (Mancini, 1979a; Watson & Kivett, 1976). Thus
far we are lacking an explanation for this somewhat unexpected
relationship, since social class differences had been ac-
counted for in the two previous studies. What social aspect
of family size contributes to lower well-being? In what ways
do the dynamics of smaller families differ from those of
larger families? It is conceivable that larger families represent more worry for the older adult, or may constrain the
parent's independence.

Parent-Child Contact

Although this paper has been primarily oriented toward the
dependent variable of well-being and how contact covaries
with it, a related question concerns what determines the
contact patterns themselves. What relational and situational
factors influence how often older parents and their adult
children interact? Factors to be considered may include geographical distance, social standing of the offpsring compared
to that of the parent, bonding between parent and child, financial constraints, and other non-family role involvements
of both parents and children.

Intergenerational Exchange: Instrumental

One aspect of how parents and children interact regards the
mutual exchange of goods and services. Certainly, both groups
can provide important services to each other in the areas of
economic assistance, home maintenance, and care in time of
sickness (Bild & Havighurst, 1976; Mancini, 1979a). What
are the implications of the exchanges for relationship quality and for the well-being of the older adult? Are there
negative consequences when exchanges are one-sided?

Intergenerational Exchange: Affective

Exchanges can also be intimate in nature. Older parents and
adult children can reciprocate with regard to providing advice on problem-solving, and understanding each other's needs
and feelings (Mancini, 1979a). In other words, each can
serve as a personal source of support on a psychological
level. What is the significance of these exchanges for life
quality? Are affective exchanges with children germane to
the older adult's adaptation?

Confronting Mortality

To what degree does a family help its older adults face impending death? We are often told that death is one of the more sensitive topics of discussion. Although this paper has focused primarily on general adjustment, for the older adult who has severe health difficulties a more specific adjustment regarding the possibility of death is critical. How can both adults and their middle-aged children adapt to movement toward death?

Relational Continuity

One of the three major orientations to explaining adjustment in old age has been termed continuity theory, which "emphasizes the importance of a relatively stable pattern of previously established role behavior" (Bell, 1976, p. 149). Older parent-adult child relations have not received much investigative attention utilizing this continuity perspective, but the approach presents considerable promise. Perhaps to better understand the present quality of parent-child interaction, we need to know something about past relational quality. If parents and children do not get along at earlier life cycle stages, why should we expect them to do so at a later point?

Communication Content

We are fairly confident that contact with other family members is not directly related to well-being. However, what is the communication like within these contact hours? The older adult may be made to feel worthwhile by others, or may be made to feel dependent and helpless. On the other hand, older parents may rebuke an adult child for some "indiscretion," in effect treating the middle-aged person as they would a younger child. What research has not yet told us is how variation in the nature of communication influences whether or not contact is productive.

Family Rituals

How important are family gatherings in the lives of older adults? Does a continued sense of "community" and family integration develop? It is often thought that these gatherings provide a source of comfort and vitality for the aged, but the true importance of these rituals requires further investigation.

Retaining the Parent Role

Some years ago, Rossi (1968) questioned whether the parent
role was ever terminated. Today, most people would agree
the role probably changes in content and context rather than
terminating. However, what might result in those families
where the older parent and adult child differ regarding what
they expect the parent role to be? What are the repercussions for well-being when the middle-aged adult rejects the
parent role presented by the aged parent? Relatedly, how
is the parent-child relational quality influenced by the various ways the parent role can be redefined? To what degree
does the former balance of power prohibit relational quality
(Hess & Waring, 1978)?

WHAT ABOUT THE FUTURE?

There is a substantial need for family life educators who
work with aged people, because by the year 2000 there will
be approximately 31 million Americans over the age of 64.
Presently, we are largely unaware of the unique characteristics of family relations in the later years. Several writers
have stated that family relationships are practically the
most important social relationships for older people (Thompson & Streib, 1961; Ward, 1978). Others have suggested that
"Family members are the greatest resource of elderly persons
for regular social interaction, for psychological and material support . . ." (Bild & Havighurst, 1976, p. 63). These
assumptions may be largely accurate under certain conditions.
However, the task before us is to explicate those situations
where family relations are facilitative of well-being. Once
accomplished, the task of building family strengths for this
age group may be made easier and the methods utilized by family life educators may be more effective. This is an exciting time for family professionals doing research on and
providing services to older adults. As Kaplan (1975) has
pointed out, "We have only begun our knowledge search on
the family in aging" (p. 385).

REFERENCES

Beard, B. Are the aged ex-family? *Social Forces*, 1949, *27*, 272-279.

Bell, B. D. Role set orientation and life satisfaction: A new look at an old theory. In J. F. Gubrium (Ed.), *Time, roles, and self in old age*. New York: Behavioral, 1976.

Berardo, F. (Ed.). Aging and the family. *The Family Co-ordinator*, 1972, *21*, 3-115.

Bild, B., & Havighurst, R. Senior citizens in great cities: The case of Chicago. *The Gerontologist*, 1976, *16*, 3-88.

Brubaker, T., & Sneden, L. (Eds.). Aging in a changing family context. *The Family Coordinator*, 1978, *27*, 301-503.

Clark, M., & Anderson, B. *Culture and aging*. Springfield, Illinois: Thomas, 1967.

Edwards, J., & Klemmack, D. Correlates of life satisfaction: A reexamination. *Journal of Gerontology*, 1973, *28*, 497-502.

Goode, W. J. *World revolution and family patterns*. New York: Free Press, 1963.

The graying of America. *Newsweek*, February 28, 1977, pp. 50-52; 55-58; 63-65.

Harris, L., & Associates. *The myth and reality of aging in America*. Washington, D.C.: National Council on the Aging, 1975.

Hess, B., & Waring, J. Changing patterns of aging and family bonds in later life. *The Family Coordinator*, 1978, *27*, 303-314.

Hill, R., Foote, N., Aldous, J., Carlson, R., & MacDonald, R. *Family development in three generations*. Cambridge, Massachusetts: Schenkman, 1970.

Kaplan, J. The family in aging. *The Gerontologist*, 1975, *15*, 385.

Kerckhoff, A. C. Family patterns and morale in retirement. In I. H. Simpson & J. McKinney (Eds.), *Social aspects of aging*. Durham, North Carolina: Duke University Press, 1966.

Kuypers, J. Internal-external locus of control, ego functioning, and personality characteristics in old age. *The Gerontologist*, 1972, *12*, 168-173.

Linton, R. The natural history of the family. In R. Anshen (Ed.), *The Family: Its function and destiny*. New York: Harper, 1949.

Mancini, J. A. *Role competence and psychological well-being among the elderly*. Unpublished doctoral dissertation, University of North Carolina at Greensboro, 1977.

Mancini, J. A. Leisure satisfaction and psychologic well-being in old age: Health and income effects. *Journal of the American Geriatrics Society*, 1978, *26*, 550-552.

Mancini, J. A. Family relationships and morale among people 65 years of age and older. *American Journal of Orthopsychiatry*, 1979a, *49*.

Mancini, J. A. Effects of health and income on control orientation and life satisfaction among older public housing residents. *International Journal of Aging and Human Development*, 1979b, *10*.

Martin, W. C. Activity and disengagement: Life satisfaction of in-movers into a retirement community. *The Gerontologist*, 1973, *13*, 224-227.

Palmore, E. Facts on aging: A short quiz. *The Gerontologist*, 1977, *17*, 315-320.

Parsons, T. The social structure of the family. In R. Anshen (Ed.), *The Family: Its function and destiny*. New York: Harper, 1949.

Quinn, W., & Mancini, J. A. *Social network interaction among older adults: Implications for life satisfaction*. Paper presented at the annual meeting of the Southeastern Council on Family Relations, Greensboro, North Carolina, April, 1979.

Rossi, A. Transition to parenthood. *Journal of Marriage and the Family*, 1968, *30*, 26-39.

Seelbach, W. Correlates of aged parents' filial responsibility expectations and realizations. *The Family Coordinator*, 1978, *27*, 341-350.

Shanas, E. Family kin networks and aging in cross-cultural perspective. *Journal of Marriage and the Family*, 1973, *35*, 505-511.

Shanas, E. Social myth as hypothesis: The case of the family relations of old people. *The Gerontologist*, 1979, *19*, 3-9.

Shanas, E., Townsend, P., Wedderburn, D., Friis, H., Milhhoj, P., & Stehouver, J. *Older people in three industrial societies.* New York: Atherton, 1968.

Thompson, W., & Streib, G. Meaningful activity in a family context. In R. W. Kleemeier (Ed.), *Aging and leisure.* New York: Oxford, 1961.

Troll, L. The family in later life: A decade review. *Journal of Marriage and the Family*, 1971, *33*, 263-290.

Troll, L., Miller, S., & Atchley, R. *Families in later life.* Belmont, California: Wadsworth, 1979.

Ward, R. Limitations of the family as a supportive institution in the lives of the aged. *The Family Coordinator*, 1978, *27*, 365-374.

Watson, J.A, & Kivett, V. Influences on the life satisfaction of older fathers. *The Family Coordinator*, 1976, *25*, 482-488.

Youmans, E. G. *Aging patterns in a rural and urban area of Kentucky.* Lexington, Kentucky: University of Kentucky Agricultural Experiment Station, 1963.

The Role of Funerals in Strengthening Family Ties

Ruby Gingles, Professor
Emeritus
Department of Human Development
and the Family
University of Nebraska-Lincoln

INTRODUCTION

The death of a loved one leaves a vast and lasting emptiness in the home that can never be completely filled. For the nuclear family, with its close but fewer interrelationships, there are many disruptions of long-standing habits and patterns of interaction. New sources of affection and companionship will be needed. Others in the family will be able to assume some of the roles of the lost member, and adjustments to the loss will be gradually made. It is at this time that the larger extended family can play a valuable role in sharing the crisis of death with the immediate family, and in helping them through their period of grief and adjustment to this loss.

When death comes to a family member, other members are faced with numerous decisions to make in a short time. One of the first questions to be answered is that of the immediate care of the body. Although there are several alternatives, the present discussion will center on funeral and burial rites as the selected avenue. The funeral, with its accompanying rites and customs, serves many functions for the family. First, the funeral serves as a dignified and respectful means of disposal of the physical body. Second it is an announcement of the death of a person, and a testimony to a life which has been lived and is now over. Third, for family and friends, the funeral is an occasion for the final goodbye, as they honor the memory and recognize the human worth of this person's life on earth. The family is saying to the wider kinship family, to friends, and others, "We loved and valued this person for the life that has been lived, and we invite you to join us in sharing our grief and joy at this time."

Finally, the funeral serves an important function in initiating the grief process (Grollman, 1974). One reason for viewing the body in an open casket is to allow each person the opportunity to face the reality of this death, an important step in the transition from the stage of shock to the stage of emotional acceptance. Also, although the person may not "look natural," he or she often looks rested and at peace, thus providing comfort to the family. This seems especially true for very elderly persons or for those who suffered great pain in their final illness. One retains a more pleasant memory than if one's last view of the person was at a time of pain and suffering.

Although the death and funeral may have the greatest impact on the immediate nuclear family, many of the extended family of relatives also may be deeply affected. The major purpose of this article will be to discuss the role of the funeral in reestablishing and strengthening ties among extended family relationships. I believe funerals can perform the following roles:

1. They provide an occasion for the extended family to give sympathy and support to the bereaved nuclear family, helping them to feel they are not alone in their sorrow.

2. They cause one to review one's relationship to the larger family, the meaningfulness of past and present relationships, and perhaps to reevaluate what one's future relationship to the family should be.

3. They serve as an opportunity for the extended family members to meet together as a family unit, somewhat as at a family reunion. There may be new members to meet, old memories to share, and family news to be brought up to date.

4. They can be helpful in teaching children about the existence and meaning of the extended family, perhaps giving them a feeling of security in belonging to this larger network of the family.

In the following review of funeral customs of the past, the role of the family is evident.

HISTORICAL PERSPECTIVE: FUNERAL CUSTOMS
OF THE PAST

The research of sociologists, anthropologists, and historians supports the hypothesis that "humanity is an animal that buries its dead with dignity" (Raether & Slater, 1977, p. 234). In Genesis, the first book of *The Bible*, there is evidence of the preparation of the dead body for burial. The recent

interest shown in the burial customs of the Egyptians, and
the viewing of the rich and elaborate furnishings of the
tomb of the King Tutankhamen is an example of the prevalence
of and importance attached to burial and funeral rites since
early times.

A review of funeral customs in the more recent past may
help one understand the influence of society and family. Since
the bereaved family wants to do what is right in honoring
their deceased member, they will consider the customs of their
religious faith, of the culture in which they live, their
ethnic backgrounds, and the views of their families. Although a younger family may view death somewhat differently
than their parents and grandparents, there will be a recognition of some of those differences, and compromises will be
made between families and generations.

Also, customs tend to change with time and we are affected by these changes. In my 60 years of experience with death
and funerals, as I have observed them, there have been several
changes in the types of funeral or death rites which people
observe and approve. As a middle child of a large German-
Irish farm family, I grew up with a feeling that funerals were
important occasions. The word of death spread quickly;
friends and neighbors called, and brought food to the bereaved family. Close friends offered to "sit up" with the
body. Sitting up with the body at night was not called a
"wake," but may have been a carryover from that custom. In
our community, there were quite a few families of Irish
descent. According to Feifel (1973), "There is a lot of folk
wisdom and emotional support in the Irish wake and the Jewish
shiva. They provide abreaction relief, a working-through and
ultimately enhanced mastery and control over one's feelings"
(pp. 4-5).

My grandfather, who lived with us, died in 1928, at 84
years of age. The custom at that time was to keep the body
in the home, with the undertaker bringing the casket to the
home, and preparing the body for burial. Funerals were sometimes held in the home, but more often in church. Looking
back, I am rather surprised to remember that as children we
took the burial rites much for granted. Death happens often
on a farm, and grandfathers are old and expected to die. We
felt somewhat in awe of his presence, but our tears were shed
for our mother's grief, not ours. Of course, he was her
father, and her relationship was one generation closer to
him.

At church funerals, it seemed that every one came. I
usually sat by my mother and, like her, I wept when the solo-
ist sang a requested hymn such as, "The Old Rugged Cross,"
"Rock of Ages," or "God Be with You 'Til We Meet Again."
From recent studies of the grief process, it would certainly

seem that these funerals initiated the grief process (Calhoun,
Selby, & King, 1976). Also, they let the family know others
cared enough to come and share their sorrow, and to honor their
loved one.

Some 15 years later when my children were small, I was
rather surprised to learn that many childhood "authorities"
believed children should be sheltered from death, not allowed
to view a dead body or to attend a funeral until they were
"older." Some mothers did not want their child to know their
pet had died, but told them it "ran away," or was "lost."
But children's curiosity seemed to be aroused by death, and,
in spite of parental protection, they learned about dead
pets. In our backyard, we have had many solemn funerals and
burials of pets, or of dead birds or animals which have been
found by children.

At about the same time, funerals seemed to become more
subdued. Obituaries were quite brief, and eulogies for the
dead were deemphasized. The funeral service was shortened,
and the songs were less emotional or perhaps omitted. The
aim seemed to be to keep the funeral as unemotional as possible, in order to spare the family _from_ grief. There seemed
to be a subtle consensus that, if there were few or no tears
shed at the funeral, one was managing his or her grief
correctly--"holding up well." Because of my earlier experiences, this type of funeral, though none was of my family,
left me with feelings of confusion and frustration. Was it
best to have only a simple, dignified service? Or should
one show grief openly for the deceased?

In the last 20 years, some gradual changes in attitudes
toward death, which have affected funerals, have been taking
place. I believe a major influence contributing to this
change has been the public awareness and interest in the
study of death and dying. Kübler-Ross (1975), in her work
with terminally ill patients, has discovered they wish to
discuss their death openly with someone. This more open attitude toward death has been accepted by others besides the
terminally ill patients, and there have been some changes
in attitudes toward funerals.

LeShan (1978) deals simply and frankly with children's
feelings about death in her recent book, *Learning to Say
Goodbye: When a Parent Dies*. She has some helpful suggestions for parents to use in communicating with their children
about death, and emphasizes the importance of being open and
honest in answering their questions. Although parents can
again feel freer to deal openly with death, they will need
to use judgment about letting children see a dead person,
or attend a funeral. A grandparent's death may be especially
traumatic for them.

The stages of dying and of grief, as described by Kübler-Ross (1969), Westberg (1976), Calhoun, Selby, and King (1976), and others are similar to each other and are comparable to the stages one goes through in other severe crises. More research is needed to help people understand these stages better. However, knowing now that there are some stages of grief which other bereaved persons experience will help us as we move through the stages of the bereavement process, and eventually make an adjustment to the loss of a loved one. At the present time, and in my experience, funerals seem to evidence a more open feeling toward death and the expression of grief. Occasionally, one hears of a person who has suggested funeral arrangements as a part of their acceptance of this final stage of life, and to help their families prepare for the actual funeral. If not too structured, these plans can then be incorporated as the family strives to have a funeral which appropriately honors the deceased, and is a comfort and source of satisfaction to the family. The body is often viewed openly in the coffin, either at the funeral home or in the church, or both (Kübler-Ross, 1974; Raether & Slater, 1977).

Funerals at the present time are not like those I remember from my youth. There is not as much stress on sadness or on eulogizing the dead. However, there is a similarity, in that they encourage grief, and acknowledge the need for tears and sadness. Though the "old" songs are seldom sung anymore, funerals tend to be more individualized, with the family playing a more active role. Recently, a young son spoke a tribute to his mother at the memorial service. This caused many tears to be shed. At another funeral, the congregation was asked to sing together as part of the service. One song, "How Great Thou Art," reminded me of some of the songs I heard many years ago.

OTHER CUSTOMS OBSERVED AT THE TIME OF DEATH

Another custom which is becoming more common is the memorial service. Raether & Slater (1977) say that, "Every funeral is a memorial service, but not every memorial service is a funeral" (pp. 201-202). They define a funeral as having the body present. The same authors believe that a memorial service without the body present may meet the needs of some individuals, but should be carefully considered and "not based on avoidance of the reality of what has happened or on the fact that it is more convenient" (p. 202).

I have attended some memorial services which seemed to me to be funerals even though the body was not present. Others, less personal in nature, were memorials, but did not seem to fulfill all of the functions of a funeral. When the body or body organs are to be donated for medical purposes, the receiving institution should be consulted about whether or not the body may be present for funeral or memorial services. Also, when the body is cremated, state laws must be observed. The funeral director should know these laws.

The family gathering after the funeral has continued to be a quite definite part of the funeral throughout these several periods of change. The larger kinship family is much in evidence here, and a kind of family reunion takes place. Church members and neighbors bring in food to the home or church, usually more than enough for the anticipated size of the group. Sharing food together plays a comforting and meaningful role in many family and cultural traditions. Thus, eating together after a funeral provides a time for expressing sorrow and shedding some tears, but also for exchanging family news, meeting new family members, and reminiscing about the past. The good times and the bad, as well as the funny and sad, are recalled. A friend says that "her Aunt Myrtle's and her paternal grandmother's were among their 'best' after-funeral family gatherings."

FUNERALS AND THE EXTENDED FAMILY

I have briefly described the functions of funerals and the roles they play in the relationship between the bereaved nuclear family and the larger family kinship network. Past and present funeral rites and customs have been discussed. History indicates that it is a part of the nature of human-kind to dispose of the dead body in a respectful and dignified manner. Over the years and in different cultures there have been many variations in the ceremonies or funerals that take place after death. The variations are due to changing beliefs about death and life after death, to religious teachings, to ethnic traditions, individual circumstances, and other factors. This article is concerned with funerals as they affect the larger, extended family unit, as well as the bereaved nuclear family.

The myths that the nuclear family is isolated, that the extended family no longer exists, and that the elderly family members are lonely and neglected have been dispelled by researchers such as Sussman (1965) and Shanas (1979). Although I was unable to find any research in the literature about funeral roles of the extended family, I thought it was an interesting area to explore. It is known that older family members often keep in touch and help meet needs of the young family in many ways. Also, they give their sympathy and support to the bereaved family during times of illness

and death. Following are some further thoughts about the
roles the funeral plays in strengthening family ties and
keeping family members in touch with each other. These
four roles were briefly discussed in the introduction to
this article.

1. The extended family gives sympathy. When death occurs
   in a family, one of the first actions is to let other family members know about it. The extended family may immediately respond by offering to help with further telephone calls, or to assist with funeral arrangements,
   shopping, tasks in the home, etc. Family members living
   nearby will probably join neighbors and friends in making
   calls to offer sympathy, to bring in food, or to help
   in other ways. Those family members who live farther
   away may call to offer sympathy and help, to ask about
   funeral arrangements, and to let the bereaved family
   know if they will be able to attend the funeral. Their
   decision about attending the funeral will depend on
   feelings of closeness, travel distance, health, and
   other obligations.

   All of these expressions of sympathy give comfort and
   support to the nuclear family of the deceased. In
   small families, they may be especially appreciated.
   My husband's older brother died recently, and, having
   no surviving widow or children, left his one brother
   with a deep sense of loss and loneliness. He very
   much appreciated calls from his brother's five nephews
   and a sister-in-law. Despite the assurance that it
   was not necessary, the oldest nephew and the sister-
   in-law came, with some inconvenience and from a distance,
   to attend the funeral, and to remain for a day to
   discuss the details of disposing of belongings and
   settling the estate. Their presence was a very real
   comfort to him; as the now oldest living member of
   that family, he was assured he was not alone.

   The sympathy and support patterns may go from older to
   younger families, or from the younger to the older. In
   either direction, the funeral brings the family together in a setting which provides a means of reaf-
   firming family ties.

2. Reviewing one's relationship to the deceased family
   member and to the larger extended family. As each
   person receives the news of a death in the family,
   memories will be evoked of one's associations with
   that person throughout the years. The cause of death,

age of the deceased, the memory of the last time spent
together, as well as one's total life involvement with
that relative will be reviewed. Especially if the relationship has been close and over a long period of time,
memories will extend to many family relationships, and
what they have meant in one's life.

This review of experiences shared with the deceased relative may be painful, sad, and joyous, as most relationships are characterized with mixed emotions. If
one attends the funeral, more reminiscing will take place.
The eventual result may be to reevaluate the meaning
of one's relationship to the extended family, and perhaps to resolve to keep in closer touch, or to reassure
oneself that the relationship you now have is satisfactory to you and you want to continue it even though
one member is gone.

3. An opportunity for the extended family to meet together
    as a family unit. The dinner served after the funeral
    to the extended family has been discussed briefly as
    another custom related to funerals. The importance of
    this custom seems verified by its existence and continua-
    tion throughout the years. The shared meal, provided
    by the church, friends, and neighbors, serves many func-
    tions. It is a way to express sympathy; it provides a
    reason for the bereaved family to spend time together;
    it is a symbol of the family's shared bonds; and it is
    a recognition of the passing of life from one generation
    to the next.

This is a time when grief may be expressed and reminiscences about the deceased family member may be shared.
These memories may be sorrowful, joyful, sometimes
humorous, and seem to help provide what Feifel (1973)
calls "abreaction relief." Recollection of humorous
events or of oddities in the deceased's personality,
which may have seemed annoying at times, may now be
viewed with affectionate acceptance.

The funeral gathering is somewhat like a family reunion
in which family members, as related above, may exchange
family news, meet new family members, and reminisce
about the past. Also family members provide support
to each other as they share some common losses. Siblings and cousins, now growing older, are experiencing
the loss of parents and spouses. Relatives of their
peer group, who had shared childhood experiences with

them, now become closer as they understand each other's concerns, and share an affectional bond.

4. An <u>appropriate</u> <u>time</u> to <u>help</u> the <u>children</u> <u>find</u> <u>their</u>
   <u>place in the extended family group</u>. LeShan's (1978)
   book is devoted to the education of children in the
   many aspects of death. Grollman (1974) has an excellent chapter about children and death in his book of
   readings. Writers in popular, as well as professional,
   publications have since been writing on this topic for
   the benefit of parents.

   The funeral serves as an excellent opportunity to share
   with your children your understanding of death, the
   meaning of funerals and other burial rites, and to talk
   about the extended family. Those children who live at
   a distance from their grandparents' homes or home towns,
   may have missed out on how they fit into the family.
   Depending upon their age and experiences with the family, and the meaning of family ties to parents, the death
   and funeral seem natural times to explain their relationship to the dead, and the place this person's life
   had in their parents' lives and in the larger family.
   It may begin to give them a feeling of security in
   "belonging" to two family kinships groups, and to gain
   some understanding of the continuity of the family life
   cycle.

   The funeral will probably arouse children's curiosity
   about death, the funeral rites, and about members of
   the family and friends. These questions may help parents
   perceive the level of the child's understanding, and
   lead to expanding knowledge to the extent that he or
   she is ready to absorb.

In all areas of family life, our hopes for building family
strengths in the future depend largely on how well we educate
the next generation. We need to broaden our children's knowledge and understanding in such areas as equality and respect
for both sexes, sex education, marriage, parenting in both
one- and two-parent families, the value of having family members of all ages, and the importance of both the nuclear family unit and the extended family. The funeral, which is a
means of recognizing the human dignity of each life and death,
can play a role by using the strengths of the extended family, if society and the family encourage involvement of the
larger family kinship network.

REFERENCES

Calhoun, L. G., James, W. S., & King, H. E. *Dealing with crises.* Englewood Cliffs, New Jersey: Prentice-Hall, 1976.

Feifel, H. Introduction. In R. David (Ed.), *Dealing with death.* Los Angeles: Ethel Percy Andrus Gerontology Center, University of Southern California, 1973.

Grollman, E. A. (Ed.). *Concerning death: A practical guide for the living.* Boston: Beacon Press, 1974.

Kübler-Ross, E. *On death and dying.* New York: Macmillan, 1969.

Kübler-Ross, E. *Questions and answers on death and dying.* New York: Macmillan, 1974.

Kübler-Ross, E. *Death: The final stage of growth.* Englewood Cliffs, New Jersey: Prentice-Hall, 1975.

LeShan, E. *Learning to say goodbye: When a parent dies.* New York: Avon Books, 1978.

Raether, H. C., & Slater, R. C. *Immediate postdeath activities in the United States.* New York: McGraw-Hill, 1977.

Shanas, E. The family as a social support system in old age. *The Gerontologist, 1979, 19,* 169-174.

Sussman, M. B. Relationships of adult children with their parents in the United States. In E. Shanas & C. Streib (Eds.), *Social structure and the family: Generation relations.* Englewood Cliffs, New Jersey: Prentice-Hall, 1965.

Westberg, G. E. *Good grief.* Philadelphia: Fortress Press, 1976.

Dr. Joan Weisman
College of Lifelong Learning
Wayne State University

INTRODUCTION

Hope for the future lies with the child: the old
man rooted in the past is the custodian of knowledge. It is this connection that binds the
society's unity throughout time. (de Beauvoir,
1972)

. . . something for which I have pleaded all my
life--that everyone needs to have access both
to grandparents and grandchildren in order to be
a full human being. (Mead, 1972)

How young children view grandparents in their families
might not be the same as how they view old people in general.
It will be the focus of this paper to explore what the attitudes are between generations within the family, outside the
family, and toward aging in general, and to propose that influencing these attitudes will benefit all family members.
The findings on children's perceptions of the elderly
are somewhat contradictory, but there is general agreement
that most young children know very few people over 75
(Phenice, 1978), and that their attitudes toward the aged
and toward their own aging is negative (Jantz et al., 1977).
Because these negative attitudes were found so early in the
child's life when the home is his/her prime influence, one
must call this a family problem and parents and grandparents
must be shown the importance of shaping children's attitudes.
Children must be taught to understand aging as a natural
developmental process of growth, and families must share their
lives with old people so everyone can benefit from the linkage with the past and from mutual support and affection.
Social contact between the young and the elderly might
ameliorate the negative attitudes (Hickey & Kalish, 1968).

355

Programs that involve the elderly and children must be initiated and existing programs expanded.

Children's books are another avenue to shape the child's
image of aging. Unfortunately, many of the books perpetuate
the myth of old people as forever sweet, passive, and dull
(Barnum, 1977).

FROM THE PERSPECTIVE OF OLD PEOPLE

Her extravagant love of the past was a way of
continuing to be a mother, now that she was only
a grandmother. (Wescott, 1962)

In the presence of grandparent and grandchild,
past and future merge in the present. For seeing
a child as one's grandchild, one can visualize
that same child as a grandparent, and with the
eyes of another generation one can see other
children. (Mead, 1972)

Quite a bit is known about the grandparent role, less
about the viewpoint of old people to children in general.

Neugarten (1968) found that the significance of grandparenting for most older people was the feeling of family
continuity. Very few people looked to the grandchildren as
a source of support. Blau (1973) has said that as far as
a supportive position goes "one real friend is worth a dozen
grandchildren."

Some of the older people in Neugarten's (1968) Chicago
study saw grandparenthood as a source of emotional self-
fulfillment. The grandparents who are increasingly apt to
be middle-aged (Kahana & Kahana, 1970) found this role as a
new chance for parenthood, this time without the stress of
career struggles or total responsibility. Some of them looked
on themselves as resource persons deriving satisfaction from
contributing to the child's welfare. There are those who
were less altruistic and looked forward to reflecting in the
glow of the child's achievements and beauty. Twenty-seven
percent of the grandmothers and 29 percent of the grandfathers were remote from their grandchildren. For them the
role had little significance; the women, primarily middle-
aged, were caught up in work and community, while the men
said they were waiting until the child was older.

In some cases there was conflict with the young family.
Robertson (1975) suggests that it is the parent generation
which brings old and young together. It is the middle generation which determines how much interaction there will be
between children and their grandparents.

When the Harris (1976) group asked people over 65 when
they had last seen their grandchildren, 46 percent answered
within a day or so, and 28 percent more said within the last
week or two. That is certainly frequent, but determining the
quality of the interaction might be more significant. The
quality of interaction differs according to how older people
perceive their role as grandparents, in what way the middle
generation mediates the situation, and according to the style
of grandparenting.

Neugarten (1968) noted five different styles of grandparenting. The first style, the formal, involves the indul-
gent, gift giving, perhaps doting, grandparent. This style
of grandparenting is a phenomenon in contemporary America
(Fischer, 1978). The second is the fun-seeker, a style which
affords mutual pleasure to child and grandparent. This probably
offers the most self-fulfillment. These are people who find
meaning in life through children (Feldman, 1977) and to whom
grandchildren are a great source of pleasure. The surrogate
parent style, a role usually taken by women whose children
are employed or ill, involves assuming various degrees of
responsibility for the rearing of the children. The reser-
voir of family wisdom is usually a role taken by a male and
an authority figure. Lastly, the distant figure role is
played by a grandparent who is remote, similar to the formal
role as far as indulging the child goes, but with infrequent
contact. Robertson (1976) suggests that the remote grandparents are generally distant characters in all their interpersonal relationships.

As far as old people's attitudes, there are undoubtedly
many who are happy to be free of the noise and problems of
young children. There are also those who find great satisfaction being involved with children. Approximately 14,000
people over 60 in the United States are involved in the U.S.
Fostergrandparent Program which benefits both older persons
and children. The success of this program attests to the
affinity of some older persons and children, and mutual benefits possible for both.

Other examples of programs where older people have enjoyed sharing affection and/or skills and wisdom with children, such as the TLC project in Ann Arbor, Michigan, and
the Foxfire concept in Appalachia, will be discussed later
in this paper.

At the February, 1979 meeting of the Detroit Women's
Forum, a young woman was pleading the cause of child care,
especially for single parents. An elderly black woman representing Seniors National Black Caucus on Aging rose and asked
why we were overlooking the great resource--people who have
already reared children, who love them, and who need employment.

Why indeed? When searching for alternatives in child care, the older person who relates well to children must be included.

There may be many old people who find even their own grandchildren troublesome and noisy. They see grandparenting as a sign of aging and they do not wish to join "SOGPP-- Silly Old Grandma with Pictures in Purse" (Huyck, 1974). But informal evidence is all around us of old people who long for contact with children. There are old people who speak of neighbors' children as their own, and they remember them at birthdays and holidays, and act as confidants to them. We see them watching the little ones in the park. In the nursing home they reach out to touch the child who has been brought to visit some lucky grandparent. Curtin (1972) recalls her childhood visits to the old folks' home: "Their hands reaching out to touch and tug and pull and exclaim over my hair, my freckles, my blue eyes . . . . Come back soon, come back and see us, we'll have a party."

FROM THE CHILDREN'S POINT OF VIEW

. . . . I could easily have impersonated, in
trance, the child and girl my grandmother had
been. (Mead, 1972)

Old people are perceived by children as very nice to children or quite mean and unkind. They are seen as lonely, bored, inactive, and possessed of much leisure time (Hickey & Kalish, 1968). Unfortunately children maintain these beliefs which determine to some degree how they will deal with older people as adults, and how they will feel about their own aging.

When three-, four- and five-year-olds were asked what the word old meant and whether they would like to be old someday, their answers were overwhelmingly negative (Treybig, 1974). Children's experience with old people outside the family is limited and they tend to ascribe more negative feelings to them (Bekker & Taylor, 1966).

Young children have mixed and confused ideas of older people, especially outside the family. "A grandfather is a man grandmother" (Huyck, 1974), and "Old people are sick, ugly, sad, rich and good" (Jantz et al., 1977) are examples of children's confused perceptions.

Sheehan (1978) found that there is more interaction between children and old people outside the family than is generally believed, and the more frequent the contact, the more realistically children identify old people. The quality

of interaction was not known, so one can assume there is much
room for establishing meaningful contacts.

Within the family, the maternal grandmother is usually
the favored grandparent (Kahana & Kahana, 1970). The reasons
given by children for favoring a particular grandparent were
based on the stage of development of the child (Kahana &
Kahana, 1970). Thus, young children would be close to the
formal style grandparent who dotes on them and showers them
with gifts and affection. A slightly older youngster, say
eight years old and less egocentric, would like to share activities and would choose a fun-seeker for a favorite grandparent.

Young people with great-grandparents are less apt to
ascribe stereotypic characteristics of old age to their
grandparents, possibly because of an expanded range of experience with aging due to their complex family structure
(Bekker & Taylor, 1966).

BRINGING THEM TOGETHER: HOW TO DO IT

Maude began by telling us about her childhood:
"We didn't have th' things that children's got
now, but we didn't have 'em and we didn't look
fer 'em." (Wigginton, 1973)

The Foxfire concept of education is based on an active
exchange of information and friendship between school children and neighboring old people. Old people have come to
the school to visit and teach the younger children. The
older youngsters go out in search of the elderly in the
Appalachian community. They establish friendships and learn
the skills and tales which are their heritage (Wigginton,
1978). The children in the project are learning that old
people can be independent, interesting, and individualistic.
This concept, perhaps in different forms for different communities, could be adopted throughout the country.

Nellie Cuellar, Detroit coordinator for Seniors National
Black Caucus on Aging, is trying to organize an Adopt-a-
Grandparent program as an alternative to day care, especially
for single parent families. Child care wages would be paid
the elderly person who would share holidays and other events
with the family. The person would also receive support and
friendship from the family to create an atmosphere of mutual
concern.

The U.S. Fostergrandparent Program is aimed at bene-
fiting both children and older persons. It has been in existence since 1975, and has been extremely successful. Participating older people report improved self-esteem, a purpose

to life, subjective feelings of greater health and vigor,
and from the stipend which each receives, a financial boost
to marginal incomes (Saltz, 1977). The children they work
with in residential institutions, hospitals, and day care
centers benefit from the strong bond of affection. Phenice
(1978) reports that although the children in a day care center
with a foster grandparent did not look more positively at
old people in general than did the children in a center without the program, they could think of more things to do with
older people and, more important, they felt less negative
about their own aging. Perhaps there was so little attitude
change because the foster grandparents had become family
and therefore were not thought of as belonging to the category of "old people." They were, instead, "my grandma, my
grandpa."

New programs are being instituted all over the country
with measurable benefits for children and for the elderly.
In Oklahoma, old people taught history to preschool children.
The children understood the concept of change more fully than
when their teachers presented the same material (Powell &
Arquitt, 1978).

As part of the war on poverty, volunteer tutorial programs were instituted in inner city schools. Many of them
used older people working in a one-to-one relationship with
children which provided real help to the children, satisfaction to the volunteers, and opportunity for intergenerational
friendships.

Teaching, Learning Communities (TLC) is an innovative
program operating in the Ann Arbor, Michigan schools. Old
people assist in the art classes, sharing their skills and
traditions. Carole Tice, project director, originated the
program to add a dimension to the lives of the children and
the older people:

> It is a mutually supportive experience, it re-
> stores the experience of the extended family in
> a society where the family structure is being
> ripped apart. It brings a sense of the past and
> the future together and allows people to feel
> more in control of the present. (Tice, 1979)

Seefeldt (1977) envisions an elderly volunteer school
program which would include orientation training for the
volunteer, the teacher, and the children. Even those persons who do not wish to be involved in relationships with
children could demonstrate crafts or help in other ways.

Established programs, such as Head Start and Senior
Citizen Centers, can try various types of collaboration
(Powell & Arquitt, 1978). Exchange visits, trips, craft

classes, and story hours would cost little and would enrich both groups.

There will have to be wider exposure to other models of aged people to influence the perceptions of old people and attitudes towards aging.

CHILDREN'S BOOKS--A ROUTE INTO DIVERSE MODELS

Grandparents must be of use to the child--they must be able to protect him, teach him, feed him; if they are not, then they are reduced to a lower form of existence. (Bettleheim, 1977)

Red Riding Hood's helpless grandmother prompted this observation from Bettleheim. Another traditional story in which old characters play important supporting roles is "The Gingerbread Boy." In examining six versions currently available to young children, I found that the word "little" was used to describe all but one couple. Two men carried walking sticks and four men and two women wore spectacles on the ends of their noses. All the women worked in the kitchen and five of the men tended the garden or worked with wood. However, in one respect, the little old people were not stereotypic at all. They had no grandchildren.

Children's books have all kinds of grandparents: stereotyped, nonsexist, swinging, friend, babysitter, stranger, senile, boring, and grandparent as guardian (Constant, 1977). There seems to be a grandparent to fit all five of the Neugarten styles, plus a few extra. Grandparents are always at home, and never doing interesting things outside the house according to Barnum (1977). Old people are depicted as passive or incompetent and these books reinforce negative stereotypes about old age.

Storey (1977) thinks that other adjectives besides old and wrinkled should be used, and that the old do not always have to be depicted bent over, white-haired, and living in antique houses.

Sadker and Sadker (1977) found quite a few books to recommend for young children, but they wish there was less constriction and limitation of role depiction. In general, the image is positive, even idealized, but dull.

An exception to the positive image is the mean old witch. She is usually in books for children in the grades beyond kindergarten, and her ugliness and extreme old age are part of her terrifying picture.

Book burning is not in order if the older person is depicted as ugly, mean, foolish, or unduly passive. Instead, the parent can be sure that the book selection has books

that show the elderly in a positive light. Among the positive
depictions, there are many that are stereotypic. The character is portrayed as loving, wearing spectacles on the end of
his/her nose, and sitting in a rocking chair by the fire. But
when firsthand experiences with the elderly are combined with
the widest variety of books, children will move toward forming their own ideas of what old people are like (Storey, 1977).

On the assumption that children's literature serves as
a major agent of socialization, Seltzer and Atchley (1971)
studied children's books from 1870 to 1960. They found there
were progressively more negative images of the elderly over
the years, but that on the whole the portrayals were neither
as stereotypic nor as negative as other gerontologists have
reported.

SUMMARY AND CONCLUSION

Everyone who lives a long time will grow old,
mothers and fathers, teens, you, the toddlers
and yes, even the baby. (Weisman, 1978)

Respectful and caring attitudes between small children
and old people in the family and in the community can offer
the family the benefits of mutual support and affection with
the sense of continuity providing new strength. It will
show children that aging is a natural developmental stage,
and it will promote positive attitudes about aging in the
children, the older persons, and the parents of the children.

In order to bring this about, the parent generation
will have to act energetically as positive mediators between
children and grandparents. Communities will have to be encouraged to devise programs and expand others which will give
children the opportunity for interaction with old people.
Children's books can present diverse models of old people and
aging.

In conclusion, awareness of the importance of intergenerational relationships must reach families, institutions,
and agencies which deal with young children and old people.
When all concerned are aware, meaningful interactions can be
arranged on an individual level, and through the schools,
community centers, churches, senior centers, and homes for
the aged. Everyone, child and adult, who actively participates in a wide range of intergeneration activities will find
rich rewards.

Young children's books as well as other media must be
selected so that children will understand that old people are
diverse, and that they are not all sick, bent, and passive,
but that they can be vigorous, involved, and interesting.

REFERENCES

Barnum, P. W. The aged in young children's literature. *Language Arts*, 1977, *54*, 29-32.

Bekker, L. D., & Taylor, C. Attitudes towards the aged in a multigenerational sample. *Journal of Gerontology*, 1966, *21*, 115-118.

Bettleheim, B. *The uses of enchantment*. New York: Vintage Books, 1977.

Blau, Z. S. *Old age in a changing society*. New York: Franklin Watts, 1973.

Constant, H. The image of grandparents in children's literature. *Language Arts*, 1977, *54*, 33-40.

Curtin, S. *Nobody ever died of old age*. Boston: Little Brown, 1972.

de Beauvoir, S. *Coming of age*. New York: Putnam, 1972.

Feldman, H., Penelope, M., & Narcissus, S. In L. Troll, J. Israel, & K. Israel (Eds.), *Looking ahead*. Englewood Cliffs, New Jersey: Prentice-Hall, 1977.

Fischer, D. H. *Growing old in America*. New York: Oxford University Press, 1978.

Harris, L. *The myth and reality of aging in America.* Washington, D.C.: National Council on Aging, 1976.

Hickey, T., & Kalish, R. A. Young people's perceptions of adults. *Journal of Gerontology*, 1968, *23*, 215-220.

Huyck, M. H. *Growing older*. Englewood Cliffs, New Jersey: Prentice-Hall, 1974.

Jantz, R. K., Seefeldt, C., Galper, A., & Serlock, K. Children's attitudes toward the elderly. *Social Education*, 1977, *41*, 518-523.

Kahana, B., & Kahana, E. *Children's views of their grandparents: Influences of the kinship system*. Paper presented at the twenty-third meeting of the Gerontological Society, Toronto, Canada, October, 1970.

Kahana, B., & Kahana, E. Grandparenthood from the perspective of the developing grandchild. *Developmental
Psychology*, 1970, *3*, 98-105.

Mead, M. *Blackberry winter: My earlier years*. New York:
William Morris, 1972.

Neugarten, B. L., & Weinstein, K. The changing American
grandparent. In B. L. Neugarten (Ed.), *Middle age and
aging*. Chicago: University of Chicago Press, 1968.

Phenice, L. A. *Children's perceptions of elderly persons*.
Unpublished doctoral dissertation, Michigan State
University, East Lansing, 1978.

Powell, T., & Arquitt, G. E. Getting the generations back
together: A rationale for development of community
based intergenerational programs. *The Family Coordinator*, 1978, *27*, 421-426.

Robertson, J. F. Interaction in three generation families,
parents as mediators: Toward a theoretical perspective.
International Journal of Aging and Human Development,
1975, *6*, 103-109.

Robertson, J. F., & Wood, V. The significance of grandparenthood. In J. F. Gubrium (Ed.), *Times, roles
and self in old age*. New York: Human Sciences Press,
1976.

Sadker, D. M., & Sadker, M. P. Growing old in the literature of the young. In *Now upon a time: A contemporary
view of children's literature*. New York: Harper &
Row, 1977.

Saltz, R. Fostergrandparenting: A unique child-care service. In L. Troll et al. (Eds.), *Looking ahead*.
Englewood Cliffs, New Jersey: Prentice-Hall, 1977.

Seefeldt, C. Young and old together. *Children Today*, 1977,
6, 21-25.

Seltzer, M. M., & Atchley, R. C. The concept of old: Changing
attitudes and stereotypes. *The Gerontologist*, 1971,
2, 226-230.

Sheehan, R. Young children's contact with the elderly.
Journal of Gerontology, 1978, *33*, 567-574.

Storey, D. C. Grey power: An endangered species. Ageism as portrayed in children's books. *Social Education,* 1977, *41*, 528-530.

Tice, C. *From childhood to old age: Four generations teaching each other.* Esalen Institute/University of Michigan Extension Service Conference, Southfield, Michigan, 1979.

Treybig, D. C. Language, children and attitudes toward the aged. *The Gerontologist,* 1974, *14*, 14-75.

Weisman, J. *How old is old?* Detroit: Program Resources, 1978.

Wescott, G. *The grandmothers.* New York: Atheneum, 1962.

Wigginton, E. *An address.* Presented at the Thirteenth National Colloquim and Workshop of the Oral History Association, Savannah, Georgia, October, 1978.

Wigginton, E. (Ed.). *Foxfire 2.* New York: Doubleday, 1973.

THE GINGERBREAD BOY REFERENCES

Galdone, P. *The gingerbread boy.* New York: Seaburg Press, 1975.

Holdsworth, W. *The gingerbread boy.* New York: Farrar, Strauss, 1968.

Rojankovsky, F. *The tall book of nursery tales.* New York: Harper, 1944.

Rutherford, B. *The gingerbread man.* Racine, Wisconsin: Golden Press, 1963.

Sawyer, R. *Journey cake, ho!* New York: Viking, 1953.

Sukkas, J. *The gingerbread man.* Racine, Wisconsin: Whitman, 1969.

VI. BUILDING STRENGTHS IN FAMILIES WITH SPECIAL NEEDS

Not all families fit the traditional form of father-bread-
winner, mother-homemaker, two children, house in the suburbs. Nor should they. Recognition has grown for the
family as a dynamic unit existing in a variety of forms.
Professionals who deal with families recognize that, while
all families benefit by enhanced relationships, improved
communication, etc., certain families have special needs.
These families need specialized programs and strategies
for building family strengths.

Sue Bean describes the Parent Aide Support Service, a
program using parent aide volunteers to help abusive or
neglectful parents. Parent aides offer friendship and
support to these parents. The philosophy of P.A.S.S. and
methods of training volunteers are given.

The next two articles deal with foster care of children. Dr. Dorothy Martin, Marty Moore, and Patricia Housley
detail a program for training foster parents. The content
of the program and ideas for establishing a similar program are shared.

Dr. Karen Edwards describes a program in which relatively mature adolescents are placed in foster care with
university students. Both the adolescents and the university students benefit.

Some ideas on providing services to families with a
handicapped member are given in the next two articles.
Dr. Lois Schwab, Virginia Wright, and Mary Cassatt-Dunn
make a case for a family-centered program of services for
disabled persons. Such a program can allow individualized planning for the disabled person and his or her family.

Dr. Marty Abramson, Dr. Michael Ash, Dr. Douglas Palmer,
and Patricia Tollison present a life-span approach to the
changing needs of families with a handicapped person. They
propose the use of trained volunteers to coordinate the
efforts of all agencies and professionals who serve handicapped persons.

Finally, Dr. Helen Cleminshaw and Dr. Gary Peterson
propose that the divorce process offers opportunities for
growth along with crises. They urge the use of those
opportunities to build strengths within those families.

The Parent Aide Support Service: How Volunteers Effect Growth in Abusive and Neglectful Parents

Susan D. Bean
P.A.S.S./Child Protective Service
Lancaster County Public Welfare
Lincoln, Nebraka

PHILOSOPHY

When I thought I would mould you, an image from
my life for men to worship, I brought my dust
and desires and all my coloured delusions and
dreams.

When I asked you to mould with my life an
image from your heart for you to love, you
brought your fire and force, and truth, love-
liness and peace.

> --Rabindranath Tagore
> *Fruit Gathering*, XXXIII

The above philosophy embodies the goals of the Parent
Aide Support Service--to help parents achieve a self, through
involvement in a relationship which encourages them to grow
and strive in ways which are meaningful to them. It also
sets the tenor of the project administration; we believe that
the way the project is run gives life and meaning to the relationship between our volunteers and parents. We know the
reasons that parent aides give of themselves and of their
time are because they want to help stop child abuse and neglect, because they enjoy nurturing others, and because it
is a satisfying, growing experience for them. We, at the project, wish to encourage the volunteers' personal growth by
our respect and caring, just as they do with their parents.
This paper discusses the process by which we provide
that support to volunteers, the relationship skills which
volunteers use naturally or that we encourage them to use,
and the process which seems to take place as the parents grow
and change within their relationship with the volunteers.

SCREENING, TRAINING, PLACEMENT

We believe that the project's screening and training process
is a very important part of our volunteer support system because:

1. It establishes an initial bond between the supervisor
    and the volunteer.

2. The self-disclosing which occurs during training not
    only helps the volunteer to know himself or herself, it
    helps each person to begin to develop a caring for the
    other members of the group.

3. The cohesive group feeling which develops during train-
    ing continues during the monthly group meetings.

   The screening and placement process is outlined in detail in Appendix A. Basically, it consists of an initial
meeting with the project supervisor, 18 hours of training, a
final screening and commitment meeting with the project supervisor, the match of parent and parent aide, a family staffing,
and finally, the referral person accompanying the aide to
meet the parent.
   During that first meeting, the supervisor explains the
program goals and expectations, and the importance of this
kind of one-to-one relationship for the abusive parent. The
supervisor also begins to establish supportive relationships
with the volunteers by helping them explore the kind of involvement they expect, and how it will fulfill some of their
own needs. We have found that, although it is important to
stress the amount of giving which is done by the volunteer
to the parent, we need to recognize from the beginning that
the aide will also be fulfilling some of his or her personal
needs and goals by this experience. If the need fulfillment
is healthy, such as "having a personal growth experience,"
it is encouraged. However, we question the involvement of
those who are in need of emotional nurturing themselves or
who are at a stressful point in their own lives.
   The 18 hours of training are divided into six sessions
of three hours each, in groups of eight to twelve. During
training, we try to maintain a balance of information giving
and personal, individual exploration. We stress that the
volunteers' greatest asset will be the natural warmth and
caring which occurs between parents; we are careful not to
"overtrain" them with skills which may interfere with that
spontaneity.

Before the second individual meeting with the supervisor, the aides will have completed the "Parent Aide Information Form," which consists of some basic personal information for the project and 11 questions designed to help them assess their readiness to volunteer. The supervisor then discusses with the volunteers their personal abilities and strengths, and assesses whether they have the following skills which we consider essential: ability to communicate, empathy, flexibility, capacity for having their own needs fulfilled elsewhere, and a sense of humor. If the aides wish to continue with the project, the supervisor also gains some specific information to help in doing a better job of matching the volunteers with parents.

Most importantly, it is during this meeting that the supervisor asks for a year's commitment to the project; this is a simple verbal statement that the volunteer will stay with us for one year. My commitment to the volunteers is to be available and to work together on the problems they encounter. It is too early at this point to ask for a commitment to their parents, so I ask for the commitment to be made to me, personally. This agreement between the volunteers and me seems to be very binding. One of the aides had a parent who was very tough to "get through to," and each visit to the home was a depressing experience. I asked the aide what kept her going, and she said the fact that she had given her word to me. Six months later, the aide and parent have a very close relationship; the parent shows some very caring feelings for her children, and she now initiates phone calls and visits with the aide.

At the end of one year, we have 22 parent aides actively working with 23 families. Six of our volunteers are Junior League members; the others were recruited in the community. Twenty of the aides are women and two are men. Nineteen of them are married, two are divorced or separated, and one has not married. Two of the aides do not have any children of their own. They range in age from 21 to 45. Eight work outside the home full-time.

Although the parent aide/parent match is done as much by the intuition of the supervisor as by objective information, we do consider the following: personalities of both the aide and parent, ages, past experiences, hobbies or activities each are involved in, needs of the parent, intensity of the relationship desired by both, work status, geographic location, and accessibility by phone.

Of the 23 families currently matched, four family situations involve abuse only, 15 involve neglect only, three involve both abuse and neglect, and one parent who referred herself because she felt she could become abusive. We have six married couples, four who are now separated, eight who

are divorced, and five mothers who have never married. The
median income range is $4,000 to $4,500 per year. The children range from just a few weeks old to 14 years, but the
vast majority are three years and under (see Table 1).

Table 1

Parent Aide Support Service Family Data

Total number of families matched with parent aides		23
Presenting problem:	child abuse only	4
	child neglect only	15
	both neglect and abuse	3
	self-referral	1
Marital status:	never married	5
	married	6
	divorced	8
	separated	4
Number of children per family:	1 child	7
	2 children	4
	3 children	10
	4 children	2

Annual income (data on eight families not available):

Range:	Number of Families
$2,500-3,000	2
$3,000-3,500	1
$3,500-4,000	2
$4,000-4,500	3
$4,500-5,000	1
$5,000-5,500	3
$5,500-6,000	0
$6,000-7,000	1
$7,000-8,000	2

The families have evidenced many of the socio-cultural and psychological factors which authorities in the field, notably C. Henry Kempe, Ray Helfer, Brandt Steele, and Murray A. Straus, have found occur frequently in abusive and neglectful families. These include isolation, low self-esteem, role reversals, poor parenting as a child, an unsupportive spouse, high stress and numerous crises, and low economic level. However, the situations which bring the families to our project vary greatly: a married woman whose one-year-old consistently had head injuries; a very depressed, single, 29-year-old who has left her daughter alone and seems to provide little emotional support; a young mother just released from jail, and working to have her three-year-old daughter returned to her from foster care; an incestuous family in which the mother knows she needs to develop some personal strengths to regain her mother role; a married woman whose two children appeared at a day care center with bruises on their necks; an alcoholic mother who is neglectful; a young teen living in a foster home with her son; and a 19-year-old mother of one who kicked her drug and alcohol addiction when she found out she was pregnant at 17.

We ask the referring person to introduce the aide to the family. As well as helping both to feel more at ease, this is a good time to discuss role expectations of each, and to ascertain that the parent knows that, although what is shared with the aide is confidential, if any abuse or neglect is observed it will have to be reported. This knowledge has not seemed to hinder the relationship once a basic trust is established. To this point, we have only had to make one such report.

Although we have not yet calculated the life expectancy for parent aides, there certainly are hazards. Recently, we were surprised that one volunteer even stayed for the introductions. At the staffing, the caseworker and I had detailed the rather chaotic life style of a particular young parent of three preschoolers. The parent aide thought we were exaggerating until she and the caseworker drove up to the house for the first visit just in time to see a burning mattress come flying out the door at the same time a fire truck arrived. One of the children had ignited it playing with a cigarette lighter. However, after three visits, the parent aide says she and the parent get along well, and talk non-stop to one another.

The volunteers submit a short report at the end of each month detailing the hours spent with their parents, what activities they participated in, and any concerns they wish us to be made aware of. These reports provide needed information for the project and make the caseworker generally aware of the aides' involvement.

On-going support is provided through once-a-month group meetings and once-a-month individual meetings with the supervisor. We feel both are equally important. The group meetings provide peer support and discussion of feelings and common problems; the individual meetings help the aide establish some direction in the relationship and work on enhancing personal skills, especially in the area of communication. I try to help the aides discover new modes of operating which may be helpful to their parent, yet are comfortable for them personally. We talk about and practice these new skills until they feel comfortable using them in relating to their parent.

OBJECTIVES AND APPROACHES

This brings us to the next major area of discussion, that of the relationship skills used by the parent aides which seem to be helpful to the parents in their growth and development. The general goals we have are:

1. to enhance the parent's self-esteem and ability to trust others appropriately, and to sustain relationships;

2. to develop problem-solving and crisis resolution skills;

3. to end family isolation and develop support systems;

4. to develop realistic expectations of the children.

Although the following methods are not presented during training or in any formal ways as "the thing to do," the aides seem to use each to some degree. Usually, the aide's natural response to a parent is "just perfect," and he or she needs only to understand how the method of relating which was chosen is helpful to the parent. Occasionally, the interaction was probably not helpful, but the aide usually somehow senses that and brings it up. We then discuss some ways to operate differently in the future, or how to reopen that same discussion and continue it with differing results.

Acceptance of the Person Apart from the Parent Role

It is our philosophy that everyone needs unconditional acceptance from at least one other person, so we stress

acceptance of each person as an individual deserving our
caring attention. Yet, we are careful not to condone the
person's present behavior as a parent. The focus is always
on the adult; if the children need some specialized services,
they are referred elsewhere. A turning point with many
families has been when they realize the volunteers were not
there because they were paid to be there, but because they
cared. One parent told her caseworker that she liked her
parent aide because, "She's the only one here for me. Everyone else comes to check on the kids." The volunteers spend
a lot of time at the parents' homes talking and sharing,
but they also try to help the parents find some personal
interests and hobbies. Some have attended classes together,
gone to the art gallery or museum, enjoyed lunch at a restaurant, gone to a move, or simply browsed through the library.
Occasionally, we arrange child care so the parent can enjoy
this rare leisure time alone.

Physical Touching

Most of our volunteers are very open people, and enjoy reaching out with hugs or pats on the arms. We encourage them to
assess the parent's reaction and then to use touching in
appropriate circumstances as they normally would.

Role Modeling

It seems that the greatest amount of learning comes from the
parents' attempts to imitate and to gain the approval of a
friend whom they trust and whom they know cares about them.
We know that many of our parents have little empathy for
their children and that they can learn it through peer interaction. It is our greatest hope that as the parent aide
expresses empathic feelings for the parent, the parent will
begin to return these feelings to the parent aide, and then
will generalize them to other relationships. We saw begin-
nings of this when a parent aide, who walks her children to
school every day, sprained her ankle. The parent volunteered
to come over and walk with the children for her. An obvious
kind of imitation happened when a parent aide visited her
family just after getting a new curly hairstyle. The next
week, the parent's hair was styled similarly. A number of
parents have begun to move very gradually toward empathy
for their children as they begin to discuss their children's
wants and needs for the first time. It is very gratifying
to see a parent develop enough self-esteem that she can begin
to move outside herself to consider the needs of others.

Exploration of Alternative Life Styles

Many of the volunteers find their own home life in sharp contrast to the parents', both economically and structurally.
There is little we can do to help the families financially,
except direct them to all the available community resources.
But we can help them learn to cope with the seemingly endless
string of crises. Many of the parents live only for today,
with few problem-solving skills and few goals for the future.
Many have very poor work histories and move frequently. We
try to help them establish some stability for their family
by learning to assess alternative solutions to their problems,
choose goals, and implement them. One parent aide agreed to
help her parent find new housing by calling the landlords
the parent had circled in the paper, getting the needed rental
information, and accompanying her to look at apartments. However, during the next move the parent aide only gave suggestions during the process. We also try to help the parents
find leisure-time activities which are free or low cost, and
encourage them to get involved in school and civic groups.

Reality Testing

The parent aides become safe people for the parents to try
out new ideas for childrearing, or new plans for the future
before suggesting them to the caseworker or the court system.
"What would you think of . . . ?" becomes a familiar refrain.
The aide learns to be very honest, but tactful, as a no-
comment is often assumed to be approval. In fact, one parent
felt the parent aide must approve of her drug usage because
when she mentioned it, the aide was left speechless. Several
weeks later, when the aide finally felt able to handle the
discussion, she brought it up again and let the parent know
she definitely did not approve. Many have been asked about
the touchy subject of spanking children. Generally, we encourage the parents to look at other methods of discipline
as being more useful as a learning experience for the child.
Parents also discuss relationships with husbands or boy-
friends, and try out tactics they wish to use to bring up
discussions on hard issues. It is during these times that
good communication skills are learned.

Feedback on Interactions with the Aide, Significant
   Others, and Systems

The difference from reality testing is that feedback is initiated by the parent aide, not the parent. Again, the communication needs to be open and honest. However, many times
the aide will not know how to handle a particular issue,

and will discuss it with the supervisor and bring it up at a later date. One parent received a telephone call while the parent aide was visiting; she said she had to leave, and would be back in a half hour. The aide waited for that length of time and then left. However, the next week she mentioned her feelings of anger and the parent apologized for being rude. Many times the parents have no one else to tell them how their behavior appears to others, and because of their limited social skills, they do not realize how they affect others. During our parent aide/parent picnic this summer, one of the parents repeatedly told me that the rolls I had baked would not have been so dry if I had thought to put them in the refrigerator to cool. She made similar comments about all the food. No wonder this parent has virtually no friends. We also try to help them understand the consequences of their behavior; for example, how their not fulfilling a court order will affect the chances of their regaining custody of their children.

EVALUATION

As supervisor, it is exciting to watch each relationship grow and develop. In our meetings, I gain some impressions of how the relationship is going, but we also ask for assessments every three months from the referral person, the parent aide, and the parent. From these assessments, we have been able to develop some ideas about how the volunteers can be most helpful and in what areas they are likely to be most effective. We ask the referring person to consider a list of variables which we feel are indicative of areas in which abusive families generally need to make some changes. This helps to indicate to us whether the family is likely to become abusive again. They are: (1) parent(s) has sufficient outside support systems; (2) parent(s) has developed appropriate parenting and disciplining skills; (3) parent(s) has good self-image; (4) parent(s) has good relationship with child(ren); (5) parent(s) has realistic expectations of child(ren); (6) parents have good marital relationship; (7) parent(s) is able to reach out to others; and (8) entire family is involved in leisure-time activities. Generally speaking, the first areas in which we note a change are improved self-image and more outside support systems, with those developing at about six months. Approximately two months later, the parents seem able to seek help when needed, and to use appropriate discipline. Changing the parents' expectations of their children, involving the entire family in leisure-time activities,

and improving the marital relationship seem to come much later,
sometimes not until 12 months.

The variables which interplay to determine whether this is
a helpful relationship to the parent are numerous, including
needs of the parent, number of hours spent together, intensity
of emotional bond developed, closeness of the parent to her
caseworker, abilities of the aide, number of significant others
involved, activities participated in jointly, and issues discussed. It is my impression that the most important variables
within the relationship are a combination of the aide's ability
to meet the needs of a particular parent, and the willingness
of both to spend a good number of hours together. Another
impression of mine would support the findings of a 1977 study
of eleven HEW demonstration projects by the Berkeley Planning
Associates. It was found that those parents who do best are
involved with a team approach; they have a number of people
who care about them working together in an organized way.

It is important to note that most of the parents and parent aides enjoy their relationship from the beginning. In
their assessments, the parents state that the most important
thing the volunteer does is to be a supportive friend, sometimes the only one they have ever had. The parent aides confirm that role. We do realize the dependencies which develop,
and we withdraw from the relationship very slowly, always
pointing out the parents' individual strengths and gains
and assuring them of our continuing availability. Usually,
the relationship comes to a very natural end, often with the
parents beginning to assert their independence. None of the
aides envisions completely ending this year-long friendship,
but know the intensity will lessen as the parents' needs
diminish. Appendix B outlines the procedure for ending the
parent aide/parent relationship in more detail.

CONCLUSION

Virginia Satir talks about making contact, of truly communicating with other people. That is really what our project
is all about--feeling the depth of another's life, becoming
intimately involved to help the parent grow and dream of becoming. We enhance our own lives by caring and giving to
another.

REFERENCES

Berkeley Planning Associates. *Study of eleven demonstration projects*. Government Document HE 1.480. Washington, D.C.: Government Printing Office, 1977.

Gray, C. *Reducing violence in families by empathy training*. Paper presented at the Second National Symposium on Building Family Strengths, University of Nebraska-Lincoln, 1979.

Helfer, R. E., & Kempe, C. H. *Child abuse and neglect, the family and the community*. Cambridge: Ballinger, 1976.

Kempe, R. S., & Kempe, C. H. *Child abuse*. Cambridge: Harvard University Press, 1978.

Steele, B. *Working with abusive parents from a psychiatric point of view*. DHEW Publication No. 75-70. Washington, D.C.: Government Printing Office, 1975.

Straus, M. A. *Family patterns and child abuse in a nationally representative American sample*. Durham, New Hampshire: University of New Hampshire, 1978.

APPENDIX A

Parent Aide Support Service
Procedures for Screening and Placement of Volunteers

1. Initial contact by phone or in group setting to explain
    basic philosophy and goals of program.

2. Mail "They Dare to Care" article to volunteer.

3. Supervisor has personal interview with volunteer to
    fully explain program and expectations of volunteers,
    answer questions, and do initial screening.

4. Volunteer attends 18-hour training program to gain know-
    ledge in the areas of child abuse and neglect, parental
    stresses and coping, communication, child development,
    discipline, relationships, and community services to
    families, and to assess their readiness to volunteer
    in this field.

5. Volunteer fills out "Parent Aide Information Form."

6. Supervisor has personal interview with volunteer to
    help him or her explore feelings about child abuse and
    readiness to help an abusive parent. At this time the
    supervisor should have assessed whether the volunteer has
    the following skills: ability to communicate, empathy,
    flexibility, capacity for having own needs fulfilled
    elsewhere, and a sense of humor. If the volunteer
    wishes to continue, the supervisor asks for a one-year
    verbal commitment to the program. The supervisor also
    gains some more specific information as to what the
    volunteer expects to give to and gain from this volunteer
    job to assist her in matching volunteer and parent,
    i.e., hours willing to give; how intense an emotional
    attachment the aide is willing to make; if aide is
    comfortable with older or younger parent, single parent,
    married couples; and activities aide will wish to be
    involved in.

7. Supervisor reviews referrals and selects parent to match
    the volunteer.

8. Supervisor calls volunteer and worker who referred
    family to seek their approval of match.

9. Staffing held with parent aide, caseworker, parent aide supervisor, and any others involved with the family to fully explain parent's needs and goals in working with him or her.

10. Worker or supervisor accompanies parent aide on initial visit to parent in order to introduce them, help establish rapport, discuss roles and need to report if additional abuse is suspected, and assure that parent is aware that all will be working together as a team.

11. Parent aides attend monthly group meetings and individual conferences with the supervisor. They also compile monthly report to keep worker aware of activities with family.

APPENDIX B

Parent Aide Support Service
Procedures for Closure of Parent Aide/Parent Relationship

1. Goals for family discussed and progress assessed at periodic staffings.

2. Parent aide and referring person agree to timetable for termination based on one of the following:
   a. Goals with family attained.
   b. Parents' statements that they are ready to end involvement or their perceived increasing independence.
   c. Parent seems unable or unwilling to be involved with parent aide despite volunteer's initiatives.
   d. Parent aide unable to follow through on commitment.

3. Several months prior to termination, parent aide prepares parent by:
   a. Discussing progress he or she has made.
   b. Increasingly encouraging parent to reach out to supportive services and significant others on his or her own.
   c. Helping parent to do individual problem solving, especially in crises situations.
   d. Assisting parent to recognize individual strengths so it is not necessary to rely on others for ego support.
   e. Assuring parent that the aide will continue to be available, but will not be visiting with as great a frequency.

4. At termination, a memo will be written by PASS supervisor to the referring person with a copy to the parent aide, stating the date of termination, why the aide is ending involvement with the family, and what parental change and growth has been noted. Referral agency assessment form will be attached.

5. A personal thank you letter will be sent to the parent aide with the above memo and a parent aide assessment form.

6. When appropriate, a personal letter and parent assessment form will be mailed to the parent.

7. File will be closed and maintained for future reference (i.e., job reference for volunteer).

Training Foster Parents: Designing and Implementing an Ongoing Program

Dr. Dorothy Martin
Department of Child Development
and Family Studies
Colorado State University, and
Marty Moore
Larimer County Department
of Social Services,
Fort Collins, Colorado, and
Patricia Housley
Colorado State University

FOSTER FAMILY LIFE

Professional and popular literature abounds with articles detailing the many pressures which plague family members today. Unfortunately, the majority focus upon the problems of families in our society, and often conclude that the family unit is in great danger. Realistically, family life is undergoing a period of change--perhaps more accurately described as a time of transition. In observing this transitional stage, it is beneficial to view the family from a positive point of view, to concentrate upon the many good aspects of family life, and to acknowledge the value of the family within society. From this perspective, it is logical to focus on building family strengths, and to address the critical issues of how to maintain a family environment conducive to optimal personal growth and development.

An often overlooked and frequently undervalued element of family life is the existence of foster home care. Foster care has existed for many years, and usually is directed toward children, but can also be important for adults who, for one reason or another, need the nurturant environment provided in a foster home. The Department of Social Services in Larimer County, Colorado, has been involved in authorizing and supervising foster care for many years, as have most social services agencies in other states. During these years, some training and support have been available for foster families. However, both the agency personnel and foster families were aware of the need for a more systematic training program to update skills and to provide necessary information. With this need in mind, an extensive training proposal was written two years ago by the Department of Social Services and the County Mental Health Center.

One of the basic assumptions of training foster parents is that the existence of foster homes and foster families is necessary for the enhanced development of children and

their families. While this seems to be a basic statement,
it is easy to ignore the far-reaching implications of such
an assumption. For example, the placement of a child in a
foster home is done with the conviction that such an environment will be conducive to the child's personal development--
physically, intellectually, socially, and emotionally. Such
placement should also provide the natural family with an
opportunity to modify elements of their present family life
and interactions. In addition, the foster family itself
should benefit from working with the foster child. Thus,
it is imperative to evaluate each foster placement with respect to the child, the natural family, and the foster family, as well as how each placement will affect the community
and society as a whole. Viewed in this manner, foster care
takes on increased importance, as does establishing high quality, appropriate training for providers of such care.

The purpose of this paper is twofold: (1) to present
an overview of an ongoing program to train foster parents within a community, and (2) to offer some general guidelines and
recommendations for establishing programs in other communities.

The Larimer County Mental Health Center, in cooperation
with the Department of Social Services, initiated a training
program for foster parents in the fall of 1977. This project
was made possible by a Title XX training grant which was awarded to the County Mental Health Center. Under the guidelines
of the grant, staff members were hired to coordinate an extensive training program for Social Services staff and providers of foster and day care services. These coordinators
were housed at the Mental Health Center, and worked closely
with both Mental Health Center and Social Services staff to
design and implement the initial training. This interagency
cooperation, in itself, was a highlight of the initial year's
program, and resulted in overall improved working relationships.

THE BEGINNING

When training began, there were approximately 90 licensed
foster homes in Larimer County, ranging in experience in
foster care from one month to 23 years. Fortunately, the caseworkers from the Department of Social Services maintained
contact with active homes through regular phone calls and a
monthly newsletter produced through the Foster Parents' Association. Using this newsletter and the enthusiasm of the
two caseworkers responsible for foster homes, parents were
alerted to the possibility of a series of training sessions.
A comprehensive assessment of the needs of foster care parents

was made at the outset. An original questionnaire, designed
by Title XX staff and the caseworkers, was mailed to each
foster home. Both foster mothers and fathers were asked to
complete the questionnaire, so that training could be planned
to meet specific needs. In all, 36 individuals returned
questionnaires. On the basis of information provided by the
parents, a rank-order list of topics of greatest interest
was made. For example, areas of greatest interest were physical aggression, dealing with child abuse and neglect, teaching children respect for selves and others, destructiveness,
dealing with feelings when a child is returned to the family,
and so forth. The wide variety of topics identified in this
original assessment supported the contention that an ongoing
program of training was needed. As the year progressed and
families became involved in training sessions, an even larger
number of topic areas were identified. This communication
of interests and needs proved to be valuable in maintaining
continuity from one phase of the program to another.

THE PROGRAM

The decision was made by Title XX staff to focus only on a
few areas of interest, in order to provide depth in training.
This approach was partially related to the possibility of
continued funding beyond the initial year. Since the Foster
Parents' Association already had regular monthly meetings,
Title XX training was scheduled at these meetings, with some
additional sessions. Communication with foster parents was
readily established; the combination of monthly newsletters
and a calling chain made it possible to disperse information
readily. The personal contacts between training staff and
parents were influential in guaranteeing attendance at training sessions. The grant provided sufficient money to dupli-
cate training materials, and to purchase books and audio-
visual material for future training or for individual use
by caseworkers and foster parents.

Separate training sessions covered eleven topic areas.
For each session, specific objectives were written by the
presenters, and an evaluation was completed by each participant. This facilitated the writing of a final report at
the end of the grant year, and provided ongoing feedback
concerning appropriateness of training.

Briefly, areas of training in the first year were:

1. Child Abuse and Neglect. Information was provided on
    the frequency and type of abuse. Feelings toward abu-
    sive parents were explored.

2. Sexual Exploration, Exploitation, and Abuse. Opportunity was provided to become comfortable with one's own sexuality in order to relate comfortably with children.

3. Preschool Development. A developmental overview of the preschool-age child was presented.

4. Adolescent Development. An overview of the development of adolescents and issues directly related to adolescents was provided.

5. Substance Abuse. Resource information on alcohol and other drug issues, as related to teens, was provided.

6. Parenting with Emphasis on Abused Children. Principles of child rearing, communication skills, action alternatives, and consequences were presented.

7. Communication. Information on family communication patterns and modification of such patterns was presented.

8. Sexual Stereotyping of Young Children. The influence of stereotyping young children on the basis of sex was discussed. Ways to determine whether or not one's own treatment of children needed to be changed were presented.

The bulk of training was provided by the staff of the Mental Health Center, with some participation by Social Services, university-affiliated personnel, and community professionals. Time provided by Mental Health personnel was donated as a match for the federal funds. Other trainers were reimbursed for their participation at the various sessions.

All members of the Social Services staff were invited to attend foster parent training; staff members who dealt directly with foster parents and children were especially encouraged to participate. In all cases where staff and parents interacted, an improved understanding for one another's role resulted, and communication between individuals became more productive.

Because of the demands of foster care, it was necessary to be flexible concerning attendance at training sessions. Ideally, participation by both parents at all sessions was encouraged. However, the normal restrictions of family life, such as school activities, lack of child care, and illness, made this impossible. All sessions were open and had no size limitation, with the exception of a three-part workshop on parenting. (This particular workshop dealt with a small group of parents, since the emphasis was on application of principles to everyday problems and situations.) While such flexibility was required, it also made planning for a group somewhat of an adventure, since anywhere from eight to fifty parents might arrive.

Evaluation of each session was extremely helpful to the Title XX staff and to each of the presenters. Not only did it provide information on particular sessions, but gave sufficient information upon which to build continuing training.

THE SECOND YEAR

After a four-month delay in funding, Title XX monies were approved for the continuation of training. The 1978-1979 grant encompassed 16 areas or modules of training; foster care parent training was one of the modules.

The proposal, submitted in April, 1978, reflected the needs of foster parents as seen by caseworkers. In addition, evaluations completed by foster parents the previous year were used in developing the outline of training. Finally, after the grant was approved, the training coordinator met with the executive board of the Centennial Foster Parents' Council before completing the training plan.

Training began in January, 1979. As in the previous year, monthly sessions were scheduled to coincide with regular evening council times. Two additional all-day sessions were planned. Training sessions were preceded by association business, accompanied by refreshments, and occasionally supplemented by a potluck supper. Child care was provided.

Topics covered at training sessions were as follows:

1. Becoming a Winner. Exploration of own values and life scripting was led by training staff member.

2. Parenting Styles. Guidance for young children (2-11 years), and communicating with older children (11 and up) was discussed by Mental Health therapists.

3. Cooperation with Other Community Agencies/Personnel. A presentation was made by a panel composed of a pediatrician who was also a member of the Child Protection Team, a natural parent of a developmentally disabled child who was in foster care, the supervisor of caseworkers who was experienced with the court system, and the school social worker.

4. Drug Abuse. A display and presentation was made by a detective from the Police Department.

5. Attachment and Early Development (birth to 3 years). This included a discussion of transitions, when children arrive in a new home, or leave a foster home. The experience and feelings of the child and the foster parents were emphasized.

6. Foster Parenting for the Developmentally Disabled Child.

7. Perceptual Handicaps and Learning Disabilities.

8. Development of Sexuality. This dealt primarily with questions children ask, and their interests/concerns in relation to their overall stage of development.

9. Understanding and Managing the Older Child Who Failed to Attach in Infancy.

As in the first year, participants in the training were asked to evaluate every session at its close, using a standard form. The evaluation entailed checking ten items, and adding comments concerning information gained and suggested improvements. Evaluations were tallied and shared with the presenters, the association board, and the appropriate caseworkers.

The involvement and cooperation of a number of professionals from the community enhanced the training. In many cases, those professionals volunteered their time. When a consultation fee was not requested, an honorarium was paid in appreciation of the contribution of their time and expertise.

PLANNING THE THIRD YEAR

After two successful years of training, funding is being sought for a third year in order to continue workshops for foster parents, as well as to provide the other training components of the grant.

As before, input from foster parents and caseworkers is being encouraged as the proposal is developed. Training topics and areas will reflect the needs of new foster parents, ongoing training for experienced foster parents, and specialized areas not previously included.

Several innovations are being considered to extend and improve training experiences:

1. Group Home Foster Parents feel that some of their needs are similar to those of other foster parents, but that they also have needs which are quite different. An

effort will be made to determine these needs and to plan training around them.

2. In-depth training in <u>Adolescent Development</u> is being explored. One session on this topic was not enough for those parents with teenagers living in their homes. These adolescents, who are always multi-faceted and often have many problems, present special challenges to foster parents.

3. An <u>Outdoor Camping Experience</u> for foster families will be developed in order to encourage family interaction while providing training.

4. <u>Adult Foster Care</u> placements are being licensed by the county. Providers will be requested to enroll in ongoing training. In addition, specialized workshops will be developed for them.

5. Experience showed that both the <u>Drug Abuse Presentation</u> by Mental Health therapists (first year of training), and the Police Department (second year of training) should be combined. This would provide a broader perspective on this issue than was given by either one alone.

WHY TRAIN FOSTER PARENTS?

The provision of training for foster parents is demanding in terms of staff and consultant time, can be frustrating, and may be costly if the number of participants is moderate. However, it seems vitally important for a number of reasons.

All parents need information about normal growth and development in order to understand and deal with their children. Very few parents, foster parents or natural parents, have had any exposure to this area, regardless of educational or socioeconomic background.

Foster parents usually do not have the benefit of watching their foster children go through step-by-step development, even if they have experienced this with their own children. Children are placed in foster care, removed, returned to their natural parents or placed in adoptive homes, or moved from one foster home to another. The foster parent suddenly encounters an individual child at a particular stage of development. A preschooler may be asking questions about sex. An adolescent may be encountering peer pressure as he or she makes decisions about experimentation with drugs.

Adolescent placements, perhaps more than all others, are apt to be difficult. These are often "hard to place" young people. Foster parents need information and support.

Foster parents are at different developmental stages themselves. They need to develop an understanding of their own selves and their needs in relation to the needs of their children. A young couple may suddenly find themselves contending with an adolescent foster child. An older couple may be trying to meet the many demands of an infant. How do they salvage time for pursuing other interests? What arrangements can they make for "relief" time, i.e., time away from children? In what ways can they preserve and develop their intimacy as a couple?

Emotional support is needed by foster children and foster parents, as they go through placement in the home, removal from the home, and changes from home to home. Foster parents can be helped to understand their own feelings and the child's experience.

As mentioned before, foster parents caring for groups of foster children have additional needs. The development of skills in behavior management and group process can provide some help. These are among the many reasons why training foster parents must become and remain a recognized priority.

CONSIDERATIONS IN PROVIDING TRAINING

In the early stages of developing training for foster parents, it is important to deal with some basic realities. These realities, both positive and negative, result directly from training or are side effects of training.

Among the positives or bonuses is the fact that bringing foster parents together reduces the isolation of families. They discover their common bonds, and recognize they have common problems. This may serve to prevent potential abuse, since one of the characteristics of abusive families is isolation.

In coming together, the families share child-rearing approaches they have found helpful and their "tried and true" solutions. Some of the most important and useful information is communicated informally, family to family. Parents tend to be more reality-bound than many "professionals."

Training may increase foster parents' sense of pride in their role. A heightened awareness of the importance of their work may be developed. Planning workshops for them can communicate the message that they are considered not only parents, but also "staff," in offering a safe and nurturing environment to other people's children.

Workshops for foster parents to which Social Services staff are invited increase the opportunities for interaction with caseworkers in an atmosphere less threatening than a home visit might be. In turn, the caseworker may view the foster parent more positively than in other situations, as it appears the foster parent is open to learning and shares common goals for the foster child.

When exposed to the positive experiences of other foster parents, a foster parent may become more willing to take on new challenges. On the other hand, hearing others' experiences may cause foster parents to become more cautious, and to avoid overzealousness in entering into situations which may exceed their present capabilities.

Other factors which need to be considered in developing training are not as positive. These include the fact that foster parents cannot take advantage of training if child care is not provided. However, child care is not an allowable expenditure under Title XX grants. Arranging for volunteers to provide care is costly in terms of staff time and involves other complications. Some projects have avoided the issue by offering all training at night, with no provisions for care of the children. The entire issue of child care needs more creative solutions.

Personalities of key people, such as caseworkers, association board members, and project staff are influential and affect all the foster parents in terms of receptivity to training. Good communication, including an appreciation of one another's needs and points of view, is vital!

Night sessions may be more convenient for foster parents, but generally are not attractive to staff. Because of heavy caseloads, workers are protective of their "free time"; building their own family strengths is of prime concern.

If the number of participants at training sessions is low, the cost of training is high. Justifying training becomes more difficult when this is true.

RECOMMENDATIONS

Based upon two years of training and a proposed third year, some recommendations can be made to those considering similar training projects:

1. Explore community alternatives for offering creative child care during training sessions. The payoffs in getting foster parents enrolled in workshops generally outweigh the obstacles in making these arrangements.

2. Combine some of the foster parent training with work-
    shops for other providers of services, such as family
    day care home parents. They share some common needs,
    such as information on growth and development. This
    increases efficiency and lowers participant costs.

3. Invite foster parents to workshops planned for staff.
    Again, training costs will be lowered. As mentioned
    before, this also heightens foster parents' sense of
    professionalism.

4. Provide specialized training to families dealing with
    developmentally disabled children, abuse, and neglect.
    These families require additional information and sup-
    port.

5. Encourage the participation of both parents in training,
    and other family members when appropriate. For example,
    teenagers benefit from the session on drug abuse. A
    family has a better chance to be cohesive and resilient
    when all family members are involved and learn to com-
    municate with one another.

6. Work towards a goal of continual, ongoing training.
    Sources of funding--"soft" money versus "hard" money--
    should be evaluated in this light.

7. Encourage the Social Services agency to define its posi-
    tion on whether or not training will be required of
    foster parents. Parents are influenced by a positive
    approach on the part of their caseworkers.

SUMMARY

The intention of this paper has been to describe an ongoing
training program for foster parents and to make recommendations to professionals considering similar projects. Staff
involved in last year's grant and the current project are
willing to consult with community personnel initiating training, and to share more specific details. Such sharing of
information and support can facilitate the smooth institution
of appropriate training programs, and ultimately result in
stronger family units.

A New Alternative: Adolescent Foster Peer Program

Karen Edwards
School of Home Economics
University of Vermont

AN ALTERNATIVE

Sally is 16 and in the custody of the state. Her widowed, alcoholic mother found her unmanageable and had conveyed custody to the state when Sally was 14. Since then, Sally has been in and out of numerous residential facilities for adolescents; she usually got out by running away. Sally tried living with a foster family, but she wasn't willing to develop a new "family" at age 16. She wanted to be independent, but she lacked the life skills to succeed on her own. What could we offer her?

The State of Vermont could offer her a Foster Peer Placement. The caregivers are graduate and undergraduate students who are licensed foster parents. They receive in-service training for university credit and participate in weekly seminars with the adolescents who share their living space. In this way, adolescents who have committed no "adult" crime can live in the community while gaining the necessary life skills for independence, self-sufficiency, and meaningful social involvement. It should be clear that only a small subset of adolescents in need of placement can be served by a Foster Peer Placement program. Since this placement is the most minimally restrictive one available in the social service system, only adolescents who have matured to a level close to independence, and who are somewhat self-disciplined and motivated, can be successful in such a placement.

RATIONALE FOR PROGRAM

Deinstitutionalization

Residential facilities for problem adolescents often become schools for learning criminal "know-how" and new ways of

393

acting out (Witherspoon, 1966). The need of the adolescent
to impress the peer group and to belong is great. We know
from social learning theory research that vicarious learning
and modeling are powerful tools of socialization. Ausubel
(1954) speculated that to escape the fear associated with
the sense of childhood helplessness, the child identified
with parents, the all-powerful beings of his or her universe,
and thus vicariously regained a feeling of power and control. If a child were denied this sense of vicarious power
through parent models, Ausubel suggested, it may be obtained
through identification with one's peers. Unfortunately, the
powerful peer models found in groups of confined adolescents
usually are not helpful in educating these young people in
constructive behavior. This is a problem in most residential treatment, even with very capable staff.

The State of Vermont recognized this problem and others
associated with institutionalized services for adolescents,
and is currently reorganizing the juvenile system. A tentative outline of the reorganized system appears in Figure 1.
One step in this reorganization was the closing of the large
state facility for adolescents called Weeks School. The
closing resulted in a scramble for alternative placements
for the adolescents previously housed there. As available
placements were filled, new placements had to be created.
If older, nonadjudicated adolescent wards of the state could
be placed with university students in a Foster Peer Program,
more traditional placements would be available for the adolescents leaving Weeks School.

University Involvement

An important contribution of this program is to provide a
model for integrating university and community services. Many
university students are seeking involvement in community and
social action programs. These programs can encourage the
commitment and idealism of students in working with other
human beings. Without interrupting traditional intellectual
pursuits, students can integrate the educational experience
of functioning as a foster peer into their overall academic
program. This assists higher education in making the transition from an "ivory tower" institution to one which serves
community needs, as mandated for land-grant institutions such
as the University of Vermont.

The University of Massachusetts sought a similar involvement in facilitating the transition to deinstitutionalized
youth programs following the shutdown of all juvenile training schools and reformatories in that state. The Massachusetts
Association for the Reintegration of Youth (MARY) is a residential treatment center for youth at the University of

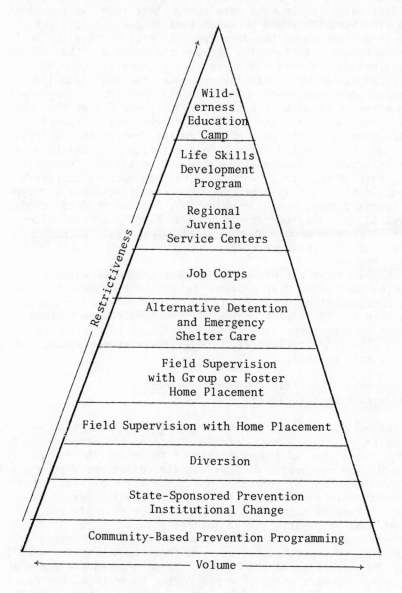

Figure 1

Continuum of Care in Vermont's Reorganized
Juvenile Justice System

Massachusetts. The program is based in two dormitories; six
student advocates in each dorm share their rooms with a youth
who traditionally would be in an institution. A resident
counselor in each of the dorms specifically deals with the
interpersonal relationships between the youth and the student.
Coordinating the entire program is a project director who
is responsible for developing resources for individualized
programs for each youth. The students have the primary responsibility of working with the youth every day of the week.
This program has brought about a positive self-image and
self-identity on the part of the youths, rather than a negative one which occurs through incarceration. It utilizes
the university resources (educational, vocational, counseling, recreation, etc.), and costs half as much as institutionalization. It also provides the students with a new type
of learning experience for which they receive academic credit
(Dye, 1973). The shortage of student housing at the University of Vermont made such a program unfeasible. Therefore,
only students living off-campus can participate in the Foster
Peer program.

        A program at the University of Massachusetts which re-
sembles the Foster Peer program is called the Advocates for
the Development of Human Potential. This provides graduate
training for 15 correctional staff and requires each staff
member to take responsibility for one youth in the department. The youth resides with the graduate student/staff and
family for one year.

Psycho-social Adventages of Developmentally Adjacent "Foster Parents"

Adolescence usually involves young people from the ages of
12 to 17. Erikson (1968) describes this as the stage of identity crisis when adolescents attempt to define their own
identity by projecting diffused ego images on one another, and
by seeing them thus reflected and gradually clarified. Adolescents help one another through this changing period in
life by forming tight peer groups in which they place a
great deal of trust. The adolescent's tendency to reach out
for satisfaction of their emotional needs to peers rather
than to adults probably stems from their desire to leave childhood dependence on adults behind. Because peers are the most
important members of their world during this stage, the Foster
Peer program offers the adolescents a peer committed to helping them meet their emotional needs, rather than an adult
figure who they may reject to assert their independence.

        The Foster Peer program uses the desire for peer accept-
ance constructively by providing the adolescents with models
who demonstrate positive social behaviors. Although the

caregivers are not exact chronological peers, they are developmentally adjacent to the adolescent. This may result in even more powerful modeling, since the adolescent can easily identify with the student as a peer, yet the student is viewed as having resources which the adolescent wants, such as independence and adult status (Whiting, 1960). Perhaps more important, many of the foster peers are involved in the same psychological self-probing that their adolescent peers are attempting; they thus may feel kinship of purpose.

When Sobesky (1976) describes the impact of stage of life on the clinical effectiveness of child care workers, he suggests several major advantages in having youth work with adolescents. He argues they are more likely to treat adolescents as individuals rather than roles. Although adolescents often stereotype themselves, their growth is not facilitated by adults who perpetuate adolescent role stereotypes. According to Erikson's (1968) theory of stage development, the adolescent looks for an opportunity to decide freely on duty and service, and is afraid of being forced into self-ridicule or self-doubt. Adolescents in the process of resolving role diffusion may be very introspective and change prone. Sobesky (1976) observes that youth are more self-observant, patient, and willing to change their behavior than older staff members. These tendencies may allow the foster peer to adapt to the changing roles of the adolescent in the relationship, and to be willing to give more freedom to alternative behaviors. Keniston (1970) describes the stage of youth as a time of trying out adult roles without making a commitment to any one of them. The foster peer roles give the university students an opportunity to change the "real world" (by their successful guidance of adolescents) without committing themselves to parenting roles in adult society.

Reduces Labeling

Most professionals who work with youngsters are aware of the power of labels in the socialization of individuals. Confinement in a training school often stigmatizes the adolescent in the eyes of the community, despite the efforts of professionals in the field. The label hinders the adolescent's return to normal life. Another stigma experienced by adolescents placed in foster families also relates to labeling. When there are "natural" children in the home, the "foster" child often feels like an outsider. By allowing the adolescent to say, "my roommate is a college student," he or she avoids the stigma of being a "foster child."

PROGRAM SET-UP AND IMPLEMENTATION

Early in January 1978, we initially discussed a Foster Peer
program, where graduate and upper-class undergraduate students would be recruited, trained, supervised, and licensed
as foster parents to share their living space with state-
committed adolescents. The program has evolved through three
periods.

Planning

For the first six months, we devoted most of our efforts to
initial planning and consultation with those who might participate or be affected by the program. At the same time,
it was necessary to assess and begin monitoring the need for
this program. Committed adolescents and students were consulted, because they were to be the program's primary users.
Their feedback, plus the feedback from various adolescent
caseworkers and student advisers, confirmed the need for
this or a similar program. It was to our benefit that both
students and adolescents were somewhat aware of what they
wanted. It was essential we understood and considered their
ideas and suggestions, in order to effectively plan on their
behalf.

This consultation verified that there were certain state-
committed adolescents who were nearly independent, somewhat
self-sufficient, motivated, and in need of an appropriate
place to live. For one reason or another, there were adolescents who no longer could live at home. Clearly, for
some, their particular needs could not be effectively met
by traditional foster family, group home, and institutional
care. Consultation also indicated that removal from the
community was unnecessary or inappropriate. Consistently,
the adolescents said they wanted either to remain in school,
work toward a Graduate Equivalency Diploma (GED), or get a
job.

Consultation also verified that there were certain graduate
and upper-class undergraduate students who wanted an opportunity to go to school and pursue professional or vocational
goals at the same time. These students had previous volunteer or paid experiences working with adolescents. Where
possible, they thought it would be an excellent idea to share
their living space with an adolescent. Some students were
particularly interested in how this type of experience might
integrate with their academic lives. They had many questions
to be answered. They wondered about the type of adolescent
that would be their housemate; how much it would cost; how
much of a reimbursement would be provided; what type of

in-service training they would receive; what amount of academic credit would be awarded; and very importantly, what
legal responsibility they would have to assume. In answering
these questions and discussing the program's potential with
them even further, we found they became increasingly supportive.

We consulted administrators and faculty from the university,
in addition to Social and Rehabilitative Services professionals, to get their input and feedback. This also proved
very helpful. Discussions centered around planning and creating some kind of cooperation between the University of Vermont and Burlington's Social and Rehabilitative Services.
Such cooperation would provide the foster placements with
easier access to Chittendent County's network of support services. Creating such access seemed to personnel of the University and in social services to be the key to optimizing
the quality and effectiveness of each placement.

The Office of Social and Rehabilitative Services committed
itself to work with, evaluate, reimburse, and license the
foster placements. It agreed to refer and help select committed adolescents needing less restrictive placements, and
to assume all of the casework responsibilities for those adolescents. Finally, Social and Rehabilitative Services committed itself to work with the program developer to continuously ensure and coordinate delivery of services to the placements.

Additional offers of assistance and commitments were made
by many of the other people who were contacted and consulted.
Most of these commitments were left open-ended; those which
were more significant and particularly useful were readily
accepted. For instance, some individuals and students in a
social psychology class at the university offered and did
help recruit potential student participants. Some youth
agency and office personnel offered to help train students,
to be guest speakers, or serve as program consultants.

The steps accomplished during the development period include the following:

1. We began a comprehensive search for literature relevant
    to the project. Such literature, which we made available
    for use by Social and Rehabilitative Services profes-
    sionals, helped to design a course curriculum.

2. We devoted much more time and effort toward establish-
    ing formal contact and support among students, student
    advisers, faculty, department chairpersons, and Uni-
    versity of Vermont administrators. Efforts also were
    devoted toward establishing similar connections with
    Social and Rehabilitative professionals. Our purpose

was to create an awareness and to provide information
and clarification of our project goals. It provided
us with a second opportunity to invite more feedback
to help with continued planning.

3. A radio interview was aired, primarily to help build
   local community awareness, interest, and support. It
   provided us with the opportunity to recruit potential
   participants and invite public feedback.

4. We designed and developed a course curriculum for the
   in-service training component of the program in order
   to help students prepare for and deal with potential
   or real problems, issues, and resolutions. The curriculum focused on adolescent psychology, counseling
   skills, and an understanding of community services.

5. We formally contacted various community resource people.
   Professionals who work with youth were scheduled as
   guest participants during the seminars. Some also agreed
   to act as program consultants.

6. We located and developed six foster peer living situations for those state-committed adolescents selected by
   Social and Rehabilitative Services. In addition to the
   radio broadcast, we circulated notices on campus to all
   graduate students and upper-class undergraduates. We
   also generated a computer printout of all off-campus
   graduate and undergraduate students, and sent out 1,500
   letters to those students with majors related to the
   project. The letter informed them of the University
   Foster Peer program and explained our goals and the
   recruitment process. Respondents were asked to complete
   an application and schedule an interview. Another recruitment strategy entailed meeting with student advisers. They were asked to refer those students they
   knew were interested in an academic field experience.
   The final recruitment approach was executed simply by
   word-of-mouth.

Personnel

The program requires one full-time coordinator. This person
is responsible for recruiting potential foster peers from the
university community, and serving as an ombudsman for those
students. The public relations work of the coordinator includes clarifying the program goals for social service professionals, the university, and the community. The coordinator
participates in curriculum design and development with the

university faculty and contacts each placement at least twice a week.

The cooperation of a university program is necessary to provide academic credit to the university students involved. In this program students can receive up to 15 credits of field experience through the Human Development program. I teach the seminar that is important for a successful field experience of this kind.

A social caseworker in the youth division coordinates the evaluation and licensing of the foster placements, selects appropriate adolescents in conjunction with their caseworker, and participates in the in-service training of foster peers.

Seminar

At the training seminars, an hour is usually spent sharing placement progress and specific problems, issues, and their resolutions. Problem-solving skills usually are worked on during this time, too. The next hour is often spent discussing readings, experiences, or insights with a special focus on adolescent psychology, counseling skills, and gaining an understanding of community services. The third hour is reserved specifically for community resource people and agency spokespersons who come to share their knowledge and expertise with the group. In addition to training, this seminar is intended to provide the social and emotional support needed by the foster peers, because living with an adolescent can be very stressful. The seminar also provides a forum for exchange of information between the university and social service personnel.

DISADVANTAGES AND PROBLEMS

Foster peer placements correct several of the faults found in institutional and foster family placements. However, there are a number of difficulties arising from foster peer placements.

Developmentally Adjacent Individuals

Some of the problems encountered in helping relationships between developmentally adjacent individuals include the possibility that the older helper will be disappointed by the immature behavior manifested. Sobesky (1976) observed some youth child care workers were unwilling to give the guidance desired by adolescents in their charge because they tried to avoid the authoritarian role they had so recently rebelled

against themselves. Furthermore, youth are still very tentative about their role in the world, and may need more support
and praise than that given by adolescents who tend to be very
inconsistent in their approval giving.

From developmental theories, we are aware that developmentally adjacent individuals share overlapping stages of
development. Both are experiencing issues of identity resolution and establishing adult intimacy bonds. The training
seminar must speak very directly to these issues to prevent
the participants from getting stuck in their mutual confusion.

The ability of adults to cope successfully with adolescents may be a real test of their own adjustment. Because
the problems faced by their adolescents may re-arouse in the
adults some of their own unresolved conflicts, they must
deal simultaneously with the child's problems, their own
adolescent problems, and the problems they encounter at middle age (Medinnus & Johnson, 1976).

Adolescents in the Seminar

Although we felt it was important to include the adolescents
in the training seminar and support group, this was a problem. The adolescents felt uncomfortable during the academic
components of the seminar and felt "talked about" when we discussed adolescent psychology. This, coupled with conflicting
work schedules, resulted in sporadic attendance by the adolescents. Because stable attendance is necessary for building trust in a support group, inclusion of adolescents in the
seminar, unless mandated, was unacceptable. Therefore, adolescents were invited to form their own support group, with
the program coordinator acting as facilitator. The topics
discussed at those meetings included employment, peer relationships, sex, drugs, and alcohol.

Coordinating Services

Adolescent wards of the state who are sufficiently mature to
be candidates for this program tend to be low priorities for
their caseworkers who deal with crisis situations every day.
University students who are hoping to work closely with social service personnel are disappointed by this.

Recruitment

Despite energetic recruitment of university foster peers
through radio broadcasts, classroom talks, and mass mailings,
the manpower resources of the university remain largely un-
tapped in terms of foster care for adolescents. At the

University of Vermont, .10 percent of the study body was willing to assume responsibility for an adolescent ward of the
state. However, these additional placements may be a real
boon to some communities.

Screening of Adolescents

The social service caseworkers must be very clear about the
limitations of foster peers in handling acting-out adolescents. The students tend to be idealistic and highly committed in their relationship to the adolescent. Termination
of inappropriate placements is very difficult for them to
accept without suffering guilt and a sense of failure. This
was demonstrated by one of the foster peers in this program,
when an adolescent, who was insufficiently screened for the
program, committed an adult crime and was sent to a correctional facility.

Length of Placement

Another limitation of the program is the potential length of
placement. The students cannot commit themselves to provide
a placement for more than nine months. For some adolescents,
this would be an insufficient commitment. However, for adolescents who will soon be released from state custody, the
opportunity to develop independent life skills through a
placement in the Foster Peer program is appropriate.

EVALUATION

So far, the Foster Peer program has been successful. All except one of the adolescents placed are gainfully employed.
None is in school, but two are working toward their Graduate
Equivalency Diplomas. The foster peers have been effective
in helping adolescents develop some life skills. For this,
the students deserve much credit. The seminars have helped
solve many problems, not only for individuals but for the
group and the program in general. The university has provided an important service to the community.

SUMMARY

The environmental conditions necessary for establishment of
a Foster Peer program are: (1) open-minded social service
personnel, (2) service-oriented university nearby, (3) a

small group of older adolescent wards of the state in need of
a minimally restrictive placement, and (4) funds to support
a program coordinator. Under these conditions a Foster Peer
Placement is a viable alternative for adolescents.

REFERENCES

Ausubel, D. P. *Theory and problems of adolescent development.* New York: Grune & Stratton, 1954.

Dye, L. The university's role in public service to the Department of Youth Services. In Y. Bakal (Ed.), *Closing
correctional institutions.* Boston: Lexington Books,
1973.

Erikson, E. *Youth: Identity and crisis.* New York:
Norton, 1968.

Keniston, K. Youth: A new stage of life. *American Scholar,*
1970, *39,* 631-653.

Medinnus, G. R., & Johnson, R. C. *Child and adolescent
psychology.* (2nd ed.) New York: Wiley, 1976.

Sobesky, W. E. Youth as child care workers: The impact of
stage of life on clinical effectiveness. *Child Care
Quarterly,* 1976, *5*(4) 262-273.

Whiting, J. W. M. Resource mediation and learning by identification. In I. Isrol & H. Stevenson (Eds.), *Personality development in children.* Austin: University
of Texas Press, 1960.

Witherspoon, A. W. Foster home placements for juvenile
delinquents. *Federal Probation,* 1966, *30,* 48-52.

Dr. Lois O. Schwab, Virginia K.
Wright and Mary Ann Cassatt-Dunn,
Department of Human Development
and the Family
University of Nebraska-Lincoln

ECONOMICS AND HUMAN RESOURCES

Economic conditions once again place a focus on the scarcity
of material resources as prices soar for energy, food, and
materials providing shelter and comfort in the immediate environment. Insatiable demands, tempered by limited resources,
threaten a change in the quality of life for a people who
have been consuming 60 percent of the world's annual marketable products while providing only six percent of the population. The next years look bleak economically if only the
consumer demand/material resource balance sheet is considered.
Innovative approaches to solving economic problems need to
be developed by persons who can accent the development of
the human resource. Alvin Toffler (1975), in his book *Eco-
spasm*, explains:

> Because the eco-spasm is more than just an econ-
> omics problem, any attempt to deal with it as
> such, applying exclusive economic remedies that
> ignore side effects, will merely make it worse.

We need a whole battery of new approaches for social
policies, family integration, personal relationships, nurturance of potential for all persons, and value systems. To
overlook any part of our population is to ignore a valuable
human resource. There is a group of individuals, consti-
tuting 12 percent of the population, that is described as
disabled. This population of persons who are physically
disabled, deaf, blind, emotionally disturbed, and mentally
retarded must be given the opportunity to develop its abilities to the fullest and to contribute accordingly.

THE POPULATION OF THE DISABLED

Total population figures on the disabled have never been
compiled. Questions included in the 1970 U.S. Census survey have provided some answers, as have various demographic
studies; however, no fully reliable data base now exists.
Humphreys (1978) assembled the following figures:

--Projections based on a New York study indicate that there are over 2,000,000 severely
disabled individuals who are homebound.

--About 24,000,000 Americans have arthritis,
of which some 5,000,000 are disabled, and
475,000 of these are receiving Social Security Disability benefits.

--There are 250,000 to 500,000 adult Americans
with multiple sclerosis.

--Some 13,000,000 Americans are hard of hearing,
of which 1,800,000 are disabled by deafness, and
of which an estimated 100,000 are low-
functioning deaf.

--Over 5,500,000 individuals are mentally retarded. Of those, about 3,500,000 are substantially handicapped by retardation.

--More than 4,000,000 Americans have epilepsy,
and 1,400,000 of these are substantially
handicapped by this condition.

--At least 2,000,000 adults with severe, persistent psychiatric disabilities reside in
their communities.

The following data, provided by Humphreys (1978),
give an estimate of the severely disabled population in
America:

Age	Number
Under 18	180,000
18-64	4,200,000
65 and over	3,900,000
Institutionalized (all ages)	1,787,000
Total	10,067,000

Some statistical information compiled by the Social Security Administration is useful in beginning to portray a profile of disability in America. The following ratios apply to totally disabled individuals in relation to non-disabled individuals (Humphreys, 1978):

Hospitalization (men)	4 times as often as non-disabled
Days hospitalized	3 times longer than non-disabled
Cost of medical care	3 times higher than non-disabled
Median cost of care as a percent of income	5 times as high as non-disabled
Average income	Half that of non-disabled

While we have some idea of the number of persons who are disabled, and the nature of their disabilities, this does not give us the complete picture. Statistics, by themselves, are misleading in that they do not fully reflect the numbers of persons directly affected by a disabled family member. A family which has a member with special needs is an entire unit with special needs.

Assuming an average family numbering four, the total number of persons directly affected by severe disability is suddenly significant. Taking only the under 18-year-old group which numbers 180,000, the actual number of persons directly affected is 720,000. This focuses the spotlight directly on the usually unseen and unrecognized need for family support services.

A FAMILY-CENTERED PROGRAM

History

A change is taking place in the delivery of services to persons with disabilities. This drastic shift in the primary focus is shown in Figure 1. As the medical model for serving the disabled developed from 1850 to 1950, there was the consideration that persons with either mental or physical disabilities should be cared for. Large institutions/farms/nursing homes as hospital-like settings were developed to care for these people. Nurses, LPNs and aides became the primary attendants. This system became well entrenched across America as large hospital settings (e.g., *One Flew over the Cuckoo's Nest, I Never Promised You a Rose Garden)*,

```
┌─────────────────────┐
│ PERSON WITH         │
│ DISABILITY          │
│ AND FAMILY          │
└─────────────────────┘

PRIMARY FOCUS
for Services

Independent Living
instruction/devicing
  in home
```

```
┌─────────────────────┐
│ PERSON WITH DIS-    │
│ ABILITY AND COM-    │
│ MUNITY SERVICES     │
└─────────────────────┘

SECONDARY FOCUS for
Supplementary Services

To replace family through:
  · Halfway Hostels
  · Visiting Nurses
  · Meals on Wheels
  · Transportation
  · Day Care
  Loneliness Reduction Programs
```

```
┌─────────────────────┐
│ PERSON IN SEMI-     │
│ AND INSTITUTIONAL   │
│ SETTING             │
└─────────────────────┘

TERTIARY FOCUS for
Independent Living

Rehabilitation/
habilitation includes:
  · Nursing homes
  · Hospitals
```

FAMILY is broadly defined as a group connected together and distinguished by the possession of common features or properties.

The above flow of services would be throughout the life continuum of persons with disabilities.

Figure 1

Delivery System for Independent Living Rehabilitation/Habilitation

and nursing homes were built to care for the physical aspects of disability. Then our programs began to change in the 1950s, as the broader concerns of individuals began to develop. The community-based programs had this broad view of the individual. Capabilities of individuals were recognized and developed for work, social, and personal living. The healthy mind as well as the healthy body was considered. Still, the emphasis was on collective programs in this second phase, even though groups were smaller than in the institutions.

A new phase is now developing; this phase is individual and family-centered. It recognizes individuals who are persons, unique in their needs. The movement is away from the collective program, because group plans just are not right for everyone. The new programs recognize the uniqueness of the individual. They are "person-centered."

Legislation

A review of some of the major legislation will give some idea of what kind of assistance is available in this individualized approach. In January, 1975, new Social Services amendments to the federal Social Security Act mandated states to furnish services directed to the goal of:

> . . . achieving and maintaining self-support to prevent, reduce, or eliminate dependency . . .;

> . . . achieving and maintaining self-sufficiency . . .;

> . . . preventing or reducing inappropriate institutional care by providing for community-based care, home-based care, or other forms of less intensive care . . . .

This law also outlines the social services to be given to individuals and/or families to help them with their responsibilities to and for themselves. In other words, the government gave notice that it no longer will serve to increase institutionalization and custodial care; persons will be given the help to learn how to "take charge" of their own lives.

Title XX has emphasized services to the target groups which are expressing local demands.

The 1973 Rehabilitation Act delineated that severely disabled persons receive services on a first priority basis by the Federal/State Rehabilitation agencies. Those described

as homebound, institutionalized, multi-handicapped, un-
served, or immobile are to be given the aid necessary to
make them independent.

This legislation has been made meaningful through the
1978 Rehabilitation Amendments, which mandate comprehensive
services in independent living. The law broadly allows:

> . . . any other service that will enhance the
> ability of a handicapped individual to live
> independently and function within his family
> and community--housing, health maintenance,
> child development services, and appropriate
> preventive services to decrease the needs of
> individuals . . . .

PL 94-142 assures the rights of handicapped children--
infants and preschool, as well as school-aged children--to
receive appropriate services and education. States are mandated to provide the necessary services in the least restrictive setting, to the greatest degree possible with non-
handicapped children, and with the intent of preventing as
many future disabling conditions as possible.

The Developmentally Disabled Assistance and Bill of
Rights Act (PL 93-103, October, 1975) further mandates that
states:

> . . . provide the early screening, diagnosis,
> and evaluation (including maternal care, de-
> velopmental screening, home care, infant and
> pre-school stimulation programs, and parent
> counseling) and training of developmentally
> disabled infants and pre-school children, par-
> ticularly those with multiple handicaps.

The years birth to school age have been shown to be a period
when appropriate intervention programs for children with
handicaps can show most significant results.

Focus on the Individual and the Family

An integrated program of services for persons with disabilities is now being devised to meet the needs of individuals.
Figure 2 shows the array of services which the above laws
may provide for individuals.

Each person is to be given just the kind and level of
services and training required. The emphasis is on the
uniqueness of each individual in regard to his or her needs.
The family, if available, becomes the first line of help
for the individual. This family support system needs to

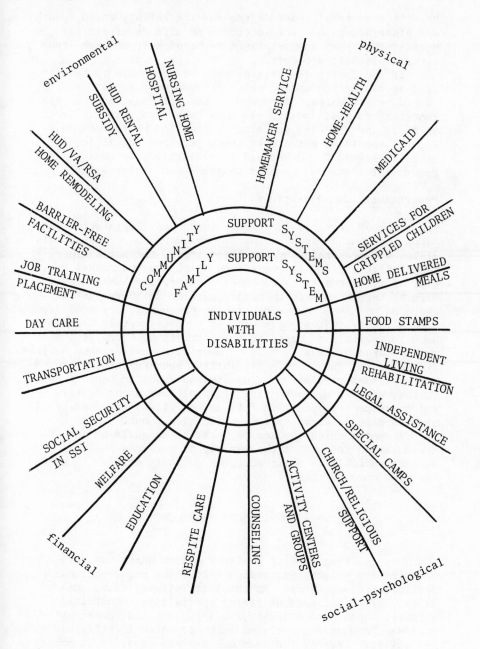

Figure 2

Array for Integrative Services

be activated to a higher degree for the infant, child, youth,
and elderly person. The services are also important for the
nuclear family as spouses learn to be of help to each other
after a disability occurs.

If the family is not available or is unable to be effective in aiding the individual, the community support system
should be activated. Information and referral services are
important so that individuals know "where to turn." Direct
services and training may also be provided by the community.
Federal subsidies often make these services available, as
shown in Figure 2. Other aid is available from non-
governmental groups, such as churches and social groups.

Programmatic Considerations

The array of services, programs, resources, legislative mandates, and human needs is vast. Consumers and professionals,
alike, are frustrated by the immensity of the bureaucracy,
technicalities, and fragmentation which are functional realities of the attempts to be helpful in meeting human needs.
Efforts have been made to create service delivery systems
which do not lose the person in the process. Very good service delivery systems have evolved to meet certain areas of
need for certain segments of the population, such as community-based programs, meals on wheels, homemaker/home health
aid services, and so on. Eligibility requirements, third
party payment regulations, and limited funds to support the
full service to all potential clientele are among factors
which frequently result in fitting the client into the available service delivery system, or doing without.

A system which focuses on meeting the goals of the individual and integrates the variety of services needed to
meet those goals is believed to be not only critically needed
but also more effective.

THE VOCATIONAL SERVICES PROJECT (VSP)

A problem-solving service delivery system which was goal-
oriented and person-centered characterized the Vocational
Services Project (VSP). An interdisciplinary team, consisting of an independent living specialist, industrial
engineer, speech pathologist, audiologist, and vocational
readiness counselor, assessed each person to identify his or
her skills. Each of the team members was equal in authority
and responsibility during assessment. Following the assessments, the team met with the person and his or her family

members, advocate, and other professionals involved. Assessment results were reported and recommendations made. An
individualized action plan was created from the recommendations, with participation from all attending the staffing.
The result was a plan outlining who would do what. In this
way, resources were identified and activated to meet the
individual's goals, regardless of where in the state the person lived. Some agencies had not provided a service or the
recommended training in such a way before, but did so following the VSP guidance. Family members learned new information and could carry out their agreed-upon part of the
task. The VSP participants learned from this kind of assessment and planning what they could do and how they could do
it. An integrated plan for assessing the various resources
resulted in the meeting of their goals.

Three team members--the independent living specialist,
the vocational readiness counselor, and the job placement
specialist--had "caseloads." At assessment, it was determined which "case manager" would work with the person, based
on that person's present degree of independence. Persons
with the greatest need for independent living training were
the responsibility of the independent living specialist (ILS);
those with some independent living skills worked with the
vocational readiness counselor; and those nearest employ-
ability worked with the job placement specialist. All participants had independent living training, either in their
homes, institutions, or from their existing service providers
following the recommendations from the plan. These "case
managers" provided the follow-through with the participants,
advocacy, and appropriate training. The VSP provided equipment, devices, job site modifications, training, and support
to the variety of persons involved in realizing the disabled persons' plans to meet their goals. As new factors
arose, goals were met, changes occurred, revised plans were
created, and the open contact and service from the team members were provided.

This was an unusual experience for most of the participants. They were regarded as participants in the assessment. They discovered what they could do, and they gained
new information. Comparative statements were volunteered,
such as, "This is the first time I haven't been told what I
couldn't do"; "I've never been told what I didn't already
know before"; "This is so together."

A coordinator provided important functions that freed
the team to work with the people and their plans. Intake,
scheduling, and budget were supervised by the coordinator.
The case managers maintained their own case notes, provided
training, counseling, worked with other resources, and taught
the participants how to do these functions themselves. The

independent living specialist, the industrial engineer, the
speech pathologist and audiologist, and the vocational readiness counselor did assessment, and individual reports and
services; the job placement specialist worked with employers
with the job placement group.

As the participants gained in independent living skills,
the case loads shifted. People started moving to vocational
readiness and job placement. Living arrangements were changed.
One person had been unemployed and living in a highly restrictive environment. He progressed to a residential workshop, and then eventually moved to an adult foster home where
household activities were shared, and to employment. The
process worked well for empowering the participants; assertiveness developed. Another participant refused post-assessments,
saying, "I don't need it, anymore; I'm doing fine. I might
come back for vocational interest and engineering if it will
get me a better job."

At the beginning of the project, none of the 70 participants was employed. After two years, 39 percent were employed.
At the end of the project, 40 percent were earning money for
work performed, 22 percent were engaged in educational programs, and 17 percent were involved in purposeful activity.
Most of the participants had initially believed they could
do nothing for a lifetime.

The funding and personnel of the VSP were used to facilitate and integrate existing resources, and were used as a
support and educational resource--all predicated on the goals
of the person. The end result was that 70 individuals with
severe, multiple developmental disabilities, and their families experienced major positive changes in their lives.

THE FUTURE OUTLOOK

Professionals interested in individuals and the welfare of
the family are appropriate experts for developing this kind
of system, if they take on the special training for meeting
the needs of the persons with disabilities. They need to
study the ways in which individuals and families interact with
the socio-cultural, political, and economic systems. This
subject-matter is important in many systems of public social
services.

The German social ethicist Dietrich von Oppen, in his
book *The Age of the Person* (1969), found possibilities for
the recovery of what it means to be a person, and to care
for other persons in the midst of a technological society.
But "the age of the person" will emerge only if people make
thoughtful and serious efforts.

Toffler (1975) wrote of the opportunities before us in planning and working out new ways for the future of life on this planet:

> Yet one might also look upon the coming years
> of trauma as the long-needed opportunity to get
> some old problems straight--to overhaul some of
> our creaking, undemocratic political institu-
> tions; to humanize technology; to think our way
> through to a fresh set of personal and political
> priorities. If we can look beyond the immediate,
> we glimpse breakthroughs to something not merely
> new, but in many ways greater and better.

Focusing on families and their strengths as educators and support systems may well be that needed breakthrough to better ways to develop persons with disabilities.

REFERENCES

Humphreys, R. *Being disabled in America*. Unpublished paper of the Rehabilitation Services Administration--HEW, Washington, D.C., 1978.

Toffler, A. *Eco-spasm*. New York: Bantam Books, 1975.

von Oppen, D. *The age of the person*. Philadelphia: Fortress Press, 1969.

Establishing Service Delivery Models for Families with a Handicapped Member: The Use of Volunteers

Dr. Marty Abramson, Dr. Michael
J. Ash, Dr. Douglas J. Palmer,
and Patricia K. Tollison
Department of Educational Psychology
Texas A & M University

INTRODUCTION

There are more than nine million handicapped individuals, between infancy and the age of 21, in the United States today (Kakalik et al., 1974). While over 50 federal programs, and literally hundreds of state and local programs, provide services to these handicapped persons, there is little indication these services are coordinated in any manner. This lack of coordination results in services which vary in quality, often are fragmented, and typically do not respond to the many needs of handicapped persons and their families.

In our numerous encounters with families of handicapped individuals, the authors have generally found these families lack information regarding what services are available, and how to go about obtaining them. Some families remark they do not know which services are appropriate for their handicapped child, while others feel they do not know what questions to ask. Other families note they have been referred endlessly from agency to agency, in their search for services. It is the rare family that has found adequate services quickly. Moreover, if services are found, it is due primarily to the sheer persistence, aggressiveness, or luck of the parents.

Our focus in this paper is twofold. First, we present a life-span approach to viewing families with a handicapped person. The environment in which handicapped people exist is constantly changing, just as it is for other persons. For example, the needs of mentally retarded persons and their families are far different in adulthood than they were in childhood. Yet, we seldom view handicaps as presenting different problems for families at different points along the life span. Hence, the initial portion of our paper describes age-related problems which often accompany handicapping conditions. In the second section of the paper, an approach for delivering services to families and handicapped persons

417

is described. The suggested model is unique, in that it is
directed toward a life-span approach, makes extensive use
of volunteer personnel, and could be established in any area
of this country.

A LIFE-SPAN CONCEPT OF THE FAMILY
OF THE HANDICAPPED

Infancy

Following birth, the family with a handicapped individual
must deal with a number of related crises in a very short
period of time. Here, the focus is on identification. If
the handicap is apparent, i.e., is readily diagnosed, there
are some immediate concerns. For example, if the infant is
physically deformed, or requires technological assistance to
survive, the mother may be unable or unwilling to hold and
cuddle the child. Several researchers (Condon & Sander, 1974;
Klaus & Kennell, 1976) have shown that a "maternal sensitive
time" exists in the first few hours after birth. During this
time, the foundation for mother/child bonding or attachment
needs to be laid. If the handicap interferes with the normal
attachment sequence, then the family may need professional
assistance to reinstate that sequence.
    The attachment sequence of the post-partum period is also
important to the future relationships of the rest of the family with the handicapped child. The father and siblings may
have difficulty in dealing with any new family member, and
these difficulties may be aggravated by the presence of a
handicap.
    The establishment of this family/infant bonding is a cru-
cial occurrence, and, if problems arise (such as a handicapped infant), the outcome can be catastrophic. For example, Kennell and his coworkers (Kennell et al., 1974) have
demonstrated that when mother and child are separated soon
after delivery for intensive care, the result is a disproportionately high number of family problems, such as child
abuse.
    Other crises which must be overcome by families of the
handicapped concern the critical aspects of infant care. Handicapped infants often require special personal care, as well
as additional technical support (e.g., mechanical devices,
special dietary considerations). When coupled with a general disruption of family life caused by time and space
intrusion, such as extensive travel to special services,
limitation of family mobility, and other sibling concerns,
the family is stressed. Without appropriate support during

infancy, the family of the handicapped child embarks on a
tortuous and difficult journey as a troubled and confused
social unit.

Early Childhood

At age three, many families of handicapped children encounter,
for the first time, the massive diagnosis and treatment bureaucracy. Government agencies and programs delivered
through the public schools and other channels begin to take
some responsibility for the child with a handicap. The first
real impact of Public Law 94-142, and its myriad of mandated
services, are now systematically available to families. Ironically, however, the availability of such services may increase the strain on the family. Often important services
are embedded in a web of bureaucratic regulation and red tape.
Cutting through these impediments can be a long, tiring, and
lonely task. Families need support and guidance in order to
receive the services they need.

School Age

For the families of children who are identified as handicapped at birth, or soon after, there are predictable difficulties and decisions to be made when a child reaches age
six. The potential crises of these families differ from
those facing families of children who have handicapping conditions which are not identified until after the child reaches
the first grade. However, in many instances, both groups of
families rely on the same community support sources for assistance.

If the issue has not been faced before, school age forces
the family of the identified handicapped child to "let go"
of some of the responsibilities for the child. Though it
may come as a relief to many, for others caught in an over-
protective system, the process of letting go can be difficult.
Many parents fear their child will not be cared for properly.
On the other hand, for the parent who has attempted to take
total responsibility for the care of a handicapped child,
there can be a sense of personal loss. In addition, handicapped children themselves may experience significant emotional problems when they begin school for the first time.
The "separation anxiety" phenomenon can be greater for a
child who has been particularly sheltered.

An additional major concern of parents is the adequacy
of the educational services for their children. Frequently,
poor communication between home and school contributes to
the problem. Although recent state and federal regulations
require that parents be included in educational program

design, traditionally there has been little effort to coordinate home and school planning for handicapped children.
Subsequently, parents have complained bitterly of being viewed
as intruders in their children's lives (Turnbull & Turnbull,
1978).

Adolescence and puberty have crisis potential for families
of handicapped children for many of the same reasons that
they do for other families. Additionally, there are specific
problems which may arise, such as the issue of sterilization
of a severely retarded individidual capable of reproduction.
Other less dramatic decisions surround questions of vocational or academic training, and the frequently specific problems
of mobility for the handicapped individual.

Adulthood

As with any of the periods along the life span, the times of
maturity and old age contain many crises for the families of
the handicapped. It is a time when the basic structure of
the family is being irrevocably changed. Handicapped individuals may be well on the way toward establishing their
own family units, thereby extending the original family group.
Moreover, the family can aid the handicapped person in establishing full citizen status, including regular voting, appropriate helping behaviors, and participation in community affairs. In all efforts, the family serves to ease the transition from a personal family focus to a broader societal family view. However, these are not easy tasks, and most families will require more information and support than is currently available to carry out this function.

In theory, the final stage of development in the life
span is death (Kübler-Ross, 1975). Certainly, within those
families with a handicapped person, the death of the handicapped member presents similar kinds of problems as those
faced by any family experiencing death. The real difficulty
lies in maintaining the family role when parents of a handicapped person die or become incapacitated. Depending on the
amount of independence the handicapped person has been able
to achieve, some portion of family support must come from
other sources (e.g., community agencies, relatives).

In spite of the fact that the problems of families with
a handicapped member can be anticipated, a preventive model
designed for these families has not been forthcoming. To
date, services which are provided have not been well coordinated or organized. Poor allocation and delivery of
community resources is most evident in the concentration of
services at the point of diagnosis, only to be followed by
ongoing assistance. In the next section, we propose a model
which, we believe, will be of great benefit to families in
need.

THE FAMILY ADVISOR MODEL

A wide variety of educational and social service agencies exists to serve handicapped persons. Medical personnel are available to assist handicapped persons with physical problems; educators assume responsibility for improving or maintaining cognitive abilities; rehabilitation specialists attempt to train handicapped persons for occupational positions, and so on. At different points in a handicapped person's life, different professional groups flow into, and out of, the family group. For example, medical personnel may have extensive involvement in the treatment of a young, severely retarded child, while educational personnel may have little or no initial contact. Later, when medical difficulties have been corrected, medical services may be reduced, while educational services increase. In like fashion, those involved in rehabilitation or vocational planning may not become involved until adolescence or adulthood. Other disciplines may contact families more frequently (e.g., social work), yet not provide extensive or comprehensive services. Those professions which are frequently involved in working with handicapped persons and their families include:

Social Work	Nutrition
Pediatrics	Psychiatry
Dentistry	Psychology
Nursing	Occupational Therapy
Speech Pathology	Audiology
Physical Therapy	Education
Rehabilitation Counseling	Law

Current Service Delivery Models

Our knowledge of handicapped persons has increased tremendously in the past few years. Along with this increase in knowledge has come improvement in assessment, prevention, treatment, and education. Typically, client-centered delivery systems have been employed to deliver these improvements in services. While seemingly admirable, client-centered approaches ignore the fact that handicapped persons do not live in a vacuum. Their handicaps are, in part, a function of the environment in which these persons live; they are environments which consist of numerous persons, different settings, and ever changing time frames. A client-centered approach has difficulty dealing with the multi-faceted environments a handicapped person encounters as a function of daily living. Yet, if handicaps are a function of environments, then treatment or remediation must also occur across environments.

One of the most highly acclaimed client-centered approaches to service provision has been the use of multidisciplinary teams. The assumption of multi-disciplinary teams is that professional responsibilities will be shared by having professionals substitute for each other. In reality, members of multi-disciplinary teams often work side-by-side rather than with each other. This occurs as a result of the "territoriality" and possessiveness found in all professional fields. Thus, factors which may not be related to the professional domain of a particular discipline, but may be related to a handicapping condition, are often not considered. In essence, it is difficult for members of teams to understand that a single discipline cannot be "all things to all people," thereby setting aside professional jealousies and rivalries.

We do not mean to suggest that client-centered approaches are necessarily inappropriate. Rather, we are suggesting that the majority of families with a handicapped person might not derive enough benefits from these types of approaches to merit their expansion or use beyond certain circumscribed areas, such as severe handicaps or comparatively minor needs of the family.

What Is Needed in a Service Delivery Model

There is little question that families with a handicapped person need service delivery systems which extend beyond those which have traditionally been available. Any service delivery model must contain certain features, including:

1. A means of initiating or obtaining services

2. Readily available diagnostic services throughout the life span

3. Appropriate treatment, education, and remediation programs

4. Access to the necessary professional disciplines

5. A means for determining the effectiveness of service delivery from the vantage point of the provider and user

Essentially, the service delivery system needs to be dynamic and able to follow handicapped persons and their families from the moment a handicap is suspected through adulthood. In earlier sections of this paper, it was noted that the difficulties encountered by families with a handicapped person change as a function of time (infancy, childhood, young adulthood, maturity), as well as the severity of the handicap (mild or severe), and the effectiveness of remediation (effective or noneffective). Currently, no system exists that has been demonstrated to be responsive to each of these factors and their concomitant variations.

The transdisciplinary model which we put forward is designed to assist families who have a variety of physical, emotional, and social needs which must be met for them to deal effectively with their handicapped person. The model is designed to serve as an organizer for the innumerable agencies and individuals who could provide services simultaneously. Such an organizational structure would result in the elimination of overlaps in services, and, more importantly, prevent the confusion which arises over the assumption of responsibility for services. Moreover, this model may be more cost-effective.

Role of the Family Advisor

The key to the model is the family advisor. These persons would be volunteers interested in working with families who have a handicapped member. The family advisors would be attached to an educational or social service agency. After some initial information had been provided to members of the professional community, referrals for identified or suspected handicaps could be made by pediatricians, teachers, neighbors, parents, etc. to the family advisor unit. A family advisor would be appointed who would then contact the family to explain the role of family advisors, and the services they could provide.

Following the referral, all responsibility for locating and obtaining services would rest jointly with the family advisor and family. If a child were identified at birth as being handicapped, the advisory unit would be notified. An advisor would be appointed who, in turn, would arrange for a transdisciplinary team to be organized, based on what appeared to be the apparent needs of the handicapped person and the family. Selecting local professionals in relevant disciplines, the family advisor would arrange for team members to provide initial diagnoses and treatment recommendations for the child and/or family (see Figure 1). After the diagnoses had been completed, treatment services would be sought, including necessary fiscal supports.

In some respects, this approach resembles many of the regional programs which have been referred to as multidisciplinary or interdisciplinary. However, it differs in several critical respects. First, the interdisciplinary team concept is primarily found in larger cities, or in those areas which have major universities or medical centers. For practical

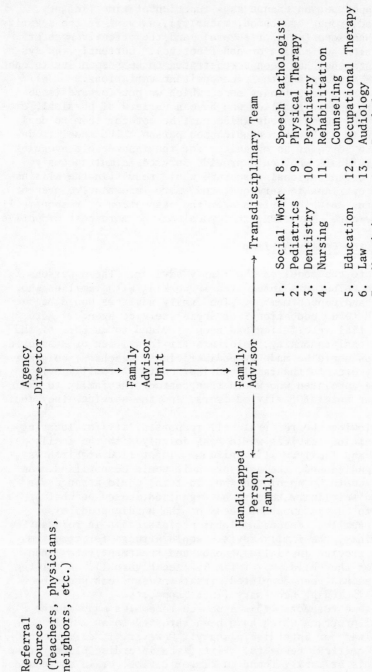

Figure 1

Organizational Structure of a Transdisciplinary Team

purposes, rural areas and smaller communities may not find it feasible, in terms of time and money, to utilize a team located in a distant city. Second, interdisciplinary teams are not equipped to deal with handicapped persons, or the families from which they come, throughout the life span. Treatment is often an ongoing process, which requires frequent re-evaluation. Most often this can best be accomplished in the community where the handicapped person lives. Third, it is frequently the case that treatment is best carried out in a number of environments, with several people. This often entails the training of families to carry out programs in the home. Such training may involve a lengthy process, requiring in-the-home visits and periodic checking to ensure that all is operating smoothly. It is our contention that a family advisor model is uniquely suited to meet these demands.

Who Shall Be a Family Advisor?

Many would point out that the last thing a family of a handicapped person needs is one more bureaucratic agency looking out for the handicapped person's "best interest." We agree, and therefore suggest that the position of family advisor be conceived of as a voluntary position rather than as a paid job. Existing programs for elderly persons (e.g., Meals on Wheels) and young children (e.g., Head Start) rely partially on voluntary participation for day-to-day operations. A similar approach would be feasible with handicapped persons and their families. Numerous groups exist whose goal is to promote the welfare of handicapped persons (e.g., Association for Retarded Citizens, Council for Exceptional Children, etc.). Individuals from these groups, or others (such as the Gray Panthers or American Association of Retired Persons), could be recruited to serve as family advisors.

Naturally, some funds would be needed. However, the initial outlay and continued costs would be minimal; such costs would be for an administrator-mental health professional, necessary secretarial help, office costs, and reimbursements for gasoline, etc. The administrator would be responsible for selection and training of the family advisors in his or her local area. In addition, the administrator would have the responsibility of insuring that a family advisor was always available to the family. Thus, as a family advisor elected to leave the program, for whatever reason, a new advisor would be assigned to continue serving the family. Hopefully, the position of family advisor would be a relatively stable one, necessitating few changes. In light of the above information, success of the program will rest, to a large degree, on the professional expertise and administrative

capabilities of the administrators. Moreover, it is recommended that these individuals reside within the administrative structure of mental health agencies because of their
life-span approach to handicapped individuals. Affiliation
to a mental-health service agency would also give the administrator access to currently established networks for
referral and treatment. It is important to reaffirm the professional background of the family advisory administrators
due to their involvement in initial training and continued
involvement in the inservice of the family advisors. It is
recommended that administrators have extensive background,
including a master's degree with years of experience, or
a doctoral level degree in one of the following areas: Special Education, Psychology, Social Work, or Rehabilitation
Counseling.

Training of the Family Advisor

Though the position would be voluntary, extensive training
will be necessary. Furthermore, it is recommended that a
competency-based training approach be adopted. Competencies
needed by a family advisor may include information and skills
in many areas. Family advisors will require information relating to all services which are available in whatever area
the family advisor unit serves. More importantly, the family advisor will need to learn appropriate interpersonal
skills, advocacy approaches, and the location of potential
sources of funding to pay for services. In addition, this
person will have to acquire management and organizational
skills, in order to deal with numerous professionals. Lastly, family advisors will need to have knowledge of techniques which can assist the family in maintaining the handicapped person in the home. Since a vast majority of handicapped persons spend a good deal of their time within the
family unit, it is critical that families view the person as
being an integral and contributing member of the family. At
least in part, the capacity to view a handicapped person in
this manner is a function of the interpersonal, social, and
emotional behavior exhibited by that individual. Families
require training in behavior management techniques designed
to promote positive behavior, while reducing inappropriate
behavior.
      In addition to the more global interests mentioned above,
the family advisor will also need training in how to assist
families with:

1. Coping realistically with problems

2. Dealing with self-pity

3. Overcoming feelings of ambivalence

4. Eliminating guilt, shame, and depression

5. Understanding the nature and extent of the handicap, and its probable cause

6. Selecting facilities and services for treatment and education

7. Determining which specific programs are most appropriate to the family's needs and the needs of the handicapped person

8. Becoming assertive advocates to ensure that the family's needs are met

9. Help the family know its legal rights

In essence, the family advisor not only has the responsibility of putting a team of professionals together, and making certain that its recommendations are compatible with the family and handicapped person, but also, making certain that the family is extensively involved in all decision-making and treatment plans.

While several programs currently in operation are similar to the one we have suggested, these programs differ from ours in several respects. First, most of the programs are client-centered. Services for families and handicapped persons are designed primarily for families with children from birth to age 21. What is not clearly understood by proponents of these models is that needs of families with handicapped persons do not end when the individual turns 21. Therefore, it is only with a life-span approach that the needs of the family can be satisfied. Second, and perhaps more importantly, the model programs we are aware of utilize paid personnel who have had experience and training in working with handicapped persons. While such personnel would be highly desirable in any program, it is improbable that fiscal resources will soon be available through local, state, or federal agencies to fund such programs on a large-scale basis. Therefore, what may appear feasible on a demonstration basis, may ignore the practical realities of inadequate revenues for major social programs. While we applaud all these efforts, and are greatly encouraged by the initial results, we question whether these demonstration projects will be applicable to a variety of settings which do not have financial resources. To our thinking, a volunteer system, utilizing minimal local

or regional financing, would seem to be the only sure way of
guaranteeing the operation of such a system.

Benefits of a Family Advisor Approach

A number of benefits are suggested by the use of the family
advisor model. Since the family advisor functions within a
prescribed catchment area, families with a handicapped person will have ready access to someone who can be responsive
to their needs and concerns. Rather than relying on a professional who may be many miles away, the family advisor will
serve as a "sounding board" and intermediary for determining
if the desired services are actually necessary.

With training, which includes a working knowledge of the
professional disciplines, family advisors will acquire a
thorough understanding of what resources are available in
their area, the relative effectiveness of those services,
and how various disciplines can be integrated to provide services. While regional services have been beneficial for dealing with exceptional or unusual situations, most handicapped
persons do not require these extraordinary types of services.
Recognition and coordination of existing services will serve
the needs of most handicapped persons and their families within their own community.

A family advisor model is a means of insuring a continuity
of services throughout the life span. Since a family advisor
will be appointed as soon as a handicap is suspected, all
successive referrals and services will be under that individual.
The provision of services will thus be centralized, with continuity being guaranteed by empowering a single group (family advisor unit) to obtain all necessary services. Thus, as
the needs of the family and handicapped person change, the
role of the family advisor will similarly change to reflect
those needs.

The final benefit to be derived involves the amount of
time the family advisor can spend in working with the families
themselves, and fulfilling their individual needs. Thus,
families will have available a means by which they can receive training in working with the handicapped member of the
family. Such training might prove to be advantageous when
the handicapped person reaches young adulthood and prepared
to enter the mainstream of society.

                              SUMMARY

Our paper has emphasized two important factors related to
the provision of services to families of handicapped persons.
First, we have noted that the needs of handicapped persons

and their families change as a function of time and age of the handicapped persons. Second, we believe that many of the service delivery models currently in existence are ill-prepared to deal with families who have a handicapped member. There is often little recognition of the needs of a family with a handicapped person, or how those needs change. As an alternative, we described and suggested the use of family advisors to meet the needs of both the family and the handicapped individual.

The next few years will witness great changes in society's actions toward handicapped persons. However, whether this awareness will mean increased expenditures for expanded services remains to be seen. If monies do not increase, means will have to be found to meet the needs of these families. A family advisor model is one approach to providing needed services at low cost.

REFERENCES

Condon, W. S., & Sander, L. W. Neonate movement is synchronized with adult speech: Interaction participation and language acquisition. *Science*, 1974, *183*, 99-101.

Kakalik, J. S., Brewer, G. D., Dougharty, L. A., Fleischauer, P. D., Genesky, S. M., & Wallen, L. M. *Improving services to handicapped children*. Santa Monica, California: Rand Corporation (R-1420-HEW), May, 1974.

Kennell, J. H., Jerauld, R., Wolfe, H., Chesler, D., Kreger, N. C., McAlpine, W., Steffa, M., & Klaus, M. H. Maternal behavior one year after early and extended post-partum contact. *Developmental Medicine and Child Neurology*, 1974, *16*, 172-179.

Klaus, N. H., & Kennell, J. H. *Maternal-infant bonding*. Saint Louis: C. V. Mosby, 1976.

Kübler-Ross, E. *Death: The final stage of growth*. Englewoods Cliffs, New Jersey: Prentice-Hall, 1975.

Turnbull, A. P., & Turnbull, H. R. *Parents speak out: Views from the other side of the two-way mirror*. Columbus, Ohio: Charles E. Merrill, 1978.

The Strength of Single-Parent Families During the Divorce Crisis: An Integrative Review with Clinical Implications

Dr. Gary W. Peterson
Department of Child and
Family Studies
University of Tennessee
and
Dr. Helen K. Cleminshaw
Department of Home Economics
and Family Ecology
University of Akron

INTRODUCTION

When the situation of parents and children involved in divorce is contrasted with the conditions of intact families, a "pathological" model is often excessively used to describe the single-parent families (Bradwein, Brown, & Fox, 1974; Josephson, 1969). In addition, accounts by other scholars have simplistically argued that problems of divorcing families are attributable either to their structural deficits, or to their changing interactional dynamics, which often appear in conjunction with marital separation (Martoz-Baden et al., 1979). A more realistic view, rather than this dichotomy, [is that problems of divorced families may result from the combined effects of both the structural deficits, and the process alterations which may occur within single-parent families.]

As discussed below, this more complex conception of the events which impinge upon single-parent families during the divorce crisis will also allow for a more positive view of the separation process. A major purpose, therefore, of the present paper is to develop a view of single-parent families which adequately portrays their potential for adjustment, stability, and internal strength in terms of a number of influential structural and process-oriented factors. When disruption in these single parent family systems becomes too extensive, certain intervention strategies which capitalize upon their potential for positive growth will also be discussed.

Such an optimistic view does not preclude the fact that the impact of divorce and separation may have destructive effects. [It should, of course, be acknowledged that several studies have indicated divorce often results in emotional trauma, persistent attachment feelings, and declines in positive psychological qualities for divorcing parents] (Brandwein, Brown, & Fox, 1974; Goode, 1956; Hetherington, Cox, & Cox,

431

1978; Weiss, 1975). A number of studies also provide inconsistent but significant support for the fact that marital
separation has several adverse effects upon children, specifically in the areas of aggressiveness, self-esteem, opposi-
tional behavior, achievement, sex-role development, locus
of control, delinquency, interpersonal relations, and personality disorders (Herzog & Sudia, 1973; Hetherington, 1972;
Hetherington, Cox, & Cox, 1978; Peterson & Leigh, 1978;
Wallerstein & Kelley, 1974, 1975a, 1975b). A realistic view,
therefore, should allow for the possibility that both negative and positive consequences may stem from marital separation.

At the heart of the present perspective is the fact that
marital separation is conceptualized as a "crisis" which
Hill (1949) has referred to as "any sharp or decisive change
for which old patterns are inadequate" (p. 51). It is noteworthy that the above definition of crisis leaves indefinite
any reference to positive or negative consequences for the
families involved. In accordance with Hansen and Johnson
(1979), the present authors prefer to consider a crisis as
being a form of disorganization resulting in either "negative disruption" or "creative regenesis." Furthermore, a
crisis will result in positive or negative consequences contingent upon the nature of three factors. Such elements
consist of: (1) the objective conditions or stressor event
under which individuals will act (the divorce), (2) the pre-
existing attitudes and coping skills of the involved individuals (crisis-meeting resources), and especially (3) the
"definition of the situation" that the concerned persons
impose on the circumstances (Hansen & Hill, 1964).

These three components create the possibility that an
objective condition or stressor event, such as divorce, might
be construed as being devastating by one individual family,
while another might view it as having creative potential.
The nature of the result would be contingent upon the particular "mix" of the three factors delineated above. Use
of the crisis concept and its situational definition also
serves to integrate the large amount of disparate literature about the impact of marital separation upon single-
parent families. Accordingly, the respective applicability
of these concepts for the situation of the child and the
custodial parent will be considered in the following sections.

THE CRISIS SITUATION FOR THE CHILD

Several studies seem to indicate that a number of factors
contribute to the child's definition of the crisis when the
stressful event of marital separation occurs. The first

aspect of the child's perception of the situation is the quality of the parents' marital relationship prior to separation. Several investigations provide evidence that if children view their parents' relationship as being a positive one, the effect of marital separation may have its most severe effects. In contrast, if children from divorced homes accurately define their parents' relationship as being dysfunctional, these young people may be more adjusted than children from intact homes who perceive their parents' marriage as being strained (Hetherington, Cox, & Cox, 1978; Landis, 1960; Nye, 1957). It would, therefore, seem probable that if children of divorce are provided a realistic view of their parents' strained relationships, this may contribute to their eventual coping abilities.

[A second aspect of the "definition of the situation" for children is the nature of their perceived relationship with the absent parent.] Children's capacity to cope with the separation crisis is enhanced when they perceive they do not have a close relationship with their absent parent (Hetherington, Cox, & Cox, 1978; Landis, 1960). Children who have a parent whom they perceive as neglectful or abusive may, therefore, have a built-in strength (or crisis-meeting resource), assuming that a distant or negative relationship will evoke less separation anxiety. Although a relationship which is perceived as close may be quite traumatic, a child who realistically views the parental relationship as destructive may actually benefit from the separation.

After the divorce, another interactional aspect of the situation is the child's perception of the quality of the parents' postdivorce adjustment. [If parents are able to moderate their disputes and avoid involving the children in conflicts after the separation, the young person's adjustment appears to be enhanced.] A family's potential for coping with the crisis would, therefore, be damaged if the parents' marital conflict continued, or escalated after the divorce. In contrast, a family strength would be apparent if the divorced couple managed to avoid extensive postdivorce conflict.

Another factor contributing to either a negative or positive definition of the marital separation crisis is the normative structure that children have internalized. In a particular subculture, socialized norms will define the degree of respectability or stigma divorced families internalize. Accordingly, studies have indicated that increasing stigma from divorce may contribute to successively lower levels of self-esteem in children (Rosenberg, 1965, 1975). In contrast, internalization of less negative norms about marital separation may function as a strength for children of

divorce because marital dissolution will be viewed as less
deviant by them.

Finally, a structural condition of the single-parent situation, which also contributes to a child's tendency to withstand separation crisis, is the availability of alternative
surrogates. Several studies indicate that positive social
behavior is enhanced when substitute models for the absent
parent are available, such as stepfathers, relatives, siblings, friends, peers, or teachers. Consequently, it appears
that surrogates for the absent parent may also serve to
strengthen the adjustment potential of children involved in
marital separation.

THE CRISIS SITUATION FOR THE CUSTODIAL PARENT

When the perspective of single-parents is considered, a number of elements also serve to define the nature of the crisis.
First of all, factors which contribute to the severity of the
marital separation crisis are the experiences of emotional
stress, despair, separation anxiety, and anger directed at
the former partner (Goode, 1956; Weiss, 1975). Of course,
another matter which contributes to the stressfulness of
the crisis for the adults involved is that the status of
being a divorced family member is often provided negative
qualities by subcultural norms (Goode, 1956; Marsden, 1969;
Rosenberg, 1965, 1975). [Changes in the family structure also
contribute to the remaining parent's difficulty in meeting
new role obligations.][Accordingly, several studies have indicated that custodial parents often experience a substantial
increase in the amount of role responsibility involving the
child socialization, childcare, provider, domestic, sexual,
and therapeutic roles] (Brandwein, Brown, & Fox, 1974; Glasser
& Navarre, 1965; Hetherington, Cox, & Cox, 1978; Nye, 1976).

With reference to the single-parent-child dyad, the degree
of disorganization the single-parent experiences during the
divorce crisis also seems to have an adverse impact upon the
caretaker-child relationship. As certain studies have reported (Glasser & Navarre, 1965; Hetherington, Cox, & Cox,
1978; Santrock, 1975) [parents experiencing divorce often become increasingly punitive, less rational in their control
attempts, and less supportive with their children.] Such alterations in parental behavior appear to stem from the emotional trauma, the stigma, and the role strain which were
previously described as consequences of the marital separation process. Parental behaviors of this nature tend to
elicit disobedient and acting out responses in children,
which, in turn, evoke further repressiveness from parents.

The result is that a reciprocal aggravation cycle often occurs between parent and child.

While certain components of the situation seem to indicate that the crisis of divorce for the custodial parent is both severe and destructive, other factors lessen the severity of the crisis and many function as family strengths or crisis-meeting resources. The first of these assets would be prevalent if a divorced parent had internalized a system of norms which did not define divorce as a deviant status. Such an attitude would alleviate many of the negative aspects of marital dissolution, and would help to moderate the crisis. Such attitudes are likely to be more prevalent as divorce continues to increase and becomes more normative.

Other strengths stem from the fact that certain special qualities of the single-parent also seem to operate as effective crisis-meeting resources for the single-parent family. [Studies indicate that such factors as marketable skills, high levels of education, substantial income, and emotional maturity serve as means to cope with, or even transcend, the negative consequences of the "crisis"](Goode, 1956; Hetherington, Cox, & Cox, 1978; Orthner, Brown, & Ferguson, 1976).

Factors serving to directly influence the single-parents' definition of the divorce situation concern the particular meaning divorced persons impose upon their circumstances. Rather than feeling overextended, certain single-parents are able to define increased role assignments as a series of challenges and increased autonomy. [Some divorced women, for ← example, seem to develop the capacity to positively define their crisis situation as one of increased freedom to engage in the parent-child relationship without the interference of the husbands](Brown et al., 1976). [Such a perspective seems consistent with the idea that new roles can be rewarding as well as obligating. Accumulation of roles, therefore, would not lead to role strain as long as the rewards grow in correspondence with the demands](Seiber, 1974).

Also supportive of the argument that certain qualities of single-parents may facilitate a family's recovery is the evidence that parental behavior often returns to supportive and rational qualities as the trauma of divorce subsides (Hetherington, Cox, & Cox, 1978). Such process-oriented characteristics of parents are especially important when they are viewed as factors which both influence and are influenced by their children's characteristics. Accordingly, it seems apparent that there are reciprocal effects between parental and child characteristics which cause the single-parent family to reestablish the particular level of positive interactions which existed before the crisis. Indeed, studies have suggested positive levels of parental behaviors and child outcomes are initially predictive of eventual recuperation

(Hetherington, Cox, & Cox, 1978; Wallerstein & Kelley, 1974, 1975a, 1975b). High initial performance in these areas should, therefore, be viewed as a family strength, because they appear to serve as a resource for the readjustment process. Since parent-child interaction patterns do return to "normal," this also indicates that families actually have crisis-meeting resources, and that the effects of the crisis may only be temporary.

Another structural factor which may serve as a strength of single-parent families concerns custodial parents who maintain extensive social relationships which can be used for outside support. Friends or kin, for example, can alleviate some of the role strain in a divorce situation by assisting with child care. Dating companions and recreational groups may help fulfill some of the single-parents' sexual and therapeutic needs. As evidence reported by Raschke (1977) indicates, high levels of social participation among postdivorce individuals are correlated with lower stress. It would, therefore, seem apparent that maintenance of substantial social networks can function to alleviate some of the worst aspects of the crisis situation by filling deficits in the single-parent family's role structure.

STRENGTH THROUGH INTERVENTION

While some divorcing families appear to have naturally operative strengths which contribute either to their coping or regenerative capacity, other families require assistance to stimulate or speed up their latent recuperative processes. Interventions which are oriented toward ameliorating many of the problematic aspects of the crisis situation will capitalize upon the enhancement of existing family strengths.

Since so many families are now experiencing the crisis of divorce, there is a great need to devise new social mechanisms responsive to the needs of such families. One method might be the establishment of community divorce clinics that are closely affiliated with the court system, and that could receive referrals from this source. While involvement in such programs should remain voluntary, strong recommendations for participation should be given by the courts and other concerned agencies. The functions of such divorce clinics would include divorce counseling, sponsorship of educational programs on divorce--as well as supplying information about welfare entitlements, housing, day care, self-help groups, and lists of helpful agencies in the community.

Divorce Counseling

Whether divorce counseling is conducted within or outside of such clinics, it can and should be used to clarify and alter objective conditions and subjective definitions which are components of the divorce situation for the family members. A major characteristic of divorce therapy, therefore, is that the problem is not some fatal flaw of character possessed by the divorcing individuals. Instead, it is the situation which is causing the difficulty, and must be redefined as an opportunity for growth rather than despair (Froiland & Hozman, 1975; Krantzler, 1974).

Divorce counseling which is truly concerned with the family's definition of the situation will often employ conjoint sessions initially focusing upon deciding whether or not to divorce in terms of the family's overall condition (Brown, 1976). In this phase, conscious thought is devoted to the possibility of divorce, and the quality of the family relationships. Such a process involves clarification of the sources and nature of the current marital dysfunction (Kressel & Deutsch, 1978). Time will be spent on ascertaining the spouses' definition of the marital situation, with reference to their commitment and involvement in the relationship. Consideration is also given to the impact of such factors as the child's perception of the quality of the parents' relationship, and the closeness of the child to the absent parent.

[If and when a decision to divorce is made and implemented, the next phase of divorce counseling has been referred to by Brown (1976) as "restructuring." Such a process has been defined as rebuilding a satisfying life style for individuals within the emotional, legal, parent-child, economic, and social relationship areas.] It is also apparent that this concept is consistent with the idea that the objective and subjective aspects of the situation must be gradually redefined as either manageable, or as an opportunity for positive growth.

In the area of emotional concerns, it is often the case that feelings of loss, grief, separation anxiety, guilt, and failure for both the adults and children must be dealt with. During this process, counselors may focus upon the trauma of family members, and assist in redefining the stigma of negative norms against divorce. The eventual objective of the counselor is to help clients use the crisis of divorce as a means to redefine the situation as one of acceptance and opportunity for growth. Restoration of the parents' emotional adjustment is also important in order to maintain constructive parent-child interaction patterns.

Because legal issues can become an inflammatory aspect of postdivorce situations, the restructuring phase of divorce

counseling will also focus upon resolving these matters. Such
an effort by counselors, working in conjunction with lawyers,
will help eliminate one of the major causes of postdivorce
conflict. Weiss (1975), for example, has argued that formerly
married individuals often find excuses to continue their conflict as an expression of their persisting attachment. [As
previously described, the quality of the postdivorce relationship also has important effects upon the adjustment of children involved in divorce.]

Divorce counselors must, therefore, develop proficiency
with interventions which encourage negotiation processes and
conflict management skills for resolving legal issues and
other factors which serve to continue postdivorce conflict.
As Kressel and Deutsch (1978) argue, divorce clinicians must
put forth extensive effort to reduce tension, establish norms
of equity during the negotiation process, and discourage
revenge-seeking tactics. Some therapists find the flow and
ease of negotiations are increased by providing a precise framework for the conduct of family bargaining sessions. Such
procedures tend to redefine the situation as one of making
equitable and constructive change, rather than one of being
stalemated by persistent vindictiveness.

Another function of the second phase of divorce counseling specifically involves the parent-child relationship. The
concern is with the maintenance of supportive parental behavior and rational control attempts, while suppressing any
coercive and inconsistent parenting which may appear. Counseling, which deals with these behavioral dimensions, is focusing upon one aspect of the family's situational context which
influences the child to respond with either positive or negative behavior. Other interventions should also seek to directly maintain the positive responsiveness of the child to
the custodial parent, which, in turn, should reciprocally
elicit more nurturant and rational behavior from the parent.

[While focusing upon the parent-child relationship during
the divorce crisis, therapists will often find that children
deny the reality of the situation, and withdraw into psychological isolation.] In order to remedy this problem, Hozman
and Froiland (1976) present a model of divorce counseling
based on Kübler-Ross' (1969) concept of loss, which assists
parents and children through the divorce process. [The model
offers the idea that many children proceed through five stages
of loss during the divorce crisis, resulting in a final stage
of acceptance.] Such a conception is compatible with ideas
expressed in the present paper, because the final stage requires that children must realistically accept and redefine
the circumstances of the divorce situation which they often
cannot control. Hozman and Froiland (1976) also recommend a
variety of interventions, which include reality techniques,

role playing, expression of feelings, and channeling the child's anger.

During the crisis of divorce, other focal points of divorce counseling pertinent to the parent-child relationship are concerned with making the separation explicit to the children, and ameliorating custody battles. In the first case, an honest, matter-of-fact approach should be used with the child/children, so that a clear definition of the family situation is acquired. Such an approach must provide children with a realistic perception of the quality of their parents' relationship. Rather than seeking to protect children from the real nature of the situation, an honest approach is crucial in order to insure that children will have a sense of trust in their parents. Divorce counseling which acknowledges such objectives helps prevent the reported feelings of guilt and responsibility children often feel for their parents' disrupted marriage. Secondly, in the area of custody decisions, a useful procedure is to employ conjoint sessions, in order that the needs and emotions of all family members, including the children, can be expressed. At times during the therapeutic process, the counselor must function as a child advocate who encourages children to express their feelings about future living and custody arrangements.

Within the economic domain, divorce counseling should focus upon defining the single-parents' role performance in the provider role. Such intervention is necessary in order to assist single-parents with their increased responsibility in this domain, and eliminate some of its incompatibility with other family roles. Areas of concern should include advisement as to child care, time use, opportunities for job training, family budgeting, living arrangements, credit, welfare, and health insurance. Counseling about these matters will provide for efficient use of economic resources, while eliminating some of the role incompatibility that is a structural problem during the divorced condition.

A final area of concern is the reestablishment of certain social relationships. With reference to the situation of divorce, one of its problematic aspects may be the absence of a partner who supplies therapeutic, affectional, and sexual needs to the single-parent. The fact that these old ties are abruptly severed underscores the need for establishment of new social relationships (Brown, 1976; Hunt, 1966). The divorce counselor's function in this area should involve helping clients to plan for their social needs. Referrals from the counselor to adult social groups will often assist single-parents to reestablish social ties.

A therapist should also seek to enlist the support of the extended family and friends, in order to alleviate ambivalence about the divorce process, and to provide emotional

support. The involvement of such individuals might be encouraged by having them attend some of the conjoint sessions
(Kressel & Deutsch, 1978). In the case of children, maintenance of social relationships is also important. As previously described, surrogates such as kin, teachers, siblings,
peers, and adult friends have been found to be significant
factors in the adjustment of children. Family therapists
should encourage the continuation of such involvements, and,
where possible, the counselor should seek their cooperation
in structuring a responsive social network of surrogates for
the child.

Education for Divorce

Besides counseling for divorced and separated families, community-based divorce clinics might also sponsor classes and
small group sessions which provide information about the
divorce situation. Such groups have been variously referred
to as "seminars for the separated" (Weiss, 1975), "situation/
transition groups" (Schwartz, 1975), or "divorce experience
workshops" (Young, 1978). The overall purpose of these educational experiences is to supply cognitive information about
the divorce crisis, as well as emotional support. Similar
to divorce counseling, these educational experiences can be
concerned with the same areas inclusive of emotional concerns, legal matters, parent-child relationships, economic
matters, and social relationships. Supplying information in
these areas will serve to clarify the ambiguity of the situation for the divorcing family. In a time where natural support systems, such as the extended family have diminished,
such alternative means of sustaining individuals through the
crisis of divorce should also be encouraged by professionals.
    While these educational support groups may not be charac-
terized by the intense involvement of divorce counseling,
they have the advantage of efficiently providing information
and support to a larger number of individuals. Examples of
their usefulness might include the alleviation of the "divorce stigma" by having group members share their experiences,
and provide information about the frequency and normality of
divorce. Instruction on parenting skills might also be provided in order to maintain the quality of the parent-child
relationship during the divorce crisis.

REFERENCES

Brandwein, R. A., Brown, C. A., & Fox, E. M. Women and children last: The social situation of divorced mothers and their families. *Journal of Marriage and the Family,* 1974, *36,* 498-514.

Brown, C. A., Feldberg, R., Fox, E. M., & Kohen, J. Divorce: Chance of a new lifetime. *Journal of Social Issues,* 1976, *32,* 119-133.

Brown, E. M. Divorce counseling. In D. H. L. Olson (Ed.), *Treating relationships.* Lake Mills, Iowa: Graphic Publishing Company, 1976.

Froiland, T. L, & Hozman, T. L. *A proposed model for divorce counseling.* Paper presented at the meeting of the American Personnel and Guidance Association, New York, March, 1975.

Glasser, P., & Navarre, E. Structural problems of the one-parent family. *Journal of Social Issues,* 1965, *21,* 98-109.

Goode, W. J. *After divorce.* New York: Free Press, 1956.

Hansen, D. A., & Hill, R. L. Families under stress. In H. T. Christensen (Ed.), *Handbook of marriage and the family.* Chicago: Rand McNally, 1964.

Hansen, D. A., & Johnson, V. A. Rethinking family stress theory: Definitional aspects. In W. R. Burr, R. Hill, F. I. Nye, & I. L. Reiss, *Contemporary theories about the family.* New York: Free Press, 1979.

Herzog, E., & Sudia, C. E. Children in fatherless families. In B. M. Caldwell & H. N. Ricciuti (Eds.), *Review of child development research* (Vol. 3). Chicago: University of Chicago Press, 1973.

Hetherington, E. M. Effects of father absence on personality development in adolescent daughters. *Developmental Psychology,* 1972, *7,* 313-326.

Hetherington, E. M., Cox, M., & Cox, R. The aftermath of divorce. In J. H. Stevens, Jr. & M. Mathews (Eds.), *Mother/child, father/child relationships.* Washington, D.C.: NAEYC, 1978.

Hill, R. L. *Families under stress.* New York: Harper, 1969.

Hozman, R. L., & Froiland, D. J. Families in divorce: A proposed model for counseling the children. *The Family Coordinator*, 1976, *25*, 271-276.

Hunt, M. *The world of the formerly married.* New York: Fawcett World Library, 1966.

Josephson, E. The matriarchy: Myth and reality. *The Family Coordinator*, 1969, *18*, 268-276.

Krantzler, M. *Creative divorce.* New York: M. Evans, 1974.

Kressel, K., & Deutsch, M. Divorce therapy: An in-depth survey of therapists' views. *Family Process*, 1978, *40*, 413-447.

Kübler-Ross, E. *On death and dying.* New York: Macmillan, 1969.

Landis, J. R. The trauma of children when parents divorce. *Marriage and Family Living*, 1960, *22*, 7-13.

Marotz-Baden, R., Adams, G. R., Bueche, N., Munro, B., & Munro, G. Family form or family process? Reconsidering the deficit family model approach. *The Family Coordinator*, 1979, *28*, 5-14.

Marsden, D. *Mothers alone: Poverty and the fatherless family.* London: Allen Lane, The Penguin Press, 1969.

Nye, F. E. Child adjustment in broken and in unhappy unbroken homes. *Marriage and Family Living*, 1957, *19*, 356-361.

Nye, F. I. *Role structure and analysis of the family.* Beverly Hills, California: Sage Publications, 1976.

Orthner, D., Brown, T., & Ferguson, D. Single parent fatherhood: An emerging life style. *The Family Coordinator*, 1976, *25*, 429-437.

Peterson, G. W., & Leigh, G. K. *The effect of marital separation upon the instrumental competence of children: A theory with social policy implications.* Paper presented at the annual meeting of the National Council on Family Relations, October, 1978.

Raschke, H. J. The role of social participation in post-separation and postdivorce adjustment. *Journal of Divorce*, 1977, *1*, 129-140.

Rosenberg, M. *Society and the adolescent self-concept.* Princeton, New Jersey: Princeton University Press, 1965.

Rosenberg, M. The dissonant context and the adolescent self-concept. In S. E. Dragaston & G. H. Elder (Eds.), *Adolescence in the life cycle.* New York: Halstead Press, 1975.

Santrock, J. W. Father absence, perceived maternal behavior and moral development in boys. *Child Development*, 1975, *46*, 753-757.

Schwartz, M. D. Situation/transition groups: A conceptualization and review. *American Journal of Orthopsychiatry*, 1975, *45*, 744-754.

Seiber, S. D. Toward a theory of role accumulation. *American Sociological Review*, 1974, *39*, 567.

Wallerstein, J. S., & Kelley, J. B. The effects of parental divorce: The adolescent experience. In E. J. Anthony & C. Koupernik (Eds.), *The child in his family: Children at psychiatric risk* (Vol. 3). New York: Wiley, 1974.

Wallerstein, J. S., & Kelley, J. B. The effects of parental divorce: Experiences of the preschool child. *Journal of the American Academy of Child Psychiatry*, 1975a, *14*, 600-616.

Wallerstein, J. S., & Kelley, J. B. The effects of parental divorce: Experiences of the child in later latency. *American Journal of Orthopsychiatry*, 1975b, *46*, 256-267.

Weiss, R. S. *Marital separation.* New York: Basic Books, Inc., 1975.

Young, D. M. The divorce experience workshop: A consumer evaluation. *Journal of Divorce*, 1978, *2*, 37-47.

VII. THE ROLE OF EDUCATION IN BUILDING
FAMILY STRENGTHS

Great potential for building family strengths lies in the
area of family life education. The articles in this section discuss the various strategies, goals, and programs
which can contribute to the most effective family life
education. Family education for a variety of audiences,
ranging from preschool to the entire family unit, is
considered.

Trudy Maas describes a preschool program which has
incorporated the parent cooperative concept. This concept
recognizes the importance of parents in the child's educational life. In this program, parents serve on advisory
boards, help as volunteers in the classroom, and help in
other ways.

The article by Gladys Helm and Ann Irvine offers instructional strategies to insure that the classroom is a
supportive, nonthreatening place to learn. Helping students to learn decision-making skills which are helpful
throughout life is discussed.

Linda Tharp discusses the classroom use of the philosophy of humanism, with its emphasis on personal worth,
positive self-concept, significant interpersonal relationships, and personal choice and responsibility for one's
own life. This strategy results in both students and
teachers learning social skills and may effect positive
change in behavior.

Dr. Joanne Everts and Dr. Vera Gershner provide an
overview of family life education in America. They describe the results of a project which identified essential competencies needed by vocational homemaking teachers.

The article by Dr. Ron Cromwell and Dr. Vicky Cromwell
proposes a family-focused philosophy of education. They
suggest that family-focused education, by reaching the
entire family unit, more effectively meets the needs of the
family. This approach could prevent many family problems,
and could also promote family strengths.

Adding Dimensions to Parent and Preschool Education by Incorporating the Parent Cooperative Concept into a Public School Setting

Trudy Maas
Jefferson County Public Schools
Lakewood, Colorado

INTRODUCTION

The parent cooperative concept is an idea that continues to find favor with parents committed to active involvement in their preschoolers' education. In a parent cooperative, parents serve on advisory committees, interview and hire personnel, pay tuition to support the educational program, and volunteer to work during the preschool sessions. They may also be involved in serving on a board of directors, organizing fund-raising activities, and helping with general maintenance, such as repair of equipment, yard work, and housekeeping.

In Jefferson County, Colorado, the cooperative concept has been incorporated into a public preschool and parent involvement program which serves 2,000 of the district's three- and four-year-old children. Entitled "Added Dimensions to Parent and Preschool Education," it is built on the belief that parents are the child's first and most effective teachers. The program focuses on providing meaningful learning experiences for each preschooler at his or her own developmental level, but it is equally committed to involving parents in all aspects of their children's education.

As in a cooperative, parents in this program are expected to work in the preschool. In addition, they are invited to participate in large group meetings, small group discussions, advisory boards, and other activities, such as making materials and planning fund raisers. Because "Added Dimensions" is tuition funded, the Jefferson County Schools can effectively serve an important segment of the parents and children in the county at a minimal cost to the district.

"Added Dimensions" is a federally-funded member of the National Diffusion Network. Consequently, materials and consulting services are available to districts and agencies interested in starting a similar program.

447

BACKGROUND

"Added Dimensions to Parent and Preschool Education" had its
start in the early 1950's, when several groups of Jefferson
County mothers, with the encouragement of the State Board for
Vocational Education, established parent education and preschool programs for themselves and their three- and four-year-
old children. Two-hour meetings were held twice monthly,
and parent participation was required if the child attended
preschool. In 1968, due to a budget crisis, the school district cut out its share of the money. In order to survive,
the parent education and preschool program became self-
supporting with the introduction of a tuition payment. Three
hundred children and parents were registered for the twice-
weekly sessions, which lasted two and one-half hours. Two
years later, it was necessary to implement a new organizational plan for three basic reasons: to keep the program self-
supporting as costs were increasing; to absorb within the
total number, some of those children whose parents could not
afford the cost; and to reemphasize the parent education aspect by allowing time for the head teacher to assume responsibility for it within the school week. It was at this time
that trained paraprofessionals were introduced successfully
into the program.

In 1971, the Title III Project, "Added Dimensions to
Parent and Preschool Education," was combined with the existing program, establishing the early intervention and home
visiting aspects. The additions proved to be so popular that
when the grant expired in 1974, the Jefferson County Board
of Education agreed to share in the future financing of these
supplementary activities. Thus, by joining the resources of
the parents, the community, and the school district, more
than 33 percent of the county preschool population could be
served by a public preschool program.

At present, the parents contribute to the financial foundation through tuition payments of $22.50 per month. This
pays for the salaries of both head teachers and teacher assistants, materials, equipment, snacks, and tuition waivers.
Parents work in the preschool, as do other members of the
community, including senior high school students. Preschool
classes meet in schools and school cottages, and in churches
which offer space for preschool centers in return for a nom-
inal rental fee.

The school district provides much in the way of support
services for the preschool. Examples of such services include supervision from an elementary school principal, building space, bus service, and administrative services. These
services enrich the program, make it available to greater
numbers of children, and greatly reduce the administrative

burdens of the head teacher, so more time can be spent in direct services to children and their parents.

PROGRAM GOALS

The underlying philosophy of both the parent and preschool components of "Added Dimensions" is that parents are the most important teachers of their children. In focusing on this principle, the parent involvement component is designed to provide opportunities for parents to:

1. become aware of their long-term responsibility as the prime educators and counselors of their children.

2. acquire further knowledge and understanding of child growth and development.

3. observe and participate in the prekindergarten so that the basic concepts of child growth and development might be understood better, and that deeper insights into human behavior be achieved.

4. progress more comfortably in their relationships with their children so they accept and enjoy them as they are, as well as encourage their individualities and share in their interests.

5. gain knowledge about where to go for help or special services in the community.

6. experience the feeling of warm support and shared concern for the welfare of their children.

7. benefit from the chance to see appropriate teaching behaviors modeled by preschool staff.

8. share concerns with other parents about the problems and demands of child rearing.

IMPLEMENTATION

In implementing the goals of the parent involvement component, "Added Dimensions" recognizes that parents have individual needs and strengths. A variety of activities is offered so that they can select the most meaningful ways to involve themselves in the educational programs of their children. Thus, just as the preschool curriculum is designed to meet the

individual needs of each child, the parent involvement program is flexible so that it can also accommodate individual
needs and interests.

All parents of participating preschools are expected to
serve as volunteers in the classroom, and to host two home
visits by a preschool staff member. They are also invited
and encouraged to become involved in any or all of the other
activities which are offered for parents at their preschool
center. Activities available at each center are described
in detail in the following section.

Classroom Volunteers

In the preschool, each family agrees to work at least two
or more school sessions during the year. These visits to
the preschool help the parents understand the program, and
allow them to see their child in a group setting. They learn
new techniques for working with children, and lend valuable
assistance to the daily program. Careful and pertinent orientation of parents is a prerequisite for an effective parent
volunteer program.

Examples of activities which parent volunteers perform
include:

1. Interacting with children at learning centers

2. Cooking with a small group

3. Sharing special talents or interests

4. Assisting on field trips

5. Directing art or craft projects

6. Tutoring a child

7. Reading stories

Home Visits

Every preschool family receives two or more home visits during
the school year. In the preschool program, the teacher assistant visits the homes of the children for whom he or she
is responsible in the center. The first visit is made at
the beginning of the year to introduce the preschool program,
and to administer the Denver Developmental Screening Test.
This is a screening instrument which points up any developmental lags a child may have. It is given in the home because the child and parent feel most comfortable and

non-threatened in their home setting. The results of this
early screening are used to plan the best instructional program for the child.

The second home visit occurs at the end of the school
year, and allows the parent and teacher assistant to discuss
the child's progress over the year. This conference is usually held in the home to emphasize the attitude of home-
school partnership which the program wishes to foster. The
conference is not only an evaluation of the child's progress,
but is a discussion of the changes observed by both the parents and the teacher assistants. In addition to these two
visits, interim visits are arranged for families who would
benefit from them.

Large-Group Meetings

Parents are invited to attend general meetings at the center
throughout the school year. An orientation meeting is planned
at the start of the year to explain the program to parents.
Open houses and dad's days are other popular large-group activities. Centers also schedule speakers or panels to discuss pertinent subjects. The input of parents concerning
topics and speakers makes these meetings more effective. Providing child care at the center during the meeting often results in increased attendance.

Small-Group Discussions

Parent discussion groups are a vital component of the "Added
Dimensions" program. Each center offers several series of
discussions throughout the school year. Groups of eight to
fifteen parents meet with the head teacher for four or five
sessions, and the agenda consists of the parents' concerns
and questions.

The discussion groups are conducted using the Child Study
Association's Education for Living group techniques. Teachers
receive inservice training in using this method. The objective of the Education for Living program is to help individuals, through group discussion guided by a trained leader, to
deepen their understanding of both the stresses and satis-
factions of family life, and to discover new, more effective
ways of handling problems.

The teacher's role as discussion leader is to help group
members share their anxieties, expectations, and problems in
dealing with their families. The leader will also add information and knowledge, so that group members realize and
are comforted by the universality of their feelings. Usually
they can suggest solutions for problems.

The areas of concern which are discussed in these groups
are wide-ranging and reflect the concerns of that particular
group. Some often-discussed areas include children learning
to accept responsibility, sibling relationships, discipline
and punishment, communication between parent and child, independence versus rebellion, and handling parental anger and
impatience.

Evaluation of discussion groups show that parents find
them extremely valuable. They conclude that the groups help
them choose appropriate solutions to specific problems, and
also help alleviate the feelings of isolation often experienced by parents of young children.

Parent Advisory Boards

The parent advisory board is yet another avenue for parent
involvement. While not a policy-making group, in the sense
of a cooperative's board of directors, the parent advisory
board communicates the concerns and suggestions of the parents to the head teachers and the Early Childhood Education
Coordinator. It helps support the program in material ways,
such as making equipment, and in less tangible ways, such
as serving as an advocate for the program goals in the community. It also serves as a sounding board for new policies
and programs.

There is a district-wide advisory board, consisting of
parent representatives from the fourteen preschool centers,
who meet with the Early Childhood Education Coordinator.
Additionally, many centers have their own boards, which communicate with the head teacher, and coordinate activities,
such as fund raisers to buy equipment and efforts to improve
the environment at the center.

Parent Library

Each preschool center houses a library with books of interest
to parents of preschoolers. Many centers also prepare newsletters, handbooks, bibliographies, and reprints for distribution to their parents. In addition, toy-lending libraries are located throughout the county. Teachers may check
out toys to lend to parents for use during home visitation
sessions and as follow-up to the visits.

PROGRAM EVALUATION

Observation and evaluation of the parent involvement component indicate that parents have participated enthusiasti-
cally in the parent education segment of the "Added Dimensions"

program, and each year support the educational programs offered in the centers by their increased involvement. Meetings of parent advisory groups are also well-attended.

An evaluation study assessed the effect of the head teacher's encouragement of parents to become involved with the preschool. It was found that two hours per week spent working with parents resulted in increased parent participation.

Parental approval of the preschool program was most effectively demonstrated when the Title III funding came to an end. At this time, parents and teachers asked the board of education for extra funds to continue the home visiting and screening aspects, which had been initiated by the grant. The fact that the preschool received this financing is a good indication the school board also realized the very real need for a program as comprehensive as the one being carried on in Jefferson County.

CONCLUSION

"Added Dimensions to Parent and Preschool Education" is a program which effectively incorporates the parent cooperative philosophy into a public preschool setting. This incorporation is reflected in the parent involvement activities which have been described in this paper. More importantly, the attitude of the cooperative movement about the unique role of parents in their children's education forms the focus of the entire "Added Dimensions" program philosophy. It recognizes that when a child enters school, both the child and parents are beginning a far-reaching experience. For the parents, it is a time filled with hopes and anxieties, which create an intense interest in the school. This is a critical period for building sound relationships between home and school. Once this relationship is established, it provides a basis for communication and cooperation throughout the child's school years.

Because of this commitment and respect for parents, "Added Dimensions" can assist them in learning ways to become involved in the educational process. Since it has public school sponsorship, the "Added Dimensions" program can offer a philosophy and a curriculum which articulate with those of the district's kindergarten and elementary programs. Also, the preschool benefits from school district resources, such as pupil personnel services, administrative expertise, transportation facilities, and warehouse purchasing of classroom materials. A further advantage is that a public school program reaches a larger segment of the preschool population than is typically served by a parent cooperative. This results in more parents becoming involved and informed about their important roles as teachers of their children.

An Approach to Teaching Family
Life Education: Tell It Like It Is,
But Keep It Safe

Gladys Helm
and
Ann Irvine
Lincoln Public Schools
Lincoln, Nebraska

Teaching family life education in the secondary schools involves two major challenges. The first challenge is to determine relevant content for the student. The second is to
select and use appropriate instructional strategies. The
first challenge is very real, but we leave it to other authors.
It is the second challenge of appropriate instructional strategies which we will address. Instructional strategies are
appropriate for family life education if they:

1. help students develop a non-threatening, supportive
    environment for learning;

2. help students gain sufficient information for making
    decisions;

3. help students assume responsibility for their own learn-
    ing, value clarification, and goal setting; and

4. help students develop thinking skills needed in making
    responsible personal decisions.

DEVELOPING A SUPPORTIVE ENVIRONMENT

By nature, the content of family life education is value-laden
and, at times, controversial. For example, when a class examines the definition of a family, the student of separated
or divorced parents does not always agree that the "nuclear
family" must be living together to fulfill family functions.
When discussing the topic of achieving Erikson's Stage of
Intimacy, some students may actually be experiencing cohabitation. This often results in conflict within families. Conflict carries into the classroom as opinions are expressed.
Emotions will arise, sides will be taken, and controversy

455

will surface. For family life education to be effective, the instructor must facilitate a change from opinion and emotion to one of factuality and objective thought. It is imperative that positive rapport be established with students and among students. The students themselves become important learning "tools" within the classroom. Regardless of which approach one is using in a family life class, positive rapport with the student is a vital element for effective learning. How the atmosphere is created will depend on the individual teacher and her or his specific teaching style. Regardless of the technique used, the following guidelines will help establish and maintain a conducive atmosphere.

1. Everyone deserves the right to be heard. (So everyone listens.)

2. Accentuate the positive. (Build on strengths. Give strokes.)

3. Eliminate the negative but be authentic. (No "put-downs" of self or others--disagree in an acceptable way.)

4. Protect the privacy of yourself and others. (Everyone has the right to remain silent or "pass" in discussions or activities when a topic is too emotionally charged for the student to handle at that time.)

If the student lacks the skills or attitudes to do the above, some experiences will need to be provided which teach the following:

1. Listening skills: listening for stated or unstated messages as well as feelings, reflective listening, and active listening.

2. Noticing and expressing the positive characteristics and ideas of others. Practice validating and affirming others. (Give positive strokes.)

3. Notice and resist statements and actions which are put-downs to oneself or others. Instead learn to describe the specific behavior in a non-blameful way and tell its effect on yourself. (Practice using "I messages.")

4. Help students feel comfortable about saying "I pass" or remaining silent during some discussions. The practice of saying "no" within the peer group may give students the added confidence to say "no" outside of class. Do not invade anyone's privacy without their permission.

Determine the difference between information and "gossip," and stay at the informational level.

MULTIPURPOSE INSTRUCTIONAL STRATEGIES

It is impossible to teach for each situation a student will face in the future. To provide the broadest knowledge base for an individual, the instructional strategies must provide students with a transferable, rational thinking pattern rather than "answers" for specific circumstances. The thinking patterns we will be describing can in fact be multipurpose. They help students (1) gather and process supportable information which can be used in making personal decisions, (2) assume responsibility for their own learning, value clarification and goal setting, and (3) develop thinking skills needed for continued learning and application to life problems.

These procedures are not new nor peculiar to family life education. Thinking is a mental "doing" which allows the information to be processed and thus becomes new knowledge or understanding, improved skills, or a changed attitude. The teacher becomes the facilitator of this learning by asking well-designed and appropriately-timed questions. The student is the "doer" or thinker. Thinking is a skill and, like other skills, it can be improved with practice.

John Dewey has been credited with being the first to formalize the idea of "doing" or experiencing fully to assure understanding. This philosophy is succinctly expressed by an old Chinese proverb:

I hear and I forget
I see and I remember
I do and I understand

Data Gathering

Thinking processes are sequential and cumulative. Thinking involves data gathering, proceeds to "doing" something with or processing the information, and culminates in the transfer of the learning to new situations. The chart below illustrates the process and identifies some of the questioning skills applicable at each level.

Data Gathering	Processing Data to Develop Knowledge, Attitudes or Skills	Interpreting and Applying Knowledge or Skills to New Situations
Observing Recalling information	Noting similarities and differences Classifying Concluding	Inferring attributes Inferring causes Inferring effects

Accurate data gathering is an essential step, without which the higher levels of thinking will be faulty or incomplete. The first skill essential to data gathering is that of observing. This idea is compatible with the thoughts of Piaget and others. The infant uses <u>all</u> five senses to the maximum in coping with the environment. This skill should be increased as we continue to learn. Society tends to stifle observation by way of the senses. It may be to our advantage to continue developing this trait of childhood. The heightened awareness of enhancing our "view" with more senses than just seeing is vital for creative thinking. Therefore, to develop the skill of observing, the student is asked to note everything he or she hears, sees, touches, smells, or tastes at the time he or she observes it. One, several, or all of the senses may be used at one time. There is no chance for failure because all <u>real</u> observations are acceptable. If the student observed it, he or she observed it! It builds self-esteem. Each person is a worthwhile human being, even though each is different. What a beautiful way to meet the instructional strategy of developing a non-threatening, supportive environment for learning.

In order to facilitate skill building in observation and to gather data, the teacher would ask, "What are some of the characteristics you notice about these (e.g., infants) ?" To tell the students the characteristics of infants may save time, but it takes away the opportunity for building the observing skills which are crucial in school and in life. It also opens new insights for teacher and student. Other examples of questions designed to help students develop the skill of observation include:

What are some of the characteristics you notice about two-year olds?

What are they saying?
What do they do when given direction? Asked a question?
What can they do physically?

What "toys" do they play with?
How do they play with toys and others things?
What do they do when with others?
How long is their attention span?
What feelings do you notice you have as
  you observe this?

Recalling or remembering relevant data previously observed, read, heard, or experienced is the second major skill
in data gathering. For example, we observe persons special
to us: the way they look, their gestures, voice qualities,
body carriage, etc., and we recall that image at will, or
recognize them far in the distance or after a long separation.
To have students recall previously stored information, the
teacher will ask:

What are some of the characteristics you recall
about __(e.g., infants)_ ? What information or
experience leads you to think that is characteristic of infants?

What is your earliest recollection of a happening
when you were young? What evidence do you have that
it really happened? How do you know that you do
remember it, and are not recalling what someone
told you?

What did you read about _____?

What did the author say was the cause of _____?

What were the problems of teenage marriages which
your book listed?

After each observation or recall question or, as needed,
ask the following clarification, probing, and support questions:

What do you mean by the term _____?

What did he say that led you to say he was _(e.g.,_
verbal)_ ?

What are some different observations that others
of you notice?

Data Processing

In addition to encouraging self-confidence, observing and
recalling helps the student collect sufficient factual information for future use. The thinking strategies of noting
similarities and differences of objects, people, ideas, and
feelings build on the two skills at the initial level. They
expand the factual base through sharing. The probability of
sharing knowledge rather than opinions is increased. Opinions are important, but it is important to recognize and
identify them. An opinion without an information base does
not promote responsible thinking.

The thinking skills of similarities and differences can
be used separately or in combination. One important factor
for such a decision is the particular learning and the objective of the class. Basically, the skills involve the
process of making comparisons and noting contrasts. Examples of questions which encourage students to compare and
contrast are listed below. When using them together, the
instructor needs to decide the more important idea. It is
important to know how they are alike or how they are different. The one to be emphasized is used last.

What are some differences of the developmental
tasks at each stage of life? What are some
similarities?

What are some similarities among the various
cultures in the way they socialize the young
child? What are some of the differences?

What are some ways you are different from the
person you were one year ago?

In what ways are our ideas different about
_____? Alike?

In what ways are our fears alike?

How are the dating customs different in various
cultures? How are they alike?

A benefit resulting from the skill of noting differences
is the awareness of the uniqueness of human beings. It also
helps guard against hasty generalizing and over-generalizing
of individuals and groups. Noting differences can be crucial
to the task of analyzing consequences in the decision-making
process.

Another data processing skill is classifying. Classifying is the ability to point out an example of a concept. It is important to know the critical characteristics of the concept. Only when the critical characteristics of a concept are known by the student can examples be differentiated from non-examples. If the student is asked to define child caregiving, he or she may be given several examples to help in the task. The examples may include day care, nursery schools, kindergarten, etc. By listing the similarities and differences of such programs, the students can state the characteristics common in all and thus define child care-giving. The retention of knowledge is increased by the "doing" within the thinking process. It is more meaningful than writing a definition from a book on a chalkboard. Classifying is basic to the decision-making process. By knowing the critical characteristics of concepts (i.e., classifying), one can categorize ideas, events, and behaviors in meaningful ways.

To aid greater insight, a non-example may be given, e.g., compare nursing care-giving with day care, nursery school, etc. This process leads us into the skill of noting distinguishing characteristics. In order to identify differences, students must see examples and non-examples. They must identify the characteristics which are critical to the concept, and also make distinctions among concepts. As mentioned above, the care-giving in nursing homes is different than in child-care situations. To reach specific sub-concepts of child care-giving, the class may distinguish between day care and nursery schools. The focus will be determined by overall course objectives and class objectives.

Concluding is another thinking skill. Individuals in life often make conclusions prematurely, inaccurately, or with insufficient information. In schools, students need to develop the skill of concluding by checking the amount of support for their conclusion. If the other thinking skills are used without concluding, the student may make insupportable conclusions or miss the main objective. Students need practice in order to make well supported conclusions a part of their thinking skills.

To use the process of concluding, the teacher asks the student to make a decision about a situation after the consideration of many new ideas. Conclusions can be used with most strategies to bring closure, however tentative.

Of all the characteristics which we have noticed and discussed about __(e.g., two-year olds)__ , which two are the most representative of that age? What reasons did you have for selecting those two over the others?

What are the major ways you and your parent(s) are
alike and different? What about _____, _____,
and _____ made you select them as the ones?

Of all the feelings that a situation like this
evokes, which one is the most common? What were
your reasons for selecting _____ as the most
common?

If you were to explain to a friend in one sentence
what a "family" is, what would you say? What about
that definition makes it a good one for a "family"?

As the students share their answers, the teacher will
want to ask appropriate questions to clarify ideas and encourage interaction among the people involved in the learning situation. This interaction must be planned to provide
students sufficient and appropriate opportunities to think
and share knowledge and feelings. The types of questions
illustrated in Figure 1 aid the students in developing and
understanding their own thinking processes as well as keeping the information understandable and well supported.
These clarification, probing, and support questions can be
used to help develop each of the other thinking skills. The
use of open and closed questions should also be noted. Closed
questions are those which bring a "yes" or "no" answer. They
start with words such as "can," "will," "would," "should,"
"do," "did," etc. Closed questions do have specific purposes in the classroom. However, questions which begin
with "what," "how," "when," "who," and "where" are much more
productive in provoking thinking and discussion. These open
questions allow for a variety of responses and verbalization
on the part of the student.

Interpreting and Applying Knowledge or Skills

Inferring is making an educated guess about an object, action,
person, place, meaning, and cause and/or effect when not all
of the needed data can be observed. Inferences are not right
or wrong; they are just more or less supportable. No one needs
to be wrong when they make an inference. This is a good step
toward achieving a feeling of self-worth. This process of
inferring provides built-in authenticity by having students
cite evidence to support the inference made.
    Inferring attributes, causes, and effects are skills es-
sential to responsible thinking and problem solving. They
help in identifying all aspects of various alternatives, and
seeing the consequences of each alternative on oneself and

When the need is to have the student(s):	Ask this type of question.
Clarify (words, situations, actions, feelings, etc.)	What do you mean by the word ____? What do you mean _____?
Refocus from one idea or level of thinking to another	You have given us an <u>opinion</u>; what information can you <u>share</u> about it? You have said how they are <u>different</u>; how are they <u>alike</u>? You have stated what you <u>think</u> she feels; what do you <u>see</u> her doing or <u>hear</u> her saying?
Narrow the focus or get more specific	We have been talking in general about _____ ; what specific information is there about ____?
Verify and support their answers	What evidence is there that this information is accurate? What experiences have you had that would lead you to say _____? How many of you can agree with that? On what do you base your reasoning? What sources did you use to get this information? What support is there for saying that is a probable cause/effect of _____?
Provide a variety of ideas or participation	What are some <u>other</u> possible causes/effects/conclusions? What are <u>other</u> similarities/differences? What do some of the <u>others</u> of you think could be the meaning of this? For those of you who agree/disagree, on what information do you base your idea?

Figure 1

Clarifying and Supporting Questions

others. Identifying possible causes is useful in understanding the complexity of issues and in possible prevention of
some future problems.
The following examples show the questions which focus on
inferences and the statements of support.

> What might be some of the characteristics of a
> single-parent family? What do you mean that there
> may be role-overload? What evidence do you have
> that role-overload exists in single-parent fam-
> ilies?

> What are the interests, abilities, and values of
> the mother in this story? What are you thinking
> about that makes you say she was _____?

> What may be some of the feelings of the pregnant
> 15-year old in the film? What do you mean by
> _____? What is there about the problems
> that 15-year olds face that makes you say she
> probably feels _____?

> What are some of the possible causes for _____?
> What do you mean by _____? What evi-
> dence or support is there for thinking that
> _____ could be a cause of _____?

> What are some of the effects of _____?
> What do you mean by _____? What sup-
> port is there for thinking that _____
> could be the effect of _____?

By the end of the discussion it is easy to conclude
which ideas are well-verified and supported and which are
not. This eliminates emotionality and personal attacks on
others. It promotes insight, differing points of view, and
plants a seed for change-of-thought. All of this can be
accomplished while the heat of controversy is diverted.
Cause and effect strategies can be extremely effective
in dealing with people's feelings. Feelings are certainly
a non-factual area! The basis for empathy and understanding
can be formed by using the skills of cause and effect.

Thinking About Controversial Issues

A controversial issue can be discussed more objectively when
the strategies of cause and effect are used. The following
technique describes one such issue.

Resource persons were used on three successive days to investigate the relationship choices of marriage, singleness, or cohabitation. This allowed students to gather additional data. The speakers included a couple who had been married eight years, a 47-year-old female who had remained single by choice, and a counselor who had worked with cohabiting couples. As the speakers talked to the class, the students were directed to complete a chart which included such questions as:

What are the positive consequences of this alternative? (recall and inferring effects)

What are the negative consequences of this alternative? (recall and inferring effects)

What values were involved? (recall and inferring attributes)

What were the life goals the speakers mentioned? (recall)

After the series of speakers was completed, the students were asked to share the information they had gathered. As the students shared, they were asked to be involved in the thinking process as illustrated below:

What do you mean by _____? (clarify statements and terms)

What have you read that supports this point of view? (evidence)

What made you think they were happy with their life style? (verify)

You have said ". . . a lot of people live together." What did the speakers say concerning this? (refocus to recall data)

How did the rest of you react to the presentation? (variety of ideas and participation)

Do you agree/disagree? Why? (variety of ideas and participation)

What are some possible definitions of cohabitation? (classifying)

How are these definitions alike? Different?
(similarities/differences)
    Note: This similarity question is a dif-
           ficult one. Some anticipated re-
           sponses might be: both are accepted
           by society; both can occur away from
           the family of orientation; both are
           for adults, etc.

How is marriage like cohabitation? Different?
(similarities/differences)

How is cohabitation like singleness? Different?
(similarities/differences)
    Note: This similarity question again is
           a difficult one. Some responses
           might be: have an element of free-
           dom, or not as acceptable as marriage.

When the facts are reviewed and clarified, the class is
ready to analyze the controversial topic with a cause/effect
strategy. This strategy keeps the discussion in an objective stance until all sides have been examined. After that,
students are encouraged to clarify their own values and judge
the issue for themselves (see Figure 2 and Figure 3).

Thinking for Personal Decisions

Learning to ask oneself questions when involved with new situations, people, or ideas can help determine what one really
thinks and feels about them. Knowing the "truth" about oneself at that point in time can give information to use in
making personal decisions. These techniques can be practiced
until they become an almost automatic approach to coping with
new experiences and making decisions. When presented with a
new idea (theory), ask yourself:

What is this really saying? (inferring meaning)

How is this idea like and different from ideas or
experiences which I already have encountered?
(similarities and differences)

If it does not "fit" with my thinking or experiences, is there any part of it that would?
(classification)

When seeking to understand causes, ask: "What are some possible reasons people would select the life style of living together?"

S.R. "rebel against authority"

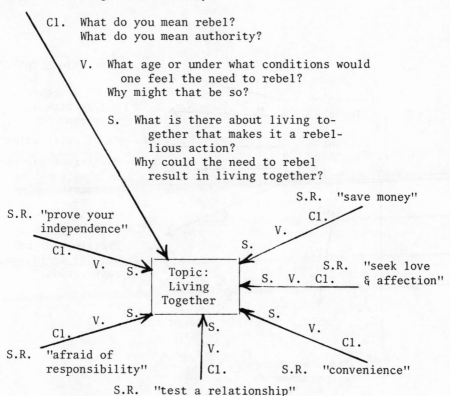

Figure 2

Diagram of a Discussion of Possible Causes

S.R. = Student response
Cl. = Clarify terms, situations, actions, etc.
V. = Verify that the action, feeling, situation, condition does/did exist
S. = Support for thinking that one could cause or be affected by the other

When seeking to understand effects, ask: "What are some results (effects) of the life style of living together?

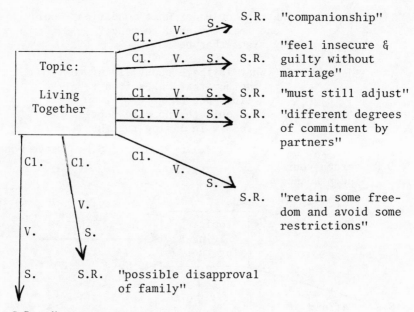

			S.R.	"companionship"
Cl.	V.	S.	S.R.	"feel insecure & guilty without marriage"
Cl.	V.	S.	S.R.	"must still adjust"
Cl.	V.	S.	S.R.	"different degrees of commitment by partners"

Topic:

Living
Together

Cl.   Cl.

V.

V.   S.

S.   S.R.   "possible disapproval
                  of family"

S.R.   "no assurance
        of permanence"

Cl.
  V.
    S.

S.R.   "retain some free-
        dom and avoid some
        restrictions"

S.R. = Student response
Cl. = Clarify terms, situations, actions, etc.
V.   = Verify that the action, feeling, situation,
       conditions does/did exist
S.   = Support for thinking that one could cause or
       be affected by the other

Figure 3

Diagram of a Discussion of Possible Effects

Is it an idea that will be useful to me in any way in dealing with myself or others? (classification) What effects will it have? (effects)

What feelings do I have as I consider this? (inferring feelings)

What will I do with this idea? (decision)

When presented with the facts, ask yourself:

What is this really saying? (inferring meaning)

What evidence do I have that it is a fact? (verification)

What are some of the causes? (inferring causes)

What are some of the effects? (inferring effects)

What feelings do I have as I consider this? (inferring feelings)

What will I do with this information? (decision)

When presented with a new experience or situation involving people, ask yourself:

What do I observe about the situation (people, place, task, etc.)? (observing)

What do I recall or infer about the people, trust level, abilities, interests, cultural influences, etc.? (recall or inferring attributes)

What is happening?

What is being "said?" (verbally, non-verbally)
What feelings are expressed?
What actions are involved?

What are the causes and/or effects of this on myself and on each other person? (inferring cause and effect)

What feelings do I have as I participate? (inferring feeling)

What will I do with the information from this
situation? (decision)

CONCLUSION

The instructional strategies described will enable students
to gather and process information in the area of family life
education in an objective, supportable way. They will also
help students develop the thinking skills needed for continued
learning, value clarification, goal setting, and problem
solving. Students will be able to learn from each other in
a supportive environment, and at the same time practice positive communication skills.

In summary, we believe that the learning procedures suggested will make it possible for students to develop their
ability to more fully understand the world about them, to
better function as effective human beings, and to continue
to learn throughout life.

REFERENCES

ASCD 1977 Yearbook Committee. *Feeling, valuing, and the art
of growing: Insights into the affective.* Washington,
D.C.: Association for Supervision and Curriculum
Development, 1977.

Ball, G. *Innerchange: A journey into self-learning through
group interaction.* (Leader's Manual) La Mesa, California: Human Development Training Institute, 1977.

Ehrenberg, L., & Ehrenberg, S. *Basics: Building and applying strategies for intellectual competencies in students.* Miami, Florida: Institute for Curriculum and
Instruction, 1976.

Elkind, D. *Children and adolescents: Interpretive essays
on Jean Piaget.* New York: Oxford University Press,
1970.

Gasda, G. M. *Human relations development.* (A Manual for
Educators) Boston: Allyn & Bacon, 1974.

Lincoln Public Schools. *Pride: A human development process
for educational systems.* Lincoln, Nebraska: Lincoln
Public Schools, 1977.

Newmark, G. *This school belongs to you and me.* New York:
Hart Publishing Company, 1976.

Schrank, J. *Teaching human beings: 101 subversive activities for the classroom.* Boston: Beacon Press, 1972.

Vorrath, H. H., & Brendtro, L. K. *Positive peer culture.* Chicago: Aldine Publishing Company, 1974.

Dr. Joanne Everts
Education Service Center
Region X
Richardson, Texas
and
Dr. Vera Gershner
Department of Child Development
and Family Living
Texas Woman's University

The challenge of the family life educator is to prepare children, youth, and adults in a world of changing technology, roles, and life styles. This preparation relates to the total being--physical, mental, and emotional--and focuses on human relationships. Although needs may be intensified by the rapid rate of change and the impact of television and mass media, the challenge is not new.

HISTORICAL DEVELOPMENT

The historical foundations of family life education are summarized here as a backdrop to one new approach. The new approach is teacher education based on desired classroom competencies. Across this century, family life education has moved from a concern for venereal disease and sex education to the specification of content and skill areas for family life educators, and to creative methods of teacher training.

Initially, the American Purity Alliance, YMCA, YWCA, and the National Education Association became involved with problems such as venereal disease and sex education. By the early 1900's, increased interest in psychiatry, psychology, mental health, and child development fostered a climate for new organizations and new emphasis on family life education. Courses in health education, home economics, and family life education began appearing in colleges and universities (Kerckhoff, 1964).

In 1908, the American Home Economics Association was formed, and immediately began to encourage seminars and workshops in the family life field. During the 1920's, organizations, such as the National Council of Parent Education and the National Child Research Center, were established. The 1930's showed an increased interest in sex education, venereal disease, prostitution, moral education, and family life

education. A growing number of professionals began to look
at the family life field as a separate area of study. In
1934, the American Home Economics Association, the American
Social Hygiene Association, and the Teachers College of Columbia University sponsored the Conference on Education for Marriage and Family Relations. Leaders in the field then established the National Council on Family Relations, and published
the *Journal of Marriage and Family* (Carrera, 1971; Kerckhoff,
1964).

The 1940's and 1950's showed continued progress in the
family life education movement. Family life educators began investigating the training needed for family education
teachers. During the 1950's, Landis and Christensen both
conducted surveys to identify the scope and needs of family
life education at the college level. In 1959, Landis' survey of colleges and universities found there were 1,027 different marriage and family courses in the 630 reporting
colleges and universities. In 1958, Christensen surveyed
475 family life educators. The participants identified sociology, psychology, home economics, child development, and
counseling as the most important subject areas for the future family life teacher. The family life educators also
identified the major tasks for the family life field and
the major goals for family life education. Two of the major
tasks confronting family life education identified by the
family life educators were improvement of teaching and development of higher personal and academic requirements for
family life educators (Kerckhoff, 1964).

The 1960's were marked with social reform, federal assistance programs, and growing concern for family life and
child development. Two legislative programs made a significant impact. The Amendments to the Social Security Act,
passed in 1962, emphasized the prevention and reduction of
dependency through rehabilitative services. The Economic
Opportunity Act, passed in 1964, emphasized civil rights and
community action. Operation Head Start was an important
component of this legislation (Brown, 1970).

Family planning programs began to expand due to the concern over world population control, and became more available to the public. Federal funds and federal programs for
birth control information and assistance were discussed and
supported in the legislature. It was not until 1970, however, that comprehensive legislation was passed (Brown, 1970).

Another important thrust arose through the Cooperative
Extension Service and through support of local agencies and
community organizations. During the 1960's, home econo-
mists expanded their work, from dealing mainly with middle-
class families, to programs designed for migrant families,
families receiving federal aid, and other low-income families.

Community organizations, such as urban leagues, consumer groups, and parent groups of many different kinds began to develop and expand (Brown, 1970).

Despite this growing support and interest, community and school family life and sex education programs met many problems. Local communities and parents were often hesitant to accept new programs and ideas relating to controversial issues. Confusion and controversy between family life educators, communities, and schools were evident. Family life education was poorly defined, and lack of accurate knowledge of school programs hindered progress. One of the obstacles to family life education identified by Sommerville (1971) was the lack of professionalism related to inadequate teacher preparation opportunities and lack of any established standards for family life and sex educators.

Family life education continued to face changing needs of families and debates on how to meet these needs. Governmental policies continued to change, and the need for advocacy for families and children became essential. Mondale (1976) reflected governmental concern for families as they were buffeted by new problems. Mondale summarized the four conclusions established through the Family Hearings of the Senate Subcommittee on Children and Youth. The first conclusion stressed the fundamental importance of the family to society; the second recognized the pressures and changes in today's society affecting the family. Problems such as increased divorce rate, single parenting, alcoholism, drug abuse, and child abuse were identified. The third conclusion recognized the impact of governmental policy on families from all levels of income and life styles. The final conclusion of these hearings was a statement of need to develop governmental family policy.

As changes and stress in the family continued, the National Council on Family Relations began to recognize the inadequacies of preparation for the family life educator. The Committee on Educational Standards and Certification for Family Life Educators (1970) developed criteria based on content and skill areas rather than on courses. These areas were as follows: family patterns and systems, family interaction, marriage preparation, human development, biological sciences, human sexuality, management of family resources, group processes, methods and materials in family life education, practice teaching in family life and sex education, field experiences, direct observation, individual and family counseling, research on the family, survey of basic laws, and community and the family.

Kerckhoff and Hancock (1971) emphasized the need for interpersonal and self-awareness training, as well as content training. They surveyed 52 members of *The Family Coordinator's*

Family Life Education Panel. The panel members identified
a need for a broader interdisciplinary training, consisting
of communication skills, interpersonal relationships, human
development, and self-understanding. These concerns for
teacher preparation in the early 1970's spawned certification efforts in some states. Authorities differed in their
reporting on certification, although they agreed on two items.
Both Kerckhoff and O'Connor (1978) and Sullivan et al. (1978)
identified several disciplines as training family life educators, and expressed dismay at the limited number of states
certifying family life educators. At the 1978 Conference
for the National Council on Family Relations, the encouragement of certification was officially referred back to the
respective state associations for promulgation.

Meanwhile, despite the lack of special certification and
the concern for adequate teacher preparation, an increasing
variety of disciplines became involved in family life education. Kerckhoff and O'Connor's (1978) survey of state education agencies identified the certified home economist as the
teacher of family life in 42 states. Twenty-one states also
identified the health educator. The social studies teacher
was specified in eight states.

The problems faced by these teachers are intense and diverse, and require special teaching skills and interpersonal
competencies. No matter which discipline originally trained
the person placed in the family life educator role, competencies are critical to their effectiveness with today's
youth. Teacher preparation, inservice or preservice, can
be effectively focused through a competency-based approach.
The research reported in the next section reflects the Family Life Education section of the Texas Home Economics
Competency-Based Teacher Education Project.

A COMPETENCY-BASED APPROACH TO TEACHER
PREPARATION OF FAMILY LIFE EDUCATORS

The need for improved home economics and family life teacher
education supported the purpose of this study. The lack of
materials for competency-based home economics and family life
teacher education was identified through reviewing the literature. Competency-based teacher education materials were developed by the Texas Home Economics Competency-Based Curriculum Project for use by colleges and universities. The
Competency-Based Home Economics Curriculum Project of Texas
is a true example of the innovative and cooperative nature
of a competency-based teacher education program. Those involved in the project include: Texas Education Agency personnel, secondary teachers, key area consultants; teacher

educators, subject-matter instructors, and students from 19 colleges and universities in Texas. The first goal of this five-year project was the identification of essential competencies needed for beginning vocational homemaking teachers. Competencies were identified and validated by teacher educators, secondary school teachers, state staff, and consultants. The second goal was the development of instructional guides for university instructors in eight subject-matter areas and teacher education. This research evaluated the competency-based instructional materials for family life teacher education developed in this project. Both instructor and student evaluations of the materials, as well as analyses on pre- and posttest data from selected competencies, were included in the study. This research was completed during the third and fourth years of the Home Economics Competency-Based Curriculum Project, funded by the Department of Occupational Education and Technology Consumer and Homemaking Division, Texas Education Agency.

Sample

Of the 19 colleges and universities with accredited vocational home economics teacher education programs, 13 instructors at 10 colleges and universities participated in the research. Those volunteering for the research taught family living course work during the spring, 1978 semester. More than 400 students were involved in the courses taught by these 13 instructors. Table 1 lists universities participating, with corresponding instructor and student populations.

The courses were within departments of home economics, and focused on preparation for marriage and marriage and family relationships. The courses in which the instructional materials were utilized varied by level, title, and course description. The instructors varied in training, discipline, experience, rank, and degree. The students varied by sex, age, major, grade point average, and classification.

Research Design

Null hypotheses were used for those evaluation components which could be tested for significant differences. Research questions were structured for the more descriptive types of data. The null hypotheses were:

1. There is no significant difference between experimental group pre- and posttest gain scores and control group pre- and posttest gain scores.

Table 1

Participating Universities with Participating
Instructor and Student Populations

University	Number of Instructors	Number of Students
Baylor University	1	21
East Texas State University	1	25
Lamar State University	1	46
Mary Hardin Baylor College	1	22
North Texas State University	2	65
Prairie View A&M University	1	47
Southwest Texas State University	1	87
Stephen F. Austin State University	3	83
Texas Southern University	1	38
Texas Woman's University	1	50
Total	13	484

2. There is no significant difference between experimental posttest-only group scores and control posttest-only group scores.

3. There is no significant correlation between student attitudes toward the materials, and instructor attitudes toward the materials.

Other issues explored in research questions were:

1. Do instructors judge the structure and content of the materials as usable and effective measured by a mean rating of 2 or more on the Instructor Form for guide evaluation?

2. Do students judge the structure and content of the materials as usable and effective measured by a mean rating of 2 or more on the Student Form for guide evaluation?

3. Do instructors and students reflect positive attitudes toward the materials measured by ratings over the 50 percentile on the semantic differential Attitude Scale?

Hypotheses one and two were analyzed in a Quasi-experimental Solomon Four-Group Design, using pre- and posttests provided in the materials for five sets of competencies. Selection of competencies were limited to those with tests of 50 reliability or above. The Solomon Four-Group Quasi-experimental Design enabled the researchers to study the possible effect of the pretest on the experimental treatment.

Limitations in this research lay in the volunteer nature of the sample, and the administration of the tests and evaluative instruments by the instructors at the ten institutions. Volunteer instructors were sought, since it is inappropriate to prescribe teaching content for methodology to college professors. Since they were willing to try something new, and explore competency-based education, they would be expected to exert a major effort and be generally favorable.

Procedures

The family living materials were submitted to 19 universities during the 1977 fall semester. The researchers discussed the materials with the family living professors during on-site interviews to the colleges and universities. Procedures explained included: selecting the competencies to be used, implementing materials and tests, and evaluating the materials. Instructors stated if they would or would not participate in the spring semester research. Application to the Human Subjects Committee was completed, and a student consent form was developed. Institutionally, all participants had previously agreed to participate in the research.

Participating instructors were interviewed at the beginning of the next semester by the researchers, using a phone interview sheet. Instructors identified the competencies which could best be tested in their course(s), and the number of students to be involved. Experimental and control groups were established, based on instructor preferences, size of classes, and flexibility of the individual instructor. Since most of the instructors preferred to use the materials and participate in the experimental groups, the researchers had to more actively solicit participants in control groups. Thirteen volunteer instructors were identified. Ten instructors participated in experimental groups, and three in control groups. The disproportionate number of experimental participants versus control participants was related to the time involved in being an experimental group participant. Those instructors using the materials were advised to test fewer competencies, due to the involved processes of testing, using, and evaluating the materials. Control group participants could more easily test more competencies.

Results

Results from the evaluation of the competency-based instructional materials for family life teacher education show general acceptance by instructors and students. Pre- and posttesting of students revealed significant differences between experimental and control groups. The students were pre- and posttested for each competency used. Students also completed a structured form evaluating the materials, using an interval data instrument. Attitudes toward the materials were assessed using a semantic differential instrument. Instructors evaluated the materials using a similar interval data form, and the same semantic differential form as the students. Instructors also participated in a structured interview.

The control groups participating in the control pre- and posttesting and posttesting-only were students in family living classes covering the same information as the competency-based family living materials, but not using the materials. Pretest/posttest control groups had pretests administered before the instructor taught content applicable to the particular content being tested. Posttests were then administered after the particular unit was completed. The posttest-only control group had the posttest administered at the end of the teaching of the family living course content.

Hypothesis Testing

The first two null hypotheses were approached by the analysis of student test scores for competencies one through five, using the Quasi-experimental Solomon Four-Group Design. The null hypothesis that no differences existed between experimental and control pretest/posttest groups was tested using the analysis of covariance. The analysis of covariance revealed highly significant differences at the .01 level for all five competencies. The null hypothesis that no significant differences existed between experimental and control posttest-only groups was tested using the analysis of variance. The analysis of variance also revealed highly significant differences at the .01 level for all five competencies. Therefore, the null hypothesis that no difference existed between experimental and control pretest/posttest groups was rejected. The null hypothesis that no significant differences existed between the experimental and control posttest-only groups was also rejected. An analysis of variance between the control pretest/posttest groups and control posttest-only groups revealed that two competencies, three and five, had significant differences between groups. Due to the results of analysis of variance of the control groups, the impact of the pretest on the control groups of competencies three and five seems evident.

Descriptive Statistics

Instructors and students evaluated the content and structure of the materials through the use of an interval data rating scale. The rating scale ranged from 0 (not applicable) to 4 (Yes always, Yes, or Definitely). A rating of 2 or more reflected a positive evaluation of the materials. Since each instructor evaluated each competency used on an individual basis, there can be several evaluations by the same instructor, but for different competencies. The student evaluations were also analyzed by competencies, so that the same student may have evaluated several competencies. Data for instructors were analyzed by item for all instructors, and over total items for all instructors. Student data were analyzed by item, by competency, and by total items for all competencies.

All items on the Instructor Form and Student Form were rated above 2, reflecting a positive evaluation of the materials. Instructor responses were higher than student responses, but had similar trends. Those areas rated highest by the instructors were related to the Terminal Performance Objectives and the Enabling Objectives. Those areas rated lowest by the instructors were related to the tests. Students rated class handouts and resources highest, and also rated areas relating to the tests lowest.

On the Instructor Form for guide evaluation, the instructor could check which parts were most outstanding and which parts needed revisions. Of 18 responses, 11 checked resources and appendices as most outstanding. The pretests were identified by 15 responses as needing revisions, and the posttests were checked 16 times as needing revisions.

Since both instructors and students rated materials above 2, the research questions "Do instructors rate the content and structure of the guide as useful?" and "Do students rate the content and structure of the guides as useful?" were both answered positively. Student data were analyzed by competency, revealing that, although they rated the materials positively, they rated particular competencies differently. Students rated Preparation for Marriage highest (3.29), and Family and Group Interaction lowest (2.58).

Summations of identical student and instructor semantic differential scales were tabulated, and means computed for each instructor group. Both instructor and student mean scores reflected scores with means above the fiftieth percentile. Therefore, the research question relating to whether instructors and students have positive attitudes toward the materials was answered positively. A significant correlation

between the students' and instructors' scores, however, was
not found.

Instructor Interviews

Preferred methodologies used by all instructors included
lecture method using transparencies, student completion of
activity sheets such as opinionnaires or information-seek-
ing forms, class discussion, and films. Other recommended
methodologies utilized were panel discussions or guest speakers, debates, group projects, small group work and discussion, role play, supportive information handouts and discussion, and student research and book reports.

Instructors indicated several ways they were presently
using the materials, and ways they planned to use them in
the future. Besides the use of selected competencies for
field testing, instructors indicated using materials from
several competencies as supportive materials with existing
course structure. Some instructors planned to evaluate the
courses offered at their campus in family living in relation to the competencies. It was also indicated that the
materials would be used to evaluate instructor methods and
individual course content and resources.

Conclusions

This research focused on the examination of the acceptance
and effectiveness of the family life instructional materials
developed in the Texas Home Economics Competency-Based Curriculum Project. Thirteen instructors at ten universities,
and their 484 students in family living classes, provided
the data during the spring semester of 1978.

The Quasi-experimental Solomon Four-Group Design revealed
highly significant gains for those students experiencing both
the tests and coursework based on the materials. Overall,
instructors perceived the structure and content of the materials as useful and effective.

Student perceptions were parallel to the instructors, but
not as high. Both instructors and students demonstrated positive attitudes toward the materials, judged by a semantic
differential Attitude Scale. Students' attitudes were generally lower, and did not correlate significantly with instructors' attitude scores. Individual instructor interviews
provided data on curriculum components used, and recommendations for improvement of the materials.

Research is needed to evaluate the published materials,
which will include revisions recommended herein. Studies
could also assess the effectiveness of the fledgling teacher

in a secondary school classroom, or the gains of different types of college students enrolled in family living courses.

As the stresses in family life intensify and accelerate, the challenge for effective family life education becomes greater. Additional research studies are needed to assess effectiveness in various settings, at different levels, with diverse students, and with varying resources.

REFERENCES

Brown, J. S. Improving family life: Action and reaction. *Journal of Marriage and the Family*, 1970, *32*, 598-609.

Carrera, M. A. Preparation of a sex educator: An historical overview. *The Family Coordinator*, 1971, *20*, 99-107.

Committee on Educational Standards and Certification for Family Life Educators. Family life and sex education: Proposed criteria for teacher education. *The Family Coordiator*, 1970, *19*, 183-185.

Kerckhoff, R. K. Family life education in America. In H. Christensen (Ed.), *Handbook on marriage and the family*. Chicago: Rand McNally, 1964.

Kerckhoff, R. K., & Hancock, T. W. The family life educator of the future. *The Family Coordinator*, 1971, *20*, 315-323.

Kerckhoff, R. K., & O'Connor, T. Certification of high school family life teachers. *The Family Coordiator*, 1978, *27*, 59-62.

Mondale, W. Government policy, stress and the family. *Journal of Home Economics*, 1976, *68*(5), 11-15.

Sommerville, R. M. Family life and sex education in the turbulent sixties. *Journal of Marriage and the Family*, 1971, *21*, 11-35.

Sullivan, J., Gryzlo, B., & Schwarz, W. Certification of family life educators: A status report of state departments of education. *The Family Coordinator*, 1978, *27*, 269-272.

Applying the Process of Humanistic Psychology to the Facilitating of Family Life Education

Linda Tharp
Fremont Senior High School
Fremont, Nebraska

THE ADOLESCENT AND IDENTITY

The quest to establish a personal identity is the major developmental task of the adolescent. This process involves becoming aware of physical, social, emotional, mental, and spiritual strengths, weaknesses, and aptitudes. It further involves clarifying an accurate perception of the self and being able to accept that self. Intertwined with these basic understandings are the questions, "What kind of job or career will be best for me?" "What kind of intimate relationships will I have with others?" "On what values will I base my life?"

However, in the fast-paced world of school, family, friends, work, and leisure activities, where there is a high need to be accepted, and where adopting society's norms is encouraged, searching out answers to the question, "What makes me unique?" may be avoided or only dealt with superficially. As the result, the young person is laying a shaky foundation for developmental tasks which will follow later in the life cycle.

Challenging the adolescent to openly confront and honestly wrestle with these issues forms the core content of many high school courses in family living. Within the curriculum, the teacher is hopefully also guiding students toward becoming fully functioning people; people who have a positive view of themselves, who are open to experiences, and who can identify with the whole of mankind. The teacher knows the students who do so will be the ones who will be able to experience freedom in their personal lives, and who will not only seek continued growth for themselves, but will reach out with support and encouragement to others.

In order to be effective in reaching these objectives, the teacher who accepts this challenge must personally ask and answer several key questions. What philosophy of education will give direction to the task of producing the best

485

possible person? How will this philosophy be applied? What
process and what methods will be most effective in achieving
the goals and objectives? What qualities, skills, and attitudes will be required of the teacher in order to facilitate
the achievement of these goals? Will students benefit from
this approach? These are the questions to which this article
has been addressed, in the hope that the reader will use this
as a catalyst for further exploration.

THE SCHOOL AND HUMANISTIC EDUCATION

The school has long been a major agent of socialization in
society. Its challenge has been to produce the best possible
person: one who can live with others in a humane way, one
with the skills necessary for effective living, and one who
can live in the physical world in a way which benefits both
the self and the world (Stanford, 1977). The American educational system can be applauded for producing a technological
society of affluence and convenience. However, the celebration must then stop to re-examine the goal of education which
sought to produce the best possible person. Reflection on
the many personal and social problems, and the inability of
so many to cope in modern society, may well cause the individual to question whether education is accomplishing the
goal it set for itself. As schools become the object of
attack, criticisms focus not so much on facilities, curriculum, or efficiency, but rather upon the schools' lack of
humanity.
      The neglect of the affective element of education can be
felt in a number of ways. The traditional school has emphasized the cognitive and/or skill orientation of the student, while the emotional and valuing part of the experience
has been neglected. In such a system, authority has rested
with the teacher, in terms of leadership, control, planning,
initiating, and evaluating. The feeling and valuing part
of both student and teacher toward content and classroom
process has been largely guarded and hidden.
      Unfortunately, the results of such methods are often
the opposite of what was intended. Apathy or rebellion result from the failure to develop potentials; low self-concept
results from unrealistic expectations and authoritarianism;
manipulation and game playing arise from the emotional dis-
honesty; impaired ability to learn is affected by a negative
view of the self. Loneliness, alienation, and lack of trust
in others and in self also occur. None of these qualities
forms the foundation for a fully-functioning person.
      Modern humanistic education seeks to provide alternatives
to traditional forms of education. Humanism developed out

of an increasing respect for the whole person. The humanist
sees the person as worthy of dignity, inherently good, future
oriented, democratic, rational, and striving for the best in
self and others. Other concepts basic to this philosophy are
positive self-concept, clear perception, living in the present
moment, developing significant interpersonal relationships,
and taking responsibility for the nature and direction of
one's own life. The humanistic educator builds a philosophy
of learning on these ideas of what it is to be human.

Operating within these guidelines, the person working with
learners moves from the role of a teacher who imparts a body
of knowledge, to a facilitator who involves the participants
in goal setting, planning, and implementation. During this
process, the facilitator is fully involved in the affective
aspects of learning.

As the facilitator does this, a number of goals become
an integral part of the learning experience. These include
becoming more aware of self and surroundings, developing communication skills, exploring emotional responses, being able
to live in the here-and-now, encouraging and developing positive relations with others, and improving skills in goal setting and accomplishment. In the process of such movement,
students are gaining valuable coping skills and positive behaviors for both present and future. Furthermore, they become
more confident and self-accepting, and these attitudes under-
lie a healthy and satisfying life. Students move closer to
achieving education's goal of helping them become the best
possible persons. Humanistic psychology offers education a
philosophical foundation of support, which can be used in
helping students become their best possible selves. Attention is now focused on the process and strategies which are
a part of the humanistic approach.

LEARNING THROUGH HUMAN INTERACTION
AND GROUP PROCESS

Humanistic educators see learning as the result of experience
and interaction. They discover that significant learning
must have meaning and importance in the life of the learner,
and that meaning is based on the perceptions and reactions
of the learners themselves. Therefore, the educator has the
responsibility of helping learners become aware of and clarify their unique needs, behavioral patterns, values, and ways
of relating to others. These are objectives which are not
imparted through lectures. They can best be discovered
through experiences and interactions which encourage self-
disclosure, provide feedback, and offer opportunities to test
one's perceptions and behaviors.

For this to happen, the classroom must change from an
aggregate to a group. This does not happen automatically,
but results from the patient nurturing of the students over
an extended period of time. This process includes trust
building, open sharing, goal setting, conflict resolution,
and task achievement. The group atmosphere and climate which
result are the consequence of the unique expressions and experiences of the particular group and its journey together.

The use of group process in the educational setting offers
exciting possibilities for growth for both students and facil-
itators. As a cohesive group forms, and as people learn to
know, trust, and care for each other, a number of significant
things happen. There is an improvement in subject-matter
learning, improvement in classroom management becomes evident,
and improved social skills become obvious (Stanford, 1977).
Other advantages of group involvement include learning from
the wisdom and experiences of others; integrating subject-
matter in a positive way; and encouraging communication skills
of self-disclosure, listening, and assertiveness. In addition, group interaction affirms the humanistic concepts which
state that people can be trusted to be self-directing, self-
motivating, and self-disciplining when given the opportunity
and guidelines.

Whether or not these expectations will be realized depends
upon how successfully the group moves through a predictable
sequence. This necessary sequence could be likened to the
developmental stages a child goes through in the movement
toward maturity. Each accomplishment is necessary in order
to go on to the next stage, and each step is contingent on
the others.

These stages are described by Stanford (1977) in his book,
Developing Effective Classroom Groups. The five stages which
he describes include: orientation, establishing group norms,
working through conflicts, productivity, and termination.

Certainly, in directing group process, knowledge of these
stages is essential. Such awareness can aid the facilitator
in recognizing where the group is, and encouraging their forward progress.

EXPERIENTIAL LEARNING

Being able to help students discover their identity, learn
to like and accept themselves, and develop positive skills for
relating are aims of humanistic education. To accomplish
this, it is recommended that the learning environment include involvement, participation, action, analysis, decision
making, and experimentation. As has been pointed out, group

process is an effective way of encouraging development in these areas.

Attention is now directed to one of the elements within group process--the use of experiential learning activities. Experiential learning encourages direct participation for the purpose of effecting awareness of personal life style and change in life style when a person desires change (Smith, 1961). Words used to describe such direct and purposeful experiences are concrete, firsthand, meaningful, specific, tangible, and personal. To provide the maximum amount of concept development, these activities should be novel, involve the senses, have emotional tone, offer personal achievement, and provide the opportunity to build on past experiences. After leading students through such experiences, the facilitator has the responsibility of processing the event in order to evaluate and develop personal concepts from the experience.

Experiential learning is based upon three assumptions:

1. Students learn best when they are personally involved in the learning experience.

2. Students must make the discovery of personal meaning if the idea is to have value or make any differences in their behavior.

3. Commitment to learning is highest when students are free to set their own learning goals and actively pursue them within a given framework (Johnson & Johnson, 1975).

These assumptions are supported by the common statement that one remembers 10 percent of what is heard, 30 percent of what is seen, and 90 percent of what is done. Dale (1972) illustrates this by his cone of experience, in which he compares the relative effectiveness of several types of learning activities. The more abstract the experience, the less permanent the learning. Unfortunately, verbal and visual symbols are most commonly used in the schools.

The more concrete the experience, the more permanent the learning; there are criteria for judging whether or not a learning activity could be called experiential. A learning activity is experiential if the experience generates concepts, rules, and principles to guide one's behavior, and if these concepts, rules, and principles can be modified to improve their effectiveness (Johnson & Johnson, 1975).

In planning such activities, Johnson and Johnson (1975) describe the process or cycle of such learning. The process involves (1) concrete, personal experiences followed by (2) observations of, reflection upon, and examination of one's

experiences, leading to (3) the formulation of abstract concepts and generalizations, leading to (4) hypotheses to be
tested in further action and further experiences. Both experience and conceptualization are necessary to be beneficial.

For the facilitator looking for sources and ideas concerning experiential activities, there is an exciting variety
available. Some of these are listed in the references. Others
can be found in current curriculum guides, in educational
journals, and in books devoted to particular aspects of group
process. The facilitator is encouraged to use his or her own
creativity and imagination in developing experiences which
will meet the particular needs of the group and the objectives
to be explored.

It is important that the facilitator become a participant
in a group which emphasizes this kind of involvement. It is
difficult for the facilitator who has not personally risked
this process to authentically encourage others to do so. The
value of such a venture can only be known by one who affirms
it as the result of personal experience. The facilitator who
is able to trust himself or herself enough to risk new growth
experiences is the facilitator who will be most capable of
generating such risk-taking behavior in students. The benefits
for both will be measurable.

THE FACILITATOR

So far, emphasis has been placed on students, and how philosophy, process, and experiences can be used to enhance their
learning and growth. The idea that the facilitator's growth
is also encouraged or discouraged by what happens in the
learning environment is frequently overlooked in such a discussion.

It is estimated that the career teacher will spend over
40,000 hours in the classroom setting. If the teacher uses
this time only as giving time, expecting, and getting little
in return, it is not unlikely that depression and anger will
be present, if only subconsciously. On the other hand, if
the teacher expects more than he or she is willing to give,
alienation is frequently the result. It is easy to detect
the teacher who has discovered the balance between giving
and receiving with students. There is a joy and enthusiasm
which are continually reinforcing. These educators have
learned and developed qualities which can be used and given
to encourage student growth. They are also aware of what
can be expected from students, and they are ready to take
personal satisfaction in such movement as it occurs. Let
us look first at skills, qualities, and attitudes necessary
if one is to offer growth-producing experiences for students.

Teaching basically means to set up conditions where students can develop clear perceptions of themselves and their world. To accomplish this most effectively, Stanford (1977) lists some requirements for a teacher:

1. Be able to facilitate relationships which are characterized by trust and openness, be genuine and congruent, appropriately self-disclosing, participate in the educational process, and be willing to be human rather than professional.

2. Have the quality of empathy--being able to perceive and feel with another person as if he or she were that other person.

3. Care for and prize the other person unconditionally.

Carkhuff (1972) reminds us that the facilitator also serves as a model to be emulated. Rogers (1969) stresses setting the mood, creating the climate, helping students reach their goals, and accepting one's own limitations. Combs (1971), from his studies in the helping professions, summarizes the role of the facilitator:

1. Know and believe the subject-matter.

2. Be able to see people as more able than unable, friendly than unfriendly, worthy than unworthy, internally than externally motivated, dependable than undependable, and helping than hindering.

3. Have personal qualities which include being more identified than apart, adequate than inadequate, trustworthy than untrustworthy, and wanted than unwanted.

4. See one's purpose as freeing rather than controlling, large-issue oriented rather than small, self-revealing rather than self-concealing, involved rather than alienated, and process oriented rather than goal oriented.

5. Take approaches to the task that are people oriented rather than thing oriented, and perceptual rather than objective.

The National Council on Family Relations (1970) gives support to similar qualities when it describes criteria for a teacher in the field of family life and sex education. In addition, affirmation is given to the importance of the teacher being familiar with and able to use group process

to help students become more aware of how they function in a
group, and their impact on group members.

This may appear to be a rigorous list of characteristics
for an effective facilitator; however, it is a realistic list.
Continual re-evaluation of one's personal traits is essential
in order to have and to maintain resources from which to give
guidance to others. When the facilitator displays the desire
for self-growth, risks can be taken, attitudes can be changed,
and skills can be learned and practiced. The results for both
students and the facilitator are well worth the effort.

What are the personal benefits the facilitator receives?
The first feedback comes as the facilitator begins to observe
and feel a difference in what is happening in the classroom
atmosphere. Individual student growth then begins to be noted
and reported. Warm relations between students and facili-
tators are evident, and small tokens of appreciation begin to
appear in assorted ways. When the final papers of evaluation
come in at the end of the semester, the statements of growth
confirm the genuine insights which were gained during the
sharing together.

Such positive results and the sense of obvious accomplishments have profound effects for the facilitator. Other benefits are as follows:

1. Skills which the facilitator learns and uses in the
   classroom transfer to other relationships, therefore
   enhancing life for the facilitator.

2. As the facilitator encourages the group to live in the
   here-and-now, the facilitator also makes a habit of doing
   so. Even the facilitator can decide to clarify perceptions of the present moment and choose happiness.

3. Trusting the students eliminates much of the fear of
   failure and the burden of overwork which plague many
   teachers. Increased confidence in students makes less
   tension and increased mental health for the facilitator.

4. While students are setting goals, making contracts, and
   taking responsibility for their lives, so too the facilitator can decide to take responsibility for his or her
   own life.

5. Ultimately, this helps to increase the self-confidence
   of the facilitator. This positive self-esteem and belief in self increase success not only in the classroom,
   but free one for creativity, accomplishment, and being
   in all other aspects of life.

The teacher who discovers the balance between giving and receiving finds a new dimension in life. Hopefully, all teachers will accept the challenge to experience the process of personal growth which opens such possibilities. By so doing, each teacher becomes a genuine model and helper for students who are seeking their own personal fulfillment.

EVALUATION OF EFFECT ON LEARNER

This article began with the statement, "The quest to establish a personal identity is the major developmental task of the adolescent." The question now must be raised, "How effective is the process discussed here in helping the individual more clearly define that identity?" Are group process, experiential learning activities, and a capable facilitator, grounded in the humanistic philosophy, able to accept and meet the challenge of helping the adolescent come closer to understanding, "Who am I?"

A number of studies have been done to discover the answer to this question. Jack Gibb (Rogers, 1969) found that validating this approach is not as difficult as some critics would indicate. From his studies, he made a number of significant findings. Those which have application to the immediate concern are reported here:

1. Group training experiences have a therapeutic or growth-promoting effect.

2. Changes do occur in sensitivity, ability to manage feelings, directionality of motivation, attitudes toward self, attitudes toward others, and independence.

3. To be optimally effective the group training must be relevant to the organizational, family, and life environment of the person.

4. There is little basis for the widespread concern among lay groups about the traumatic effects of group training.

From his own work, Rogers (1969) found that group encounters had the following effects on students. Students will:

1. feel more free to express both positive and negative feelings in class;

2. tend to work through these feelings toward a realistic
    relationship;

3. discover they have responsibility for their own learning;

4. feel free to take off on exciting avenues of learning with
    more assurance, knowing that the teacher will understand;

5. find that both their awe of authority and their rebellion
    against it diminish; and

6. find that the learning process enables them to grapple
    directly and personally with problems of the meaning
    of life.

Other changes which occur as the result of group participation are:

1. Individual changes:
    a. Self-concept increases as the result of being
        accepted by the group.
    b. More of one's own potential is realized and brought
        into being.
    c. New directions for life are chosen on the basis
        of decisions.

2. Relationship changes:
    a. There is an increased depth of communication with
        others, both in and outside of the group.

3. Organizational changes:
    a. Those who participate in growth experiences are able
        to share similar experiences with others.

The author gives support to each of these effects of the
humanistic educational process. These outcomes have been
validated daily in the classroom. They happen with ordinary
students during ordinary semesters; however, they prove that
the ordinary can be very extraordinary. The qualities of
surprise and excitement, searching and discovering, expecting and finding are qualities which give education its meaning and energy. When one considers the vast potential for
a rich and rewarding life available to each person, how can
we do anything less than strive for its attainment?

We must first experience the process of our own growth.
We must be deeply knowledgeable of our subject-matter and
develop the skills necessary for facilitating group process
and experiential learning. We must understand and feel comfortable with principles of humanistic education. If we are

moving in this direction personally, if school systems are requiring teachers to grow, and if institutions of higher learning are offering such experiences to student teachers and to veteran teachers, then we are offering hope and direction to our young people and to our culture in a time of rapid change and uncertainty. Let us accept the challenge.

REFERENCES

Alschuler, A. S. Humanistic education. In D. A. Read & S. B. Simons (Eds.), *Humanistic education sourcebook*. Englewood Cliffs, New Jersey: Prentice-Hall, 1975.

Association for Supervision and Curriculum Development. *Perceiving, behaving, becoming: A new focus for education*. Washington, D.C.: The Association, 1962.

Bernard, H. *Personality*. Boston, Massachusetts: Holbrook Press, Inc.

Bloom, B. S. *Human characteristics and school learning*. New York: McGraw-Hill Book Company, 1976.

Carkhuff, R. R. *The development of human resources*. New York: Holt, Rinehart, & Winston, Inc., 1971.

Carkhuff, R. R. *The art of helping*. New York: Human Resources Development Press, 1972.

Combs, A. W. Humanistic goals of education. In D. A. Read & S. B. Simons (Eds.), *Humanistic education sourcebook*. Englewood Cliffs, New Jersey: Prentice-Hall, 1975.

Combs, A. W., Avila, D. L., & Purkey, W. W. *Helping relationships*. Boston, Massachusetts: Allyn & Bacon, Inc., 1971.

Dale, E. *Audiovisual methods in teaching*. New York: Holt, Rinehart, & Winston, 1969.

Dale, E. *Building a learning environment*. Bloomington, Indiana: Phi Delta Kappa, Inc., 1972.

Egan, G. *Interpersonal living*. Monterey, California: Brooks/Cole Publishing Company, 1976.

Gorman, A. H. *Teachers and learners: The interactive process of education*. Boston, Massachusetts: Allyn & Bacon, 1974.

Halpin, A. W., & Croft, D. *The organizational climate of schools.* Chicago, Illinois: University of Chicago Press, 1963.

Johnson, D. W. *Reaching out.* Englewood Cliffs, New Jersey: Prentice-Hall, 1972.

Johnson, D. W., & Johnson, F. T. *Joining together.* Englewood Cliffs, New Jersey: Prentice-Hall, Inc., 1975.

Luft, J. *Group process: An introduction to group dynamics.* Palo Alto, California: Mayfield Publishing Company, 1970.

Luft, J. *Of human interaction.* Palo Alto, California: National Press Books, 1969.

National Council on Family Relations, Committee on Educational Standards and Certification for Family Life Education 1968-69. Family life and sex education: Proposed criteria for teacher education. *The Family Coordinator,* 1970, *19,* 183-185.

Read, D. A., & Simon, S. *Humanistic education sourcebook.* Englewood Cliffs, New Jersey: Prentice-Hall, 1975.

Riesman, D. *The lonely crowd.* New Haven, Connecticut: Yale University Press, 1961.

Robert, M. *Loneliness in the schools.* Niles, Illinois: Argus Communications, 1973.

Rogers, C. R. *Freedom to learn.* Columbus, Ohio: Charles E. Merrill Publishing Company, 1969.

Saulnier, L., & Simard, T. *Personal growth and interpersonal relations.* Englewood Cliffs, New Jersey: Prentice-Hall, Inc., 1973.

Schmuck, R. A., & Schmuck, P. A. *Humanistic psychology of education: Making the school everybody's house.* Palo Alto, California: National Press Books, 1974.

Silberman, C. E. *Crisis in the classroom.* New York: Random House, 1970.

Smith, J. M. *Leading groups in personal growth.* Richmond, Virginia: John Knox Press, 1961.

Stanford, G. *Developing effective classroom groups.* New York: Hart Publishing Company, 1977.

Stanford, G., & Roark, A. *Human interaction in education.* Rockleigh, New Jersey: Allyn & Bacon, Inc., 1974.

Stein, J. *Effective personality: A humanistic approach.* Belmont, California: Wadsworth Publishing Company, 1972.

Dr. Ronald Cromwell
and
Dr. Vicky Cromwell
Department of Child and
Family Studies
University of Tennessee

The most basic assumption in this paper is that the family, however one chooses to define it, is our nation's most valuable natural resource. The family is the raw material upon which this society is built. As professional educators, we must commit ourselves to its exploration, cultivation, support, and growth. Any society is only as strong as the most basic units which comprise it. We must begin to focus far more attention on helping families strengthen their interpersonal relationships. Novak (1977) stated:

> . . . the family is the seedbed of economic money habits, attitudes toward work, and the arts of financial independence. The family is a stronger teacher of the religious imagination than the church. Political and social planning in a wise social order begins with the axiom: What strengthens the family strengthens society. . . . (p. 3)

The family group can learn to utilize resources more effectively, generate additional resources, and maximize inherent energy potentials for relationship growth and development. Efforts must be increased to help the family cope with constant changes experienced both within and outside its boundaries. Family-focused educational intervention is one means toward accomplishing these goals.

Families can, and do, learn from their struggles, and from the struggles of other families. Family members possess a wealth of personal experiences which facilitate the integration and retention of both cognitive (factual) and affective (experiential) domains of learning (Bloom et al., 1971). Family members, as students together, bring to the educational setting a common past, present, and future. In most cases, family members share common vocabulary, values, and rules which govern their interaction. The family, then,

is an ideal educational unit with the potential for frequent
and continuing interaction among the "students." However,
it is only recently that attention has been directed to total
families as "students" in the educational process (Cromwell,
1978; Cromwell & Bartz, 1977; Cromwell & Cromwell, 1976;
Cromwell & Cromwell, 1979).

FAMILY RESOURCES AND RELATIONSHIP ENERGY

The family is conceptualized as an energetic system, requiring an ongoing supply of resources in order to do productive
and efficient relationship work. Resources generate energy
in a cybernetic manner, such that the greater the supply of
resources, the greater the potential energy output, given
that the system has learned to efficiently utilize available
resources. Once efficiency has been learned, then the energy
output feeds back on the resources to create even greater
resources for energy generation and the system can regenerate
itself.

The challenge in family-focused education involves helping families harness their inherent energy potential, so it
can be used to promote relationship change and growth. Professionals who intervene with families have as their primary
job channeling energy resources of the system in ways which
will illuminate both the home and the individuals who live
in it. The emphasis is on helping families learn efficient
use of relationship resources to generate the energy necessary for relationship building.

One of the primary functions of the family is the allocation of the resources contained within it and generated by it.
When asking students to identify resources within the family,
they typically mention expendables like money, housing, health
care, automobiles, food, etc. Less frequently mentioned are
the resources of affection, love, self-verification, education, and open and honest communication. These intangible resources serve to build family strengths and maintain a store-
house of relationship energy. Both tangible and intangible
resources are necessary, but not always sufficient to assure
a maximum quality of life.

The point we wish to make is, that while the family system is energetic, the resources which contribute to that energy
source are finite. Resources can be expended in non-productive,
non-growthful ways, to the extent that the energy source becomes weak and depleted, making it difficult to perform tasks
or build relationships. Families frequently use up their natural resources which could produce relationship energy.

The constant and unrelenting forces of change, both within and outside the family, contribute to random expenditures

of energy in attempts to adjust, adapt, and realign to situations generally foreign and unfamiliar. In many cases, contemporary families lack the resources necessary to generate the energy or strength necessary to constructively utilize the change process. When viewing the family in a context of change, it becomes fundamentally important to help families acquire necessary resources (or to learn to use the resources they have more efficiently) to facilitate relationship growth. This is precisely the goal of family-focused education.

Implied in the discussion above is that tangible resources (like money, shelter, health care) and more intangible resources (like affection, love, open and honest communication) are mutually important in the overall functioning of families. In our biased opinion, families spend infinitely more time and energy in the pursuit of tangible resources (which can be used up), while putting the intangibles (which can grow and regenerate) on the back burner.

The skills necessary to efficiently manage tangible resources of relationships differ from those necessary to efficiently manage intangible resources in relationships. The number of family members necessary for successful educational intervention also differs by type of resources. While the more tangible resources are necessary for various levels of quality of life, they are not sufficient in and of themselves. Put another way, simply having access to monetary resources, and all that they can provide, does not necessarily assure the family a quality interpersonal life.

In addition, family members can learn efficient financial management skills, and those skills are important and probably transfer or overlap to other areas. Families can also learn to better manage their more intangible resources by learning (and practicing) relationship skills in areas like communication, problem solving, affection giving, and conflict management. Learning to manage the financial resources of the family may require the active participation of only one member of the group. It is conceivable that one person delegated the authority to manage the financial intake and outgo for the family could do an efficient job with that task. However, it is inconceivable (to us) that one family member could improve the process of conflict management in the family without participation of each member involved in the conflict (it takes two or more to engage in relationship conflict). Managing the intangible resources requires participation by everyone involved in the relationship. Much more will be said about this when we focus on the components of a philosophy for family-focused education. Attention now shifts to the emerging political interest in the family in regard to family resources and social policy.

FAMILY RESOURCES AND SOCIAL POLICY

There is considerable talk and interest in the area of "social policy and the family," and it appears that many policy
makers are primarily concerned with providing a minimum level
of tangible financial resources for American families. Without question, the family has been recognized politically, as
evidenced in the party platform statements of both the Democrats and Republicans during the last Presidential campaign,
the promises of a White House Conference on the Family, the
mad scramble of family-focused organizations and professionals to get on the political band wagon, and the increasing
rumbles by legislators to do something for the "folks back
home." Somewhere in this political process, the interpersonal
aspects of the family seem to have been forgotten.

In a recent guest article in the *COFO Memo* (Coalition
of Family Organizations), Gilbert Steiner (1979) analyzes
government positions on "Family Stability and Income Guarantees." This essay examines how a politically-inspired focus
on the tangible resources of income maintenance can over-
shadow and actually exclude the more tangible relationship
resources (which also "keep the family going").

Political interest in the family appears to be economically
motivated and tied closely to inflation and government spending. According to Steiner (1979), the President's formulation of a "government action--family strength trade-off" is
one where "government steps in by necessity when families
have failed" (p. 2). To "fail" means to be either welfare
dependent, or to be functionally dependent (to require protection outside the family circle). Are we then to assume
the families who are welfare dependent lack family strengths,
and the ability to utilize intangible resources and build
intimate relationships? Are we also to assume that families
who have not "failed" (economically) do in fact reflect "family stability?" What then is family stability in the social
policy sense of the term?

"A good deal of what is discussed as family policy actually refers to ways of making dependent families more like
non-dependent families. . . ." Accordingly, "If there were
no indigent families, or at least no indigent families dependent on public assistance, a substantial part of the interest in family policy would disappear" (Steiner, 1979, p. 2).
The assumption is that non-dependent families are stable.
We simply must face the fact that financial stability (not
costing the government more than a fixed amount) and relationship stability are very different. Obviously, there
are many "successful" families in the ghettos of our nation
who are financial failures and many "non-successful" families (in the relationship domain) who are financially

successful. Both types of families, in fact, all families, can benefit from educational intervention to help them manage the tangible and intangible resources at their disposal. To provide educational intervention on behalf of families is the primary concern of family-focused education. Before outlining the components of such a philosophy, a closer look will be taken at how educational intervention, focused on families' interpersonal resources, could supplement efforts directed toward meeting the more tangible needs of families.

In 1976, the Advisory Committee on Child Development, commissioned by the National Academy of Sciences, published a volume entitled *Toward a National Policy for Children and Families*. Although the report centered primarily on policies directed toward families with children under six years of age, and was primarily child-focused, it does represent an attempt at recommending government policies for family support. In summary, the committee recommended that:

> the federal government take the lead in developing a comprehensive national policy for children and families, the essential components of which include: (1) employment, tax and cash benefit policies that assure each child's family an adequate income, (2) a broad and carefully integrated system of support services for families and children, and (3) planning and coordination mechanisms to insure adequate coverage and access of families to the full range of available services. (1976, pp. 4-5)

The Carnegie Council on Children, headed by Kenneth Keniston, also developed a policy statement at roughly the same time the Advisory Committee on Child Development was preparing their statement. *All Our Children: The American Family Under Pressure*, published in 1977, acknowledges, "American social science habitually has studied the psychological, social and intellectual development of children in relative isolation from the social context in which they live" (Keniston, 1977, p. xxiii). The Council viewed the family to be the primary social force in America:

> We [the Carnegie Council] believe families--and the circumstances of their lives--will remain the most critical factors in determining children's fate. To support children almost always requires supporting their families; to understand the development of children, the lives of their parents must be understood. Keeping a family going does not come easy. (Keniston, 1977, p. xiv)

Like the report of the Advisory Committee on Child Development, the Carnegie Council on Children placed heavy emphasis on guaranteeing every American family (for their children's sake) a liveable income and decent jobs, equal access to available services, including health, and protection of rights under the law. Both of these commissioned reports call for federal intervention in the form of legislation to "help keep the family going."

"Keeping a family going" is a primary goal of family-focused education. This is a formidable task indeed, but we are not without educational resources and knowledge to assist us in the process. Family-focused education can be, should be, and perhaps must be included in the implementation phase of any future public policy programs to improve the quality of family living in our country. Full employment, minimum income allowances, the Equal Rights Amendment, child care legislation--all of these and other government programs stand a better chance of success with addition of complementary educational programs directed toward the development of interpersonal resources inside the family.

We agree with Keniston (1977) in his assertion that most of our efforts to help children and families have emphasized reform of the victims rather than reform of the victimizing forces. Educating and reforming are time-honored American traditions, but we know now that they are not enough to bring about significant and lasting change. On the other hand, we must guard against an extreme reaction which would suggest the conception and implementation of public programs without educational consideration. The numerous failures of the War on Poverty illustrate how education for mothers and job training programs did not, in themselves, produce jobs, income, or social opportunity. One focal point of government policy now appears to be correcting injustices of our economic system to obtain full employment, income supports, and full access to health and educational services with varying degrees of success.

We believe these programs will also fail without a family-focused educational component. Obtaining an adequate income will not guarantee the use of that income to achieve the goals of a particular family. Having an adequate income will change many aspects of life among economically-deprived families, including interpersonal relationships. We know too, that disagreements and conflicts about finances exist in families with adequate and substantial incomes. The point is that an income support system may have a negative impact upon family life unless educational programs are available to help families learn how to prepare for and cope with anticipated changes within the family. Thus, it becomes imperative to: (1) include family-focused education in any discussion of public policy which will have impact upon the family, and (2) promote the development and implementation of continuing education for families in every community to supplement family policy programs.

To date, the perspective of policy makers has generally ignored an educational approach to family life (or social policy, for that matter). Anglo-Saxon political philosophy-- both liberal and conservative--has historically tended to ignore the family as the focus of political impact. Conservatives feel that emphasis upon the family is simultaneously a constraint upon the state (Crosby, 1975); and to liberals, emphasis upon the family is a constraint upon the individual (Novak, 1977).

In actuality, most public policies have been developed to serve specific individuals: the elderly, handicapped children, low income mothers, the unemployed, or dependent children. We agree with Keniston that it is erroneous to assume "that the problem of individuals (in the family) can be solved by changing the individuals with the problems" (1977). Only recently have we stopped forcing working mothers to seek day care outside the family realm. Tax credits are now allowed for child care payments to relatives. In half of the states, low-income families may be better off if the father leaves home, because his presence disqualifies them for welfare payments. One relevant question needing an answer is, to what extent does the father "desert" knowing that his family will be economically better off without him?

In an assessment of "The Need for a National Family Policy," Maroney (1977) concluded:

> Social services that attempt to support the family have received lower priority than those that replace the family . . . . If policies and programs are categorized by purpose and function, the State has placed greater emphasis on these which in essence substitute for the family, an emphasis that is expressed in both the scale of social welfare expenditures and the type of service developed. (p. 12)

Historically, the United States has exhibited a preoccupation with the health and welfare of its children, almost to the exclusion of the family. This point was eloquently expressed by Max Lerner in *America as a Civilization* (1957): ". . . it is evident that in no other culture has there been so pervasive a cultural anxiety about the rearing of children." There is, in America, a tremendous ". . . overconcentration on the child."

When government leaders and professional "experts" become overwhelmed with the problem of family instability in the face of economic constraints, they frequently call for an emphasis on assisting children rather than families. The two commissioned reports on family social policy which were briefly outlined earlier were, in essence, inspired by a concern for children, not families. Even Steiner (1979), in his review essay on "Family Stability and Income Guarantees," concludes: "If family stability and children's needs cannot readily be accommodated, let the way be open to support the children's cause" (p. 6, emphasis added). One problem permeating conclusions of this kind appears to be a difficulty in "thinking relationships," especially family relationships. When the going gets tough, the tendency is to splinter off individuals who are members of relationships in attempts to focus on the "individuals with the problems." This logic has failed time and time again. We are not individuals in isolation, but are involved in relationship structures. We simply must give relationship intervention a try at the family level.

The tenuous announcement of the White House Conference on Families, the formation of coalitions of family-focused organizations, the creation of new organizations and commissions concerned about the social impact of policies on the family and the development of new family policy, and the general reawakening of the masses to the importance of the family in our society all combine to create a unique and challenging situation for family professionals. To be sure, the United States is entering a new and exciting era of family consciousness.

The time is right to propose organized family-focused education offerings, directed to families as students, to supplement and complement large-scale social policy intervention. There needs to be a balanced plan directed toward developing both macroscopic and microscopic support systems for families. Assuming that the federal government will fulfill its promises at the macro level (to assure at least minimum tangible resources), it becomes imperative for educators to focus on supplementing those efforts by developing educational opportunities to help families learn to more effectively utilize and create relationship resources inside the family. It is this educational goal which creates the challenge of, and responsibility for, professionals engaged in educational intervention, while reinforcing the societal need to develop relationship education for families.

In short, the social service system, government family supports, and proposed social policies for families will become oppressive in extent and expense without an accompanying emphasis upon promoting satisfying family development

and preventing problems by planning for positive, constructive change, as opposed to treatment and remediation. A
similar point was eloquently expressed by Maroney in the conclusion of his report on "The Need for a National Family Policy": "Society is fortunate to have families who care. The
corollary to this is that families should also be supported
by a caring society" (Maroney, 1977, p. 14).

The family deserves equal access to support systems and
experience which will help them adapt and realign in the face
of both internal and external forces of change. Families need
help in learning to utilize the change process constructively.
Education programs for families must be developed to assist
in overcoming what Keniston (1977) refers to as the "myth
of the self-sufficient family" (p. 7).

The family can no longer be taken for granted. It will
increasingly become the role of educators to provide the educational models necessary to help families reach their maximum relationship growth and potential. This is perhaps the
fundamental challenge facing educators today and in the future. The family will increasingly need help in maintaining
internal balance and practicing new behaviors in the process
of changing and growing (Cromwell & Cromwell, 1979). Components of a philosophy for family-focused education are outlined in the following section.

PHILOSOPHY FOR FAMILY-FOCUSED EDUCATION

The attitude professionals assume when considering education
programs for families has far-reaching program implications.
If educators misinterpret contemporary "doomsday" data about
families, this may lead to a philosophy of education which
revolves exclusively around the alleviation of problems. What
we advocate is a preventive and promotive model of education
which focuses on the normal developmental processes of change
over the life cycle. Most existing educational models are
"reactive"; they focus on what to do after a problem occurs.
A preventive and promotive educational model is "proactive"
and focuses on preparing for those changes which are predictable over the normal course of family development. The
latter model "learns about life" to prepare the family for
the process of "lifelong learning" (Cromwell, 1978).

It has been our experience in working with couples and
families, in both educational and therapeutic contexts, that
the tendency is to focus on problems or what is wrong in their
relationships. Family members need help in focusing on the
positive components of their relationships, and encouragement to promote those positive attributes. When families
begin assessing the "what is going right" or positive aspects,

the negative aspects become less all encompassing, burden-
some, and overwhelming to them.

When educators view family living as a constant process
of change and redefinition of relationships within the family system, and between the family and the larger social
context, a comprehensive philosophy of education begins to
emerge. Although we envision the development of the capacity to learn, and thus to change, to be a primary goal of
education, the fact remains that our educational system is
geared primarily to the transmission of knowledge or cognitive aspects of learning. While the family group provides
a natural arena for cognitive learning, it also has a wealth
of personal experience to draw on in the affective domain.
A promotive program of sequential development can be achieved,
capitalizing on both cognitive and affective modes of learning. We envision the development of a model for family-
focused education to include at least five major components.

Components of a Philosophy for Family-Focused Education

First, family focused education must begin with the assumption that it is normal for families to need assistance in
order to realize an optimum quality of family life. It has
become clear that the demand for treatment of various individual and family pathologies will not be met by expanding
the supply of trained therapists, clinicians, and social
workers (Spoon & Southwick, 1972).

In response to the need for more preventive approaches,
family-focused education is distinctive, and will remain distinctive from other "helping" professions, through an emphasis upon promoting "normal" family development and preventing problems by planning for positive, constructive change,
as opposed to treatment and remediation. A similar position
was recently echoed by David Mace, co-founder of the Association of Couples for Marriage Enrichment: "Our remedial services to families, while prompted by the best motives, have
not been effective enough" (Mace, 1978a, p. 1).

Professionals who study, treat, or educate families seem
to know more about families than families know about themselves. The cumulative body of knowledge about families is
not getting to families as effectively as it might. Just a
few years ago, the public was generally unaware of research
findings in dentistry. Today, preventive dentistry is present everywhere; much of the water we drink is treated to
help preserve the teeth, toothpastes and toothbrushes have
been improved, and television and other media sources educate the public in preventive dentistry. But, much of what
we currently know about family relationships is locked away
in professional journals or on a researcher's desk, and not

being applied to the family. In this regard, families do not have access to the information which might improve their quality of life.

Secondly, we need to focus on families as the basic unit for education, as opposed to individuals who happen to be family members. Family life education in the United States has traditionally been directed to individual students in public schools, colleges, and universities (Kerckhoff, 1964), where the majority of participants were female (Somerville, 1971). And, the majority of participants in adult family life education have been middle-class women (Houle, 1963; Rudd & Hall, 1974). Family-focused education is different from education about families; it is education in families. It should be obvious that a mother/wife alone, for instance, cannot improve the quality and clarity of family communication as effectively as when all family members understand the need for change, and together practice new ways of communicating.

When family interaction is viewed as part of a "system" of interconnected roles and relationships, it follows that all (or most) family members should be involved in family education. Attempting to change family functioning by way of only one member of a system is inherently risky and has low potential for success.

Several years ago, Houle (1963), in a review article on "Adult Education and Family Life," described the benefit to be gained by focusing upon family units in parent education:

> A child who learns with his parents is very likely to have both a sense of companionship with his mother and father and a respect for the process of learning which will endure in his own later life. Parent education should not just be parents studying about children; it should also be parents studying with children. (p. 228, emphasis added)

Most parenting education programs are basically "reactive," emphasizing what to do after a behavior occurs. Frequently, parenting education includes only one parent and none of the children. It seems reasonable that, since the children are the primary focus for the educational program, they should be equal participants in the process. It also seems logical that children might better live by the rules which are intended to govern their behavior if they have a role in establishing those roles. When the educational focus is supposedly on the family, isolating family members from one another is a questionable procedure at best. Involving the total parenting system, parents and children, will necessitate changing both the content and process of the educational

experience as it has been traditionally conceived and implemented.

One promising and encouraged exception to traditional
models for family life education is the emergence of voluntary education programs directed to the total family. Examples of these educational models include: "family growth
groups (Anderson, 1974; Papp et al., 1972), "family cluster
education" (Otto, 1971, 1972; Sawin, 1972), "family enrichment" (Kreml, 1970; Prunty, 1976), "family enrichment week-
end" (Bowman, 1976; Wilson & Wilson, 1976), "family camping"
(Branch, 1976; Clarke & Kempler, 1973), and "developing resources for family potential" (Cromwell & Cromwell, 1976).
Certainly, the National Symposium on "Building Family Strengths"
is designed to enhance this movement. In addition, there
are numerous voluntary education programs which focus on
marriage enrichment (see Mace, 1978b; Otto, 1972; Smith et
al., 1976, for a review of these programs).

While most of these family focused educational programs
are relatively unique, and have received limited exposure,
they represent an important and evolving family process model
for education. Anderson (1974) describes this type of educational experience as one in which ". . . families view themselves as participants in, not subjects of, the process,
coming to an awareness that the resources for growth and problem resolution lie within themselves" (p. 11). By focusing
upon whole family systems, this model of education ". . .
provides opportunities for families to increase their awareness of their unique strengths and resources and then to
actualize their dominant capabilities in family living" (p. 8).

In summary, we are advocating that education for families should be preventive and promotive in focus, and designed
to include as many members of any given family system as possible. Total family units cannot be the only audience for
family life education, but they do deserve greater emphasis
than in the past. Continuing to emphasize educational intervention to individuals, who just happen to be family members,
denies the potential for growth and development inherent in
the family, and lessens the likelihood that motivation, confidence, and a feeling of capability will generate within
the family system. Certainly, one of the goals of educational intervention into family functioning should be to promote family strengths which may eventually preclude the need
for intensive, direct assistance.

A third component of a family process philosophy for education involves accepting and advocating the notion that
effective family relationships do not just happen, but are
the result of deliberate efforts by members of the family
units. Relationships require extremely hard work and large
expenditures of energy! Individual efforts can be enhanced

through learning and practicing skills necessary to cope with family interaction, and in developing an understanding of family change and development.

In this regard, there are at least two central obstacles facing educators who focus on family units as students in educational intervention. First, the educator must reach family units to motivate them to take advantage of educational opportunities. This is particularly difficult, because families seem unaware of the resources available to them either inside or outside their system. There is increasing evidence that this situation is changing, and that families are themselves beginning to realize the potential for growth offered in family life education programs (Bartz, 1975).

A second obstacle to overcome is helping families identify their needs, so they may voluntarily choose to explore and experience education offerings. Recruitment of participants may be difficult, but there is a growing constituency voluntarily selecting programs of this type. For example, in many cities there are waiting lists of couples desiring a marriage enrichment experience.

Educators have perhaps defaulted in responding to the challenge to develop educational programs for families by assuming the family is a private domain. A long history of taboos and misinterpretations lies behind the belief that the family is sacred and self-sufficient, and not amenable to educational intervention (Keniston, 1977). The idea that quality marital interaction, parenting, and communication skills "come naturally" will not fade rapidly in the near future. The contemporary facts on American family life provide overwhelming evidence that relationship skills do not come naturally, but require careful observation, education, practice, and continual work on the part of all participants.

If change is expected and approached positively, family concerns will be indicative of a transitional process, and not necessarily interpreted as failure of family members to handle their lives. A family-focused approach to education can help total family units achieve self-directed change in a supportive, non-threatening educational environment.

When family living is viewed as a process of continuing change and redefinition of relationships, both within the family system and between the family and the larger social context, a process philosophy of education emerges. If, as we believe, family life education has a primary goal of preparing family members to adapt to changes at the broader societal level, as well as those at the interpersonal level, then the concept of a lifelong learning process becomes fundamental to educational intervention with families.

Fourthly, techniques of family life education and delivery sites must be expanded beyond organized, teacher-
guided offerings on college campuses or other traditional
educational settings. Educators are now realizing that to
best address the normal needs of families, "Muhammad must
go to the mountain." It is now widely accepted that the
majority of adult learning takes place outside organized
"schooling" situations (Tough, 1971). Educators are challenged to meet family needs at the time their needs are most
pressing and, consequently, most motivating. Motivation to
learn more about the processes of family living often does
not coincide with courses scheduled to begin each September
and January. The requirement to commit the family to an extended period of time--eight, six, or even four weeks--may
be a deterrent to participation in organized educational programs.

Professional experience in designing and implementing a
comprehensive model of education for families (Cromwell &
Cromwell, 1976) indicates it is difficult for families to
set aside blocks of time. Consequently, it is suggested that
program models be reduced in size (offerings and time commitment), and decentralized so specific sessions can be offered
at specified times in a variety of community settings. A
reduced and decentralized model would be more effective, in
the long run, in attracting family group participation. In
fact, the model utilized in the National Symposium on "Building
Family Strengths" can be implemented in your communities by
selecting specific offerings, and making them more family-
focused. The model could then be implemented by working
through existing organizations like clubs, churches, schools,
business and industry, to list but a few.

In addition, family members may learn more readily and
effectively through a self-designed program, involving easily
accessible materials and self-determined scheduling. This
approach to education does not relieve the educator of responsibilities. The educator moves from teacher to facilitator, helping participants select and organize their learning experiences, suggesting resources, and assisting in evaluation of their personalized learning. Emphasis is placed
on both the cognitive and affective dimensions of learning
within the context of the family. The "students" have the
advantage of ongoing interaction, discussion, and practice
in their natural home environment.

A final component in our philosophy for family-focused
education involves utilization of existing community resources.
Educators can facilitate the development of a support system
for families by promoting the delivery, coordination, and
integration of family development resources at the local,
state, and national level. This process will help families